BRITISH
MUSIC HALL

ROYAL
STANDARD

FACING VICTORIA STATION.

Proprietor — Mr. THOMAS SAMUEL DICKIE.

Notice: Whitsuntide Festivities, June 7th, 1897.

A 'ROYAL STANDARD' RECORD HOLIDAY CO.

Important Engagement of the incomparable

Marie Lloyd

LESTER KING
The Popular Baritone Vocalist

PASSMORE BROS.
The Great Eccentric Comedians.

Daisy De Roy
Charming Serio Vocalist.

PAT RAFFERTY
The Popular Irish Comedian.

LILLY MARNEY
Charming Character Vocalist.

DUTCH DALY
Eccentric Comedian and Instrumentalist.

Prof. HARCOURT
The Mysterious Marvel

FLORRIE WEST
The Popular Comedienne.

FRED DARBY
Eccentric Comedian and Dancer.

The Donnells
The Exceptional Two Comedy Artistes and Dancers.

NELLIE GERTINE
Lady Character Baritone Vocalist.

Jess BURTON
Vocal Comedian.

ALFRED HURLEY
The Popular Tenor Vocalist.

An Original Screaming Absurdity, entitled,

THE ACADAMY
Introducing the Celebrated

COLLINSON COMBINATION
Comprising Six Ladies and Three Gents.
And Others.

NOTICE.—During the Holidays Doors open 6.45; Afterwards, Time and Prices as usual.

NOTICE.—Seats may be booked and reserved on application.
Telephone No. 503, Westminster.

Manager — Mr. FRED LAW

GRAND BILLIARD & GRILL ROOMS

BRITISH MUSIC HALL

An Illustrated

WHO'S WHO

from

1850

to the

PRESENT DAY

Roy Busby

Paul Elek   London and
New Hampshire USA

For my godsons,
Peter Sharman and Gary Colton

First published in 1976 by

Paul Elek Limited
54-58 Caledonian Road
London N1 9RN

and Paul Elek Inc.
10 South Broadway
Salem
New Hampshire 03079
USA

Copyright © 1976 Roy Busby

All rights reserved. No part of this publication may be reproduced, stored in a retrieval system or transmitted in any form or by any means, electronic, mechanical, photocopying, recording or otherwise, without the prior permission of the publishers.

ISBN 0 236 40053 3

Produced by computer-controlled phototypesetting using OCR input techniques and printed offset by
UNWIN BROTHERS LIMITED
The Gresham Press, Old Woking, Surrey
A member of the Staples Printing Group

Acknowledgements

In compiling this book I have drawn from books noted in the text, and from newspapers and theatrical journals dating from 1850. I am particularly indebted to *The Performer*, the official organ of the Variety Artistes Federation from 1906 to 1957. Its pages contained much valuable information and contemporary comments, and its *Who's Who* was a useful means of verifying incidents in the careers of certain artistes appearing in variety in 1948.

My thanks are due to the following: to the curators and staff of the Enthoven Collection of the Victoria and Albert Museum; the British Museum Library; the Newspaper Library at Colindale; and the Library and Museum of the Performing Arts, New York. To Lord Olivier for his comments on George Robey, Professor John Munro of the American University of Beirut for advice and suggestions on research, and to Don Ross for the inspiration of *Thanks for the Memory*. To the many variety artistes who kindly gave details of their careers and supplied photographs, and the anonymous photographers whose work contributed so greatly to the interest of this book.

Although a rather dilatory member of the British Music Hall Society, I have received much valued help and kindness from many of its members, especially from the late Mrs Pacey, the charming widow of variety agent Tom Pacey, and Mr Reg Aubrey who, until his death a few years ago, ran his own music hall museum at his home in Wimbledon.

Last, but certainly not least, my very sincere thanks to my good friends Dennis Colton and Ellen and John Crampton for their encouragement and advice, and hours of hard work typing the manuscript. Without them this book would not have been possible.

Foreword

This book really began in 1948 with the arrival at the Golders Green Hippodrome of Don Ross's *Thanks for the Memory*. I was only 12 at the time, but the magic of Nellie Wallace, Gertie Gitana, Ella Shields, Talbot O'Farrell, G.H. Elliott, Randolph Sutton and Billy Danvers cast a spell which has never been broken.

Music hall came and went in less than a hundred years, but during that short period a unique chapter in the history of British popular culture and entertainment was written. The greatness of Dan Leno and Marie Lloyd, the consummate art of Vesta Tilley, the honest vulgarity of George Robey and Billy Bennett are as much a part of Britain's theatrical heritage as the histrionics of Garrick, Siddons and Irving.

With the exception of *Who's Who in Variety*, published by *The Performer* in 1950, which included only artistes active in the profession in 1948, this is the first comprehensive book of reference on music hall and variety. It includes details of the careers of all the greats, most of the major and many of the 'wines and spirits'. American and continental artistes who appeared on the British music-hall stage are also included.

The British Music Hall Society with its proud motto 'Cherishing the jewels of the past and actively supporting the interests of the future', does much to preserve the spirit of music hall, and variety is enjoying a great renaissance in clubs and pubs up and down the country. I hope this book will be useful to students of the theatre, and contribute to the growing interest in modern variety shown by the popularity of the television programmes 'The Good Old Days' and 'New Faces'.

Introduction: from pleasure-gardens to variety

C.H. Simpson, Master of Ceremonies at the Royal Gardens, Vauxhall

British music hall technically came, thrived, and died in less than a hundred years. In fact, its origins go back at least to the eighteenth century and its spirit survives today in public houses and clubs throughout the country.

The ancient fairs of St Bartholomew, Southwark, and Smithfield had singing booths which presented shows ranging from scaramouch dancers, clowns, and contortionists to low comedy singers. These were suppressed in 1700 on the grounds of alleged obscenity, which 'provoked undesirable behaviour in the audience', a charge familiar throughout the history of music hall and variety.

Modern music hall (which can be said to date from about 1860) was an amalgam of three popular elements: the pleasure-garden with its saloon theatre, the song-and-supper room, and the catch and glee clubs and harmonic meetings of tavern concerts. Of the early pleasure-gardens Vauxhall had the strongest influence on the development of popular musical entertainment. Originally opened in 1660 as the Spring Gardens, Foxhall, they were enlarged by Jonathan Tyers and re-opened as the New Spring Gardens, Vauxhall (a cockney corruption of Foxhall) in June 1732. The charge for admission to the gardens, which were designed to attract an aristocratic patronage, was two shillings and sixpence. An orchestra played nightly as visitors strolled among the sham Gothic ruins and painted architectural façades. Concerts were held in the Rotunda, a semicircular bandstand with room for tables and dancing on a small central stage. The success of Vauxhall resulted in similar ventures all over London: the Marylebone and Ranelagh Gardens; Islington Spa; Whale's in Bayswater; the Highbury Barn; the White Conduit House, Clerkenwell; Bagnigge Wells, King's Cross; and the St Helena Gardens, Rotherhithe. The New Spring Gardens had by 1831 become the Royal Gardens, Vauxhall, presided over by C.H. Simpson who acted as Master of Ceremonies for a total of 35 years. The price of admission was reduced to a shilling and variety concerts were held in the Rotunda, which was enlarged to include boxes, pit and gallery, with a stage on one side and an arena for displays of horsemanship, clowns and acrobats. Simpson died in 1835 and in 1837 *tableaux vivants*, described as 'groups of sculpture by male and female artistes', took their place beside the comic vocalists.

Another famous pleasure-garden, Cremorne in Chelsea, was granted a music licence in 1837 and developed along the lines of Vauxhall. A Saloon Theatre advertised a 'Grand Amazon Ballet', a Russian circus and a *burletta* entitled 'Low Life Above Stairs'. Firework displays, balloon ascents, parachute jumps, and dancing took place in the grounds.

Of the smaller gardens, the Shepherd and Shepherdess Tea Gardens in the grounds of the Eagle Tavern in Shepherdess Walk, City Road, played the most important part in fusing saloon theatres, concert rooms and pleasure-grounds. The Eagle, immortalised in the children's rhyme 'Pop Goes the Weasel', was famed for its harmonic meeting, vying for popularity with its close neighbour, the Royal Albert Saloon and Standard Tavern. The Eagle Tavern was taken over by Thomas Rouse in 1831. A builder by profession, he turned the grounds and the adjacent Adam and Eve Tea Gardens into a miniature Vauxhall. At the southern end he built the Grecian Saloon, which became the most celebrated of London's saloon theatres. The Royal Eagle Coronation Pleasure Gardens and Grecian Saloon, which was decorated with the trappings left over from the coronation of William IV, boasted: 'Dancing and vaudeville, set paintings, cosmoramas, fountains, grottos, dripping rock, elegant buildings, arcades, colonnades, statuary, singing, music, and other delightful amusements which render it a fairy scene.' The Grecian was enlarged in 1844 and Rouse, known as 'Bravo' Rouse for his habit of leading the applause from the stage box, engaged the best concert-room vocalists and dramatic and burletta players. At the same time the Eagle Tavern continued to prosper as a 'free and easy' concert tavern, and survived as a music hall until 1887. Other leading saloon theatres, which like the Grecian were later licenced as legitimate theatres, included the Britannia, Hoxton; the Effingham Saloon, Stepney; the Bower Saloon, Stangate; the Albion Saloon, built on to the Yorkshire Stingo Public House, St Marylebone; and the Albert Saloon.

The clown Tom Matthews sang Grimaldi's 'Hot Codlings' at the Cremorne in 1845 and by 1847 the variety concerts at Vauxhall and Cremorne included Sam Cowell, the Great Machney, J.W. Sharpe, and W.G. Ross, the leading vocalists at London's tavern concerts and song-and-supper rooms.

The song-and-supper rooms which abounded in the West End of London from the end of the eighteenth century were led by Evans in Covent Garden, the Cider Cellars in Maiden Lane, the Coal Hole in Fountain Court (off the Strand) and the Dr Johnson Concert Room, Bolt Court, Fleet Street.

Evans, at 43 King Street, was originally the town house of the Earl of Orford, converted into a tavern in 1773. It boasted 'stabling for a hundred noblemen and horses'. By 1800 it was being run by a landlord named Joy and when the basement was turned into a song-and-supper room by W.C. Evans, it became known as 'Evans, late Joy's'. A concert hall was later built

The Eagle Tavern, City Road, in about 1825

in the grounds but it was not until Evans retired in 1844, and it was again rebuilt by his musical director John Green, that it reached its full glory with Sam Collins, Sam Cowell, and J.W. Sharpe on its late-night variety bills. (It was later taken over by the National Sporting Club and during the 1930s became the home of the Players Theatre Club which, as a link with the past, became known as 'The Players, Late Joy's'.)

In less prestigious premises, the Coal Hole

Evans Song and Supper Rooms, Covent Garden, in about 1850

and the Cider Cellars (also known as the *Cyder* Cellars) were opened by brothers John and William Rhodes during the early 1820s. At both the clientèle was exclusively male and entertainment was run at first on the lines of the old 'Cosmus's Court', with the customers expected to sing for their suppers by contributing their own turns to the evening's revelry. Later, in rivalry with Evans, Rhodes engaged the best concert artistes of the day, Charles Sloman, Tom Hudson, Robert Glindon, John Caulfield, J.A. Cave, and J.W. Sharpe.

During the 1840s the notoriety of W.G. Ross's harrowing rendering of the gruesome ballad of the condemned chimney sweep 'Sam Hall' attracted huge crowds to the Cider Cellars—and the censure of the moralist. The Coal Hole is considered to have been the original of Thackeray's 'Cave of Harmony' where scurrilous songs were sung to the outrage of Colonel Newcome's moral susceptibilities in *The Newcomes.* The self-styled 'Baron' Ranton Nicholson contributed to the Coal Hole's decline by transferring his infamous Judge and Jury Society from the Garrick Head, Bow Street, in 1853. Calling himself 'Lord Chief Baron', Nicholson presided over a grotesque parody of legal procedure, 'trying' cases, usually of seduction and adultery, which were thinly veiled skits of society scandals of the time. The woman 'witnesses' were men in drag and the show was 'spiced only too frequently by the ribaldest of wit and the rankest of obscenity'. Nicholson also introduced 'Poses Plastiques' (early nude shows) and offered private rooms for dinner and beds for the night at one shilling and sixpence. In 1858 he took over the management of the Cider Cellars but, like the Coal Hole, its days were numbered. Both had their licences revoked in 1862, the Coal Hole being run as the Occidental Tavern until Terry's Theatre was built on the site in 1876, and the Cider Cellar, where Charles Sloman once sang 'The Maid of Judah' and 'The Daughter of Israel', became a synagogue.

The passing of the Theatre Act of 1843 put the saloon theatres under the jurisdiction of the Lord Chamberlain and with the decline in popularity of the pleasure-gardens the field was clear for the tavern concerts held in bars and upper rooms to expand into full-scale music halls. As early as 1829 the Rotunda Assembly Rooms in the Blackfriars Road, Southwark, provided variety entertainment and when in 1838 John Blevoitt took over the management he described it on his bills as a 'music hall'. The Grapes public house at Southwark Bridge Road also billed its saloon as the Surrey Music Hall but later changed its name to the Winchester to avoid confusion with another hall built in the grounds of the Surrey Gardens. The greatest consolidating influence in the rise of music-hall entertainment was Charles Morton, dubbed by Clement Scott as 'The Father of the Halls'. Born in Hackney on 15 August 1819, he gained early theatrical experience at the Pavilion, Whitechapel, and in the early 1840s became the landlord of the St George's Tavern, Belgrave Road, Pimlico, and later of the Crown, Pentonville, and India House Tavern in

Left: 'Lord Chief Baron' Nicholson   Right: a bill for the Coal Hole Tavern, 1856

Leadenhall Street. He acquired the Canterbury Arms in Upper Marsh, Lambeth, in December 1848.

The Canterbury owed its name and ancient reputation as a pilgrim's rest to its close proximity to Lambeth Palace, the London residence of the Archbishop of Canterbury. Under the management of Morton and his brother-in-law, Frederick Stanley, it was soon popular for its 'free and easy' harmonic meetings, chaired by Morton's brother Robert. Originally for men only, a 'Ladies' Thursday' was later introduced and proved so successful that Morton built a new hall on the old inn's bowling green. Opened on 17 May 1852 with actor and vocalist John Caulfield as chairman, its first star attraction was Sam Cowell, who drew large crowds to hear him sing 'Villikins and His Dinah' and 'The Ratcatcher's Daughter'.

In the days before the term became synonymous with red-nosed comics the Canterbury was literally a music hall. Morton lived up to his motto of 'One quality only—the best', forming a resident choir and company of solo singers who performed glees, cantatas and part songs. In contrast to his high-minded entertainment, Morton also ran a 'book', listing the entries and prices of runners in forthcoming race meetings (the law put an end to 'listmen' in 1853). The Canterbury was famed for its hot baked potatoes, which Morton served from burning ovens wheeled around the hall between the glees and cantatas.

Morton opened a larger and grander Canterbury in December 1856, built on the same site at a cost of £25,000. Admission was

Charles Morton, 'The Father of the Halls'

The Canterbury Music Hall, 1856

sixpence to the body of the hall and ninepence to the well-furnished gallery, which included a collection of paintings valued at £10,000 and christened by George Augustus Sala 'The Royal Academy Over the Water'. In the main hall refreshments were served at tables with the Chairman's table stretching the full width of the stage. Morton continued to offer the highest musical entertainment with ballet and opera in concert form on the bills. Here Gounod's *Faust* was sung in England for the first time and Morton was largely responsible for the popularity of Offenbach in this country. There was plenty of variety, serio-comediennes followed prima donnas and comic singers, turgid tenors. Blondin, 'The Hero of Niagara', crossed the crowded hall on a tightrope between renderings of 'The Jewel Song' and 'The Soldier's Chorus'.

Besides Sam Cowell, who remained at the Canterbury until he left to tour the USA in 1859, other comic singers included Sam Collins singing 'The Rocky Road to Dublin' and 'Limerick Races', Robert Glindon famed as 'The Literary Dustman', and E.N. Mackney, the 'Negro Delineator' whom Morton styled 'The Great Mackney'.

Following the success of the Canterbury, music halls mushroomed all over London, unimpeded by the restrictions of later town planning regulations. The first to challenge the supremacy of the Canterbury in the West End was Edward Weston, who converted the Six Cans and Punch Bowl Tavern and the adjoining National Hall School in High Holborn into Weston's Music Hall. It opened on 16 November 1857, with Morton's old chairman John Caulfield as musical director, and just as Morton had pinched Cowell from Evans, so Weston lured Sam Collins from the Canterbury to be his first star attraction. The hall was 103 feet long but made to look longer by a mirrored wall at the back of the stage which reflected the gallery decorated with carved gold-painted cupids and four large crystal chandeliers, one at each corner of the hall and an even larger one in the centre.

The Royal Panopticon of Science and Art in Leicester Square was converted by E.T. Smith in 1858 into the Alhambra Palace and let to Howes and Cushing's American Circus. Leicester Square was then the heart of London's French colony and did not enjoy a very salubrious reputation. On 27 June 1859 *Peeping Tom* reported:

London cannot boast of another spot where an equal amount of aspiring fallen humanity vegetates, lives, breathes and has its being. What a chronicle of misery and woe, of aspiration and disappointment, of loyalty and treachery, of innocence betrayed and vice made more vicious would not Leicester Square yield could it be made to speak. . . . Its internal filth and outward show are all French and even the dirty urchins who wallow in its gutters are tainted with French notions, 'Ici on parle français' is written on every front, upon every window, on every shopwoman's and shopman's countenance.

The writer ended his tirade with what he considered the final affront to national pride: 'Even the blackman at the Alhambra Palace would fain make you believe he is an African by French parents!'

On the north side of the square stood Savile House, a one-time royal residence, which during the 1820s and 1830s was used for gaming and as a song-and-supper room. It was reformed by a Miss Linwood, who turned the ground floor into the Linwood Gallery, exhibiting needlework and tapestry. It eventually returned to its 'evil ways' and as the 'Walhalla' housed Madame Warton's troupe of 'Poses Plastiques' and advertised such diverse attractions as wax figures, marionettes, a clairvoyant lady, and an incubating machine. In 1847 it was purchased by Richard Pridmore, who ran it as a casino until 1858 when, to cater for the 'Frenchified' tastes of the area, it was

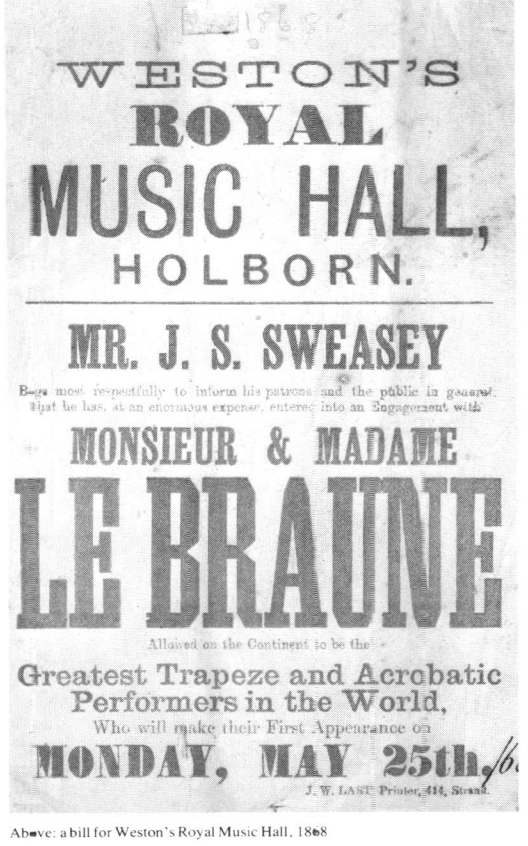

Above: a bill for Weston's Royal Music Hall, 1868

Below: Weston's Music Hall, 1857 (*Victoria and Albert Museum, Crown copyright*)

Posters outside the London Pavilion, 1902

converted into the Café Du Globe, and run with a licence from the Middlesex Justices in the name of George Reeve (for the Linwood Gallery) as a cross between a music hall and a café chantant.

This is how a contemporary newspaper describes this example of the smaller halls of the period:

> The Café Du Globe is a magnificent salon reached from Leicester Square by alternate flights of stone steps. The visitors on entering are at once struck by the air of elegance, comfort and convenience with which they are surrounded. On every side immense gorgeous plate-glass mirrors reflect surrounding objects and massive glass-drop chandeliers, suspended from the salon. Against the walls on either side are erected stuffed seats, in front of which are marble-topped tables. From end to end rows of similar tables are fixed at convenient distances from each other with as many chairs as would seat some thousand loungers. The admission to the Café Du Globe is free, but the visitor must indulge in some creature comfort to the amount of not less than sixpence.

The site of the Café Du Globe was later rebuilt as the Empire Theatre of Varieties.

In 1858, the Lord Chamberlain refused E.T. Smith, the eccentric showman and lessee of Drury Lane, a licence to run the Alhambra Palace as a theatre, but the following October the magistrates granted him a music licence. He converted the circus ring into an area for tables and in place of the original grand organ, which he sold to St Paul's Cathedral, he built a stage 70 feet deep and 50 feet wide with a proscenium of Moorish design to match the Alhambra's architecture. The hall was opened on 10 December 1860 as the Alhambra Palace Music Hall and the following year saw the London debut of the sensational Leotard, the original 'Daring Young Man on the Flying Trapeze'.

Emil Loible and Charles Sonnhammer took over the management of the Black Horse Tavern in Tichborne Street, Haymarket in 1859, which they ran as a 'sing-song' and café chantant. In 1860 the hall was rebuilt at a cost of £12,000 and with a capacity of two thousand opened on 23 February 1861 as the London Pavilion.

With this growing West End competition to the Canterbury, Charles Morton built a music hall at a cost of £35,000 on the site of the Boar and Castle Inn, near the junction of Tottenham Court Road and Oxford Street. It opened on 26 March 1861 as the Oxford Music Hall. Here he presented programmes on the same successful lines as the Canterbury. His singers were led by Miss FitzHenry, the music-hall name of mezzo soprano Emily Soldene, Madame Parepa, the wife of Carl Rosa, and Miss Russell, who sang the part of Marguerite in the first performance of *Faust* at the Canterbury. Comic singers included Harry Liston, a cockney singer of 'When Johnny Comes Marching Home', and 'Naughty Naked Cupid', and 'Nobody's Child'. The tragic A.B. Hollingworth scored a great hit with 'The Man With the Carpet Bag', Harry Rickards sang 'Oxford Joe', and 'Captain Jinks of the Horse Marines', and the Great Vance sang of 'Costermonger Joe' and 'The Chickeleery Cove'. In the summer of 1861 Morton paid Sam Cowell's passage home from New York so he could appear at the Oxford. The American tour had left him broken in health and a mere shadow of his former greatness.

As the success of the Oxford seemed assured, Morton sold the Canterbury in 1867 to William Holland, known as the 'People's Caterer' because of his success at the Surrey Gardens. Holland redecorated the hall and invited his patrons to come and spit on a thousand-guinea carpet. Under his management the hall changed its policy, replacing classical music with variety on broader music-hall lines. Thanks to the success of George Leybourne's singing of 'Champagne Charlie', the Canterbury and Holland prospered, but a month after the sale Morton was faced with disaster. The Oxford was gutted by fire on 10 February 1868. He recouped some of his losses by selling what was left of the hall to M.R. Sayers and W. Taylor, who rebuilt and re-opened it on 9 August 1869. Although Morton was never to build another music hall he went on to run the Philharmonic Hall, Islington, and at various times revived the flagging fortunes of the Alhambra, Tivoli, and Palace

The Oxford Music Hall in about 1898

Theatre of Varieties. After 60 years of stage service he died on 18 October 1904.

By 1875 there were more than 300 music halls in the London area alone. These ranged from public houses with music halls licenced by the Middlesex and Surrey justices to lavish palaces of variety. A law was passed in 1878 requiring music halls to hold a 'Certificate of Suitability' issued after inspection by the Metropolitan Board of Works. Without this the magistrates were not allowed to renew licences and from then on there was a rapid decline in the number of smaller halls. At about the same time the sale of drinks in the halls was restricted to bars open to the auditorium but divided by a promenade from the stalls, which had replaced the tables of the earlier period. Thus the music halls were replaced by variety theatres, often run by syndicates and companies led by such luminaries of the variety stage as Edward Moss, Oswald Stoll, Richard Thornton, John Barrasford, Walter de Frece, Walter Gibbons, George Adney Payne, Charles Gulliver, George Black, Val Parnell and the present-day descencant of them all, Bernard Delfont.

For a scholarly and fascinating study of the origins of the music hall *The Early Doors* by Harold Scott (1946) is recommended. Mr G.J. Mellor's *Northern Music Hall* (1970) fills a long-neglected gap in the history of the provincial music halls. A comprehensive list, *London Theatres and Music Halls 1850–1950*, was compiled by Diana Howard and published by the Library Association in 1970.

List of terms

Burlesque. A satirical play which parodied popular plays or current events. Burlesque in this country dates from Buckingham's satire of Dryden in *The Rehearsal* of 1671. By the nineteenth century burlesque, or 'extravaganza' as it was often billed, had developed along broader lines and although lacking the wit and sophistication of earlier productions was less bawdy. During the 1870s and 1880s the London home of burlesque was the Gaiety Theatre under the management of John Hollingshead and later George Edwardes. A strong element of burlesque survived in the revue skits of the 1940s and 1950s.

Burlesque (USA). Entertainment of a decidedly lower tone than vaudeville and popularly known as 'burleycue' or 'leg show'. Said to have been devised by Michael Bennett Leavitt during the 1860s, its strongest influence was the minstrel shows. The programmes consisted of singing and dancing chorus girls, bawdy comedy routines known as 'bits', monologues and burlesques of current plays. Acrobats, comic singers and magicians appeared in the olio (qv). From the 1920s burlesque became synonymous with striptease, and in New York with Minsky's. It was finally outlawed in New York by a barring statute passed in 1942.

Burletta. Originally, during the eighteenth century, a mixture of burlesque and operetta but later legally defined as any piece in three acts with at least five songs.

Café concert. French term for entertainment in restaurants and boulevard cafés. It ranged from sedate singers with orchestras to red-nosed comics. Many stars of the French music hall began their careers in café concerts, including Yvette Guilbert and Maurice Chevalier.

Ciné variety. During the 1920s and 1930s variety shows which preceded the films. The most famous surviving ciné variety theatre is the Radio City Music Hall, New York.

Corner men—bones and tambo (USA, endmen). The 'bones' and tambourine players in a minstrel show. They sat at each end of the stage line up and engaged in banter with the interlocutor, usually a white faced compère who sat in the centre. This chat across the platform became known as 'cross talk'.

Dime museum (USA). The early dime museums were developed on the lines of P.T. Barnum's American Museum opened on the corner of Broadway and Ann Street, New York in 1842. There jugglers and ventriloquists appeared on the same bills as educated dogs and industrious fleas. In the Curio Hall, albinos, fat boys, giants and bottled embryos were displayed. By the 1880s dime museums flourished throughout the USA, presenting freaks and 50-minute variety shows. In London the nearest thing to a dime museum was the Royal Aquarium, Westminster.

Fit-ups. Itinerant companies who set up their stages in village halls, market places and barns. Their melodramatic plays and exaggerated histrionics established the nineteenth-century 'barnstorming' tradition.

Free-and-easys. Taverns and early music halls run on casual free-and-easy lines with the customers supplying their own impromptu entertainments. With the growth of regular music halls the free-and-easy engaged professional acts but still relied on local amateur talent as support and many future stars of music hall gained experience in this way.

Lion Comique. A term used to describe the 'heavy swell' and swaggering singers of the 1860s and 70s. The phrase was invented by music hall manager J.J. Poole to bill the greatest of the 'Lion Comiques', George Leybourne.

Mashers. Term for the fashionable man-about-town and the 'lardy-dah city toff', ridiculed by the 'masher songs' of the 1860s and 70s. Probably derived from 'smasher'.

Medicine show (USA). Street-corner variety or minstrel show given to attract crowds for the sale of patent medicine.

Olio (USA). Originally the variety acts between the two parts of a minstrel show, later applied to the variety acts in burlesque.

Penny gaff or blood tub. Improvised theatre which presented lurid melodrama and thrived in the East End of London during the nineteenth century.

Poses plastiques. Motionless exhibitions of living statuary which introduced women to the platforms of the song-and-supper rooms of the pre-music-hall era. Led by The Seldoms and La Milo, these studies of classical sculpture were popular on music hall bills of the 1900s and were the forerunners of the tableaux and nude shows which survived in variety until the mid-1950s.

Sand dance. Comedy burlesque of Arab dancing.

Smalls and spits. Small music halls which were often little more than a raised platform in the saloon bars of public houses. The term 'spits' was applied to the roughest of these which had spitoons strategically placed on the sawdust-covered floors.

Revudeville. A mixture of non-stop variety and revue. The London home of revudeville was the Windmill Theatre which commenced its policy of 'non-stop flesh-and-blood vaudeville' on 4 February 1932.

Top banana (USA). Principal comedian of a burlesque show.

Vaudeville (USA). The American equivalent of music hall. The origin of the word has been given as 'voix de ville' or songs of the city streets. The Charles Morton of vaudeville was Tony Pastor (1837–1908), who brought together the finer elements of the dime shows, burlesque, and beer-hall vaudeville and on 24 October 1881 staged a variety show as 'clean as a hound's tooth' at his new 14th Street Music Hall, New York. Vaudeville was soon controlled by managers with circuits of theatres from coast to coast. The most powerful of these was A.F. Albee and B.F. Keith, who with F.F. Proctor virtually held the monopoly in New York and the north until challenged by Marcus Klew and his partner A.L. Erlanger. On the west coast Martin Beck's far-flung Orpheum circuit held sway with Kohl and Castle as the vaudeville potentates of the Middle West. In the no-man's land in between, small-time vaudeville houses were known to seasoned pros as the 'death trial' and 'aching heart' circuits. The most famous vaudeville house was the Palace Theatre, New York, opened by B.F. Keith in 1913.

Wines and Spirits. Supporting acts whose names appeared low on the bill or programme and often in smaller type than the bar prices.

Who's Who

A

John Abbott, bass baritone, born Vernon John in West Virginia in 1896. He first appeared in England in 1931 as one of a successful vocal and musical act, 'The Three Virginians'. When the trio broke up he worked in variety as a solo act, and appeared in musical comedy. Later he turned legitimate and created the role of John Blandish in *No Orchids for Miss Blandish*, at the Prince of Wales Theatre, London. During a national tour of the play, he died in Edinburgh on 1 April 1943.

Afrique, vocalist and impressionist of variety and revue. Born Alexander Witkins in Johannesburg on 2 February 1907. He gave up the study of law for a stage career and trained as a singer for five years, making his debut in 1928. He came to London in December 1930 and became a member of the Vic-Wells Opera Company in March 1931. He made his first variety appearance at the Windmill in 1934 and appeared at the London Palladium in 1936. As the popular pantomime character Abanazer, he appeared in six consecutive Tom Arnold productions of *Aladdin*. In cabaret he appeared at the Ritz Carlton Hotel, New York in 1937–38 and then teamed with Larry Adler to tour South Africa. On his return to London he appeared in revues for George Black, including *Black Vanities* and *Black Velvet*.

Fred Albert, topical vocalist and comic singer of his own songs, 'The Mad Butcher', 'Take Care of the Pence', 'I Knew that I was Dreaming' and 'Perverted Proverbs'. Born on 9 November 1845, he made his earliest appearance as an amateur at the Goldsmith's Arms in Little Sutton Street, Clerkenwell, and as a pro at Macdonald's, Hoxton. He died at the age of 42 on 12 October 1886.

The Great Alexander Troupe, Hungarian acrobats originally known as the *Magyar Troupe*. They appeared in Budapest in 1925 and in London at the Dominion Theatre in 1929, making frequent tours of this country until 1938. After the war they returned as The Great Alexander Troupe and appeared in Bernard Delfont's International Variety at the London Casino on 23 February 1948, taking part in that year's Royal Variety Performance at the London Palladium.

Hadji Ali, speciality act, born in Egypt in 1892. He had the bizarre ability to swallow live mice, frogs, fish and so on and then regurgitate them unharmed. He first appeared at exhibitions and fairs in Cairo and Alexandria in 1910, and later went to the USA. Billed as 'The Egyptian Enigma' he appeared as a dime museum attraction and then toured in vaudeville as the star of Robert L. Ripley's *Believe It or Not*. During the 1930s he toured the world in variety, headlining in Australia for Frank Neil. Revue comedian and producer Frank O'Brien brought him to England to star in *New Faces*, making his first appearance in this country at the Theatre Royal in Chatham in June 1937. During the tour of the show he died in Wolverhampton in November 1937.

Sheik Ben Ali, 'The Comedy Prince of Magic'. Born in Calcutta on 26 August 1906. He first appeared at the Calcutta Exhibition of 1928 and after tours in India appeared in Japan, the USA, France and Germany. He made his London debut at the Pavilion in November 1933 and presented his own show in summer seasons at Great Yarmouth in 1936 and Skegness in 1937. He made his first solo variety appearance at Collins Music Hall, Islington, in January 1940, and with his comedy magic routine and catch phrase 'Nobody Inside, Nobody Outside', he remains a popular act in cabaret, pantomime and variety. In 1972 he appeared in a successful season of music-hall entertainment at the Lyceum, London.

Maud Allan, classical and exotic dancer, born in Toronto, Canada in 1879. Studied the piano in San Francisco and later in Berlin under the distinguished Italian pianist and composer Ferruccio Benvenuto Busoni. An interest in classical sculpture led her to a study of classical dancing, and she made her first stage appearance in Vienna in May 1903. In September 1907 she gave a private dance recital in Marienbad for King Edward VII. She made her London debut at the Palace Theatre of Varieties on 9 March 1908. Bare-footed and dressed in diaphanous costumes she danced to the music of Chopin's 'Valse Caprice' and Mendelssohn's 'Spring Song', but the most popular part of her act was 'The Vision of Salome'; danced to a waltz by Archibald Joyce, it

Maud Allan as Salomeé, 1908

caused a sensation. Not that it was in any way salacious. The criticism arose from the use of a property head of St John the Baptist which she swayed and gloated over and finally embraced. Opinion was divided as to her dancing ability but all agreed that she gave a highly dramatic performance which packed the Palace for eight months.

Following successful appearances at other London halls, she was booked by Walter de Frece for the Palace Theatre, Manchester, but at the last moment the city's Watch Committee, who wrongly thought she wore nothing under her rows of pearls and veils of crepe de chine, banned her from appearing. This guaranteed her success across the city boundary at the Victoria Theatre, Salford, and 'house full' notices for the rest of her provincial tour.

In 1909 she appeared in Moscow and St Petersburg and the following year toured the USA and Canada, appearing at Carnegie Hall, New York, on 20 January 1910. Her return to the Palace, London, in February 1911 was followed by a music-hall tour of the UK. In April 1918 she appeared in the title role of Oscar Wilde's *Salome*, presented by J. T. Grein's Independent Theatre Society, which gave two private performances at the Royal Court Theatre, Sloane Square. The play, translated from the French original by Lord Alfred Douglas, was still unlicensed by the Lord Chamberlain, and gave rise to a sensational criminal libel action brought by Maud Allan against Noël Pemberton Billing MP who, because of her association with the play, insinuated in his newspaper *The Vigilante* that she was a lesbian. She lost the case.

Between world tours she made frequent music-hall appearances in England. She retired from the stage at the age of 50, making her last variety appearance at the London Coliseum in May 1928. She returned to London in April 1932 to play the Abbess in *The Miracle*, at the Lyceum.

Chesney Allen *see* **Flanagan and Allen**

Jerry Allen, theatre organist, born Deryck Neil Allen, in Hemel Hempstead, 5 August 1925. He began his career as a cinema organist at the age of 14, playing at the Regal Cinema, Margate. Booked for the Tommy Trinder road show, he made his first stage appearance at the Theatre Royal, Chatham, in March 1940. Later formed the Jerry Allen Trio and was engaged by George Black for his revue *Strike a New Note*, which opened at the Prince of Wales, London, on 18 March 1943. Also worked summer shows and toured in revue with Issy Bonn, Tommy Trinder, and Alec Pleon. Turned solo in 1949 and became well-known in variety and on radio's 'Variety Bandbox' as Jerry Allen and his Hammond Organ.

Curtis D'Alton, baritone, born in 1857. After six years spent as a blacksmith he joined Sam Hague's Minstrels and made his first appearance at the Free Trade Hall, Manchester, in 1878. During the next eight years he split his time between singing with Moore and Burgess Minstrels at the St James's Hall, London, and acting as entertainer and later musical director of Llandudno Promenade Concerts. In September 1887 he went on a concert tour of America for Leo Dockstader. He made his music-hall debut at the Royal Holborn in June 1888, followed by four months at the Alhambra and six months at the Empire. He was the original singer of 'Our Jack's Come Home Today' and popularised 'The Longshoreman'. He died on 24 August 1911.

Ted and Barbara Andrews (and their daughter Julie), songs-at-the-piano act, popular in variety and on radio during the 1940s. Tenor Ted Andrews was born in Toronto, Canada, on 1 April 1907 and made his stage debut as a singer in 1928. He came to England to work as a musical arranger in 1937 and in 1939 teamed with pianist Barbara Morris. They were billed as 'Ted Andrews, the Canadian Troubador, with Barbara at the Piano' and made their first variety appearance at the Metropolitan Music Hall, Edgware Road, in 1940. Ted and Barbara later married, and after the war were joined in the act by Barbara's 12-year-old daughter. Billed as 'The Amazing Child Singer Julie Andrews', she made her solo debut in *Starlight Room*, which ran for a year at the London Hippodrome and on 1 November 1948 appeared at the London Palladium in the Royal Variety Show. The following Christmas she appeared with Vic Oliver in Emile Littler's *Humpty Dumpty* at the London Casino and during the early 1950s came to wider fame as the radio friend of Archie Andrews, Peter Brough's dummy in the top BBC show 'Educating Archie'. Ted and Barbara Andrews are now retired from active show business and Julie is an established star of musical comedy in the USA.

The Seven Ashtons, Risley and Tumbling Acrobats. A family troupe from New South Wales, the Seven Ashtons were managed by their parents, Dorothy and Hay Ashton. After touring the Tivoli Circuit of Australia for David N. Martin and South Africa with the Boswell Brothers Circus, they were booked by Leslie and Lew Grade for the 1948 Christmas season at the Tower Circus, Blackpool. Their original circus routines were adapted for the variety stage by Hay Ashton and they made their first London music-hall appearance at the Hackney Empire on 14 March 1949, and later that year played two engagements at the Palladium. On 7 November 1949 they took part in the Royal Variety Performance at the London Coliseum.

Arthur Askey, mini-comedian whose talents in variety, revue, radio and pantomime, make up for his lack of inches, and have earned him the billing of 'Big-Hearted Arthur'. Born in Liverpool in June 1900. After eight years as a clerk with Liverpool Education Office, he joined a touring concert party. He made his first stage appearance at Colchester, and

Arthur Askey

in London at the Crystal Palace in 1924. After 10 years of hard slog, small variety dates, touring revue and seasons with seaside concert parties, notably Powis Pender's 'Sunshine' at the Summer Theatre, Shanklin, IOW, his first real success came in 1938 when he broadcast with Richard Murdoch in the BBC's first weekly 'Same time, Same station' show 'Band Waggon'. This led to his own radio, and later TV, shows and established him at the top of variety bills at all the main music halls. In pantomime he is a good all-round performer in every comedy role from Buttons to Widow Twankey. He appeared in six Royal Variety Performances at the London Palladium between 1946 and 1968. On 17 October 1974 he was guest of honour at a Variety Club luncheon to celebrate his 50 years of show business.

Athleta, gymnast, born in Antwerp, Belgium, in 1867. Her parents were circus performers and at an early age she worked an act with her sister as a hand-balancer and equilibrist. On the death of her sister she took up weight-lifting and appeared in Antwerp with strong man John Marx. She made her first appearance in London in 1893, billed as 'The Strongest Woman in the World'.

Sam Auckland, concertina player and originator of the singing canary act. Born in Warrington on 27 December 1876, he spent over 20 years in the civil service before forming a double act with his wife Betty, and making his debut at Pringle's Palace, Edinburgh, in 1919. As 'The Aucklands Concertina Act' they toured in Scotland in variety for the next two years and then made their first London appearance at the London, Shoreditch, on 25 September 1912. In 1924 Sam Auckland introduced 'Little Tweet' into the act. A canary which sang to the accompaniment of a concertina and later to a full orchestra proved such a novelty that 'Little Tweet' records were issued.

George Auger, sketch artist. Born in Cardiff, Wales, he went to the USA as a child and later became an American citizen. Over eight feet tall, he wrote his own sketch material with parts to suit his height. His most successful was 'Jack the Giant Killer', which ran for 18 months in New York with Auger as the giant and a cast of midgets led by three-foot-tall Ernest Rommel as Jack. Auger and his company made their first appearance in Britain at the Glasgow Coliseum in August 1908.

'Auntie' (P. L. Clark), music-hall comedian who cleverly combined the art of the comedy dame with the skill of trick cycling. At the age of nine he was apprenticed to the Villions Acrobatic Troupe, making his first appearance at Rowley's in Huddersfield. After 14 years with the Villions, spent touring the world in circus and variety, he teamed in 1910 with W. E. Ritchie, an American well-known in the halls of this country as 'The Original Tramp Cyclist'. Together they worked two cycle acts, 'Ritchie's Reckless Rough Riders' and a similar routine billed as 'Clark's Crazy Comedy Cyclists'. In May 1911 Clark appeared solo at the Kingston Empire, but continued for many years to tour the UK and Europe with his cycling act. In his famous dame role of 'Auntie', Clark first appeared in his 'A gate, a bike, and a gamp' act with Marie Lloyd's variety company at the Willesden Hippodrome in June 1921. 'Auntie' opened the Royal Variety Performance at the Victoria Palace in February 1927.

Charles Austin, comedian, born Charles Reynolds in the East End of London in 1879. He made his music hall debut at Sebright's, Hackney, in 1896 as part of the double act

Charles Austin, 'Parker, PC'

of 'Lytton and Austin, The Stage-Struck Waifs'. He later appeared as a solo comic vocalist and in 1902 played Abanazer to Marie Lloyd's Aladdin at the Crown, Peckham. It was with his own comedy-sketch company, featuring the exploits of 'Parker, PC', that he scored his greatest success. He toured these crazy police station sketches for many years, the original 'Parker, PC' being followed by 'Parker's Progress', 'Parker on the Panel', etc. When the Garrick Theatre, London, staged a season of Old Time Music Hall in 1934, Austin acted as its genial chairman. A member of the Grand Order of Water Rats, he was highly regarded in the profession, serving as King Rat six times. He died on 14 January 1942.

B

Babette and Raoul, adagio dancers, Elizabeth and Hugh Duff McLauchlan. Babette, born in Glasgow on 7 April 1925, appeared at the age of seven as a dancer in concerts with Sir Harry Lauder and George Formby. At 16 she was engaged as principal dancer at the Glasgow Pavilion, appearing for a 20-week run with G.H. Elliott in 1941. Raoul, born in Hamilton, Scotland, on 2 December 1920, first worked with the acrobatic trio known as 'The Three Brightons'. He teamed with Babette just before the war. The act broke up when Raoul joined the army in 1939. Re-formed in 1947, they became popular in revue, cabaret and variety.

Max Bacon, comedian and drummer. Born in London 1 March 1904, he began his career as a dance-band drummer, joining Ambrose in March 1927. Played with the band on radio and on tour in variety with the Ambrose Octet. He then teamed with Sam Browne and Evelyn Dall as the variety act 'Stars of Radio', which was later joined by Gloria Brent and Maudie Edwards as 'Stars of the Air'. As a solo comedian he was well known in variety and on radio, distinguishing his act with a drum solo finale. During the latter part of his career he turned to straight character acting, including a West End appearance in *The Diary of Anne Frank*.

Hylda Baker, comedienne, born in Farnworth, near Bolton, on 4 February 1908. First appearance at the Opera House, Tunbridge Wells, in April 1918. From the age of 10 she toured as a single variety act, singing, dancing and doing impersonations, making her first London appearance at the Hippodrome, Poplar, in 1923. Starring in revue from the age of 15, she produced her own touring shows from 1939, the most successful being the 1948–55 editions of *Bearskins and Blushes*. After her success in Barney Colehan's BBC television show 'The Good Old Days' in 1955, she became a regular television performer, appearing with her silent friend Cynthia, a tall man in drag, who although never saying a word prompted Hylda's frequent asides, 'She knows y'know'. In 1961 she appeared in her own television show 'Our House' followed by 'Best of Friends' but her greatest success was the long running ITV show 'Nearest and Dearest' in which she co-starred with Jimmy Jewel (qv). A good character actress, she gave a notable performance as the back-street abortionist in Tony Richardson's 1960 film *Saturday Night and Sunday Morning*; her other films included *Up the Junction* and *Oliver*. In 1968 she returned to the West End in *Fill the Stage with Happy Hours* and in 1969 she appeared at the Palace Theatre in *Mr & Mrs*, a short-lived musical based on Noël Coward's *Brief Encounter* and *Fumed Oak*.

Josephine Baker, American-born star of French music hall. Born in St Louis, Missouri, on 3 June 1906. By the age of 10 she was appearing in New York at Harlem night-clubs, and at 16 she toured with the Sissle and Blake (qv) all-negro musical *Shuffle Along*. On 1 September 1924 she opened at the Colonial Theatre, New York, as a sort of black Fanny Brice in Sissle and Blake's new musical *The Chocolate Dandies*. When the show closed in May 1925, Baker set out on a tour of Europe with Lew Leslie's *Blackbirds* which, as *La Revue Nègre*, opened at the Théâtre des Champs Elysées, Paris, on 22 September 1925. Although described by one Paris critic as looking like 'a cross between a boxing kangaroo and a piece of chewing gum', her eccentric dancing was an overnight success and she was booked by Paul Derval for the Folies Bergère. In 1927 she starred in *Un Vent de Folie*, where her feline grace, accentuated by two cheetahs on a leash, and superbly lithe body, naked except for a girdle of bananas, took Paris by storm. Her success as a dancer was ratified by her singing of 'La Petite Tonkinoise' and 'J'ai Deux Amours', which established her as one of the most exciting stars of the Folies Bergère and Casino de Paris.

Her success was reported with interest in the USA and in 1936 she returned to New York to appear with Fanny Brice, Bob Hope and Gertrude Neilsen in the Ziegfeld Follies of 1936. Billed as the 'St Louis-born Flame of Paris' she had two good solo spots, singing 'Maharani' and dancing in the exotic production number 'An Island in the West Indies'. The New York critics were unimpressed. What New York

Max Bacon

lost, Paris gained. After 118 performances the show temporarily closed because of the illness of Fanny Brice, and by the time it reopened in September Josephine Baker was again the toast of Paris.

Between revues she toured the world, making successful appearances in both cabaret and variety. In 1938 she topped the bill at the London Palladium, followed by a tour of the Moss Empires. In 1940 she joined the French Women's Army and when France fell was actively involved with the Resistance and Free French forces, and entertained the Allied Armies with ENSA. For her services to France she was awarded in 1946 the Légion d'Honneur, the Croix de Guerre and the Rosette de la Résistance.

On 3 June 1947 she married French orchestra leader and arranger Jo Bouillon and together they rented the Château Milandes in the Dordogne. There they adopted an international family of 12 orphans, and from then on most of Josephine's time was spent looking after the children, though she found time for occasional revues and concert tours to boost the Milandes coffers. She announced her retirement in 1956, but in 1959 returned to the Paris Olympia in the spectacular 'Paris Mes Amours', and in 1964 appeared in New York. To raise £100,000 to buy Milandes from which the family was about to be evicted, she made another come-back in May 1968 at the Olympia and recorded four new songs for issue by Columbia. These ranged from a moving tribute to Edith Piaf, 'La Vie en Rose', to a brilliant new arrangement by Delanoe of 'Hello Dolly'. In 1972 she was engaged by the BBC to appear at the City of Varieties Music Hall, Leeds, in 'The Good Old Days' television programme.

HYLDA BAKER *Exclusive Decca Recording Artist*

Above: Hylda Baker and 'Cynthia'
Below: Josephine Baker at the Olympia, Paris, 1959 *(photo, Viollet)*

To celebrate her golden anniversary in show business she returned to America in June 1973 to give five shows at New York's Carnegie Hall. In the past she had found her most appreciative audiences outside the USA but now, plumed in the grand tradition of the French music hall, and mocking her 67 years in a sequinned body-stocking, singing 'Look at the Old Girl Now, Fellas', she brought the house down. Singing a little, talking a lot and nostalgically doing the Charleston, she was acclaimed by the world press. After an absence of 35 years she returned to top the bill at the London Palladium for the week of 19 August 1974. Sensationally dressed in a tight-fitting trouser-suit of turquoise blue with matching jewelled turban, topped by three-foot-high ostrich feathers, her entrance brought a gasp from the audience. Her repertoire spanned her long career, each song linked by reminiscences of Sissle and Blake and 'I'm Just Wild About Harry', of her friends Helen Morgan in *Show Boat* and Ethel Waters at the Cotton Club, remembered with 'Bill' and 'Stormy Weather'. The Paris of Hemingway, Cocteau and Picasso introduced 'J'ai Deux Amours' and Edith Piaf's 'La Vie en Rose'. Appropriately she summed up with 'There's No Business Like Show Business' and from her it was no cliché. As *Daily Mirror* critic Clifford Davis wrote the morning after: 'If you want to know what show business is all about—see Her, there won't be another.' In November she returned to the Palladium to appear in the Royal Variety Performance, a fittingly distinguished occasion on which to make her final London bow. To mark her 50th year on the Paris stage, she opened on 6 April 1975 in *Josephine*, a lavish revue at the Bobino Music Hall. Four days later she suffered a severe stroke and died on 12 April 1975.

Charles Baldwin, sketch artist and part author of Fred Karno's famous sketches 'Mumming Birds', 'Saturday to Monday' and 'The Diving Birds'. Born on 1 November

1870, he made his first stage appearance in a walk-on part in a production of *The Sultan Mocha* at the Strand Theatre in 1887. From 1890 to 1897 he gave parachute exhibitions and staged productions for Isaac Cohen at the Princess and Crown Theatres, Peckham, and later toured with his own sketch company.

Harry Ball, comic vocalist, born Harry Powles. A one-time pottery decorator for the Royal Worcester factory, he entertained friends with comic songs and musical selections on the violin and piccolo in his spare time. With his pet dog Fathead he gained a local reputation as an entertainer, and in 1865 left Worcester to manage a small music hall in Gloucester, becoming manager and chairman at St George's Hall, Nottingham, in 1868. He was the father of Vesta Tilley (qv) and as the popularity of 'The Great Little Tilley' spread through the Midlands, he gave up the Nottingham hall to tour with his daughter. Billed first as 'Harry Ball, the Tramp Musician with his wonderful performing dog Fathead' and later as 'The Great and Original Temperance Band Comedian and Vocalist' he wrote all his own songs including 'I'm Mourning for Jemima', 'What in the Name of Goodness is England Coming To Today' and 'Katie Trips the Dell'. He died on 10 October 1888.

Barbette, famed female impersonator and trapeze artist. Born Van der Clyde Broadway in Round Rock, Texas on 20 December 1899, he began his career as a circus wire-walker and aerialist with the Ringling Brothers. When one of the Alfaretta Sisters trapeze act was taken ill Van der Clyde took her place. As a female impersonator on a low wire he toured as a single act in vaudeville and in 1923 appeared at Thomas Barrasford's Alhambra Music Hall, Paris. Later that year he caused a sensation in the revue *Y a qu'a Paris* at the Casino de Paris and, billed as 'Barbette the Enigma', remained one of the greatest stars of the French music hall for over 20 years. In *Les Folies du Music Hall* (1960) Jacques Damase gives a vivid description of Barbette the 'man-woman':

Barbette, London, 1926

> On stage against black velvet curtains appeared a young woman in a silvery-gold wig topped with plumes and feathers with a train of rich lamé and silver lace, undressing on a couch of rich oriental carpets. The woman then rose, naked except for the gems on her breast and belly, and began walking a tight rope. Her eyes shaded green like some mysterious asiatic jewel, she walked backwards and forwards along the tight rope, dispensed with her balancing pole, and contorted her thin nervous body as the entire audience held its breath. Then Barbette leapt down on the stage, gave a bow, tore off her wig and revealed a bony Anglo-Saxon acrobat's head: gasps from the astonished audience shattered by the sudden brutality of the action.

Barbette made his first London appearance with Bertram Mills Olympic Circus on 20 December 1926 and later made several variety tours of the UK. After 20 years at the top of the bill at the leading music halls of London, Paris, Berlin and New York, he returned to the USA at the outbreak of war and while appearing in vaudeville in 1942 fell and injured his spine. Forced to retire from active stage work he became a producer with the Ringling Brothers, Barnum and Bailey Circus. He died at his home in Austin, Texas, on 5 August 1972.

George Barclay, cockney step-dancer and comedian of the team 'Barclay and Perkins—The Brewers of Mirth'. Born in 1868, he married the coster comedienne Kate Carney (qv) in 1885 and later became a successful variety agent. He died on 30 January 1944.

Wilkie Bard, comedian, born William Augustus Smith in Manchester in 1874. After gaining experience as an amateur at the local Ship Inn, he left a job as a clerk in a cotton spinner's office and made his first professional appearance on 11 February 1895. He was then working under the name of Will Gibbard but by the time he arrived in London a few months later had changed to Wilkie Bard. His London debut was at Collins Music Hall, Islington, in June 1895 as a coster comedian singing 'E Aint the Bloke I Took Him For', 'Never 'Ave a Lodger for a Pal' and 'All Becos E's Minding a 'Ouse'. He soon developed his own style of comedy, adopting the eccentric but distinctive make-up of a high bald forehead with black spots painted above each eyebrow. He presented a wide range of character studies and sketches including 'The Turkish Bath Attendant', 'The Night Watchman', 'The Park Keeper', 'The Beauty Parlour', and 'The Boot Shop'. Perhaps he was at his best in droll dame roles ranging from stage cleaners to haughty duchesses—and the would-be prima donna who confides to the audiences:

> I want to sing in opera, if I could have
>   my choice,
> I want to sing in opera, I've got that
>   kind of voice,
> Signor Caruso told me I ought to do so,
> So that's why I want to sing-in-opera,
> Sing-in-op-op-oper-a-a.

During his long and successful career in pantomime he twice appeared at Drury Lane, in 1908 as Idle Jack in *Dick Whittington* and in 1909 as Widow Twankey to Marie George's Aladdin. He started a vogue and panto tradition of tongue-twisting songs like 'She Sells Sea Shells on the Sea Shore' and was the originator of the 'interrupted turn' used by double acts ever since. He took part in the first Royal Variety Performance at the Palace in 1912, singing 'The Night Watchman'. Other successful comic songs included the anti-suffragette 'Put Me on an Island Where the Girls are Few', the policeman's song 'I'm Here if You Want Me' and 'O, O, Capital O'. He made several top-line tours of America receiving up to £300 per week and when the great music-hall vogue began to decline he turned to revue, appearing in *The Bing Girls* at the Alhambra in 1918. Returning later to variety, he continued on the halls and in pantomime until shortly before his death on 5 March 1944.

Fred Barnes, light comedian and character vocalist, born in Birmingham on 1 May 1884. Educated at Beechfield College, Malvern, he made his first stage appearance in December 1907 at the Gaiety Theatre, Birmingham, and in London at the Empress, Brixton, in 1908. He was an immediate success and in the heyday of his career was one of the brightest stars of the variety stage. A polished artiste with a good light baritone voice, dashingly handsome and always immaculately dressed, he played at the top of the bill at almost every theatre of note in London or the provinces. He also toured with considerable success in Australia, South Africa and America, singing such song hits as 'Ragtime Violin', 'Floating with my Boating Girl', 'Wedding Bells Ringing for Sammy', 'The Black Sheep of the Family', 'Two Dirty Little Hands', 'What You Never Have You Never Miss', 'There's a Friend in Every Milestone', 'Give Me a Million Beautiful Girls', 'Sally—The Sunshine of our Alley' and 'Give me the Moonlight', originally made famous by Elsie Janis and kept green by Frankie Vaughan (qv). With Randolph Sutton (qv) he was the original singer of 'On Mother Kelly's Doorstep' but, not making much of a hit with the song, relinquished it to Sutton who made it very much his own. In a less tolerant age, a scandal in Fred's private life caused his popularity to decline and by the mid-1930s he had passed out of the limelight. Suffering from tuberculosis, he retired to his small flat in Southend-on-Sea where he died of gas poisoning on 23 October 1933.

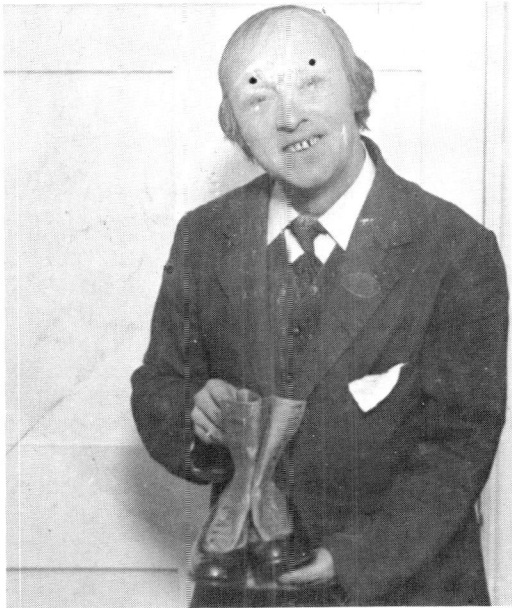

Above: Wilkie Bard, 'The Boot Shop', 1912

Below: Fred Barnes

Ida Barr, comedienne, born Maud Barlow at the Albany Street Barracks, Regent's Park, London, on 17 January 1882. Preferring the ups-and-downs of the stage to the discipline of her father, a sergeant-major in the Life Guards, she ran away from home at the age of 16 to make her first stage appearance in the chorus of the Theatre Royal, Belfast, in 1898. A strapping girl of nearly 14 stone, resplendent in tights, tassels, green sequinned shamrocks and Irish harps, she was a great success and remained in Ireland for six years. Returning to London she appeared as the Sultan of Morocco in pantomime at the Pavilion Theatre, Whitechapel and made her first solo music-hall appearance at the Middlesex about 1906. She was then working as Maud Laverne but, after deciding to change her name, first appeared as Ida Barr at the Bedford, Camden Town, in January 1908. To get away from an unsuccessful marriage to comedian Gus Harris who billed himself as 'The Only Yiddisher Scotsman in the Irish Fusiliers' and resented his name slipping to the bottom of the bill while his wife's rose to the top, Ida left for the USA in 1910. By 1912 she was topping vaudeville bills from New York to San Francisco and later repeated her success in South Africa and Australia. Billed as The Ragtime Girl' she returned to London on the crest of the 'Ragtime' dance craze and was a great hit with the songs 'Everybody's Doing It' and 'Oh, You Beautiful Doll'. After many years of virtual obscurity, she was 're-discovered' by Daniel Farson and with G.H. Elliott, Billy Danvers, Albert Whelan, Marie Lloyd Junior and Hetty King made a record ('Music Hall') at the Metropolitan Music Hall, Edgware Road. At the age of 81 she took part in the last performance at the Metropolitan, on Good Friday, 12 April 1963, and on 8 January 1964 opened at the Comedy Theatre in Daniel Farson's short-lived music-hall entertainment *Nights at the Comedy*. She died on 17 December 1967.

T. W. Barrett, 'A Nobleman's Son'

Water Rats, he was Prince Rat for 1927–28. He died on 26 November 1942.

Nora Bayes, American syncopated vocalist of 'Shine on Harvest Moon' fame. Born in Milwaukee, Wisconsin, in 1881, she toured in vaudeville both as a single act, billed with typical American modesty as 'The Greatest Single Woman Singing Comedienne in the World', and with her husband as 'Nora Bayes, Assisted and Admired by Jack Norworth'. Although one of the greatest stars of vaudeville and musical comedy in the USA her first appearance in London at the Palace Theatre in 1905 was not a success. She tried again in

Jack Barty, 'The Burly Burlesquer'

T. W. Barrett, popular comedian, born in 1851. Although his father was a Birmingham shoemaker, almost from his first London appearance at the Pavilion, Mile End, he was known on the halls as 'A Nobleman's Son'. He is credited with being the originator of the deadpan style of comic delivery. His songs included 'The Marquis of Camberwell Green', 'I Don't Like London', 'I've Been and Got Married Today', 'Jolly as a Sand Boy' and the number which gave him his aristocratic billing, 'A Nobleman's Son'. He toured with the second edition of De Courville's *Veterans of Variety*, and died on 19 April 1935.

Jack Barty, variety, revue and musical-comedy comedian. Born in London in 1888, he made his earliest music-hall appearances as part of a double-comedy act in 1907. After army service he resumed his variety career in 1918 as a single turn billed 'Jack Barty—The Burly Burlesquer', and became well known as a revue comedian for his performance in the record-breaking *Our Liz*, which ran in London from 1922 to 1924. During 1925 and 1926 he made a variety tour of South Africa, Australia and the USA. In musical comedy he was successful in *White Horse Inn* (1931–32) and *Casanova* at the London Coliseum (1932–33). Returning to variety, he became an early member of the 'Crazy Gang' at the London Palladium, and appeared with them in the Royal Variety Performance of 1933. A member of the Grand Order of

Nora Bayes *(photo, S. Georges, London)*

1914 but again flopped at both the Empire and Victoria Palace. Undaunted, she was resolved that sooner or later she would overcome this apathy and establish herself as a star in London. However, in the summer of 1923, Charles Gulliver, the managing director of the London Theatres of Variety, found himself short of head-lining acts and booked her for a month at the London Palladium. At the end of the engagement she was still far from being a success but had at least managed to break the London ice, and made the unprecedented offer to Gulliver that if he would let her stay on at the Palladium she would take a 50 per cent cut in her already reduced salary, accept low billing, and change her material weekly. He accepted, and as the weeks went by she built up a regular following, until at the end of her 10 weeks she was doing a longer and longer turn and receiving a standing ovation nightly. Her top billing and salary restored, she played to full houses for the last month of her run and on the last night, 6 October 1923, sang each of the 35 songs she had introduced during the previous 12 weeks. It had taken 20 years but at last she was a London success.

A strikingly large woman, with an exuberant and expansive personality, she had a powerful voice somewhere between soprano and contralto. While never great masterpieces of originality, her songs ranged from syncopated jazz to a burlesque version of 'Softly Awakes my Heart' from *Samson and Delilah*. She could belt an Al Jolson number, or softly sing the blues. She returned to London in 1924 to top billing at the Oxford and Empire Theatres, and again in 1926 to star in Maurice Cowan's revue *Life* at the Palladium, and to appear in variety at the Alhambra. In cabaret at the Café de Paris, London, she was one of the first established vocalists to include the songs of Noël Coward in her act. She died in New York on 19 March 1928 at the age of 47.

George Beauchamp, comedian born in 1863. He made his first appearance in 1879, touring the provinces barnstorming in Shakespearean and melodramatic roles. As a comic singer he first found success in America where he appeared at the Casino Theatre, St Louis, in 1886. After a three-month variety season at Koster and Bial's Concert Hall on 23rd Street, New York, he toured through the USA, playing ten states in six months, under the management of Tony Pastor. His return to England did not bring him the acclaim he had enjoyed in the USA and in 1886 he returned to New York to appear for Pastor and make another tour under the management of Fred Hart of Harlen and Hart. By 1880 he was singing character songs almost exclusively, in a style which established him as a star on both sides of the Atlantic. He is best remembered as the original singer of the all-time classic, written and composed by T. W. Connor, 'She Was One of the Early Birds and I Was One of the Worms'. For years he concluded his act with this song, its still-famous chorus being sung all over London:

She was a sweet little dicky bird,
Chip, Chip, Chip, she went
Sweetly she sang to me,
Till all my money was spent,
Then she went off song—
We parted on fighting terms—
She was one of the early birds,
And I was one of the—

When he came to the last line, which he sang as if it were a question, he would go to the footlights, pause at the last word, cock his ear, and wait for the audience to roar 'worms'. In 1889 he married serio-comedienne Nelly Lingard, and died in 1901 at the early age of 38.

Harry Bedford, red-nosed comedian, born in Pimlico, London, in 1873. He made his first stage appearance at the age of seven with Mamley's Variety Company at the Magpie Music Hall, Battersea, followed by child parts in the stock company of the Elephant and Castle Theatre and the Britannia, Hoxton. After breaking apprenticeships as diverse as boat-building and wig-making, he joined a touring theatre company at 6s 6d a week and later worked the beach shows of the south coast as a burnt-cork minstrel and clown. At 15 he played the Cat to the 14-year-old Vesta Tilley's Dick Whittington at the Theatre Royal, Portsmouth making his first solo music-hall appearance under the name 'Fred City' at Vento's Varieties, Portsmouth, in 1889. In 1895 he appeared at the Middlesex Music Hall, London, with James Graydon's 'Rip Van Winkle Sketch Company' and soon afterwards as a solo comedian and dancer. A popular low comedian, his earliest song successes were 'Cock of the North' and 'When I Get Some Money' but his greatest hit was 'A Little Bit off the Top', which he first sang at Southampton in December 1898. Tame by today's standards, it was considered very saucy in the not-so-naughty nineties. The first verse told of his liking for roast pork and his request to a waiter to:

Carve a little bit off the top for me, for me!
Just a little bit off the top for me, for me!
Saw me off a yard or two, I will tell you
   when to stop,
All I want is a little bit off the top.

By the fourth verse he was in the embarrassing situation of being sat on by a courting couple while sleeping in a hayfield, and letting out the anguished cry,

Move a little weight off the top for me, for me!
Shift a little weight off the top for me, for me!
Take away the gentleman, the lady she can stop,
All I want is a little weight off the top.

He toured with the Veterans of Variety Company and died on 17 October 1939.

Bessie Bellwood, one of the greatest music-hall comediennes, whose tremendous popularity during the 1880s and 1890s has been overshadowed by the fame accorded to her successor as 'Queen of the Halls', Marie Lloyd. Famous for her outrageous cockney humour, she was born Elizabeth Ann Katherine Mahony in Monkstone, Northern Ireland, in 1857. She was brought up in Bermondsey, London, and employed as a child as a rabbit-skinner in the New Cut. For an extra few shillings a week, she sang Irish ballads at The Jolly Tanners in Southwark, which led to her earliest professional music-hall appearance at the Winchester and Star, Bermondsey.

Described by Arthur Roberts as a veritable Jekyll and Hyde among comediennes (*Fifty Years of Spoof*, 1927), she was always ready to give as good as she got in the rowdy days of the early music halls, where you had to be both good and loud to survive. Her mastery of repartee and her tempestuous personality which stood no nonsense are vividly illustrated by Jerome K. Jerome's recollection of her debut at the Star, Bermondsey, published in *The Idler Magazine* in March 1892:

Introduced by the Star's Chairman as 'The World's Famous Zither Player Signorina Ballantino', she was at once heckled by a hefty-looking coalheaver who made it clear that he had no intention of allowing his drinking to be disturbed. A slanging match ensued with Bessie declaring

Bessie Bellwood, 1889

her intention of 'wiping down the bloomin' 'all with him and making it respectable'. For over five minutes she let fly, leaving him gasping, dazed and speechless. At the end, she gathered herself together for one supreme effort, and hurled at him an insult so bitter with scorn, so sharp with insight into his career and character, so heavy with prophetic curse, that strong men drew and held their breath while it passed over them, and women hid their faces and shivered. Then she folded her arms and stood silent, and the house, from floor to ceiling, rose and cheered her until there was no more breath left in its lungs.

Her patter was often 'blue' and her songs suggestive, but without the finesse of Marie Lloyd. However, she was idolised by her audiences and generous to those in need. Her most successful song, 'What Cheer Ria', dating from 1887, tells of a young cockney coster girl's visit to a music hall, and how she decided not to sit in the 'gods' with her friends, but spend a shilling to sit at the Chairman's table. The chorus ran:

What cheer Ria! Ria's on the job.
What cheer Ria! Did you speculate a bob?
Oh Ria, she's a toff and she looks immenskoff,
And they all shouted, What cheer Ria!

All her songs were in the pure music-hall tradition, with themes and sentiments which were repeated over and over again during the 100 years or so of music-hall history. There was 'I'm a Lady', 'I'm a Lady Who Has Seen Better Days', 'The Organ Grinding Girl', 'The Duchess of Petticoat Lane', 'Has Anybody Seen My Mary Ann?', 'Aubrey Plantagenet' and, in the days when a music-hall pro had the problem of getting to as many as six halls a night, 'The Pro's Coachman':

First he's at the Tivoli,
Then he's at the Pav,
Then comes out and begins to shout,
Fifteen minutes you have,
Then he drives like hell to the Paragon.

CANTERBURY
THEATRE of VARIETIES, WESTMINSTER BRIDGE ROAD.
Managing Director — Mr. G. ADNEY PAYNE

"Our own Bess!"—Vide "Referee."

MISS
BESSIE BELLWOOD
Has the pleasure of announcing that her
FIRST COMPLIMENTARY
BENEFIT
In London will take place at the above Establishment
TO-NIGHT
WEDNESDAY EVENING, APRIL 3rd
WHEN A GRAND
DOUBLE ENTERTAINMENT
Introducing the leading Celebrities of the Theatrical, Musical, and Sporting Worlds will be presented under the Experienced Supervision of Mr. HUGH J. DIDCOTT.

One Hundred Artistes will appear
INCLUDING
MR. ARTHUR ROBERTS
(By permission of H. Watkin, Esq., Avenue Theatre)
MISS
HARRIET VERNON
(By permission of Augustus Harris, Esq.)
MR. DAN LENO
(By permission of Augustus Harris, Esq.)
MISS
BESSIE BELLWOOD
By desire, will sing "The Kerry Dancers."
TED PRITCHARD
And
W. GOODE
(Chesterfield)
WILL SPAR THREE ROUNDS.
MR.
CHARLES COLLETTE
MR.
CHARLES GODFREY
The Beautiful Geraldine
Frank Hinde's Light Weight Lancashire Wrestlers
JOHN BARKER
Of Lees.
JACK MASSEY
Of Oldham.
KREMSER
The Miraculous Stilt Vaulter.
CHARLES ROSS
(From the Gaiety Theatre).
MISS JENNY HILL
MR. G. H. MACDERMOTT
MISS ADDIE CONYERS

Manager — Mr. J. ARTHUR TRESSIDDER.
Musical Director — Mr. EDWARD BOSANQUET.

DOORS OPEN AT 7. COMMENCE 7.15.
PRICES FROM SIXPENCE TO FIVE GUINEAS

WEDNESDAY, APRIL 3, 1889

Billy Bennett, 1937

She visited America in 1895, scoring a great hit at Koster and Bial's Music Hall, New York, but alas her reign as 'Queen of Comedy' was all too short. On her return to London she made her last appearance at the Pavilion in July 1896 and died on 24 September of that year, aged 59.

Billy Bennett, outstanding star comedian whose bawdy forthright humour was the essence of music hall. Born in 1887, his father was one of the double act of Bennett and Martell (qv) and he made his first appearance as the rear end of a donkey. However, he was not over-enthusiastic about following in his father's footsteps, so after a brief career as an acrobat he signed on as a regular soldier. Completing his term of army service, he returned to the stage as a burlesque comedian, until he re-enlisted at the outbreak of the First World War. From 1919 he worked the halls as a soldier comic, specialising in absurd parodies such as:

There's a cock-eyed yellow poodle to the north
  of Waterloo,
There's a little hot cross bun that's turning green,
There's a double-jointed woman doing tricks in
  Chu Chin Chow,
And you're a better man than I am Gunga Din.

With his shaggy moustache, black hair plastered into a quiff, ill-fitting dress-suit, a suspender posing as a fob below a seedy looking waistcoat which struggled to contain an egg-stained dickey and, as a last touch of sartorial elegance, brown hob-nailed boots, he was, as his billing announced, 'Almost a Gentleman' As a solo act he made three Royal Variety appearances, the first at the Alhambra in 1926, and at the Palladium in 1933 and 1934. In 1930 he teamed on a part-time basis with James Carew (qv), forming the BBC radio black-faced cross-talking act of 'Alexander and Mose', which was first broadcast from Savoy Hill and followed the old tradition of the nigger-minstrel corner man. Together they took part in the Royal Variety Show of 1931, and when James Carew returned to America his place in the act was taken by Albert Whelan (qv). Billy Bennett made his last stage appearance in George Black's *Black Varieties* at the Opera House, Blackpool, on 23 May 1942, and died on 30 June of the same year.

Bennett and Martell, slapstick comedy act. John Bennett, born in Scotland, was at the age of 15 apprenticed for seven years to the Trowbridge Ballet Troupe but, after only a few months spent playing a 'swell' in a comic ballet, broke his apprenticeship and teamed with an original member of 'The Three Karnos'. As 'Bennett and Harley, the Murderous Knockabouts' they made their debut at the Parthenon, Liverpool, in 1890.

Robert Martell, born in Coventry, made his first stage appearance at the age of 17, working a concert-party double act with Jack Manley. In 1886 he teamed with T. E Dunville, and as 'The Two Martells' they appeared for five months as two comic policemen with Fred Stinson's 'Flint and Steel' Company. After two years of provincial smalls doing a high-kicking comedy routine they were engaged by James Payne for a tour of the USA and on their return appeared with Sidney Cooper's pantomime company as bailiffs in *Babes in the Wood* at Leicester. When Dunville turned solo in 1888, Martell worked for a time with another partner as 'Martell and Olive' until he teamed with Bennett in 1890. They were a sound knockabout, slapstick comedy act on the halls and in pantomime for many years, appearing in both Drury Lane and Surrey Theatre pantomimes. Bennett was the father of Billy Bennett (qv) of 'Almost a Gentleman' fame. Martell died on 29 April 1925, and Bennett on 17 February 1936.

Jack Benny, outstanding vaudeville and radio comedian, born Benjamin Kubelsky in Chicago on 14 February 1894. Brought up in Waukegan, Illinois, where his father was a haberdasher, he studied the violin as a boy and at 13 fiddled with a Waukegan dance orchestra At 17, as Benny K. Benny, he teamed with Cora Salisbury and for 18 months toured as a straight musical act in vaudeville. In 1911 Salsbury left the act and Benny teamed with pianist Lyman Woods, with whom he made his first appearance in England at the Palace Theatre, London, in 1912, followed by a

12-week tour of the UK. The Woods-Benny partnership lasted for six years until Jack joined the US Navy in 1917. As there was not much demand for a straight violinist in the navy, he first introduced comedy into his act in a service revue, which toured the training camps of the USA.

On his discharge he returned to vaudeville as a stand-up comedian and in 1921 appeared as Proctor's Music Hall, a well-known 'break-in house' on Fifth Avenue, New York. He later made the Orpheum circuit and headlined at the Palace Theatre, New York, for the first time in 1929, making his solo London debut at the Palladium in August 1931. In 1932 he was invited by Ed Sullivan to broadcast for CBS and although insisting that he knew nothing about radio, his first words on the air were a Benny classic, 'This is Jack Benny speaking. Now there will be a brief pause for everyone to say "who cares"'. For the next 18 years, Benny, together with Phil Harris, Mary Livingstone, and his famous negro feed, Eddie 'Rochester' Anderson, remained one of the most popular comedians on the air and many of his programmes were broadcast by the BBC Home Service during the war. With his radio partners Jack Benny topped the bill at the London Palladium for the weeks of 19 and 26 July 1948, and from then on made frequent variety appearances in this country, including a number of Royal Variety Shows. His perennial comedy line hinged on his meanness, his vanity about his age (a perpetual 39), and his excruciating playing of the violin. His first television appearance was at the opening of the Hollywood TV station in March 1949 and his first show was screened on 28 October 1950. During the next 20 years 'The Jack Benny Show' guest-starred many celebrities, among them most of the greats of stage and screen. Marilyn Monroe made her television debut as Jack's guest in 1953 and later the same year Humphrey Bogart appeared in Benny's burlesque of *Detective Story*. Other guests ranged from Harry S. Truman to the Marquis Family of Chimpanzees. His stage and television appearances in Britain became an almost annual event; the last one in London was at the Palladium on 17 June 1973. In November 1974 plans were going ahead for Jack to star with Walter Matthau in a film version of Neil Simon's Broadway success *The Sunshine Boys* but after a short illness he died at his home in Beverly Hills on 26 December 1974. The perennial 39-year old was almost 81.

George and Bert Bernard, American dancers and pantomimists, remembered in this country for their mime-to-records comedy act, popular in variety during the late 1940s and early 1950s.

George Bernard, born in Cumberland, Maryland, July 1912, began as a child tap dancer in the 1920s, graduating to juvenile tap dancing with revue and floor shows. While appearing in cabaret in Washington DC, he met Bert Maxwell, a 15-year-old vaudeville and musical comedy dancer from Boston, and in 1932 they teamed as 'The Bernard Dancers', touring North and South America with a modern and satirical ballet routine. In 1938 they appeared at the Folies Bergère, Paris, and made their London debut in a floor show at the Dorchester Hotel in September that year.

Bert Maxwell joined the US Army in 1941 and Bernard worked solo, entertaining the troops at USO camp shows. In 1946, as George and Bert Bernard, they devised their record mime act, assisted behind the scenes by George Pierce. After success in the USA they played for 10 months at the Lido, Paris, and in November 1947 appeared in revue at the London Casino. Comedy mime acts were then a novelty and the Bernard Brothers, as they came to be billed, were an instant success with their parody of the Andrews Sisters. Their popularity increased during their first London variety

Blondin, 1861

season at the Palladium, opening 16 April 1948. Later that year they appeared in the Royal Variety Show at the Palladium and after engagements in Paris were again at the Palladium starring in Val Parnell's pantomime *Cinderella*. A summer season at the Opera House, Blackpool, was followed by *Puss in Boots*, their second Palladium pantomime at Christmas 1949.

Blondin, French tight-rope walker, born in 1824. Billed as 'The Little Wonder', he first appeared at the Ecole de Gymnase at Lyons in 1831. His international fame was established by crossing Niagara Falls on a wire at a height of 160 feet on 30 June 1859. A great showman, he repeated his feat in July, and in August crossed the falls blindfolded with a man on his back. His last crossing, on 14 September 1860, was on stilts and was watched by the Prince of Wales, who had to be restrained by his equerry from accepting Blondin's offer of a piggy-back ride across the falls. Billed as 'The Hero of Niagara' he made his first appearance in England at the Crystal Palace on 1 June 1861, when in addition to his usual skill on the low and high wires, he appeared as Jacko the monkey in a melodramatic pantomime-cum-ballet entitled 'The Child of the Wreck'. After a provincial tour he made his music-hall debut at the Canterbury, followed by a very successful engagement at the Alhambra. Between world tours he made frequent music-hall and pleasure-garden appearances in England, eventually making London his home. Retiring to 'Niagara Villa', Northfields, he died in 1897.

The Two Bobs, American duettists, Bob Alden and Bob Adams, born in 1882 and 1876 respectively. Pioneers of ragtime, they first appeared in England in 1908 and soon became headline attractions billed as 'The Two Bobs'. Making their home in England, they remained popular in variety for over 20 years, singing songs at the piano, such as 'The Trail of the Lonesome Pines', 'Our Village', 'Casey Jones', 'On the 5.15', and 'If You're Going Back to Dixie'. They retired in 1927, Bob Alden dying in 1932 and Bob Adams in 1948.

The Two Bobs, 1910

Walford Bodie, flamboyant variety artist, who during his career was variously considered to be a great showman, miracle worker and blatant charlatan. Whichever description was true, theatre managers did not give a hoot; the name of Dr Walford Bodie at the top of their bills meant record-breaking business in both the UK and America for over 40 years. Born Sam Bodie in Aberdeen on 11 June 1870, he was apprenticed at the age of 14 as an electrician with the National Telephone Company. He first appeared as a Saturday evening entertainer at the Town Hall, Stonehaven, in December 1886, demonstrating the new-found wonders of electricity. But it was not until his sister married Werner Walford, who ran the Connaught Theatre of Varieties, Norwich, that he made his professional debut as a conjurer and ventriloquist. By 1901 he had obtained an American degree of dubious provenance and, adding his brother-in-law's name to his own, toured in the 'Royal Magnet's Variety Company' as 'Dr Walford Bodie', assisted by his wife 'Princess Rubie', his sister 'Mystic Marie' and 'La Belle Electra'. He made his first London appearance at the Britannia Theatre, Hoxton, in 1903, with such success that during the next six months he was booked for three return engagements and appeared at other leading London halls luridly billed as 'The most remarkable man on earth, the great healer, the modern miracle worker, demonstrating nightly "Hypnotism, Bodie force and the wonders of bloodless surgery"'. He claimed to have treated 900 cases of paralysis that had been given up as hopeless and incurable by the great London hospitals. When the wonders of electricity ceased to be wonders he toured his own variety shows. Once more turning to ventriloquism he was billed in 1921 as presenting a new historical comedy drama ventriloquial scene, 'The Merry Monarch, or Nell Gwyn's Haunted Boudoir', and in 1930 was billing himself as 'The Talkies' Only Rival'. When 'Princess Rubie' died on 24 January 1931, Bodie married Florrie Robertshaw, a 22-year-old chorus girl. He continued to tour in variety and made his last appearance at the Olympia, Blackpool, a few weeks before his death on 19 October 1939.

The Boganny Troupe, company of five boys who presented a music-hall slapstick comedy routine known during the early 1900s as 'The Lunatic Bakers'. The troupe was formed by Joe Boganny, the son of a one-time acrobat who appeared as a slack-rope performer with both Sanger's and Henglar's circuses. Joe Boganny first worked as one of the 'Three Brothers Clifton' doing acrobatics in full evening dress, and continued with his own troupe at the Alhambra in 1905. He died on 28 July 1943

George Bolton, comedian and leading pantomime dame. Born Portsmouth 12 June 1900. Began his stage career with a juvenile troupe at the Palace Theatre, Jarrow-on-Tyne in April 1913. By the age of 18 he was touring in revue as

principal comedian, making his first London appearance at the Palace, Hammersmith, on 7 August 1925. For the next 10 years he toured the UK and in 1936 went to Australia. Turning solo he made his first variety appearance at the Metropolitan, Edgware Road, in 1937, and became one of the most popular pantomime dames.

Issy Bonn, comedian and vocalist, born Benjamin Levin in London on 21 April 1903. Success as a boy singer during the First World War led to his first professional appearance at the Mile End Empire in 1923 as one of the 'Three Rascals', a singing and comedy trio. As a single act he worked the small

'Dr' Walford Bodie and a patient, before and after treatment, 1906

Joe Boganny and his troupe

halls and in cine-variety as Benny Leven. BBC variety producer John Sharman heard him singing in an East End cinema, and he was given his first radio spot in 1936. As Issy Bonn he became well known on the air and in variety singing sentimental ballads of the 'My Yiddisher Momma' type. During the war he toured with ENSA. In 1948 he toured his own road show, 'And So We Go On!', and in the following year 'The Melody Lingers On'. On Good Friday 12 April 1963, he took part in the last bill at the Metropolitan, Edgware Road.

Webster Booth *see* **Ann Ziegler and Webster Booth**

Fred Brezin, light-fingered magician who specialised in stage pickpocket routines on the London halls and throughout Europe during the early 1900s. Born Max Frederick Brezinski on 26 September 1886, he made his first appearance as 'Master Fred Brezin—the Boy Magician' at the Music Hall, Charlotte Street, Portsmouth, in 1887, and in London three years later at the Middlesex Music Hall. Later he acted as stage assistant to a number of well-known illusionists, notably Curtis Leo and Valezzi, and in 1904–5 worked the halls as 'Prince Kuroki'. He introduced his deft pickpocket routine while on the bill of the Canterbury Music Hall in 1906 and later presented the act in variety and cabaret throughout Europe.

Brinn, extraordinarily adept juggler who specialised in spectacular feats of balancing hefty pieces of artillery on his chin and neck. These included shells of progressively larger size, balanced on an iron rod. After each balance he let the shell fall, catching it upon the back of his neck. When he appeared at the Palace Theatre, London, in August 1904, he was assisted by his own company dressed as soldiers and sailors, with a stage set representing the deck of a battleship. After the shell-balancing warm up, he balanced a cannon on an iron rod perched on his chin. This he also let drop and as he caught it on the straining muscles of his neck, it automatically fired. The climax of his act was the balancing on his chin of the cannon fitted in its gun carriage, which was hauled into position by special tackle manned by six sailors.

Peter Brough, ventriloquist, born in Ealing, London, on 16 February 1916, the son of Arthur Brough, who with his dummy 'Tim' worked as a ventriloquist from 1903 to his retirement in 1922. Peter Brough made his professional stage debut at the New Theatre, Oxford, in December 1938 and shortly afterwards auditioned unsuccessfully for the BBC. During the war he served in the RASC and toured with ENSA but was invalided out of the army in 1942. He was then given another BBC audition, and booked to broadcast in John Sharman's 'Music Hall'. With his cheeky schoolboy doll 'Archie Andrews', he toured for the next year in variety for Stoll, and while appearing at the Brixton Empire was seen by Charles Maxwell, who engaged him to appear in his popular radio programme 'Navy Mixture'. Other radio shows followed, including the famous 'Variety Bandbox', and in 1948 he was given his own 20-minute radio spot entitled 'Two's a Crowd'. Supported by the 'voice of them all' impressionist Peter Cavanagh, it was such a success that in June 1950 he was awarded his own radio variety show 'Educating Archie'. Appearing with Peter Brough and the star of the show 'Archie Andrews' were among others Max Bygraves, Hattie Jacques, Robert Morton and the 14-year-old Julie Andrews. The show was only intended as a six-week replacement for 'Take It From Here' but eventually ran for 30 weeks and won a silver mike in the National Radio

Above: Issy Bonn
Below: Brinn, 1904

and Television Awards as the top variety series of 1950. Other series followed, and established Peter Brough and Archie Andrews as household names and a top-of-the-bill attraction at variety theatres up and down the country. 'Educating Archie' helped to establish many young comedians, notably Tony Hancock, who replaced Robert Morton as Archie's tutor on 3 August 1951.

Brown, Newland, and Le Clerq, black-faced sketch trio of 'Black Justice' fame. Ben Brown, born 1848, James Newland, born 1843, and George Le Clerq, born 1849. During the mid-1870s Brown and Newland were a well-known double act appearing both in variety and with minstrel concert parties, touring Australia and New Zealand in 1880 with Hiscock and Hayman's 'Australian Federal Minstrels'. George Le Clerq was originally paired with Sam De Voy (1842–1907) and became popular on the halls and in pantomime playing black-faced 'robbers and broker's men'. After many years the partnership broke up and Le Clerq went to America to appear with G. W. Moore's minstrels and Tony Pastor's vaudeville company. On his return to England he teamed with Brown and Newland. As 'Brown, Newland and Le Clerq' they became some of the most successful exponents of the three-handed sketch combinations. The greatest success was 'Black Justice' with Le Clerq playing a policeman, the black-faced Brown as the Judge and Newland as a confused barrister. Other memorable sketches included 'Go as you Please, or Eat as you Chews', 'Killing Indians', and 'The Coffee Can Brothers'. Brown and Le Clerq died in 1911, and James Newland in March 1931.

Teddy Brown, xylophonist, saxophonist and drummer, born Abraham Himmebrand in the USA in 1900. Trained as a classical musician but, after four years with the New York Philharmonic Symphony Orchestra. left to play with a dance band, later forming his own. On coming to England he appeared in cabaret at the Kit Kat Club and the Café de Paris, becoming a popular heavyweight single act in variety and on radio. He appeared in the Royal Variety Performance at the London Palladium on 11 May 1931. A popular member of the Grand Order of Water Rats, he served as Prince Rat in 1945 and was crowned King Rat the following year. Alas, his reign was soon over. While touring with Lew and Leslie Grade's *Road to Laughter,* he died in Birmingham in April 1946.

Tom Brown, American siffleur, who made his debut in England in 1893 with such success that he was commanded to entertain the Prince of Wales. He toured Europe between 1894 and 1897, returning to London in 1898 to work a new routine with partner Edith Hoyt, a dancer and coon singer. Brown accompanied his whistling on a grand piano and did impressions of musical instruments including the piccolo, cornet and trombone.

Douglas Byng, revue, cabaret, pantomime and occasional variety artist, famed for his delightfully outrageous comedy songs which established him during the 1930s and 1940s as the high priest of camp. Born in Nottingham on 17 March 1893, he made his professional stage debut with Greville Hayes's concert party 'The Periodicals' at Hastings on 17 July 1914, and in London at the Gaiety in May 1917. From August 1922 to June 1924 he toured the twice nightly variety theatres with Harry Day's revue *Crystal.* At Christmas 1924 he played Eliza the Cook in the pantomime *Dick Whittington* at the New Oxford Theatre (formerly the Oxford Music Hall), London. The pantomime also starred Wilkie Bard and the Egbert Brothers, but the hit of the show was Dougie Byng singing 'Oriental Emma of the 'Arem', the first comic song

Teddy Brown, 1935

he wrote. Although managements sometimes argued that he was too sophisticated for children, he appeared during his career in 27 Christmas pantomimes and must be regarded as one of the finest dames in pantomime history. In April 1925 he was engaged by C. B. Cochran for *On With the Dance* at the London Pavilion, produced by André Charlot, with music, lyrics, and sketches by Noël Coward. The highlights of the show were Alice Delysia singing 'Poor Little Rich Girl' and the sketch 'Oranges and Lemons', in which Byng and Ernest Thesiger played two rather passé spinsters getting ready for bed in their Bloomsbury hotel on New Year's Eve. He went on to star in all the Cochran revues at the Pavilion between 1925 and 1931. In 1926 he appeared in cabaret doing a double act with Lance Lister at the Chez Henri Club in Long Acre, singing topical duets, burlesquing sister acts and ending with 'The Cabaret Boys', which he later described as the first slightly queer number to be sprung on the public.

As a solo act he soon became one of the most popular cabaret performers, singing such comic gems as 'The Pest of Budapest', 'Mrs Lot', 'Sex Appeal Sarah', 'Boadicea', and 'Milly, the Messy Old Mermaid'. In 1931 he made his New York cabaret debut, billed as 'London's most important and expensive cabaret star', and in 1934 played at the Monte Cristo, Paris, as 'Douglas Byng, l'acteur extraordinaire anglais'. His first solo variety appearance was at the Alhambra, London, in a one-man pantomime burlesque 'Cinders, or Hop o' My Thumb', in which he made his entrance on a flying wire singing 'I'm Doris the Goddess of Wind'. He went on to play practically every music hall in the British Isles, sharing the top of the bill with some of the greatest names in variety, including George Robey and Gracie Fields. During the Second World War he continued to play variety dates and revue and was a great attraction at the Café de Paris, London, billed as 'Dougie Byng, Bawdy but British'. His most successful song of the period was 'Blackout Bella' which he sang at ENSA concerts in India and Burma. In 1955 he appeared in London and New York in Feydeau's *Hotel Paradiso* and in 1967 starred in the BBC television series 'Before the Fringe', singing many of the songs he made famous in revue. He now lives in semi-retirement at Brighton.

C

Big Bill Campbell, Western-style entertainer and showman, born Medicine Hat, Alberta, Canada on 13 July 1893. Well-known on radio before the war as 'The Happy Philosopher', he made his first London appearance at the Coliseum in 1935. He is best remembered for his hill-billy shows, popular in variety and on radio during the 1940s and 1950s, in which he was billed as 'Big Bill Campbell and his Rocky Mountain Rhythm'.

Herbert Campbell, famous comedian of music hall and pantomime. Born in Lambeth, London, in December 1846. He began his career with a nigger-minstrel troupe, making his music-hall debut as one of the burnt-cork trio of 'Harman, Campbell, and Elston', and his solo bow at the Alhambra, Shoreditch, and Collins Music Hall in 1868. The epitome of music-hall fat men, his first song success was a parody of G.H. MacDermott's 'By Jingo':

> I don't want to fight,
> I'll be slaughtered if I do,
> I'd let the Russians have Constantinople.

He was a popular music-hall singer of dame songs, of which one of his best was 'At My Time of Life'. He sang this at up to six halls a night, dressed as 'homely body' poking fun at the so-called 'new woman' of the 1870s:

> Fancy me a-smoking 'fags',
> A-riding bikes and wearing 'bags',
> And leaving off my bits of 'rags',
> At my time of life.

One of the greatest of all pantomime artistes, he appeared in seven pantomimes at the Grecian Theatre (under the management of the Conquest family), two at the Theatre Royal, Liverpool, two at Covent Garden, and 22 at the Theatre Royal, Drury Lane. He was first engaged by Augustus Harris to play Kabob in *Sinbad* at Drury Lane in 1882, and the following year teamed with Harry Nicholls as the Ugly Sisters, a pantomime partnership which lasted until 1890. In 1891 he appeared in the first of the famous double scenes with Dan Leno (qv), the 19-stone Campbell making a perfect foil for the diminutive Dan for the next 14 Christmas pantomimes. With Harry Randall and Dan Leno, Campbell went into music-hall management, taking over a number of suburban London halls, and in 1898 they built the Granville Theatre of Varieties in Fulham Broadway, Walham Green. After a number of successful years, during which the three comedians topped their own bills when the halls were in need of star attractions, they found the cut-throat competition from the big variety combines too great, and eventually sold their interest at a loss. On Boxing Day 1903, Campbell as the King and Leno as the Queen opened in *Humpty Dumpty* at Drury Lane. On the last night of the show Leno and Campbell clasped hands and sang:

> In the panto of old Drury Lane,
> We have both come together again,
> And we hope to appear
> For many a year,
> In the panto of old Drury Lane.

It was not to be. Herbert Campbell died on 19 July 1904, and Dan Leno three months later.

Herbert Campbell with Dan Leno

Cardini, magician who specialised in playing-card, lighted-cigarette, and billiard-ball manipulation, born Richard Valentine Pitchford in South Wales in 1895. He became interested in conjuring and developed a skill at performing intricate card tricks during convalescence at the Royal Victoria Military Hospital, Netley, recovering from injuries received on the Somme. After his army discharge he made his first music-hall appearance at the Swansea Empire in 1918, followed by a tour of the halls of South Wales and a visit to Australia, which did not result in engagements. On his return to London in 1920 he was again unable to get variety bookings so went to work demonstrating tricks in the magic department of Gamages. In 1921 he returned to Australia and for the first time used the name 'Cardini'. At that time he was accompanying his magic tricks with comic patter ill-suited to his personality but during his Australian tour he dropped this side of the act. Using a minimum of props he developed a sleight-of-hand routine of silent perfection, which established him as one of the leading variety magicians. His wife, dressed as a page boy, introduced the act by 'Paging Mr Cardini'. Going to the USA, he was booked to tour the Keith-Albee vaudeville circuit, appearing at the Palace Theatre, New York, in 1926. His success was so great that A. E. Keith gave him a contract to headline at his variety theatres throughout America and during the next four years he made six return appearances at the Palace. He made his London debut at the London Palladium in 1932, appearing for five weeks in a George Black revue, followed by variety dates at the leading London and provincial halls. On 22 May 1932 he took part in the Royal Variety Performance at the Palladium, an honour shared by few other magicians. He also toured the continent, making highly successful appearances in Berlin and Paris. He died in New York in December 1973.

James Carew, actor and comedian, born in Goshen, Indiana, USA, in 1872. He made his first appearance at the Irving Theatre, Chicago, in 1897. In May 1904 he appeared as Lieutenant Richard Redstone in *Two Little Sailor Boys* at the Academy of Music, New York, and then joined Maxine

Elliott's company playing Sam Coast in *Her Own Way*, making his London debut in the part at the Lyric Theatre on 25 April 1905. In March 1906 he played Captain Hamlin Kearney in *Captain Brassbound's Conversion* at the Royal Court. The part of Lady Cicely Waynflete was played by Ellen Terry, who the following year visited the USA and married Carew in Pittsburg on 22 March 1907. From 1907 to 1910 he toured the British music halls presenting various sketches including 'The Westerner', 'Moments Before', 'Zangwills', 'The Odd Number', and 'The Case of Johnny Walker'. In 1930 he teamed with Billy Bennett (qv) as the black-faced comedy cross-talking act of 'Alexander and Mose', at first purely a radio act from Savoy Hill, and then as a double turn in variety. The act contained all the elements of cross-talk in the tradition of the corner men in the nigger minstrels, and toured the halls with great success. As 'Alexander and Mose', Carew and Bennett appeared at the Royal Variety Show at the London Palladium on 11 May 1931. The part of Alexander was later taken over by Albert Whelan (qv). Carew died in April 1938.

Maxwell Carew, quick-change artist and character singer. Born in Leeds on 1 November 1882, he began his career as a coster singer at the Tivoli, Bristol, in July 1896. By the time he reached London in September 1898 he had developed his act on broader comic singing lines and made his first appearance at the Old Vic, then being run as the Royal Victorian Coffee Music Hall by Emma Cons. In 1900 he teamed with his brother as 'Carl and Carr', touring a cross-talking comedy routine for the next eight years. In 1910 they appeared at the London Coliseum on a bill topped by Sarah Bernhardt. In 1949, Maxwell Carew's 53rd year on the stage, *The Performer* noted that he had played 46 pantomimes, 36 of them as dame.

The Great Carlton, 'The Human Hairpin', card manipulator and juggler, born Arthur Carlton Philps in Holloway, London, in 1881. In 1900 he got a job at the Westminster Royal Aquarium as doorman and barker, enticing passers-by to view the 'Oriental beauties from the far far East End of London in the '"Turkish Harem"'. Later he toured his own conjuring act of card manipulation and fake hypnotism, making his first professional stage appearance at the St George's Drill Hall, Newcastle, on 21 December 1901, and in London at the Crystal Palace Café Chantant in 1902. This was followed by a trial turn at the Bedford, Camden Town, with the result that the next week he was booked for the Alhambra Palace, Middlesex, and Metropolitan music halls. He was very tall and thin, 6 feet 2½ inches in height and only just over nine stone in weight. He billed himself as 'The Human Hairpin', and accentuated his physique with elevated shoes, a high bald skull cap and a black leotard. He toured Europe with his own company of freaks, including Bobby Dunlop, 'The American Fat Man', who weighed over 40 stone, and a number of dwarfs. (When Dunlop dropped dead at the Winter Garden, Berlin, his place was taken by a giant named 'Scotty' who was seven feet tall and weighed over 30 stone.) In addition to his comedy magic, his act included the illusions 'The Mysterious Cross', 'The Four Queens', 'The Inquisition', and the old Maskelyne and Cooke box trick (escaping from a locked and corded box). Later he put on weight and turned to playing dame roles. He died on 26 June 1942.

George Carney, comedian, born in Bristol on 21 November 1887. He made his first stage appearance in December 1906 in *Aladdin* at the Theatre Royal, Nottingham, and in London at the Holborn Empire in November 1907. He was then

Left: George Carney Right: The Great Carlton as Dame Durden

working a double act, 'Carney and Armstrong', which toured the United Kingdom, Australia, and South Africa for a number of years. With Jewish comedian Sam Harris, he later toured his own revues, in 1913 presenting *The Prize Fight*, rather strangely described on the bills as 'A New Musical Comedy Athletic Revue'. Turning solo in 1926 Carney starred in variety with his comedy studies 'The Fool of the Force', 'The Stage Door Keeper' and, in the oldest music-hall tradition, the broken-down swell in 'I Live in Leicester Square'. His last variety appearance was in 1933, but he continued to appear in revue both in London and New York. He appeared in a number of films, notably John Baxter's *Music Hall* (1934) and as Henry Hardcastle in Baxter's classic *Love on the Dole* (1941). He died on 9 December 1947.

Kate Carney, coster comedienne, born in London in 1869. Her father was an old-time comedian who worked with a partner as 'The Brothers Raynard'. In 1885 she married George Barclay (qv), a comedian then working the double act of 'Barclay and Perkins, The Brewers of Mirth', who later became a successful variety agent. Although later famous for her cockney character songs, she made her first stage appearance at the Albert Music Hall, Canning Town, on 10 February 1890 as a singer of Irish ballads. Her first song hit was 'Here's My Love to Old Ireland', but it was 'A Donkey Cart Built for Two', 'Sarah', and 'Three Pots a Shilling', which established her at the top of the bill and her reputation as the 'Cockney Queen'. A buxom woman, dressed in a coster dress of pearly and a large hat trimmed with enormous ostrich plumes, she was the perfect Donah to the costers of Albert Chevalier, Gus Elen and Alec Hurley. Her songs combined a ripe humour with the pathos of East London life, telling of street markets selling anything from a cauliflower to a cock linnet, jellied eels, the smell of hot bagels and salt herrings, and of ''Arrys and 'Arriets' out for a summer stroll in Victoria Park. There was a richness of social history in Kate's songs: 'Has Anyone Seen My Yiddisher Boy?', 'Oysters a Shilling a Dozen', 'Liza Johnson', 'When the Summer Comes Again' and the most plaintive of all her songs, 'Are We to Part Like This, Bill?'. A good businesswoman, she formed her own company of step-dancers and cake-walkers who backed her act. After a brief spell of retirement she returned to the halls in the early

1920s, this time working with a mouth-organ band. In 1935 she and George Barclay celebrated their golden wedding and later the same year she appeared in 'Cavalcade of Variety', the finale of the Royal Variety Performance at the London Palladium which marked 45 years on the stage. She continued to perform until shortly before her death at the age of 80 on 1 January 1950.

Russ Carr, born Frederick Russell Parnell in 1889. Son of the great ventriloquist Fred Russell (qv), he followed his father's footsteps onto the halls, when as a prize in a talent contest he won a week's engagement at the Camberwell Empire. He made several world tours with his ventriloquist act, later giving up the stage to work as a variety agent. He died at the age of 84 on 29 August 1973.

Norman Carrol, character actor and comedian, born Sydney Edward Brandon in Manchester in 1890. Modelling his act on that of Bransby Williams (qv), he first appeared at the Grand Theatre, Manchester, in 1907 and in London at the Bedford, Camden Town, on 6 June 1909. Billed as 'Sydney Brandon—The Boy Barry Sullivan of the Music Halls', he presented character impressions until 1919. He then changed his act to comedy and, billed as 'Norman Carrol—Never 'Eard of Him', toured in variety burlesquing the act of 'Sydney Brandon'.

The Great Carter, Charles J. Carter, born in the USA in 1875, who first appeared as 'Carter the Boy Magician' in 1885. Sponsored by Houdini, he toured five continents with an elaborate and well-presented show. He died in Bombay on 3 February 1936.

Morny Cash, dialect comedian, born in Manchester in 1872. He started his professional life as an engineer making amateur appearances with a friend as comedy duettists. Appearing at a charity concert they were seen by a variety agent who booked them for their first professional engagement in Blackpool at five shillings per head. Turning solo he established a local reputation working the small halls of Manchester: Liston's, The Ship Inn, and The Hen and Chickens. The turning point in his career came when he appeared at the Roscommon Music Hall, Liverpool, and was booked for a tour of the South. Billed as 'The Lancashire Lad', and singing 'All of a Do-Da', 'Beautiful Beautiful Bed', 'Married a Year Today', and 'I Live in Trafalgar Square', he became one of the most popular of the Northern dialect comedians. He died on 16 October 1938.

The Cassons, husband-and-wife musical and dramatic sketch artists who graduated to the halls via the legitimate stage. Edie Benson (Casson) had previously been a member of Sir Frank Benson's company playing Lydia Languish, Kate Hardcastle, and Ophelia to Benson's Hamlet. Walter Casson was a one-time member of Joseph Eldred's and Miller and Elliston's companies. They turned to the music hall in 1896 and were popular with their well-acted variety sketches.

Peter Cassons, hypnotist who claimed to be the first to present genuine hypnotism on the English stage. Born in Bridlington on 13 December 1921, his first professional exhibitions of hypnotism took place at Butlin's Theatre, Skegness, on 29 June 1946 and in variety at the Bedford Music Hall, Camden Town, in November the same year. During 1948–49 he presented his one-man show at many London and provincial theatres and created a good deal of interest, not only as an entertainer but also as a lecturer to the

Kate Carney, Collins Music Hall, 1935 *(Tony and David Oaks photo collection)*

BMA and to groups of psychiatrists and dental societies. He later established a 'psychological clinic' in Yorkshire.

Harry Champion, cockney comedian, born Shoreditch, London, in 1866. He first appeared on the halls as a negro comedian at the Royal Victoria Hall, Old Ford, London, in 1882 at the age of only 15. He continued to work the act for a number of years while developing his own style of rich quick-fire cockney patter with songs to match. Finally abandoning his burnt cork make-up, he made his debut as a cockney comedian at the Queen's Music Hall, Poplar, and the Parthenon, Greenwich, on 27 February 1888. He was an immediate success with such songs as 'Any Old Iron',

Harry Champion, 1931

'Boiled Beef and Carrots', 'I'm Henry the Eighth, I Am', 'What Cher My Old Brown Son', 'The Old Dun Cow', 'With the End of My Old Cigar', 'Ginger You're Barmy', and remained so for over 50 years. His style was wholly original; he sang his songs at breakneck speed, with words coming out of his mouth like bullets out of a machine gun. He never seemed to tire, although singing up to six songs a turn at three or four halls a night. He had a great liking for songs about food: apart from the famous 'Boiled Beef and Carrots', there was 'Baked Sheep's Hearts', 'I Like Pickled Onions', 'Icum, You Cum, Cu-cu-cu-cum, Cu-cu-cu Cucumber', 'All Because There Wasn't Any Crackling on the Pork', 'Hot Tripe and Onions' and 'Hot Meat Pies, Saveloys and Trotters'. In 1931 he toured with Lew Lake's *Stars Who Never Fail to Shine*, and at the London Palladium on 31 October 1935 made a belated first appearance in a Royal Variety Show, taking part in the 'Cavalcade of Variety' finale. In 1937 he returned to the Palladium to appear with the 'Crazy Gang' for the three months run of *London Rhapsody*. He continued to appear in variety and give concerts for charities connected with the war until shortly before his death at the age of 76 on 14 January 1942.

The Three Charlivels, acrobatic instrumentalists, John, Charles, and Valentino Andrew, born in 1923, 1925 and 1926 respectively. Their father was Charles Rivels, an acrobatic clown who as 'The Chaplin of the Trapeze' toured the world in circus and variety. In 1937, when John was 14, Charles 12, and Valentino 11, they made their debut as 'The Three Charlivels' in Buenos Aires. Their first appearance in England was at the Palace Theatre, Blackpool, in April 1947 and in London at the Casino in September the same year. Between the three of them, they played 16 different musical instruments and soon established their act in variety and revue, appearing in the Royal Variety Performance at the London Coliseum, in 1949.

Albert Chevalier, coster comedian, born in Notting Hill, London, on 21 March 1862. His mother was Welsh and his father French, which perhaps explains why he was baptised Albert Onesime Britannicus Gwathveoyd Louis Chevalier. It was as Albert Knight that he first appeared with the Roscius Dramatic Club at the Ladbroke Hall Notting Hill, in January 1876 and made his professional debut on 29 September 1877 with the Bancrofts at the Prince of Wales's Royal Theatre (rebuilt in 1905 as the Scala). During the next 10 years he appeared under the management of the Kendals, John Hare, Edgar Bruce and Sir George Alexander. In 1887 he toured with Willie Edouin in his own adaptation of H.J. Byron's burlesque 'Aladdin or the Wonderful Scamp', which opened at the Strand Theatre, London on 25 February 1888. In this Chevalier sang 'Our 'Armonic Club', the first cockney song he performed in public. In 1889 he appeared as principal comedian at the Avenue Theatre, London, singing 'Tink a Tin' and 'Funny Without Being Vulgar', written by his brother Charles Ingles (Auguste Chevalier). The following year he toured with John Beauchamp in 'Socks and Buskins', a musical and dramatic entertainment of 'Recitations, Original Humorous Songs and Burlesque.' He made his first music-hall appearance at the London Pavilion on 5 February 1891. Dressed in a chequered jacket, peaked cap, neckcloth and bell-bottomed trousers, all trimmed with the velvet and pearl buttons of the coster comedian, he sang 'The Coster Serenade', 'The Nasty Way 'E Sez It', and 'Funny Without Being Vulgar'. He was an immediate hit, hailed by the press as 'The master among variety artistes', 'The Kipling of the halls' and 'The Coster Laureate'. Although lacking the genuine cockney personality and earthy quality of his fellow comedian Gus Elen—he was strictly a stage cockney, as true to reality as the stage Irishman, Jew, or Scot—he was a fine artist, conscientious in points of detail like make-up and wardrobe, and with a stage presence that managed to create a receptive atmosphere for his incredibly mawkish songs such as 'My Old Dutch'.

In 1898 Chevalier gave a series of special matinee recitals at the Queen's Hall, London, The Dome, Brighton, and the Free Trade Hall, Manchester. These gave him the opportunity of playing before audiences that would never have visited a music hall. These audiences included members of the royal family, which by this late period in Victoria's reign had reached a huge total. When the future Queen Mary confessed a liking for his song 'Knocked Em in the Old Kent Road' he became the social vogue and even Mrs Ormiston

Albert Chevalier, 'The Coster Laureate'

Chant, the Mary Whitehouse of the day, approved his act. In June 1906 he and the great French diseuse Yvette Guilbert appeared together for a season at the Duke of York's Theatre, London, Chevalier singing his cockney songs and Guilbert performing her repertoire of the songs of old France. They were such a success that in October 1906 they went on a concert tour of the USA and Canada. Of their opening at Koster and Bial's, New York, Guilbert wrote in her autobiography *The Song of My Life* (1929):

> Albert Chevalier was rather more skilful than actually talented, his style was what I should call 'theatre de drama ambigu populaire' (it would correspond to the old fashioned type of Lyceum melodrama). It was already very much out of date but he was the first artist who specialised in cockney with both humour and pathos. In three or four of his interpretations he was first rate, the rest were stereotyped and harked back to 1870. He was a delightfully cultured man and knew how to choose his music and contrive an excellent make-up.

In New York the pair appeared at Carnegie Hall followed by

a 7000 mile tour, playing 42 engagements in six weeks. During much of his later career Chevalier appeared in London and on tour with a dramatised version of 'My Old Dutch' and later in a sketch based on another successful song, 'A Fallen Star'. He was married to Florrie Leybourne, a one-time music-hall comedienne and daughter of George Leybourne. He died on 11 June 1923.

Maurice Chevalier, the most celebrated and internationally famous of all French music-hall artistes. Jean Cocteau wrote 'Paris has two monuments, the Eiffel Tower and Maurice Chevalier'. Born in the Menilmontant district of Paris on 12

Maurice Chevalier, the London Hippodrome, 1948

September 1888, by the age of 12 he was singing comic songs at a local café and in December 1901 made his first professional appearance as Paris's youngest red-nosed comedian, at the Tourells Casino on the Avenue Gambetta. In 1904 he was engaged for the back row of the chorus at the Parisiana Music Hall in the revue *Satyre Bouchonne*, in which the principal part was played by Harry Fragson. After six months at the Parisiana he was back touring the café concerts, becoming a favourite with the audiences at the Eden Café in Asnières.

Influenced by the comic dancing of Little Tich, then as popular in Paris as he was in London, and the step dancing of Norman French, Chevalier introduced an eccentric dance routine which evolved into a strictly individual technique known as the 'Chevalier style'. Billed as 'Chevalier M', the turning point in his career came in 1907 when he was booked to replace Dranem as principal comedian of the Eldorado, Paris, with such success that he was signed by P. L. Flers to appear for three consecutive winter seasons at the Folies Bergère. The 1911–12 Folies featured the famous comedy dance 'Valse Renversante', bringing together Chevalier and Mistinguett (qv), the start of a famous stage and personal partnership which lasted for the next 10 years. He made his first appearance in England at the Palace Theatre, London, in February 1919, replacing Owen Nares in *Hullo America*, which starred Elsie Janis and Billy Merson. Inhibited by his limited English, learned while a prisoner-of-war in Germany, he was only a moderate success. Returning to Paris he signed a contract with the Casino de Paris which gave him equal billing to Mistinguett and from then on professional jealousy marred their relationship. She took a new partner, the American Earl Leslie, and Chevalier did a solo speciality for the first time in the simple costume which became his trademark, a dinner jacket and straw hat. In 1925 he appeared with the Dolly Sisters in a revue at the Casino which introduced one of his greatest song successes, 'Valentine'. In May 1927 he returned to London to star in *White Bird*, which only ran for as long as two months because of the personal success of Chevalier. In 1928 he made his American debut at the Ziegfeld Roof Garden, New York, in a revue with Helen Kane and Paul Whiteman. His first film, *Innocents in Paris*, made in 1929, featured the song 'Louise' which became one of his greatest hits and signature tune. During the next six years he made a total of twelve films for Paramount Pictures.

Billed as the 'Highest Paid Artiste in the World', he presented the first of his one-man shows at the Dominion Theatre, London, in December 1930. From then on he split his time between filming in Hollywood and revue, variety, and cabaret in Paris, London, and New York. In 1938 he was created a Chevalier of the Legion of Honour (no pun intended) and after the war returned to London to repeat the

G.H. Chirgwin, 1904

success of his one-man show at the London Hippodrome. He took part in the Royal Variety Performances of 1949 and 1961. Announcing his retirement at the age of 80 in 1968, he made a farewell tour of the UK and principal cities of Europe and America. He died in Paris on 1 January 1972.

G. H. Chirgwin. Of all the eccentric music-hall comedians, with their grotesque costumes and strictly individual make-up, George Chirgwin stands supreme as 'The White-Eyed Kaffir'. Born in 1854, he first appeared with his six brothers in an act known as 'The Chirgwin Family' at the Swallow Rooms, Regent Street, in 1861, and later toured with his brother Jack in a double cross-talking nigger-minstrel act. His solo debut occurred by accident. The 'Bros Chirgwin' were billed to appear at De Frece's Hall, Liverpool, when at the last moment Jack was taken ill. Undaunted, George strode onto the stage and proceeded to chat with the audience in the informal manner which was to establish him later as one of the greatest idols of the halls. He explained with great aplomb that he *was* the 'Bros Chirgwin'; his mother, having expected twins, was so disappointed at his lone arrival she gave him the name 'Bros'. This delightful piece of impromptu foolery completely won over the rowdy Scouse audience and he worked solo for the rest of the week. He continued to work a double act for the next few years, in variety with Jack Chirgwin and in pantomime at the Britannia Theatre, Hoxton, with the veteran comedian Fred Lay. His first real solo success in London was at the Oxford on 10 June 1878, and for the next thirty years he played up to six halls a night, earning as much as £100 per week.

How he came by his famous black face make-up with a white greasepaint diamond painted around his right eye, is music-hall legend. Like all legends, there is more than one version but the one that George told was this: While waiting to do his act at a fete in a small town in Gloucestershire, he wiped a fly from his eye, unwittingly rubbing off the burnt cork as well. The white patch produced a bizarre but comical effect, the potential of which he was quick to realise. Wearing black tights to emphasise the height of his very thin figure, he made his entrance with his right eye concealed beneath the brim of an enormously high top hat. Even after he had been known as 'The White-Eyed Kaffir' for a score of years, when he jerked his head back to reveal the celebrated white lozenge, he was greeted by roars of delight and cries of 'good old George'. Apart from reversing his colour scheme from time to time, wearing a white suit, top hat, and a black diamond on a white make-up, he used the same basic costume throughout his career, even when in middle age he put on a good deal of weight and tights made him appear rather gross.

Chirgwin played a wide range of musical instruments including violin, cello, bagpipes, piano, banjo, a one-string fiddle, and other strange contrivances of his own invention. He had an extraordinary voice which ranged from baritone to a strangely haunting falsetto. One has only to listen to the recordings of his two great songs, 'My Fiddle is My Sweetheart' and 'The Blind Boy', to understand why he remained such a firm favourite for 50 years. He had a remarkably strong command over his audience who he greeted with the words 'Good evening ladies and gempmums', the 'ladies' in a deep baritone and the 'gempmums' in a shrill falsetto. He would ad-lib with the stalls and answer the friendly banter from the 'gods' with many a pun and humorously topical retort. During his act he would be bombarded by demands of 'Give us the blind 'un, George' and an equal clamour for 'the Fiddler', and seldom left the stage without singing both. He celebrated his silver jubilee on the stage at the Oxford in 1911 and in 1912 appeared in the garden party scene of the first Royal Command Performance at the Palace Theatre, London. On his retirement he became the landlord of The Anchor at Shepperton, and died in 1922.

Paul Cinquevalli, music-hall juggler superb, born Paul Kestner in Lissa, Poland. In 1859, his father was forced for political reasons to leave Poland and re-settle in Germany. Paul was educated in Berlin, and at 13 was apprenticed to gymnast and aerialist Cinquevalli. Billed as 'The Little Flying Devil', he made his first public appearance at Odessa, Russia, in 1873. While appearing in St Petersburg he fell from the trapeze and crashed 50 feet to the ground. After 10 months in hospital, he returned to the circus ring as a juggler. As a form of self-imposed physiotherapy, he worked on a few basic tricks picked up from fellow circus performers, eventually developing the act of juggling to a standard which has never been surpassed. Adopting the name of his old tutor Cinquevalli, he first appeared in England in 1885 with such success that he made London his home and became one of the greatest stars of music hall. Billed as 'The Human Billiard Table', he could play billiards on his own back better than most people play on a regulation table. He juggled with cues and balls of all sizes, ending his act by throwing a cannon ball into the air and catching it on the nape of his neck. Unlike

Paul Cinquevalli, 'The Human Billiard Table'

most speciality acts he had a 'star' personality with a fine sense of comedy. On a bill to mark the 38th anniversary of the Royal Holborn on 19 November 1895, 'Paul Cinquevalli l'incomparable' was given star billing over Marie Lloyd and 40 other leading variety artistes. At Christmas 1896 he played the Slave of the Lamp to Dan Leno's Widow Twankey and Herbert Campbell's Abanazer in *Aladdin* at the Theatre Royal, Drury Lane. He appeared before the royal family on many occasions and presented his 'Human Billiard Table' routine at the first Royal Command Performance at the Palace Theatre in 1912. His last appearance in England was at New Brighton in June 1912, followed by a tour of

Australia. Wrongly thought to be a German, he suffered from the backlash of the First World War and retired from the stage in 1915. He died at Brixton on 14 July 1918.

Harry Claff, baritone, who after establishing a reputation in musical comedy and light opera during the 1900s turned to the music-hall stage with even greater success. He studied singing under Garcia, won a scholarship to the Royal Academy of Music and while appearing in a RAM operetta was heard by Richard D'Oyly Carte and given a three-year contract to appear at the Savoy. From parts in Gilbert and Sullivan, he went to George Edwardes at the Gaiety, singing the baritone leads in *The Shop Girl*, *The Circus Girl*, *A Gaiety Girl*, and *San Toy*. He made his first variety appearance with Sir Alexander Mackenzie's 'Knights of the Road' at the Palace Theatre, London. Soon afterwards he turned solo, touring the variety theatres singing operatic arias in character. In a lighter mood he presented a double act with his wife, Winnie Wager, billed as 'Harry Claff and Lady—The Demon and the Fairy'. His most famous act, 'The White Knight', was followed by a series of historical musical sketches, 'King Henry VIII', etc., with which he toured America, Australia, New Zealand and South Africa. He was very proud of being chosen to lead the singing of the National Anthem at the first Royal Command Performance at the Palace in 1912, and from then on made it a feature of his publicity. A great pantomime favourite, he appeared for 12 years in Howard and Wyndham's productions and in six pantomimes at the Theatre Royal, Drury Lane. He died on 8 May 1943.

Above: Harry Claff, 'The White Knight'
Below: Clapham and Dwyer, 1930

Clapham and Dwyer. Straight man Charlie Clapham and inarticulate Billy Dwyer teamed up in 1925 as semi-professional entertainers at private functions. They broadcast from Savoy Hill in 1926 and soon became popular for their absurd cross-talking routines which, whatever the subject of their confused conversations, always got mixed up with the doings of 'Cissie the Cow'. Their first appearance in variety was at the Shepherds Bush Empire in 1928, and they remained firm favourites in variety and on the air until Dwyer's death in 1943. Charlie Clapham continued as a solo turn, presenting an act of nonchalant nonsense.

Johnson Clark, ventriloquist, born in Ripley, Derbyshire, in 1886. Began his career with a pierrot troupe on the beach at Skegness in 1903, making his music-hall debut at the Granville, Walham Green, the following year. Booked for a Moss and Stoll tour, he appeared at the Oxford and Tivoli, London, in 1906. Billed as 'The Sportsman Ventriloquist' and known as the 'Squire', he toured in variety for many years with his two dolls, 'Giles' and 'Hodge the Yokel'. His act was presented in a sketch format with rural settings, 'The Orchard Thief', 'The Barge Boy', 'Romany Rye', and 'Wishing Well Farm'. He appeared in the Royal Variety Show in 1931. During the 1940s he toured with Morris and Cowley (qv) in 'The Squire's Party'.

George Clarke, comedian, born in Bromley, Kent, in 1886. He began his career with his father, appearing as patter comedians and dancers billed as 'George Clarke and His Half'. Later known as 'Clarke and Clements', the father-and-son partnership lasted until 1910, when Clarke senior retired and George, turning solo, became well known as a 'Dude Comedian'. *The Performer* wrote of him in 1946:

> He was a past master in the art of giving full rein to the most priceless verbal inanities, was always impeccably attired on the stage, and with his monocle typified the 'silly ass' character so vastly enjoyed by the average man in the street. Clarke also had the art of creating laughter by exploiting the nit-wit, and never resorted to blue material. His most outstanding sketch was undoubtedly 'His First Car', in which he drove an Austin Seven about the stage with almost uncanny skill, yet conveyed the impression that the plunging of the vehicle was the result of gross mishandling on the part of a character that even P. G. Wodehouse would have been proud to create.

After success in variety, not only in this country but also in South Africa, Australia, and the USA, he played in his first revue, *Step This Way*, followed between 1913 and 1923 by a series of shows under the management of Harry Day. He appeared in three Royal Variety Performances at the London Palladium, in 1930, 1932, and 1934. In later years he appeared in musical comedy, mainly with touring versions of West End successes. He died in December 1946.

Harry Clifton singing 'Mr Double Stout', 1880

Clayton and Jenkins, two grotesque comedians who appeared with great success during the 1890s. Their most famous routine was 'Darktown Circus' in which, dressed as negro ballerina and clown, they performed a mock equestrian act with their mule, Jasper.

Harry Clifton, music-hall and 'drawing-room vocalist', born in Hoddesden, Hertfordshire. A popular singer of motto songs, sentimental in tone but much in vogue in the 1860s, including 'Work Boys, Work and be Contented', 'Up with the Lark in the Morning', and 'Put Your Shoulder to the Wheel is a Motto for Every Man'. His style can be fully appreciated from the following verses of three of his most successful songs, 'Pulling Hard Against the Stream', 'Paddle Your Own Canoe', and 'Wait for the Turn of the Tide':

Then do your best for one another,
Making life a pleasant dream,
Help a worn and weary brother,
Pulling hard against the stream.

Then love your neighbour as yourself,
As the world you go travelling through,
And never sit down with a tear or a frown,
And paddle your own canoe.

Then try to be happy and gay, boys,
Remember the world is wide,
And Rome wasn't built in a day, boys,
So wait for the turn of the tide

He died at his home in Shepherd's Bush on 15 July 1872.

Jimmy Clitheroe, 'Cheeky Kid' comedian, born in Clitheroe in 1916. Brought up at Blacko, near Burnley, he took dancing lessons as a boy in Manchester. On winning a talent competition at the Nelson Alhambra, he was engaged to tour with a juvenile troupe, playing the accordion, roller-skating and doing female impersonations for seven shillings a week. Pantomime at Liverpool with Lucan and McShane was followed by summer shows, variety and touring in revue, his early career including bit parts in films starring George Formby, Vera Lynn, Old Mother Riley, and Frank Randle. In the summer of 1945 he appeared in a revue on Blackpool's South Pier with principal comedian Albert Burdon. They worked so well together that for years they were regarded as a perfect revue and pantomime partnership. Jimmy was given his first broadcast part in the Manchester radio show 'The Mayor's Parlour', which led to appearances in Ronnie Taylor's radio and television series 'Call Boy'. In the Manchester studio he met an old pal from juvenile touring days, James Casey, the son of Jimmy James (cv). Casey was then a BBC light entertainments producer, and following Clitheroe's success in 'Call Boy' worked on a new series starring him as a precocious Lancashire lad which brought him overnight fame as 'The Clitheroe Kid'. The obvious successor to Wee Georgie Wood, he continued his 'little boy' act well into middle age, appearing in his own radio and television shows, as well as touring in variety and working each Christmas in pantomime. Just as Wee Georgie had Dolly Harmer, the Clitheroe kid was well stage-mothered by Mollie Sugden. In 1959 he took part in the Royal Variety Performance, held that year at the Palace Theatre, Manchester. 'The Clitheroe Kid' made history as the longest-running radio show, ending a 15-year run in 1972. Unmarried, Jimmy lived with his mother in Blackpool and she helped greatly with his career. Her death had a bad effect

Left: Jimmy Clitheroe, 1928
Right: George Clarke

on his own failing health and he died on the day of her funeral, 6 June 1973, at the age of 57.

Charles Coborn, comedian who introduced two of music-hall's greatest songs, 'Two Lovely Black Eyes' and 'The Man Who Broke the Bank at Monte Carlo'. He was born Colin Whitton McCallum in Mile End, London, on 4 August 1852 and made his first part-time music hall appearances in 1872, being paid half-a-crown a night to act on Monday and Saturday as chairman, vocalist and dramatic monologuist at the Alhambra, North Greenwich. He soon accepted an 'Irishman's rise' to two shillings a night for a regular twice-weekly engagement at William Lusby's Sugar Loaf Tavern, Whitechapel. Adopting the name of Charles Coborn, from Coborn Road, Bow, he got his first full week's booking at the Gilbert Music Hall, Whitechapel, and shortly afterwards another week at The Rodney's Head. (The Gilbert

Charles Coborn, 'The Man Who Broke the Bank at Monte Carlo', 1891

was a small hall at the back of the Lord Nelson Tavern, Whitechapel Road. Whitechapel Underground Station now stands on the site. The Rodney's Head was a slightly larger hall a few doors west of the Gilbert. A public house of the same name now marks the original site.) This led to two weeks at the Oxford, Gravesend, and at Christmas 1875 he played Pantaloon and Cassim Baba in *The Forty Thieves* at the Alhambra Music Hall, Sandgate, Kent. In October 1879 he was given a trial turn at the Oxford, where the manager, J.H. Jennings, was so impressed that he signed Coborn for six months' work, billing him as 'The Comic of the Day'. Not all managements were as impressed by Coborn. He was an active campaigner for the improvement of music-hall working conditions and was largely responsible for forming the Music Hall Artists' Association in 1885, and later the Music Hall Benevolent Fund. His union activities made him unpopular with the Managers' Association and he was often out of work.

At the Paragon Music Hall, Mile End, on 21 May 1886 he sang 'Two Lovely Black Eyes' for the first time. It was his own parody of Edmund Foreman's mawkish ballad 'My Nelly's Blue Eyes', which had been made famous in America by the Christy Minstrels. Although the management of the Paragon claimed to be unimpressed, the East End audience liked it well enough. The song subsequently went down well at Belmont's, Deacon's, and the Metropolitan Music Hall, Edgware Road, and when in July 1886 Coborn sang it at the Trocadero, it was so popular that his original two-week booking was extended to a total of 14 months. It became a great hit and, as the two black eyes were received for 'praising the Conservatives frank and free', a popular subject for political cartoons in *Punch*. Even the Salvation Army got into the act, substituting the words 'My Jesus has Died' for 'Two Lovely Black Eyes'. During the 1880s Coborn was working as a coster comedian and from 1887 included in his repertoire 'Our 'Armonic Club', of which author Albert Chevalier (qv) had given him the sole music-hall performing rights. When in 1890 Chevalier turned to the halls, Coborn returned the song to him and out of friendship for Chevalier gave up the coster side of his own act.

Following his success at the Trocadero he was engaged to appear at the London Pavilion for three years, and when the popularity of 'Two Lovely Black Eyes' began to pall, introduced his other great song 'The Man Who Broke the Bank at Monte Carlo'. Written in 1891, with words and music by Fred Gilbert, it was based on Charles Wells' book *How I Broke the Bank at Monte Carlo,* and was first offered to Albert Chevalier. He tended to look down on music-hall audiences and turned it down, thinking it too highbrow for their tastes. Coborn bought it instead, and although he did have some trouble getting it accepted by the Oxford audience, its swaggering chorus, in the great tradition of the Lion Comique, was soon as widely sung as 'Two Lovely Black Eyes'. On 15 October 1900 he appeared at Tony Pastor's Music Hall, New York, followed by dates at Hyde and Behman's Vaudeville Theatre, Brooklyn, Proctor's Fifth Avenue Theatre and Shea's Variety Theatre, Toronto. Returning to England in 1901, he toured with his own concert party 'Charles Coborn's High Class Variety Entertainments'. Revered as 'The Father of the Profession', in 1932 he celebrated 60 years on the stage. He continued to make occasional appearances until shortly before his death at 93 on 23 November 1945.

Walter Colberg, German contortionist and acrobat. Born Walter Bojorski at Spandau on 23 December 1904, he began his career with Leo Spurgat, with whom he made his debut at the Cinema Prenzlauer-Allee, Berlin, on 27 February 1925. They were then working a 'devil' act as 'The Norman Brothers'. In 1929 they changed their name to 'Leo and Walter', and made their first London appearance at the Holborn Empire on 2 February 1932. Later the same year Leo's wife joined the act and as 'The Three Spurgats' they toured the USA with Barnum and Bailey and the Ringling Brothers. When Leo Spurgat and his wife left the act in 1935 Colberg teamed up with his daughter, with whom he appeared in variety as 'The Crystal Wonders'. The act broke up in 1946.

Lottie Collins, serio-comedienne, the originator of the famous 'Ta-ra-ra-boom-de-ay!' song-and-dance craze which swept three continents during the 1890s. Born in London in 1866, the daughter of a nigger minstrel, she first appeared on the halls as a skipping-rope dancer in 1877. With her two younger sisters, Lizzie and Marie, she worked the halls as 'The Three Sisters Collins', appearing in the dancing sketch 'Skiptomania' at the Oxford and in three consecutive pantomimes at the Pavilion, Whitechapel. In 1881 she turned solo, singing and whistling minstrel numbers, notably 'The Whistling Coon'. In 1886 she played the part of Mariette in Richard Henry's Gaiety burlesque 'Monte Cristo Junior', and during the next four years worked the halls billed as 'The Kate Vaughan of the Music Halls'. In 1891 she toured the USA without any great success, but while there she heard a ditty which took her fancy and she returned to London with 'Ta-ra-ra-boom-de-ay'. The American origins of the song are obscure, having its roots in the negro folk music of the deep south. Henry J. Sayers, one-time member of the Thatcher's Minstrels, heard it sung in St Louis with the refrain 'Tin-a-ling-a-ling boomderay'. He arranged it for the nigger minstrel troupes and it was later used in George

Thatcher's minstrel musical *Tuxedo*, performed at a club in Tuxedo Park, New York. The English version, arranged by Angelo Asher with words by Richard Morton, was first sung by Lottie Collins at the Tivoli Music Hall, London, in October 1891. Starting slowly on rather a demure note, she would pause at the end of the verse, place her hand defiantly on her hip and whirl into a furious high-kicking apache can-can style dance which sent the audience wild and often left Lottie fainting in the wings. Its first verse and chorus ran:

A smart and stylish girl you see,
The belle of good society.
Fond of fun as fond could be,
When it's on the strict QT.

I'm not too young, not too old
Not too timid, not too bold,
But just the very thing I'm told,
That in your arms you'd like to hold.

Ta-ra-ra-boom-de-ay, Ta-ra-ra-boom-de-ay, etc.

It caused a sensation, in which accusations of vulgarity from the purity league were mixed with the bravos of music-hall audiences, and did much to establish the reputation of the so-called 'Naughty Nineties'.

While Lottie was still Ta-ra-ra-boom-de-ay-ing for Charles Morton at the Tivoli she was engaged by George Edwardes to sing the song as a specially interpolated turn in his burlesque *Cinder-Ellen Up to Date* at the Gaiety. At Christmas 1891 she appeared at the Grand Theatre, Islington, as Alice Fitzwarren in *Dick Whittington* in which Harry Randall made his first London pantomime appearance. Lottie was the hit of the show, taking innumerable encores until she was exhausted. When the craze for the song began to decline she repeated her London success in New York, followed by a seven-month tour from Boston to San Francisco. The following year she returned to the USA with her own variety company, billed as 'Lottie Collins Troubadours', and toured for three years. Although she was never allowed to forget 'Ta-ra-ra-boom-de-ay', she toured the halls during the mid-1890s with the sketches 'The Coachman's Wife', 'The Little Widow', The Girl on the Run-dan-dan' and 'Gertie the Gaiety Girl'. Lottie Collins's third husband was James W. Tate, later well known as 'That' of the music hall act of 'Clarice Mayne (qv) and That'. Her eldest daughter was Josie Collins, who after a brief career in variety became famous as Teresa in the original production of *The Maid of the Mountains*. Lottie Collins died at the age of 44 on 2 May 1910.

Sam Collins, comic vocalist and music-hall manager. Originally a chimneysweep by the name of Samuel Vegg, he is now regarded as the prototype of the stage Irishman although he was born in London in 1827. A genial man, he earned a considerable reputation singing and dancing at free-and-easy and concert rooms in the London of the 1840s. He was popular at Evans's Song and Supper Rooms, singing 'Paddy's Wedding', 'Limerick Races', and the 'Rocky Road to Dublin', and was one of Charles Morton's first stars at the Canterbury Music Hall. In 1885 he appeared at the newly opened Weston's Music Hall, and later the same year took over The Rose of Normandy Tavern, Edgware Road, turning

Lottie Collins, 1900

Sam Collins, 1858 (*Victoria and Albert Museum, Crown copyright*)

it into the Marylebone Music Hall. In 1861 this hall passed to Frederick Botting, and Collins returned to the stage to appear with J. W. Pell and Pat Feeny in *Donnybrook Fair* at the Alhambra. In 1861 he took over the Lansdown Arms, Islington, which he converted into a music hall to seat a thousand and opened as Sam Collins' Music Hall on 4 November 1863. He died aged 39 on 25 May 1865.

Collins Music Hall, 'The Chapel on the Green', was rebuilt and much enlarged in 1897. It remained a popular hall throughout the Second World War under the management of Lew Lake, and survived until it was destroyed by fire in 1958. The front bar, decorated by ephemera recording its history, served as a public bar until an office block was built on the site in 1962. Part of the 1897 frontage remained, marked by a blue plaque put up by the GLC.

Tommy Cooper, comedy magician, born in Caerphilly in 1922. After joining the army in 1939 he served seven years in the Horse Guards. Encouraged by his success as a barrack-room comedian, on leaving the army he went to be auditioned by Miff Ferrie, who suggested that he dropped mediocre comedy impressions for a comedy magic act. This he did, and was booked by Ferrie for his Windermere Floor Show in November 1947. With his now-famous comedy routine—fumbled conjuring punctuated by ridiculous patter and maniacal laughter—he went over well. On 24 December 1947 he made his television bow in Leslie Henson's 'Christmas Party', and between dates at the Windermere, where he played for 18 weeks of the first six months of his career, he worked other good West End cabaret spots. His first variety appearance was at Collins Music Hall in November 1948, followed by a tour of the Stoll and Syndicate halls. In 1949 he acted as a resident comedian at the Windmill, going from there each night to fill cabaret dates at many of London's top night spots, including Churchill's, The Coconut Grove, The Albany, and Café Anglais, doing as many as 52 shows in one week. In March 1951 he opened at the London Hippodrome in the revue *Encore de Folies*, which ran for nearly a year, and in July 1952 made his first appearance on the bill of the London Palladium. This led to a head-lining tour for Moss Empires and in the spring of 1953 he toured with the revue *Peep Show*. On his return to London he was booked for the Coronation Variety Season at the Palladium and in November 1953 took part in the Royal Variety Show. At the Prince of Wales Theatre he co-starred with Benny Hill in *Paris by Night*, which ran for 17 months. In March 1959 he returned to the Prince of Wales to co-star for 10 months with Shirley Bassey. He has starred in his own summer shows almost every year since 1957, and topped the bill at the Palladium both in variety and his own revues. His first regular television appearances were in the BBC series 'It's Magic', screened in 1952, and the first of many 'Cooper' television programmes went out on ITV in March 1957. He was voted ITV Personality of the Year by the Variety Club in 1969, and in November 1975 started yet another 'Cooper' television series.

Bert Coote, comedian remembered for his music-hall sketch 'The Lamb on Wall Street' (i.e. a 'sucker amongst the bulls and bears'). Born in 1868, the son of the composer Robert Coote, he made his first stage appearance as one of the 'Babes in the Wood' at the Sadler's Wells Theatre on 26 December 1873. His first music-hall appearance was in 1896 and during the next 35 years he presented 'The Lamb on Wall Street' over 20,000 times. He died on 2 September 1938.

Coram, ventriloquist, born Thomas Whitaker near Halifax in 1883. On leaving school he worked at a local cotton mill, then joined the army as a bandsman in 1898. In his spare time he worked on a ventriloquist act using a pair of Chinese dolls as hand puppets, and on completion of his term of service,

Tommy Cooper, 1970

Coram and Jerry, 1931

entertained on Morecambe sands. Billed as 'Le Roi' he made small-time variety appearances and worked with a pierrot show at Portrush, Northern Ireland. His first London appearance was at the Lyceum Theatre in 1906, under the management of Thomas Barrasford, who ran the theatre as a music hall between December 1904 and December 1906. Originally booked as an 'extra turn', he remained on the bill for nine weeks, and was then engaged for an extended tour of the USA. Just before the First World War he introduced the doll, Jerry Fisher, into his act. Made by Coram, he was bigger than most ventriloquist's dolls and with a little help from Coram was able to walk with a natural gait, cry tears, wink an eye, smoke, and in less refined moments, spit into a spitoon. Billed as 'Coram, the Military Ventriloquist' or as 'The Great Coram', he appeared as an army or naval officer with Jerry as one of the other ranks. Closing the act in the scarlet of a Life Guardsman he sang:

> I'm Jerry Fisher, one of the old militia,
> I'm Jerry Fisher in the morning,
> One of the rank and file, no wonder the ladies smile,
> But I'm every inch a soldier.

Coram appeared with Jerry in the Royal Variety Performance at the London Palladium on 22 May 1930, and in the radio programme 'The White Coon's Concert Party', the first ventriloquist to broadcast. When Coram died on 25 March 1937, Jerry was presented to the London Museum's Theatre Collection.

The Three Cossacks, American roller skating act, formed in 1933 by the Chicago-born Johnny Gaynor, Jean Ross, and Wilton Ferguson. Johnny Gaynor began his career with the 'Ross Kress Four' then teamed with Joe Byron and another partner as the 'Gaynor Byron Trio', later working with Byron alone. When Byron left the act he was replaced by Wilton Ferguson, who had previously appeared for five years with the 'International Four' skating act. Before teaming with Gaynor and Ferguson, Jean Ross toured for two years with the Sandy Lang vaudeville skating team. 'The Three Cossacks' made their first appearance in Winnipeg in 1933 and their European debut at the Paramount, Paris, in June 1935, appearing in London at the Palladium two weeks later. On an elevated stage platform they reached a speed of 200 miles per hour. They appeared in the Royal Variety Performance of 1935.

Tom Costello, comedian and vocalist, born in Birmingham on 30 April 1863. He made his first appearance at the Prince of Wales Theatre, Wolverhampton, and in London at the Bedford, Camden Town, in 1886. The following Christmas he played Mephistopheles Muldoon in George Conquest's pantomime *Jack and the Beanstalk* at the Surrey Theatre. During a long and successful variety career he sang many good songs, the best remembered being 'At Trinity Church I Met My Doom', and 'Comrades' He appeared with the 'Veterans of Variety' company both on tour and at the London Palladium in 1922, and later toured his own road show, 'Veteran Stars of Variety'. He died on 8 November 1943.

Sam Cowell, one of the earliest music-hall performers and the first star of the Canterbury Music Hall. Born in London on 5 April 1820, the son of Joseph Leathley Cowell (1792–1863), an actor at the Theatre Royal, Drury Lane. In 1821 Joseph Cowell went to America with his family and by 1826 had established a reputation as one of the leading

Above: Sam Cowell, 1858   Below: Tom Costello

41

comedians in the USA, renowned for his performance as Crack in *The Turnpike Gate*. Sam Cowell made his first stage appearance at the age of nine at a benefit performance for his father. He later toured with his father playing Shakespearean roles billed as 'The Young American Roscius', entertaining between the acts by singing negro songs. Returning to England in 1840 he made his first British appearance at the Adelphi Theatre, Edinburgh, on 1 July 1840 playing Pierre in *Robert Macaire*. The following Christmas he appeared at the Theatre Royal, Edinburgh, with the famous clown Tom Matthews in the pantomime *Harlequin King of the Cannibal Island*. His first appearance in London was at the Surrey Theatre in 1844. On becoming well-known as a comic vocalist, he appeared at Cremorne in 1846, Vauxhall Gardens in 1847, and in burlesque at the Olympic Theatre the following year. By 1850 he had given up the legitimate stage for the more lucrative engagements at the London song-and-supper rooms—the Cole Hole, Cider Cellars, and Evans's, in Covent Garden. He specialised in character comedy songs, his greatest success being 'Villikins and His Dinah' and the tragic tale of 'The Ratcatcher's Daughter'.

A rather squat and ungainly man, but with a good stage presence, Cowell has been likened in appearance to Edmund Kean, a likeness which added to the success of his burlesque of *Richard III* and his sketches 'The Life and Death of Bad Macbeth' and 'The Tragical History of Hamlet the Dane'. He was a great success at the Grecian in 1851 and soon afterwards appeared at the Canterbury Music Hall, gaining such popularity that Charles Morton was forced to build a larger hall in 1854. In 1859 Cowell left England for a tour of the USA, opening on 28 November 1859 at the French Theatre, New York. During the next 20 months he toured a small variety company throughout the USA and Canada. The ups and downs of the tour were recorded in great detail by his wife and the diaries provide a fascinating picture of life in America just before the Civil War. The tour was a great strain on Cowell's health; he was both consumptive and alcoholic. He returned to London during the summer of 1861 and appeared at Morton's Oxford Music Hall. He died at Blandford at the age of 44 on 11 March 1864.

Right: Whit Cunliffe *(photo, Fielding of Leeds)*

Left: Claude Dampier

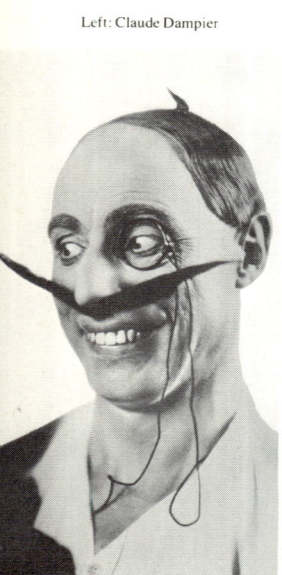

The Craggs, acrobatic troupe founded by J.W.Cragg, who first appeared with a partner in 1862. They were then working a trapeze act, appearing for 'Lord' George Sanger's Circus during the 1866–67 season. On being joined by their wives they worked the music halls as an acrobatic quartet, appearing at the Oxford on the night it was destroyed by fire, 1 November 1872. In 1873 Cragg's original partner left the act and it was re-formed with Cragg's wife, two sons and a daughter. That year they toured New Zealand, Australia, and the Middle East. J. W. Cragg retired in 1893 and took over the management of the Leigh Theatre, but with various members of the family 'The Cragg's Acrobatic Troupe' continued in variety for over 30 years.

Frank Craig, American negro entertainer, born in New York on 1 April 1870. From the age of 13 he gave boxing exhibitions at halls and fairgrounds in the USA, later boxing as a professional. He came to England in 1894 to beat both Ted Pritchard and John O'Brian. Turning from the ring to the music halls, he made his debut in 1896 at the Oxford and Washington as an immaculately dressed song-and-dance man. He then formed his own variety troupe of negro acts, including, in 1899, the black female impersonators Cropp and Johnson. Between 1900 and 1910 he toured the UK for Moss and Thornton, also appearing in Paris at the Casino and Folies Bergère.

Whit Cunliffe, elegant Edwardian singer of 'girl' songs, 'If the World Were Ruled by Girls', 'Girls, Girls, Girls', etc. A stage dandy in the older tradition of the Lions Comiques, he sang his songs strolling around the stage resplendent in a fine frock coat, topper and spats of brown, grey, or mauve. In a summer mood he has been described as a 'straw-hatted symphony in brown' when he would sing 'There's Something in the Seaside Air' and his most successful number, 'Who Were You With Last Night?'. He retired after the First World War and died in 1965.

D

Alexandra Dagmar, actress and music-hall singer who, although born in London, made her first stage appearance at 'Lord' George Sanger's Theatre, Westminster Bridge Road, on 15 November 1884 grandly billed as 'Important engagement of the great American actress Miss Grant Washington as *Richard III*. Her first appearance in Europe.' Later, on her first tour of the USA, she found herself billed as 'Alexandra Dagmar, the great Russian Beauty. The Favourite of the Czar.' A strikingly handsome woman with a strong singing voice, she turned from dramatic roles to the variety stage in 1886, becoming popular on the halls and as one of the finest principal boys of the 1890s. She appeared as Dandini in *Cinderella* at the Theatre Royal, Drury Lane in 1895–96. Later she worked a music act with her husband as 'Dagmar and De Celli, Operatic Duettists'.

Dudley Dale, comedian and dancer famous in the 1930s for his juvenile troupe of boy singers and dancers, 'Dudley Dale and his Gang'. Began his career as a patter comedian at the Argyle, Birkenhead, in 1914, making his London bow at the South London Palace the same year. His greatest success came with the formation of the 'Gang', which over the years toured the world with a succession of singers, dancers and comedians who later became well-known solo acts. Dudley Dale with or without his gang appeared in pantomime for Lew and Leslie Grade, Andrew Melville and other top managements.

Claude Dampier, comedian famous in variety and on radio for the catch phrase 'Well if it isn't Mrs Gibson!' Born in Clapham, London, he made his first stage appearance at the Grand Theatre, Birmingham, in 1896, and in London at the Theatre Royal, Drury Lane, later the same year. He spent 17 years working in variety in South Africa and Australia, and on his return to England in 1927 toured in revue and variety as a 'Dude Comedian'. During the 1930s he was popular on the radio with his amiably idiotic 'Mrs Gibson' act, in which he was partnered by Billie Carlyle. After the war he appeared regularly in the long-running radio series 'Up the Pole' with Jewel and Warriss.

Bebe Daniels *see* **Ben Lyon and Bebe Daniels**

Billy Danvers, red-nosed comedian, born William Mikado Danvers in Liverpool. As his name suggests, he came from a theatrical family; his father was Jimmy Danvers, a popular comedian in the North, his grandfather Edwin Danvers, a burlesque actor of the 1860s, and his uncle the eccentric comedian Ramsay Danvers. His first appearance, at the age of four, was in a music-hall comedy routine played by his father and Little Tich at the Tyne Theatre, Newcastle. He began his career as part of the double act of 'Billy and Frank Bass', making his first London appearance at the Bedford, Camden Town, in 1911. Turning solo in 1918 and billing himself as 'Cheeky, Cheery and Chubby', he was very much the red-nosed comic of the old school. His success was not confined to variety; he worked in concert party, revue, and musical comedy, including two tours of *Miss Hook of Holland* and *The Belle of New York*. He was a great pantomime artiste, appearing as Buttons at the Theatre Royal, Drury Lane in 1934. In 1948–50 he toured with Don Ross's show *Thanks for the Memory* appearing with the company in the Royal Variety Performance in November 1948. He never retired and in 1964 toured with another *Thanks for the Memory* company which included Hetty King, Sandy Powell, Marie Lloyd Junior, Cavan O'Connor, and Trevor Moreton. For the week of 2 March 1964 the show played the Granada in Brixton (late Empress), where in February 1948 the original company had commenced its successful tour. Billy died two weeks later on 20 March 1964.

Sonny Dawkes, female impersonator, born Wolverhampton on 17 July 1921. First appeared with a Bert Aza juvenile troupe at the Empire, Penge, on 3 September 1935. From 1937 to 1941 he worked as a light comedian in concert party and appeared as dancer and juvenile lead in touring revue. His first serious switch to drag came during the war while working with Ralph Reader's RAF 'Gang Show'. In 1946 he was booked by Jack Lewis as 'leading lady' for his all-male ex-service shows 'The Army Wore Skirts' and 'This Was the Army', which toured until they ran out of variety theatres in the late 1950s. A great pantomime dame, he has played the ugly sister to countless uglier ones all over the country.

Charles Deane, comic vocalist and song writer. Born Edward Saunders in Aldgate, East London, in 1866, he was for five years a Billingsgate fish porter by day and amateur entertainer by night. While appearing at a club in Hoxton, he was seen by G. H. Chirgwin (qv) who advised a music-hall career and arranged Deane's first professional appearance at Forester's Music Hall in 1890. His first song successes were 'Lovely Woman' by Harry Anderson and 'Strolling Round the Town' by Harry Castling. He later wrote his own material as well as supplying songs to other artists including 'One of the Girls' to Marie Kendall and 'Woa Emma' to Kate Carney. He died on 17 October 1910 at the age of 54.

Jeanne de Casalis, comedy actress, variety and revue comedienne. Born in Basutoland, South Africa, 22 May 1897. She studied the piano, but gave it up in favour of acting, making her first stage appearance at the Casino, Cannes, in *La Poudre aux Yeux* in 1919. Her London variety theatre debut was at the Coliseum in *Packing Up* in 1927, and she appeared the following year in the Charlot *1928 Revue* at the Vaudeville Theatre. Her famous scatter-brained character Mrs Feather originated from a revue sketch at the Alhambra in 1934 and became the mainstay of her career in

Billy Danvers, 'Cheeky, Cheery and Chubby'

Jeanne de Casalis, 1928

variety, gaining her nation-wide fame on radio during the war and the early 1950s.

The Deep River Boys, American singing act, Edward Ware, Vernon Gardner, Harry Douglas, George Lawson, with Cameron Williams at the piano. The boys met as members of a college glee club while students in Virginia and became famous on American radio. They made their first stage appearance in New York in 1936 and in London at the Palladium on 18 July 1949. In October 1953 they returned to the Palladium to star with George Formby in *Fun at the Fair*.

The Three Delevines, acrobatic brothers act. Born in Yorkshire, Harry, Percy and Dennis Delevine made their first appearance in London at the Alhambra in 1887 and became a popular act in Europe and America during tours of 1889 and 1890. During the early 1900s they combined their act with 'The Two Sisters Winterton' and as 'The Five Delevines' presented 'Flirtations', an acrobatic dancing and musical act.

Henri De Melvin, female impersonator who won wide acclaim on the halls during the 1870s billed as 'The Wonderful Baritone, The Wonderful Soprano, The London Star.' When he appeared at the London Pavilion in April 1872 the *Era* commented: 'A word of praise is also due to Mr Henri De Melvin who is decidedly one of the best female impersonators of the day. This gentleman neither by word, look nor gesture oversteps the bounds of propriety. His singing of the famous duet "The Gypsy Countess" in two different voices is admirable, and cannot fail to amuse . . .'

Florence Desmond, variety and revue artiste, born Florence Dawson in Islington, London, on 31 May 1905. She first appeared in variety in 1920 doing a precocious low comedy routine 'á la Nellie Wallace' (qv), followed by a top hat and tails song and dance number. In 1925 she was engaged by C.B. Cochran as one of his 'young ladies' and on 30 April opened at the London Pavilion in *On With the Dance*. This was followed by Cochran's 1926 revue, which after a short

Henri de Melvin, 1872

Florence Desmond

London run was toured by Tom Arnold under a new title, *Piccadilly*. Desmond was engaged to play the combined roles originally played by Spinelly and Hermione Baddeley and the new comedian of the show was a provincial discovery of Arnold's by the name of Max Miller. She made her New York debut on 7 November 1928 with Noël Coward and Beatrice Lillie in *This Year of Grace* which, after its run of 157 performances at the Selwyn Theatre, toured the USA and Canada. On her return to London in 1929 she devised a cabaret act of songs and impersonations of leading musical-comedy stars, and made regular variety and cabaret appearances. When in 1933 she was booked by the BBC to broadcast from Savoy Hill she hastily prepared a radio act, doing impersonations of Janet Gaynor, Zazu Pitts, Jimmy Durante, Greta Garbo, Marlene Dietrich, Marie Dressler, Gracie Fields, and Tallulah Bankhead. It was a great success and the following day HMV recorded 'A Hollywood Party', which became the bestseller of 1933. Later that year she returned to the USA touring her variety act on the Fox Theatre circuit with Eddie Cantor, and on her return to London in 1934 topped the bill at the Victoria Palace. On 24 April 1934 she opened at the Palace Theatre in *Why Not Tonight?* and stopped the show with her send-up of Mae West singing 'I'm No Angel' and her burlesque of Greta Garbo's 'I Want to Remember Everything in this Room' scene from *Queen Christina*. Between revue and cabaret engagements she starred in variety, appearing in the Royal Variety Performance at the Victoria Palace on 15 November 1937. In 1938 she toured her own road show 'Taking Off', in 1940 starred in *Sunny Side Up*, and on 5 March 1941 opened with Max Miller and Vera Lynn in *Apple Sauce* which ran for 462 performances at the London Palladium. After the war she spent at least four weeks of every year on the bill of the

London Palladium, and on 29 October 1951 made her second Royal Variety appearance. She retired in 1954 but made a comeback in 1958 to appear with Beatrice Lillie in *Auntie Mame* at the Adelphi Theatre, London.

Jerry Desmonde, elegant straight man and comedy feed to a number of leading comedians, notably Sid Field (qv) and Norman Wisdom (qv). Born James Robert Sadler, in Middlesbrough on 20 July 1908, he began his career at the age of 11 with the family act of 'Sadler Elsie Four', making his first appearance at the Palace Cinema, Armadale, on 15 November 1919. He appeared with this act until 1928 when he went into the chorus of musical-comedy road shows including a tour of the USA with 'This Year of Grace'. On his return to England he teamed with his brother Jack, appearing in variety as the 'Desmonde Brothers', and then worked in revue, concert party, and variety with his wife as 'Peg and Jerry Desmonde'. In 1942 he joined the great Sid Field for an eight-week road show. Sid was then still a struggling comedian trying to break into the West End but not making it any further than the Holborn Empire. It was the turning point of both their careers. When Sid Field was seen by George Black and engaged for the revue *Strike a New Note* at the Prince of Wales Theatre, Jerry Desmonde went too. *Strike a New Note* (1943) was followed by *Strike it Again* (1944) and *Piccadilly Hayride* (1946). The immaculately dressed Desmonde with his superior air was the perfect foil for the quaint cockney camp of Field. They appeared together in 'Golf' at the Royal Variety Performance at the London Coliseum on 5 November 1945, and repeated their success in 'Billiards' at the Palladium's Royal Performance the following year. In 1946 Desmonde appeared in the film version of *London Town* with Sid Field in the lead and in 1947 they were together again in Walter Forde's film *The Cardboard Cavalier*.

At the time of Sid Field's untimely death in February 1950, Jerry Desmonde was playing pantomime at the Grand Theatre, Brighton. Later that year he worked as a straight man to Nat Jackley and subsequently appeared at the Palladium and Prince of Wales with Bob Hope. In November 1952 he made his third Royal Variety appearance, acting as compère to the 'Songs that Made the Halls' finale, which included Vera Lynn, Maurice Chevalier and Gracie Fields. In 1953 he appeared in the film *Trouble in Store*, the first of a successful series of films made between 1953 and 1966, starring Norman Wisdom as the accident-prone and slightly vulgar 'Norman', with Jerry Desmonde giving excellent support in a variety of long-suffering roles. In 1958 he appeared with Norman Wisdom at the Palace Theatre in *Where's Charley?*, a musical version of Brandon Thomas's famous farce *Charley's Aunt*. A spot from the show was included in the Royal Variety Performance held that year at the Coliseum. During the 1950s he became a well-known television personality, perhaps best remembered as the quiz master of '64,000 Dollar Question'. In May 1961 he appeared at the Strand Theatre as George Lasher, the MC of the Bedford, Camden Town, in *Belle*, the greatly underrated 'music-hall musical' of Doctor Crippen and his ill-fated wife. Jerry Desmonde took his own life in 1967.

David Devant, stage conjurer and illusionist, born at Holloway, London, on 22 February 1868. His first music-hall appearance was at the Albert Palace, Battersea, in 1886. On 5 February 1891 he appeared as a trial turn at the London Pavilion, which led to a three-year contract to appear for eight weeks each year at the Pavilion and Oxford Music Hall. At the Crystal Palace in 1892 he presented his first original illusion, 'Vice Versa', in which he appeared to change a man into a woman. When some months later he was booked by Sam Adams to perform the illusion at the Trocadero Music Hall, Devant invited John Nevil Maskelyne, the doyen of British magicians, to attend a performance. He was so impressed that in August 1893 he engaged Devant to replace Charles Morritt as his assistant in his 'magical sketches' at the Egyptian Hall, Piccadilly. In July 1904 David Devant became Maskelyne's partner and on 7 August 1905 the first production of 'Maskelyne and Devant's Mysteries' opened at the St George's Hall. The highlight of the programme was the first performance of 'The Mascot Moth', considered to be Devant's most sensational illusion.

In addition to managing the St George's Hall, Devant organised three companies to tour the UK, Europe, and the USA. On 11 November 1907 he produced a new programme entitled 'The Magical Master', which included what is claimed to have been the first stage performance of the legendary 'Indian rope trick'. In 1910 Julian Wylie suggested to Devant that he should return to the music-hall stage during the summer closure of St George's Hall. With some reluctance he agreed to top the bill of the Brighton Hippodrome with a 50-minute programme of magic including variations on the 'Mascot Moth' and 'Artist's Dream', an adaptation of the original 'Vice Versa' sketch. From then on, when his London commitments permitted, he

David Devant, 1910

toured in variety, topping the bill at the opening of the Golders Green Hippodrome on Boxing Day 1913. On 1 July 1912 he represented the world of music-hall magic at the first Royal Command Performance at the Palace Theatre. A nervous breakdown made him decide to leave the St

George's Hall in 1915, but he continued to headline in variety until a serious nervous disorder forced him to retire from the stage in 1920. He continued to teach and write about magic until his death on 13 October 1941.

Deveen, magician, born in London on 24 April 1900. His first stage appearance was at the Orpheum Theatre, New Orleans, in 1919. After touring Australia, New Zealand and South Africa he returned to England in 1920 and made his London music-hall debut at the Bedford, Camden Town. Billed as 'Deveen, The Distinguished Deceiver, Assisted by his "New York Blondes"', he toured in variety and was one of the first magicians to make a television appearance from Alexandra Palace.

The Diamond Brothers, knockabout comedy, singing and dancing act. Hughie, Tom and Harold Diamond were born at Wilkes-Barre, Pennsylvania, where their father, a one-time vaudeville dancer, ran a cinema and theatre. Hughie, the eldest brother, first appeared with 'The Five Avalons' wire-walking act, and then with his wife and two brothers formed a straight song-and-dance act which headlined in vaudeville as 'The Four Diamonds'. After nine years Hughie's wife Phoebe left the act, which was then reformed on comedy lines as 'The Diamond Brothers'. They appeared with success at the Palace, New York, and in 1931 with Schwab and De Sylva's burlesque revue *Take a Chance*. They made their London variety and cabaret debut at the Palladium and Dorchester Hotel on 22 January 1934, and for the next eight months appeared in variety, cabaret, and in C.B. Cochran's revue *Not Tonight* at the Palace Theatre. They opened their second season in London at the Café de Paris in March 1935, appearing that October in the Royal Variety Performance at the London Palladium.

Phyllis Dixey, actress-manager, although better-known as 'Peek-a-Boo' fan dancer. Born in Raynes Park, London, in 1914, she trained as a dancer, making her first stage appearance at the Birmingham Hippodrome in August 1930. Pantomime and revue followed and by the age of 21 she was starring as leading lady in her own road shows. After three years as leading lady with Ernie Lotinga she teamed with Jack Tracy to appear in variety with 'The Sap and the Swell Dame' act. She and Tracy were married in 1937. In 1940 she appeared in her own show at the Phoenix Theatre and during the next five years of war became a welcome diversion at the Whitehall Theatre, where the Phyllis Dixey 'Non-Stop' revues played to full houses. In May 1944 she took over the lease of the theatre, where in addition to her 'Peek-a-Boo' shows she put on the very successful *Worm's Eye View*, which ran for a total of 2,245 performances. Between 1948 and the mid-1950s she toured the variety theatres with 'Peek-a-Boo', playing the Metropolitan, Edgware Road, Collins Music Hall, etc., but finally gave up in the face of competition from less artistic nude shows, all-in wrestling, and finally, bingo.

Reg Dixon, 'Proper Poorly' comedian who, although born in 1915, has a lugubrious style of comedy in the tradition of much earlier music-hall artistes such as George Formby Senior, Alfred Lester, and Jack Pleasants. He made his first appearance, aged 10, at the Scala Theatre in his home town of Coventry. From the age of 16 he appeared with a number of touring revues, first as one of the company and then working a piano act with a partner, billed as 'Scott and Dixon'. During the late 1930s he toured his own fit-up company throughout the North of England and Scotland, until he joined the RAF at the outbreak of war. He served in

T.E. Dunville, 1892

India, Burma and the Middle East and toured with Ralph Reader's RAF 'Gang Show'. He made his first London stage appearance at the Stoll Theatre on 10 May 1946, but his first real break came in 1949 when he became the resident comedian of that famous springboard to fame, the BBC's Sunday evening radio show 'Variety Band Box'. With his popular signature tune, 'Confidentially', and catch phrase 'proper poorly', he became a well-known radio and variety comedian, taking part in the Royal Variety Performance from the London Coliseum on 7 November 1949. In April 1952 he got his first starring part in the West End, taking over the lead from George Formby in *Zip Goes a Million* at the Palace Theatre. In November that year he made his second Royal Variety appearance in the 'Songs That Made The Halls' finale from the London Coliseum. In 1953 he appeared in Charles Saunders' film *Love in Pawn* and in 1955 made *No Smoking*, directed by Henry Cars. He is now a popular entertainer in the Midlands and Northern clubs and star of summer shows, variety and pantomime.

The Donaldson Brothers and Ardel, sketch artistes and knockabout comedians. Born in the USA, the three Donaldson brothers made their first appearance as contortionists at Grand Rapids, Michigan, in 1878 and later toured the United States with the Barnum, Forepaugh's, and Sell Brothers circuses. After touring Australia and New Zealand, they came to England, opening as contortionists at the London Pavilion in 1890. In 1892 they teamed with Tom Ardel, a fellow American who had previously worked in Britain with Alf West as 'Ardel and West', and together formed a comedy sketch act. Their most successful routine was 'Scenes from the Zoo', in which they combined contortions with comedy, wearing skins and performing monkey tricks in a large animal cage, advertised as constructed for a cost of £750.

Leo Dryden, singer of patriotic ballads, notably 'The Miner's Dream of Home'. Born George Dryden Wheeler in Limehouse, London, on 6 June 1863, he made his first appearance as a semi-pro at Forester's Music Hall, London, in 1881. Influenced by Charles Godfrey (qv), he toured a similar act but without any great success. While appearing at the Albert Music Hall, Sheffield, he was seen by Jenny Hill (qv). She arranged a meeting with her agent Hugh J. Didcott, who booked him for the Oxford on 4 February 1889. From then on his career improved and his singing of 'The Miner's Dream of Home' sent him to the top of the bill during the Boer War (1899–1902). Supported by his own band of flag-waving supers, he sang his songs dressed in a variety of costumes, ranging from a Rajah for 'India's Reply' to a pith helmet for 'What Britishers are Made Of'. For his song 'The Great White Mother' he appeared in the headdress and warpaint of a Canadian Indian singing a jubilee tribute to Queen Victoria:

> Great White Mother, far across the sea,
> Ruler of the ocean may she ever be,
> Long may she reign, glorious and free,
> In the great white motherland.

Other songs of the same jingoistic nature included 'The Gallant Gordon Highlanders' and 'Bravo Dublin Fusiliers'. Appearing during the 1930s with the Veterans of Variety company, he again scored a great success with 'The Miner's Dream of Home' and later acted as Chairman of Collins Music Hall. He died on 21 April 1939.

'Professor' Duncan, animal trainer of 'Duncan's Collies'. Born John Patterson in Dundee in 1856, he first worked the smalls of the North during the 1880s with a 'dumb dog' act. More dogs were added to the routine and as 'Duncan's Collies' they played at the Palace Theatre, London, for nine months. Regarded as one of the best exponents of animal acts in variety, Duncan toured America, Australia, South Africa and most of Europe. After giving a performance for Edward VII at Buckingham Palace, Duncan changed the billing to 'Duncan's Royal Scots Collies'. When he retired in 1926 Duncan's act was carried on by his son Victor, who was on the bill during the successful Danny Kaye season at the Palladium in 1948. Duncan died on 17 January 1936.

T. E. Dunville, eccentric comedian born in Coventry in 1870. As a young man he formed a nigger minstrel trio, locally known as the 'Three Spires'. In 1866 he teamed with Robert Martell and as 'The Two Martells' they joined a touring pantomime company as knockabout comedians with such success that they were booked to tour the USA. On their return to England in 1887 they appeared as the two broker's men in *Babes in the Wood* at Leicester. When the act broke up in 1889 Dunville made his first solo appearance at the Victoria Music Hall, Bolton, and in London at Gatti's-Under-the-Arches on 30 June 1890. At first attired in conventional evening dress singing comic songs, he later changed to the most eccentric of costumes, hideously clownish make-up and sang nonsensical songs such as 'Pop Pop Popperty Pop', 'Dinky Dee', 'Bunk-adoodle-I-do', and songs composed of short sharp sentences delivered staccato fashion:

> Little boy,
> Pair of skates,
> Broken ice,
> Heaven's gates.

Not to everyone's taste, he made a poor impression on Max Beerbohm, who after seeing him at the Oxford in July 1901 wrote in the *Saturday Review*: 'Who is this loathsome object? This seedy Scaramouch, lank-haired, red-nosed ... Ugliness of appearance, ugliness of manner, ugliness of jokes—such is the panoply of Mr Dunville.' Despite Beerbohm, he was a popular artiste in variety and pantomime for over 30 years. Not able to make the switch to revue, all the rage after the First World War, he found bookings hard to come by. While appearing at the Clapham Grand in March 1924 he heard himself referred to as a 'fallen star' and drowned himself in the Thames at Reading.

May Moore Duprez, comedienne and dancer, born in the USA in 1889. She first appeared in England in 1900 and with Fanny Fields was a leading performer of 'Jolly Little Dutch Girl' routines, singing in a ridiculously broken Dutch accent 'Leetle Meester Baggy Breeches'. She retired in 1916 and died in 1946.

E

Jack Edge, variety and revue comedian, born Jack Haylon in Manchester, on 18 October 1891. First appeared with the 'Eight Lancashire Lads' at the Alexandra Theatre, Birmingham, at Christmas 1904, and in London in 1905 at the Tivoli, Collins, and Oxford Music Halls. First worked a solo act at the Queen's Park Hippodrome on 8 February 1908. From 1913 he appeared in London revues, including *Three Cheers* with Harry Lauder at the Shaftesbury Theatre in 1917, and played George Robey's role in *Zig Zag* at the London Hippodrome in 1918. He toured in variety throughout the UK, South Africa and Australia and for over 20 years starred as principal comedian in pantomime for Julian Wylie.

Jimmy Edwards, popular comedian, born in Barnes, London, 23 March 1920. While an undergraduate at Cambridge he took part in the 'Footlights Revue' and played the trombone in the University dance band. After the war, during which he served in the RAF, winning the DFC at Arnhem, he attended one of Vivian Van Damm's auditions and was booked to appear at the Windmill Theatre in May 1946. During 18 months as resident comedian at the famous Soho home of 'Revuedeville', he played six shows a day six days a week and built up a 10-minute spot lecturing on the art of playing the trombone in a mixture of Cambridge English and RAF service slang. In 1947 he was engaged by the BBC to broadcast in their revival of the wartime comedy programme 'Navy Mixture', which led to the phenomenally successful radio comedy series 'Take It From Here' and national stardom for Jimmy Edwards, Joy Nichols, and Dick Bentley. At the end of 1949 Edwards toured with George and Alfred Black's revue *Sky High*, and appeared on variety bills with Dick Bentley and Joy Nichols. In October 1950 the 'Take It From Here' trio appeared in Jack Hylton's revue *Take It From Us* at the Adelphi Theatre, which ran for three months with Nichols and Bentley, and a further nine months with Edwards starring alone. On 29 October 1951 he appeared in the Royal Variety Performance at the Victoria Palace, and in April 1952 returned to the Adelphi to star with Tony Hancock and Vera Lynn in *London Laughs*. It ran for 1,113 performances and was followed in November 1954 by *The Talk of the Town*. Once more in a mortarboard and academic gown, like a latter-day Will Hay, 'Professor' Jimmy Edwards appeared in 1956 as the headmaster of Chiselbury School in the BBC television series 'Whacko'.

At Christmas 1958 Edwards starred with Tommy Steele in Harold Fielding's spectacular production of Rodgers and Hammerstein's *Cinderella* at the London Coliseum. 'Whacko' ran for a total of six series, followed by 'The Seven Faces of Jim', 'More Faces of Jim' and 'The Fossett Saga'. In 1966 he appeared, minus his famous handlebar moustache, in the name part in a television adaptation of R.S. Surtees's *John Jorrocks Esq*. West End stage appearances include *Big Bad Mouse*, in which he appeared with Eric Sykes at the Shaftesbury Theatre, and later toured South Africa, and *Half Way Up the Tree* at the Queen's Theatre, London. At the General Election of 1964 he stood unsuccessfully as Conservative candidate for North Paddington, while other improbable roles included General Malana, the Governor of Santo, in Emile Littler's production of *The Maid of the Mountains* at the Palace Theatre. In October 1972 he appeared with the drag duo Rogers and Starr (qv) in the revue *Hulla Baloo* at the Criterion Theatre.

Gus Elen, comedian and singer, probably the greatest of the select band of coster comedians of the 1890s. Born in Pimlico, London, on 22 July 1862, he began his career as a draper's assistant by day and a programme seller at the Royal Aquarium by night. As an entertainer his career had humble beginnings, first as a London street busker, dancing and singing to a barrel organ in the Strand, and then as a pub singer, passing the hat at The Black Dog, Lambeth, and The Magpie and Stump in Cheyne Walk, Chelsea. He made his earliest appearances on a variety bill at the Bow Music Hall and Sebright's, Hackney, and during the late 1880s played with a nigger minstrel troupe on Ramsgate sands. Returning to London by way of the provincial halls, where he appeared as a solo 'coon' comedian, he had his first real success as a coster comedian at the Middlesex Music Hall in 1891. His cockney songs were far truer to life than the idealised and rather mawkish emotions expressed by his rival, Albert Chevalier. Although full of pathos they were rescued from cloying sentiment by a sharp dash of irony. One of his best was a nostalgic ditty about his little East End terrace house with a backyard which had such 'nobly distant views' and 'wiv a ladder and some glasses, you could see the 'Ackney Marshes, if it wasn't for the 'ouses in between'. Another, 'It's a Great Big Shame', was an exquisite elegy to his newly wedded friend, Jim:

It's a great big shame, and if she belonged ter me,
I'd let 'er know who's who,
Nagging at a feller wot is six foot free,
And 'er only four foot two,
Oh! they adn't been married not a month nor more,
When underneath 'er fumb goes Jim,
Oh, isn't it a pity as the likes of 'er,
Should put upon the likes of 'im?

Other great songs included 'Never Introduce Your Donah to a Pal', ''Arf a Pint of Ale', 'It's a Marvel How 'E does It But 'E Do', and 'You Can Almost Shut Your Eyes and 'Ear Them Grow'. He made his first appearance in the USA touring for Klew and Erlinger in 1907. After more than 30 years on the halls he went into retirement, but made a comeback in the Royal Variety Performance at the London Palladium in 1935, and later played the regular variety bills of the Palladium and the Holborn Empire. He soon chose to return to contented retirement on the South Coast, where there were no ''ouses in between'. He died on 17 February 1940.

The Elliotts and the Seven Musical Savonas, one of the most successful and original of the early music-hall speciality acts. J.B. Elliott was originally a solo trick-cyclist during the 1860s, later forming a family troupe with his three sons and three daughters. They all played a number of musical instruments and during the 1880s worked a cycle-mounted band, which was so well received that they later divided their talents into two separate acts, 'Elliotts, the World's Cycling Wonders' and 'The Seven Musical Savonas'. They were quick to realise the entertainment value of electricity and while it was still considered the wonder of the age, built a high stage set fitted with over 1,000 electric light bulbs. Dressed in colourful Watteau-esque eighteenth-century court costumes, they each played a saxophone, and billed themselves as 'The Only Saxophone Band in the World'. They played 50 different wind, string and percussion instruments among the seven of them, many of primitive and foreign origin. In addition, their illuminated set concealed three organs, which when played together sounded like a cross between Notre Dame and a fairground. So individual and accomplished were the two acts that the audiences were slow to realise they were performed by the same troupe, partly because trick-cycling and musical virtuosity rarely go hand in hand, but also because the jockey-like garb of their first turn contrasted dramatically with the powdered wigs and brocaded satins of the second. They made two world tours and for nearly 30 years this

Gus Elen

gloriously original if bizarre troupe remained unchallenged as the greatest exponents of the musical variety act. J. B. Elliott died on 22 May 1906, Ralph Elliott on 7 August 1909 and Thomas and May Elliott on 2 and 5 September 1929.

Chick Elliott, one of the few successful 'black-faced' comediennes, born in Sydney, Australia, on 26 February 1900. From the age of four she appeared with her mother's act, in which she made her debut in Melbourne. From 1916 she worked as a 'coon' singer in variety, pantomime and revue, and first appeared in London at the Islington Empire in December 1930. Later she toured as a solo act in variety, working a black-faced act and as a stand-up comedienne in evening dress. She also worked in revue, musical comedy and operetta, including parts in *Merrie England* at the Princes Theatre, London, in 1946, and *The Kid from Stratford* with Arthur Askey at the Princes and then the Winter Garden in 1946–48.

G. H. Elliott, the original 'Chocolate Coloured Coon', who carried the music-hall 'coon' singing tradition of Eugene Stratton (qv) into the 1950s. Although born in England on 3 November 1884, George Henry Elliott made his first stage appearance as a child in the USA, playing Little Lord Fauntleroy in Newark, New Jersey, and at the age of nine became a singer and dancer with the Primrose West Minstrels. On returning to England in 1901, he appeared that summer with Harry Reynolds's Minstrels at Colwyn Bay, doing his own American 'coon' speciality, singing ballads and comic songs and appearing in burlesques and sketches. He and a partner also presented a musical double act, in which he played several instruments. His first London appearance was at Sadler's Wells Theatre on 10 March 1902, and later that year he was engaged for Gatti's, Westminster Bridge Road, at £4 for the week. He was a worthy successor to Eugene Stratton, who died in 1918, and rose to a pre-eminent position as music hall's leading singer of sentimental 'coon' songs, notably 'I want to go to Idaho', 'Sue, Sue, Sue', 'Hallo Susie Green', 'I'se a Waitn' for you Josie', 'Rastus Brown', and his most famous 'I Used to Sigh for the Silvery Moon'. He also revived many of Leslie Stuart's fine songs, including 'Lily of Laguna' and 'Little Dolly Daydream', always acknowledging Eugene Stratton as the original singer, and offering them as his personal tribute to 'The Dandy Coloured Coon'. Elliott appeared in the Royal Variety Performance at the Alhambra on 12 February 1925, and 23 years later, in February 1948, he joined Don Ross's *Thanks for the Memory* company at the Empress, Brixton. After a tremendously successful national tour it was featured in the Royal Variety Performance at the London Palladium on 1 November 1948. G. H. Elliott died at his home in Brighton in 1962.

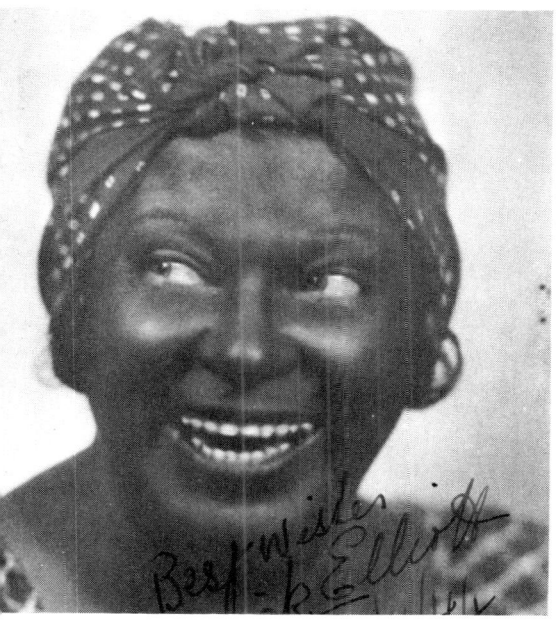

Above: Chick Elliott, 1944

Below: G.H. Elliott, 'The Chocolate Coloured Coon', 1948

Joe Elvin, cockney comedian born in Crown Street, London, on 29 November 1862. His father was the Irish actor Joseph Keegan who in 1863 joined Charles Kean's company at the Princes Theatre, and also appeared with Samuel Phelps and T. P. Cooke. Later Keegan left the comparative refinement of Oxford Street for the stock company of the Bower Saloon, a notorious rough-house that specialised in melodrama of the most lurid kind. While at school in Tottenham Court Road Joe Elvin took his first steps toward a stage career under the tuition of Paddy Fannin and, billed as 'Little Elvin', made his first stage appearance in the pantomime 'Hop O' My Thumb' at the Theatre Royal, Brighton, in 1871. The following year he appeared as juvenile comedian and clog dancer at Crowder's Music Hall, Greenwich, and soon afterwards joined his father in a sketch act billed as 'Keegan and Little Elvin'. They became particularly associated with the Standard Music Hall, Pimlico, their sketches during the next 10 years including 'The Unpolished Boots', 'Peter and Paul', 'The Brummagen Bruiser', 'The Boy Baronet', 'Rival Lodgers', 'The Marble Hall', and a free adaptation of Dickens's *Bleak House*, entitled 'Poor Joe'. In 1882 they appeared at Tony Pastor's, New York, and finding that American audiences clearly preferred their vaudeville entertainment to be of a lighter vein than their usual melodramatic sketches, Keegan and Elvin turned to comedy. On their return to England they played in *Puss in Boots* at the Grand Theatre, Islington, in 1884, and the following year at the Marylebone Theatre presented 'The Tinker's Holiday', which established them as a leading music-hall sketch act. Many of their greatest successes were first presented at the Middlesex, including 'The Hansom Cabby' in 1890. Others included 'The Broker's Man', 'A Dreadful Tragedy', 'The Clock', 'The Village Maiden', and 'I Ain't Barmy'. Although Keegan and Elvin had been working the halls for nearly 20 years, most of their success had been in the provinces and suburban London halls. However, in 1890 they appeared at the Oxford Music Hall, a successful engagement which resulted in a three-year contract for the Oxford, London Pavilion, and Tivoli. They now began to branch out into spectacular sporting sketches, notably 'Toffy's Trotter', a big racing scene set at Alexandra Park. Written by Elvin and Wal Pink, it was first produced in pantomime at the Paragon, Mile End, with a cast of six principals, 100 extras, and several prize-winning 'trotters'. A similarly ambitious production was 'Over the Sticks', which—complete with a spectacular hurdle race—was the Christmas attraction at the Oxford in 1893.

When Joseph Keegan retired in 1895 (he died on 6 October 1901), Joe Elvin continued with his own company, presenting the sketches 'Obedient Billy', 'A Day's Sport', 'The Bookie', 'Who Sez So', 'Trespassers Beware', 'The Holy Friar', 'Riding to Orders', 'Billy's Money Box', 'Uncle Izzy', 'Sailor Lad', and ''Appy 'Ampstead'. The last sketch ended with a scene of Hampstead Heath on a Bank Holiday which W. MacQueen Pope considered would have done credit to Drury Lane. One of Elvin's most famous catch phrases was 'I'm obliging my brother', a motto which he certainly lived up to off the stage. A tireless worker for show-business organisations, he was one of the founders of the Grand Order of Water Rats, the Variety Artistes Federation and the Variety Artistes Benevolent Fund, of which he was elected the first president in 1907. In 1909 he set up the fund and made the first donation of £500 to build a home for aged music-hall and circus artistes, resulting in the purchase of Brinsworth House. Joe Elvin died on 3 March 1935.

Above: Joe Elvin, 1898

Fred Emney, character actor and music-hall comedian remembered for his famous dame sketch 'A Sister to Assist 'Er'. The nephew of comedians Arthur and Fred Williams (qv), he was born in Islington on 5 March 1865 and made his first appearance in *The Ticket of Leave Man*, and *The Forty Thieves* at the Sadlers Wells Theatre on 25 May 1885, followed by a tour with Nellie Farren's company in the Gaiety burlesques *Aladdin* and *Ariel*. From 1887 to 1889 he toured in the play *Dorothy*, playing the part of Lurcher, originally created by Arthur Williams. An outstanding burlesque comedian, he played in West End productions almost non-stop for over 20 years. Excelling in musical comedy and comic opera, he appeared in *Jaunty Jane Shore* at the Strand Theatre in 1894, *All Aboard?* at the Criterion, 1895, and *The Yashmak* at the Shaftesbury in 1897. Although a successful pantomime dame in the role of Clorinda in *Cinderella* at the Lyceum in 1894 and as Nurse in *Sleeping Beauty and the Beast* at Drury Lane in 1900, it was not until 1906 that he made his first regular music-hall appearance with 'Man the Brute'. In *Sinbad the Sailor*, the Drury Lane pantomime for 1906–07, Emney as The Empress of all the Saharas appeared with Harry Randall as Mrs Sinbad. The hit of the show was a tea-party scene in which the two sat and imbibed numerous cups of tea, well laced with whisky. The climax was a riotous quarrel and slanging match that went down so well that Emney later developed it into the sketch 'A Sister to Assist 'Er', which as such he first presented at the Tivoli Music Hall in 1907. It was so

Below: Fred Emney

successful that like John Lawson's "Humanity" and Fred Karno's 'Mumming Birds' it soon ranked as one of the classic sketches of the halls.

From 1912 Fred Emney appeared mainly in variety. 'A Sister to Assist 'Er' was followed by 'The Arrival of a Rival' and 'The Plumbers', a hilarious slapstick sketch of the havoc caused by Emney as the Plumber arriving with his mate 'Erb two weeks late to mend a burst waterpipe, carrying tools to mend a gas leak. 'Erb was played by Harry Gratton, who also wrote the sketch. In 1915 he appeared in the revue *Shell Out* at the Comedy Theatre, and was the hit of the show with a solo comedy dame routine 'Getting Over a Stile', which he later worked with success in variety. At Christmas 1916 he played the Baroness in *Cinderella* at the London Opera House. On the opening night, while appearing in the whitewashing scene with the Brothers Egbert, he slipped on some soapsuds and fell heavily on to the stage. The audience, thinking it part of the comedy routine, laughed and applauded. Fred carried on with the show, but it was his last performance. As a result of the fall he died a week later, on 7 January 1917.

His son, the popular rotund comedian Fred Emney Junior, was born in London on 12 February 1900. He made his first appearance as a page boy in *Romance* at the Duke of York's Theatre in 1915 and at Christmas 1916 played a small part in *Puss in Boots* at the Theatre Royal, Drury Lane. Developing both in style and girth he turned solo as a variety comedian and performer of songs at the piano. In 1920 he left London for New York and was such a success in vaudeville and cabaret that he remained in the USA for nearly twelve years. On his return to England in 1931 he toured in variety and from the mid-1930s in revue and musical comedy. His postwar successes included *Starlight Roof* at the London Hippodrome and the long-running West End comedy *Blue for a Boy*.

Bert Errol, music-hall's greatest female impersonator. Born on 11 August 1883, he received a good musical education as a child and began his career in his home town of Birmingham in 1901 as a concert singer and after-dinner entertainer. In 1908 he became a member of Adler and Sutton's Concert

Bert Errol, 1935

Ethardo, 1865

Party, and early in his career appeared with Harry Reynolds' Minstrels. He had a remarkably versatile singing voice, ranging from falsetto to robust tenor, which during the 12 months he spent with Harry Reynolds was put to good use as the minstrels' female impersonator in the traditional black-faced, court-dressed, prima donna burlesques. Discarding the black make-up but remaining a 'lady', he made his first London music-hall appearance at the London Pavilion in 1909, billed as 'The Famous Male Soprano and Double-Voiced Vocalist'. He was the first female impersonator to achieve fame in variety and his popularity in this field was only surpassed in recent years by Danny La Rue (qv). Beautifully dressed, he managed to look glamorous without being camp. Although he sang many of his songs, such as 'My Sahara Rose', perfectly straight, he scored his greatest success with his burlesques of musical comedy actresses. In variety he toured extensively throughout the UK, Australia, New Zealand, South Africa and Canada, playing for years at a time in vaudeville throughout the USA. In pantomime he worked nine seasons for Wylie and Tate in both London and the provinces. He appeared at the London Hippodrome in 1922 as Minnie Mumm to Dolly Harmer's Maxi Mumm, the Ugly Sisters in *Cinderella*. He died on 29 November 1949.

Ethardo, Italian acrobat, born in 1835. He first appeared in England at the Crystal Palace, London, in 1865. Billed as 'The Spiral Ascensionist', he balanced on a globe 30 inches in diameter and worked his way up and down a foot-wide spiral track 130 feet long, climbing to a height of 50 feet. He made his first London variety appearance at the Strand Music Hall on 26 September 1866 and appeared at the Canterbury in 1865. He was popular for a number of years and even had a waltz named after him. He died in 1911.

David Evans *see* **Tony Fayne and David Evans**

Norman Evans, variety comedian and pantomime dame of 'Over the Garden Wall' fame. Born in Rochdale in 1901, he began his working life as a commercial traveller and like all good salesmen had a ready supply of funny stories for every occasion. Gaining a reputation as a comic after-dinner speaker, he decided, when selling got a bit rough, to become a funny man for a living. He first appeared professionally at 'smokers' and local masonic functions. While appearing with a northern concert party, he was seen by his home town's pride and joy, Gracie Fields, who arranged variety dates which led to his first London appearance at the Alhambra on 5 November 1934, and Number One variety tours for Stoll and GTC. Although one of the finest of the modern dame comedians, he favoured the older 'bonnet-and-shawl' tradition rather than the glamorous vulgarity of latter day drag artists and was a great pantomime favourite in the North. Norman Evans is perhaps best remembered for his 'Over the Garden Wall' sketch which he toured in variety and broadcast as a weekly comedy series in 1948 and 1949. During this period he also toured his 'Good Evans' road show, making his first appearance in America at the Palace Theatre, New York, in 1949. He scored a big hit in the USA and in May 1950 returned with a British variety company for a season at the El Capitan Theatre, Hollywood. He appeared in three Royal Variety Performances, at the London Palladium in 1937 and 1947, and in 1951 at the Victoria Palace. He died in 1969.

Will Evans, one of the finest music hall slapstick comedians. Born in London on 29 May 1875, he made his first stage appearance in the traditional theatrical family manner, being carried on to the stage as a baby during a pantomime at Drury Lane, in which his parents, Fred Evans and Amy Rosaling, famous clowns and pantomimists, were appearing. At the age of six he appeared in the Harlequinade of *Robinson Crusoe*, the Drury Lane pantomime for 1881–82, with Fanny Leslie as principal boy and Arthur Roberts as dame. He received good early training as a knockabout comedian and instrumentalist with his father's pantomime troupe, touring the UK and Europe with the 'Cats on the Tiles' acrobatic comedy act. Later he and his older brother Fred Evans Junior, with another partner, turned to the music halls as a musical trio. When Fred Evans married Minnie Jee and joined her and her two brothers to appear in variety as 'The Florador Quartette', Will Evans married Ada Luxmore and the couple worked a comedy musical act as 'Evans and Luxmore'. In 1894 his wife became fatally ill (she died on 11 May 1897) and he turned solo, becoming famous for his eccentric clown-like make-up and series of slapstick sketches and monologues, 'The Derby Winner', 'Building a Chicken House', 'Harnessing a Horse', 'Whitewashing a Ceiling', 'Papering the Parlour', etc. At his funniest in pantomime, he is considered to have originated the now traditional slapstick kitchen scenes and knockabout routines.

He was a popular Christmas attraction in London and the provinces for nearly 30 years. He appeared in every pantomime at Drury Lane between 1911 and 1919, playing Potterini in *Hop O' My Thumb* (1911–12), Pompos for three consecutive years of the Arthur Collins *Sleeping Beauty* (1912–14), the Grand Duke in *Puss in Boots* (1915–16), the Grand Duchess in *Puss in Boots* (1916–17), the Slave of the Ring in *Aladdin* (1917–18), Little Flossie, one of the 'Babes In The Wood' (1918–19), and the Baroness in *Cinderella* (1919–20). He was part author of the very successful farce *Tons of Money*, first produced at the old Shaftesbury Theatre in 1922, with Tom Walls and Ralph Lynn. Transferring to the Aldwych in 1923, it was the first of an era of famous farces associated with that theatre and ran for nearly 800 performances. Will Evans retired on his share of the proceeds, and died on 11 April 1931.

F

W. B. Fair, William Burnham Fair, comedian and singer of 'Tommy Make Room For Your Uncle'. Born in Camden Town, London, in 1850, he later moved with his family to the north of England, getting his first professional engagement as a call boy at the Queen's Theatre, Manchester, where he also appeared between calls in low comedy parts at a combined wage of nine shillings per week. In 1872 he returned to London and made his first appearance at the East London Theatre in a sketch entitled 'Sitanas'. The East London was then run by George Leybourne and frequented by many old music-hall friends, including William Holland. Holland liked Fair's performance and booked him to appear with James Fawn and Nelly Power, playing Lively Boy in his Christmas pantomime *Jack and the Beanstalk* at the Surrey Theatre. This was the first of a series of pantomime roles. Fair appeared at the Surrey the following year in *Forty Thieves* and later at the Surrey Gardens in a burlesque 'Crusoe the Second' by T. S. Lonsdale, which introduced the song 'Tommy Make Room For Your Uncle' and made Fair one of the most popular music-hall artistes of the day. He sang the song with phenomenal success at up to six halls a night for over ten years. Between 1878 and 1880 he managed the Winchester Music Hall in Southwark Bridge Road, where he was a popular chairman. Alas, his table was always surrounded by fairweather friends and Fair and his 'Tommy' money were soon parted. He made several attempts at a variety comeback, trading on his old fame with the billing 'W.B. ''Tommy Make Room For Your Uncle'' Fair'. But tastes had changed since the 1870s and he was never able to regain his lost stardom. He was reduced eventually to opening cab

Will Evans as Flossie, one of the 'Babes in the Wood', 1918–19

doors outside the Coliseum for a living. He died on 22 July 1901.

El Nino Farini, trapezist born 1855. He first appeared in London at the Alhambra and Cremorne Gardens in 1866, working with his father, acrobat and tightrope-walker G. A. Farini. Billed as 'El Nino Farini—the Infant Prodigy', he played a drum solo while suspended by the nape of the neck from a high trapeze. He appeared with his father as 'The Flying Farinis' at the main London and provincial halls and in the spring of 1869 performed at the Crystal Palace in a benefit for the artists and staff of the Oxford Music Hall, destroyed by fire the previous February. On a rope stretched between the balconies of the centre transept, G.A. Farini emulated the feats of Blondin, walking the wire blindfolded with his nine-year-old son on his back.

When Nino outgrew his prodigious attraction he appeared at a Paris circus in 1870, billed as 'Mlle Lulu—The Beautiful Girl Aerialist and Circassian Catapultist'. On 11 January 1871, 'Lulu' appeared in London at the concert hall of the Cremorne Gardens, in an act which involved being catapulted from the stage to a high trapeze, flying perpendicularly a distance of 25 feet and turning a triple somersault. Soon afterwards 'she' became the star attraction at the Holborn Amphitheatre, described by an enthusiastic press as a 'beauteous little blonde of seventeen, her slender figure most symmetrical and graceful', and as 'The Eighth Wonder of the World'. 'Lulu's' true sex was not revealed until 1878, when he was 25, apparently causing much embarrassment to 'royalty, commoners, peers and plebeians', who were reported to have surged to lay 'just tribute at the feet of the marvel of the age'.

Photographs of Nino Farini in the Gabrielle Enthoven Collection of the Victoria and Albert Museum, taken about 1880, show him as a strangely effeminate young man with blonde hair falling over slender shoulders.

G. F. Farini managed the Westminster Royal Aquarium during the 1880s and according to T. McDonald Rendle in *Swings and Roundabouts* (1919) Nino went to Canada and became a photographer and portrait painter.

El Nino Farini as, left, 'The Infant Prodigy', 1866, and, right, 'Lulu, the Beautiful Girl Aerialist', 1871

W.B. Fair, 1878

Billy Farrel, American negro dancer who introduced the famous 'cake-walk' dance into American vaudeville at the Grand Opera House, Brooklyn, in 1886 and a few years later to the British music hall at the Alhambra Theatre, London.

James Fawn, comedian and comic vocalist of 'If You Want to Know the Time Ask a Policeman' fame. Born in 1849, he made his first stage appearance with J. R. Newcomb's company at the Theatre Royal, Portsmouth, in 1865. As a low comedy actor he played with Charles Matthews and Madam Celeste at Drury Lane, the Princes, and the Adelphi, and was with Marie Lytton at the Imperial Theatre, Westminster, for three years. Turning to the music halls he appeared at the Old Vic, then being run on variety lines by J. A. Cave, acting as a low comedian in sketches and singing songs as low as the comedy. In 1877 he formed a double act with Arthur Roberts and worked the halls singing comic duets which, to use Roberts's own expression, were 'very near the knuckle'. They appeared together in three

James Fawn, 1870

pantomimes at Drury Lane: *Mother Goose* in 1880, *Robinson Crusoe* in 1881, and *Sinbad* in 1882. When Roberts turned to musical comedy, James Fawn worked for a short time with Sam Wilkinson, and as a solo artiste was one of the first stars of the new Alhambra Theatre of Variety, opened in 1884. Billed as 'The Prince of Red-Nosed Comedians' he sang drunk songs of a gentlemanly variety in top hat and tails, protesting between rather refined hiccups that 'it must have been the lobster, it couldn't have been the wine, for I hardly had enough to drown a fly'. He sang his famous song 'If You Want to Know the Time Ask a Policeman' for over 30 years and added a new expression to the English language. His last appearance was at the South London Music Hall in 1922, less than a year before his death on 19 January 1923.

Tony Fayne and David Evans, impressionists well known in variety and on radio during the 1940s and early 1950s. Born in Bristol, they made their first appearance at the Bristol Empire in November 1940, and in London at the Criterion Theatre on 27 February 1941. After war service they re-teamed in 1949 with a new act of sporting and double comedy impressions, ranging from fast-talking sports commentaries to the soft singing style of Flanagan and Allen.

Sid Field, comedian, born in Edgbaston, Birmingham, on 1 April 1904. At the age of 12 he became one of the 'Fourteen Royal Kino Juveniles' and made his first appearance at the Empire, Bristol, in July 1916. At 14 he toured as understudy to Wee Georgie Wood (qv), but outgrew the job without ever having to appear in place of the irrepressible George. During the 1920s he appeared as comic feed in Clara Coverdale's revues, and toured as principal comedian for William Henshall. After 27 years of hard slog, he was 'discovered' in March 1943 by George Black and made his first West End appearance in *Strike a New Note* at the Prince of Wales Theatre. Although hailed by the press as 'London's new comedy star', he was using the same material with which he had toured in variety for years, presented in a rather camp style that was years ahead of its time. His character studies of the cockney spiv 'Slasher Green', the 'Golfing Rabbit', the 'Cinema Organist', and 'Society Photographer' established him as one of the greatest comedians since Dan Leno. *Strike a New Note* was followed by *Strike it Again* and in October 1946 he returned to the Prince of Wales to star in one of the first post-war musical successes *Piccadilly Hayride*. On 5 November 1945 he appeared in the Royal Variety Performance at the London Coliseum and the following year joined the select band invited to appear in the Royal Show for a second year in succession. In 1946 he starred as Wesley Ruggles in the film version of *London Town*, and in 1947 played a seventeenth-century equivalent of 'Slasher Green' in Walter Forde's film *The Cardboard Cavalier*. In January 1948 he topped the bill at the London Palladium, replacing Mickey Rooney, who cut his booking short and returned to the USA.

In January 1949 he opened at the Prince of Wales Theatre in Mary Chase's Pulitzer Prize-winning comedy *Harvey*. In the part of Elwood P. Dowd he proved to be a fine actor, but in August ill-health forced him to leave the cast and to take a sea trip to South Africa. During his absence his part was taken by J. E. Brown. With health seemingly restored he returned to the cast of *Harvey* on Boxing Day, 1949, but died suddenly on 3 February 1950. Sid's tragic death at the age of 45 robbed variety of one of its brightest and best-loved stars. A memorial service was held at St Martin's-in-the-Fields on 20 February, at which the lessons were read by Sir Laurence Olivier and Ted Ray. As a lasting tribute a bronze plaque was placed in the foyer at the Prince of Wales Theatre. It reads:

To the memory of the great comedian Sid Field who made his first appearance in the West End at this theatre on 18

Sid Field, 'The Cardboard Cavalier', 1947

March 1943 and who played his last performance here on 2 February 1950.

In June 1951 the stars paid their own respects to Sid at a midnight benefit at the London Palladium. Attended by the Duchess of Kent escorted by Noël Coward, the star-studded bill was brought to a close by the 81-year-old George Robey singing 'If You Were the Only Girl in the World'. The show raised £17,000 for Sid's wife and children. As Sid Field would no doubt have put it, 'What a performance!'

'Happy' Fanny Fields, American comedienne born in 1884. Billed as 'The Happy Little Dutch Girl', she established a vogue for character songs sung in a heavy broken Dutch accent, popular on the London halls during the early 1900s. Singing 'By the Side of the Zuider Zee', she took part in the first Royal Command Performance at the Palace on 1 July 1912. She married in 1913 and returned to the USA where she died in 1961.

'Happy' Fanny Fields

Gracie Fields, comedienne and singer, the worthy successor of Marie Lloyd as 'Queen of the Halls'. Born Grace Stansfield in Tweeddale Street, Rochdale, on 9 January 1898, she made her first stage appearance at the age of seven in a singing contest at the Circus of Varieties, rebuilt as the Rochdale Hippodrome in 1908. As the protégée of Lily Turner, a music-hall artiste who worked the Midlands using the name 'Rose Bush', she toured the halls of the Rochdale area, singing the chorus of Lily's songs from a seat in the balcony.

Gracie Fields, 1931

She made her first professional appearance at the New Rochdale Hippodrome in 1910, and was held over for a second week billed as 'Young Grace Stansfield, Rochdale's Own Girl Vocalist'. Two years with 'Charburn's Young Stars' as 'Gracie Fields, Versatile Comedienne' were followed by a season in a concert party, 'Cousin Freddy's Pierrots', at St Anne's on Sea. After six weeks in variety she toured in the revue 'Yes I Think So' in which she made her first London appearance at the Middlesex Music Hall in 1915. The revue toured for 18 months with Archie Pitt as principal comedian. At the end of the run Pitt produced his own road show *It's a Bargain*, with Gracie as second leading lady. She later took over the lead from Mona Frewer and the show ran for two-and-a-half years. In 1917 Archie Pitt produced his famous revue *Mr Tower of London*, which toured for a total of nine-and-a-half years. In August 1923 Archie Pitt and Gracie Fields were married and in 1925 *Mr Tower of London*, then in its sixth year, was booked by Oswald Stoll for a week at the London Alhambra. The day after it opened Gracie Fields was elevated from the ranks of an unknown revue artiste and acclaimed as London's new star. Hannen Swaffer, the 'Pope of Fleet Street', wrote in the *Express*: 'Gracie Fields is an English girl of whom the West End had never heard until last Monday. Yet gifts which amount to genius show her as a Beatrice Lillie, Florence Mills, an Ethel Levey and Nellie Wallace all rolled into one.' As she had a 20-minute wait between her appearances in *Mr Tower of London*, Oswald Stoll booked her for a ten-minute variety spot across the road at the Coliseum. Archie Pitt paid her £28 a week in revue, but Stoll offered her £100 for her first London variety appearance at the Coliseum, and she was soon topping bills at other London halls. In February 1928 Sir Gerald Du Maurier engaged her to appear as Lady Wier in Walter Ellis's play *S.O.S.* at the St James's Theatre. Lady Wier committed suicide at the end of Act I, leaving Gracie free to appear in variety at the Coliseum and Alhambra, followed by late-night cabaret at the Café Royal.

On 1 March 1928 she made her first Royal Variety appearance, and on 3 September her London Palladium debut on a bill to mark the return to 'new look' variety under the management of George Black. She sang 'My Blue Heaven' and 'Romona' and during the second week of her engagement introduced into her act comic songs in broad Lancashire dialect. Her original London reputation was founded on straight songs but her comic singing was such a success that it led to the comedy gems, 'Walter', 'In My Little Bottom Drawer', 'Heaven Will Protect an Honest Girl', and 'The Biggest Aspidistra in the World'. While appearing at the Metropolitan, Edgware Road, in 1931 she bought the song 'Sally' from composers Leo Towers, Bill Hains and Harry Leon. It became her signature tune, inseparable from her name ever since.

She made her first film, *Sally In Our Alley*, in 1931, which led to a series of highly successful films made both in England and Hollywood, and by 1938 was ranked as the world's highest paid star. In 1938 she was awarded the CBE by George VI. During the war she toured extensively for ENSA, entertaining in practically every zone of the war between 1942 and 1945. Vera Lynn may have been the 'Forces Sweetheart' but to everyone Gracie Fields was simply 'Our Gracie'. In 1947 she made a series of broadcasts for the BBC entitled 'Gracie's Working Party' and on 3 November appeared in the third of her eight Royal Variety Performances. After an absence of 10 years she returned to the London Palladium at the top of the bill for the weeks of 4 and 11 October 1948. From then on she spent much of her time in semi-retirement on the Isle of Capri, making occasional concert and television appearances, including an award-winning television performance in J. M. Barrie's play *The Old Lady Shows Her Medals*.

Tommy Fields, light comedian, born Thomas Stansfield in Rochdale, 28 June 1908. Began his career touring with Archie Pitt's famous road show *Mr Tower of London*, making his first London appearance with the show at the Alhambra in 1925. In 1927 he teamed with Nino Rossini and for more than ten years they were a successful comedy double act in variety as 'Fields and Rossini'. Turning solo in 1938, he was billed in the South as 'London's Lancashire Comedian' and in October 1949 appeared at the Palladium on a bill topped by his sister, Gracie Fields. In 1949 he also toured the USA with Gracie, followed by a six month tour of a revival of *Mr Tower of London*. Apart from variety and revue, he was a popular summer show comedian and pantomime performer, also appearing with success in musical comedy, including *Maid to Measure* with Jessie Matthews at the Cambridge Theatre in 1948 and in the lead of the Australian production of *Where's Charlie* in 1950.

Fips, eccentric comedian and circus clown. Born in Berlin on 7 August 1878, to parents who were Finnish circus performers appearing with the Renz Circus, Hamburg. He made his debut with this company at the age of four. He came to England with the Zaro Acrobats in 1890, making his first London appearance at the Standard Music Hall, Pimlico. Later he worked with the famous clown Gobert Billing at the London Hippodrome, and as a single turn in variety and pantomime.

Flanagan and Allen, popular singing and comedy duo, both as a double act in variety, and later with the Crazy Gang at the Palladium and Victoria Palace. Bud Flanagan was born Reuben Weintrop in Whitechapel, London, on 14 October 1896. At the age of 10 he got a part time job as a call boy at the Cambridge Music Hall, Commercial Street, Shoreditch, and in 1908 made his first stage appearance at the London Music Hall, billed as 'Fargo the Boy Wizard'. He was not a great success as a conjurer, and a few weeks later he appeared at the Cambridge singing 'If You Want to be Somebody', in the soft cockney style of Alec Hurley (qv).

When he was 14 he went to the USA and joined the vaudeville schoolboys act 'Campus Days' doing a Jewish comedy routine under the name of Bobby Wayne. When this act broke up he teamed with Dale Burgess, Bud in burnt cork and Dale with white make-up. They devised an act at the piano, Dale opening as a solo pianist until Bud poked his head out of the piano and started a cross-talking comedy routine. On their return to San Francisco in 1915 after a tour of Australia they were greeted by a large notice in their agent's office which read 'Notice to English Artistes. We don't need you, your King and Country do'. Taking the hint, Bud sailed for England in the *Lusitania* and Bobby Wayne became Driver Winthrop of the Royal Field Artillery. Bud was posted to France in 1916 where, between ammunition deliveries to Passchendaele and Vimy Ridge, he took part in divisional concert party shows which incldued singing a duet with the great French star Mistinguett. Discharged from the army in 1919, he toured in variety and revue with a succession of partners, with Roy Henderson as 'Flanagan and Roy', Jack Buckland as 'Flanagan and Poy' and with Tommy Hunter as 'Flanagan and Hunter'. In 1924 he toured with Florrie Forde's (qv) revue 'Flo and Co', acting as comedian to straight man Chesney Allen.

Born in Brighton on 5 April 1894, Chesney Allen first appeared at the Grand Theatre, West Hartlepool, in 1910, making his London debut at the Bedford, Camden Town, the following year. After war service as an officer in the Royal West Kents, he appeared at the Criterion, London, in the farce *You Never Know, You Know*. He then toured in variety as the straight man of the comedy double act of Stanford and Allen. Early in 1920 he joined Florrie Forde's company in partnership with Stanford, and when Florrie Forde left the show during the summer months of each year to star at the Isle of Man, Allen toured her show as manager.

When Flanagan replaced Stanford in 1924, Flanagan and Allen became popular members of 'Flo and Co', and later decided to work in variety as a double act, making their debut with their 'Underneath the Arches' act at the Argyle,

Marc Fleming

Flanagan and Allen, 1935

Birkenhead, in February 1931. Two weeks later they appeared at the Hippodrome, Sheffield, and the following week were booked by Val Parnell for the Holborn Empire. Billed as 'The New Star Comedians', they were given an eight-minute spot which was such a success that they over-ran by 16 minutes, and were engaged by George Black for the London Palladium. They were soon established as the leading double act in variety and as top recording artistes for HMV. In 1932 they appeared in George Black's *Crazy Month* at the London Palladium, which also included the comedy teams of 'Nervo and Knox' (qv), 'Naughton and Gold' (qv) and 'Caryll and Mundy'. From then on they were inseparable from the Crazy Gang, appearing together in a long series of George Black revues at the Palladium: *Life Begins at Oxford Circus* (1935), *Round About Regent Street* (1935), *All Alight at Oxford Circus* (1936), *OK for Sound* (1936), *London Rhapsody* (1937), *These Foolish Things* (1938), and *The Little Dog Laughed* (1940). During the war Flanagan and Allen toured in variety and with ENSA singing 'We're Going to Hang Out the Washing on the Siegfried Line', 'Umbrella Man', 'Run Rabbit Run' and 'Underneath the Arches'. They also worked in the revues *Top of the World* with Pat Kirkwood and Tommy Trinder at the Palladium, *Hi de Hi* with Wilson Keppel and Betty and Eddie Gray at the Palace, and *Black Vanities* at the Victoria Palace. When in 1945 Chesney Allen was forced by ill health to retire from the stage and become the managing director of the Reeves and Lamport Agency, Flanagan turned solo, appearing that Christmas in pantomime at the Adelphi and touring in variety.

In 1947 the Crazy Gang was re-formed by Jack Hylton and on 17 April *Together Again* opened at the Victoria Palace. It ran for 1,566 performances, to be followed during the next 15 years by *Knights of Madness* (1950), *Ring out the Bells* (1952), *Jokers Wild* (1954), *These Foolish Kings* (1956), *Clown Jewels* (1959), and in December 1960 the final show, *Young in Heart*.

Bud Flanagan was a great favourite with the royal family, succeeding to Dan Leno's old title of 'The King's Jester'. With Chesney Allen and the Crazy Gang he made 15 official Royal Variety appearances and gate-crashed a number of others. When one afternoon in 1960 Bud went to Buckingham Palace to receive the CBE, he looked around the crowded Throne Room and remarked to Prince Philip 'That's a smashing house you've got for a matinee'. He retired with the Crazy Gang in 1962 although he did continue to make occasional appearances in charity shows for the Grand Order of Water Rats of which he was a past King. In May 1967 he took part in a nostalgic tribute to Sophie Tucker at the Victoria Palace. He died on 20 October 1968.

Neville Fleeson, American song writer and variety artiste, born in 1887. Toured in vaudeville as a light comedian and during 1917-18 with Irving Berlin's all-soldier show *The Yip Yip Yaphanks*. With a girl partner he appeared in 1924 at the Victoria Palace, London, billed as 'Fleeson and Folsam' and later toured the USA with impressionist Sheila Barrett. As a song writer he is remembered for 'I'll Be With You in Apple Blossom Time' and he worked in Hollywood collaborating on a series of musical films. He died in Chicago in October 1945.

Marc Fleming, 'Your very own Aunty Flo', female impersonator of cabaret, summer shows and pantomime. Born in 1926 he is a popular London pub entertainer, especially at The New Black Cap, Camden Town, a famous 'drag' pub a few doors from the site of the old Bedford Music Hall. His act falls into the 'vulgar but honest' category, too candid perhaps for the comfort of those in the front, bringing something of the low comedy of the early halls back to its grass roots, the local pub. If it was ever true that music hall was buried with Max Miller, it was dug up again with Marc Fleming.

57

Cyril Fletcher, popular comedian in variety and on radio with his 'Odd Odes' act. Born in Watford on 25 June 1913, he made his first appearance with a concert party at the White Rock Pavilion, Hastings, and in London at the Holborn Empire in 1939. As well as being a well-known variety and radio comedian, he is a popular pantomime performer, playing everything from Buttons to dame.

Flotsam and Jetsam, famous double act at the piano, introducing themselves on stage and on the air with the ditty:

> We'll tell you our names,
> In case someone forgets 'em,
> I'm Jetsam (I'm Flotsam)
> He's Flotsam (He's Jetsam)
> We want them to be recognised
> By anyone who spots 'em
> I'm Flotsam (I'm Jetsam),
> He's Jetsam (He's Flotsam!)
> Flotsam and Jetsam.
>
> As kind fate allots 'em
> The songs sung by Jetsam,
> Are written by Flotsam,
> I sing all the low notes,
> (You'd wonder how he get's 'em.)
>
> At the keyboard is Flotsam,
> So I must be Jetsam!
> Yours very sincerely,
> Flotsam and Jetsam!

B. C. Hilliam (Flotsam) was born in Scarborough on 6 November 1890. He began his career as an entertainer at the piano at local functions using the name Lloyd Holland. In 1910 he went to Canada and formed the 'Canadian Follies'. During the war he served as a lieutenant in the Canadian army, forming service concert parties and working a double act with Hugh Aitchison Green. (The father of Hughie 'Opportunity Knocks' Green, he sang songs of the Harry Lauder and Will Fyffe type and was famed for his spirited rendering of the monologue 'The Cousin of the Corpse'.) After the war Hilliam toured the Keith vaudeville circuit of the USA and appeared for three months at Florenz Ziegfeld's New Amsterdam Roof, New York. In 1919 he wrote the music for *Buddies* which played for 15 weeks to capacity audiences in Boston and ran for two years at the Selwyn Theatre, New York. His second musical, *Princess Virtue*, opened at the Central Theatre, New York, in May 1921 and closed 16 performances later. After further vaudeville tours partnered by singer Molly McIntyre and later tenor Horace Ruwe, he returned to England in January 1926. In February that year he met singer Malcolm McEachern.

Flotsam and Jetsam *(photo, Lewis of London)*

Malcolm McEachern, born in Australia, appeared as a concert singer early in his career and toured Australia and Canada with Nellie Melba. By 1926 he had established a London concert reputation and was also getting good spots on the bills of so-called 'higher class' variety theatres. Between houses at the Coliseum, where McEachern was appearing in February 1926, he and Hilliam discussed the idea of a double act and a few weeks later made their debut at the Victoria Palace. They went over well and were engaged for the Coliseum and Alhambra. Now billed as 'Mr Flotsam and Mr Jetsam' they appeared in the Royal Variety Performance on 24 February 1927. Between top-of-the-bill variety tours they recorded for Columbia and made regular broadcasts from Savoy Hill, at one time giving out nightly news bulletins in verse. Later they starred in their own radio shows, 'Our Hour', 'Round the World with Flotsam and Jetsam', 'Signs of the Times', and 'The Wedding of Maud Marie'. They remained a popular act until Malcolm McEachern's death on 17 January 1945. Hilliam later formed his own summer show, 'Flotsam's Follies'.

The Amazing Fogel, Maurice Fogel, mind-reading act. Born in London on 7 July 1911, he made his first variety appearance at the age of 18, doing a straight magic act at Collins Music Hall, Islington. He developed his thought-transmission routine while serving in the army and used it as an intriguing form of entertainment with George Black's famous service show *Stars in Battledress*. In 1946 he toured the act in variety, topping bills for Moss and Stoll, and has since led the field in this kind of speciality; touring the world with his own show and presenting a top spot in variety and cabaret.

Ford and Sheen, the oldest established double drag act, which after 35 years is still appearing in variety, revue and pantomime. Chris Sheen, born Christopher Shinfield, in Tibshelf, Derbyshire, in 1908, began his career with Jo Boganny's 'Boys', making his first appearance at the Alexandra Theatre, Hull, on 1 March 1933, and in London at the South London Palace in 1935. Joining the famous all-male revue *Splinters* he met Vic Ford and in 1936 they

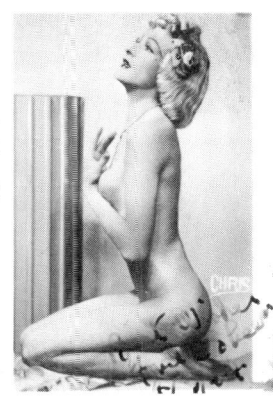

Ford and Sheen, 1944

teamed as female impersonators in variety. Popular in pantomime, they were as successful as grotesque Ugly Sisters as they were in glamorous drag. During the war they entertained the troops and during the late 1940s and early 1950s toured with the leading all male revues, including 'Soldiers in Skirts', 'Showboat Express', 'Forces Showboat', 'Forces in Skirts' and 'Misleading Ladies', in the last of which they gave Danny La Rue his first speaking part. They also toured South Africa with Tommy Trinder, and in 1949 appeared with Max Bygraves and Hal Monty in Stafford Dickens's full-length feature film *Skimpy in The Navy*. In recent years they have made overseas tours with Chris Shaw, and continued to appear in summer shows and pantomime. In variety their rather old-fashioned cross-talk act, perfectly timed and polished by constant repetition, makes a quaint contrast to the brasher style of modern drag acts. In the old tradition, they take their bow at the finale as well-groomed males.

Florrie Forde, famous singer of music hall chorus songs. Born Florence Flanagan in Fitzroy, near Melbourne, in 1875, her first appearance was at the Polytechnic, Sydney, in 1893, singing 'He Kissed Me When He Left Me and Told Me I Had to be Brave', and in 1894 she became a member of Dan Tracey's Variety Company. The following Christmas she sang and danced in the chorus of George Reynolds's pantomime at the Theatre Royal, Sydney, and was re-engaged the next year to play the first of a long career of principal boys. As a member of C. B. Westmacott's drama company she took leading soubrette parts, playing William in *Black Eyed Susan*, and toured in variety for Harry Rickards billed as 'The Australian Marie Lloyd'.

Florrie Forde's first appearance in England was at the London Pavilion on 2 August 1897, playing the same night at the Oxford and South London Palace. Described by MacQueen Pope as the 'female epitome of music hall gusto', she was a fine buxom woman, splendid in feathers, sequins and tights. Walking up and down the stage, she kept time with her jewelled chorus stick, leading the audience in one after another of her famous songs 'like a sergeant-major with an awkward squad'. What great songs they were: 'Oh Oh Antonio', 'She's a Lassie from Lancashire', 'Hold Your Hand Out Naughty Boy', 'Down at the Old Bull and Bush', and Good Bye'ee'. At the height of her fame during the First World War, she chased away wartime blues with 'Pack Up You Troubles in your Old Kit Bag', 'Take Me Back to Dear Old Blighty' and 'It's a Long Way to Tipperary' The last was first sung by its composer Jack Judge but owes its continuing popularity to Florrie Force.

In addition to variety and pantomime, she ran her own touring revue company 'Flo and Co', and during the summer months she was a great favourite on the Isle of Man, where for 36 consecutive years she wooed generations of holiday-makers with 'Flanagan' and 'Has Anybody Here Seen Kelly?'. She appeared in the Garden Party scene in the first Royal Command Performance in 1912, and in the Royal Variety Show of 1935.

A great pantomime artiste, she was the darling of the old school which considered that from bosom to thigh a principal boy could not be too massive. At Christmas 1935 she appeared for the umpteenth time as principal boy in *Forty Thieves* at the Lyceum Theatre, London. She was then a large lady of sixty and discreetly modified the traditional costume, much to the disappointment of James Agate who 'Tauberishly' admitted in the *Sunday Times* that she was his heart's delight, but regretted that she had allowed discretion to be the better part of valour.

Her popularity never waned and she was all set to cheer up the troops of the Second War as she had done in the First, by demanding 'What's the Use of Worrying', and urging them to 'Smile, Boys, that's the style', when she died suddenly on 18 April 1940. Her memory is kept green by 'Down at the Old Bull and Bush' and although 'Appy 'Ampstead' is now more camp than cockney, a few years ago the public bar of The Old Bull and Bush in North End Road, Hampstead, was

FLORRIE FORDE

renamed the 'Florrie Forde Bar' and decorated with photographs, bills, etc. On the outside wall two painted signs show her in typical pose, a worthy tribute to the pub's greatest advertisement.

George Formby Senior, the famous father of a famous son, born James Booth at Ashton-Under-Lyme in 1877. In 1889 he went to work in a Manchester ironfoundry but his job as a blacksmith's striker was far too heavy for a boy of 12 and the toxic sulphur fumes inhaled for 10 hours a day affected his lungs for the rest of his life. Life was hard for young Jimmy. His mother was a drunkard and he was often forced to sing for

George Formby Senior, 1913

his supper in the streets of Ashton. While still a small lad he teamed with a friend and toured the free-and-easies as the 'Glen Ray Brothers'. Later, while singing at the Hen and Chicken in Manchester, he was seen by Danny Clark and booked as a solo turn at the Argyle, Birkenhead.

Adopting the name of Formby from the Lancashire town of that name, he toured with the Walford Bodie Royal Magnet's Variety Company. In 1900 he married Eliza Hoy and made his home in his wife's native town of Wigan, becoming popular at the Wigan Empire, and inventing the town's famous landmark 'Wigan Pier'. Billed as 'The Lad From Wigan' or 'The Wigan Nightingale', a comic reference to his painfully croaky voice, he was one of the first Lancashire dialect comedians to win popularity in the South. In London he appeared as the gormless John Willie, an innocent at large in the big city, the prototype of the 'Up for the Cup' Northerner. Dressed in an unfashionable and ill-fitting jacket and trousers, with cut-down bowler two sizes too small, boots on the wrong feet, and a black spot painted above each eyebrow, he confided to his audience that he was 'Playing the game in the West'. This involved spending money on champagne for the girls, strolling along the Strand knocking policemen's hats off, and what's more, he added defiantly, 'I'm not going home to a quarter-to-10, 'cause it's my night out'. All his songs were in the same genre, telling of his adventures while 'Leaning on a Lamp Post at the Corner of the Street', and how since he parted his hair in the middle he was such a great hit with the girls—until his wife spotted him and exclaimed 'John Willie, Come On!'

Very popular in pantomime, particularly as Idle Jack, he starred in 1907 with George Robey in Newcastle and later worked in revue, notably in Albert de Courville's *Razzle Dazzle* at the Theatre Royal, Drury Lane, in 1916. By 1918 he was earning £300 per week in variety and was so highly regarded that Moss Empires gave him a bonus of £1,000 to buy a house at Stockton Heath, Warrington. Like Jimmy James and Max Wall, George was very much the comedian's comedian. Marie Lloyd once said that, of all the artistes she appeared with during her career, the only two acts she would bother to watch from the wings were Dan Leno and George Formby. 'John Willie' suffered from a bronchial cough, the legacy of the Manchester iron foundry, which he passed off as a comic feature of his act, and ironically his trademark. His asides to the orchestra, 'coughing better tonight'—'coughing summat champion', and his comedy routine of stopping in the middle of a song or patter to 'have a good cough', always had the audience rolling in the aisles, and left George gasping for breath in the wings. The cough won in the end. While appearing in pantomime at the Empire Theatre, Newcastle, he burst a blood vessel, and died on 8 February 1921 at the age of 44.

George Formby Junior, popular singing comedian with a toothy grin and ukulele who kept the name 'George Formby' at the top of variety bills for 60 years. Born George Hoy Booth in Wigan on 26 May 1904, he was apprenticed at the age of seven to a racing stable, riding in his first race at Lingfield Park in 1915 at a weight of 3 stone 13 pounds. He later raced in the colours of his father, of Lord Derby, and other noted owners, but although he was placed on 27 occasions, he never won a race. Increasing weight forced him to give up the turf, and on the death of his father in February 1921 he decided on a career in variety. Using the name George Hoy, he made his first stage appearance as a trial turn at Harrison's Picture House, Earlstown, on 21 April 1921, followed by a week's engagement at the Argyle, Birkenhead. His first London appearance was at the Shepherds Bush Empire later that year.

Although he never saw his father perform, when he began in variety he based his act on George Senior's gramophone records, wore his stage clothes, and was coached by his father's pianist, Harry Duckenfield. In 1923 he went into partnership with Sam Paul to tour the revue *Chip off the Old Block*. Not a great success at first, he slowly developed his own style and stage personality, a sort of up-dated John Willie, singing comedy songs to his own high speed ukulele accompaniment. In 1924 he married Beryl Ingham of the dancing duo 'Beryl and May—The Two Violets', and from then on his wife handled all his business affairs and helped greatly in the development of his career. In 1926 he signed a five-year contract to tour for a part of every year in revue, appeared each Christmas in pantomime, and during 1931–32 toured his own variety road show. With such popular songs as 'Chinese Laundry Blues', 'When I'm Cleaning

Windows', 'Auntie Maggie's Remedy', 'The Lancashire Toreador', 'Mr Wu', 'Fanlight Fanny', 'Leaning on a Lamp-post' and 'It's Turned Out Nice Again', he became one of the greatest stars of modern variety.

In 1934 George made his first film *Boots, Boots*, for the Mancunian Film Company, followed by *Off the Dole* in 1935. These led to a contract with Associated Talking Pictures to make a series of films produced by Basil Dean, which featured many of his song hits built into spectacular production numbers and established him as the top box-office cinema attraction for six consecutive years.

A favourite of King George VI, he appeared in the Coronation year Royal Variety Performance at the London Palladium in 1937, and gave several command performances at Windsor Castle. During the war he toured extensively for ENSA, playing troop concerts in Europe, North Africa, and the Middle East, being awarded the OBE for his services in 1946. In that year he was paid £1,000 per week to tour Australia, an offer repeated in 1949 for a variety tour of Canada, followed by a second tour of North America in 1950. On 20 October 1951 he opened at the Palace Theatre, London, in Emile Littler's *Zip Goes a Million*. In this, his first West End musical comedy appearance, George starred as Percy Piggot, the unworldly heir to the Brewster millions who could only inherit if he managed to spend a million pounds in four months. The hit song of the show, 'Ordinary People', was in the old tradition of his father's John Willie, and like his father's, George's career was dogged by ill health. In May 1952 he suffered a coronary thrombosis and was replaced in *Zip Goes a Million* by Reg Dixon. It looked as though his career was finished but he fought his way back to health, touring Rhodesia in the spring of 1953, and making his variety come-back at the top of the bill at the Garrick Theatre, Southport. In October he returned to the West End to star with Terry Thomas and Billy Cotton in *The Fun of the Fair* at the London Palladium. In 1954 he made a not too successful television appearance as a replacement for Gilbert Harding in the panel game 'What's My Line' and in the summer starred in *Turned Out Nice Again* at the Blackpool Hippodrome. Early in 1955 he toured South Africa, fund-raising for cancer research. On his return he took part in a Royal Variety show held before the Queen and Prince Philip at the Blackpool Opera House, and in May made a 10-day charity tour of Canada. Later that year he made his debut in a straight play *Too Young To Marry*, and at Christmas returned to the Palace Theatre to play Idle Jack in his first London pantomime *Dick Whittington*. In 1956 he again toured in *Too Young To Marry*, and in 1958 appeared in a farce entitled *Beside the Seaside*. He played a summer season at the Windmill Theatre, Yarmouth, in 1959 and appeared in *The Time of Your Life* at the Queen's Theatre, Blackpool, in 1960. The death of his wife Beryl on Christmas Day 1960 caused another heart attack, but two months later he had recovered sufficiently to set tongues wagging by announcing his engagement to a 36-year-old school teacher. He had the spirit but literally not the heart for it. He died on 6 March 1961 at the age of 56.

Bruce Forsyth, popular comedian, born Bruce Joseph Forsyth Johnson in Edmonton, North London, in 1928. He left school at fourteen and made his first stage appearance on a variety bill at Bilston, near Birmingham, doing a page-boy tap dancing act, billed as 'Boy Bruce, the Mighty Atom'.

Years of hard slog followed, playing run-down variety theatres with third-rate revues, gaining experience from end-of-the-pier shows and from two-and-a-half years at the Windmill, the comic's RADA. When the war ended, 'Boy Bruce' was still only 17 and overshadowed by the new wave

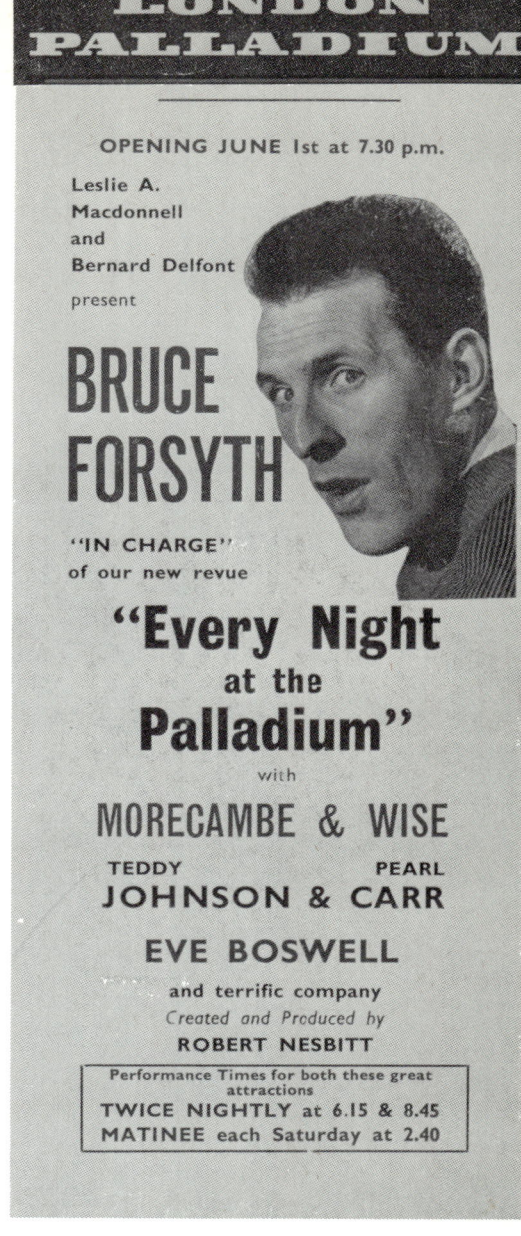

Bruce Forsyth, top of the bill, 1959

of ex-service comedians, Tony Hancock, Jimmy Edwards, Tommy Cooper, Frankie Howerd, and the Goons, who began to dominate postwar variety, revue, and radio. He was picking up some good provincial press notices and was a popular seaside comic from Blackpool to Babbacombe, which gave him invaluable experience of audience participation and the art of ad-lib. While playing summer season at Eastbourne in 1958 he was engaged by ITV to compère their new all-star variety show 'Sunday Night at the London Palladium'. Immensely successful, each Sunday the Palladium hosted the top names in show business, but it was Bruce's expert handling of the 'giveaway' spot, 'Beat the

George Formby Junior

Clock', that was the real hit of the show. For three years he was firmly 'in charge' of 'Sunday Night at the London Palladium', coming to be regarded as the first real TV comic and voted ITV Personality of 1958 by the Variety Club of Great Britain. Again at the London Coliseum on 3 November 1958 he made the first of many Royal Variety appearances and compèred the show at the Victoria Palace in 1960 and at the Prince of Wales in 1961.

His Palladium appearances were not confined to Sunday nights. He appeared there in pantomime and was a star attraction in variety, topping the bill in June 1962, supported by Morecambe and Wise. A versatile entertainer with his own distinctive walk, talk, song and dance routine, during the 1960s he appeared in his own TV shows, played in cabaret and at top clubs, notably The Talk of the Town at the Old London Hippodrome, and on 18 November 1964 made his musical comedy debut playing seven roles in *Little Me* at the Cambridge Theatre, London.

After reaching such a high note his career seemed in danger of getting into the doldrums. The first step in his comeback was the not too promising prospect of an early Saturday evening family show 'The Generation Game'. Originally a Dutch TV programme, the idea was for two members of a family, father and daughter perhaps, bridging the 'generation gap' by competing against other family couples, performing various activities calculated to have amusing results. Without the expertise of Bruce Forsyth the show could easily have developed into another embarrassing charade but he brought to the programme all his old summer show experience and by not taking the show, the contestants, or himself, seriously, has achieved a remarkable success. As a bonus, Bruce married one of the show's hostesses, the lovely Anthea Redfern.

In 1973 Bruce starred in the London summer show 'Palladium 73' and in 1975 proved his virtuosity in the hardest test of all, a one-man show. After a short tour he opened at the New London Theatre and was a smash hit. In November 1975 he compèred the Royal Variety Show at the London Palladium and was such a success that for this and his one-man show he received the Variety Club award of Show Business Personality of the Year.

The Sisters Fortescue, a double male-impersonating 'masher' act, worked during the 1890s by two sisters, Veni and Daisy Fortescue. Born in the Edgware Road district of London, Veni trained at the age of eight with Katie Lanner's Ballet Troupe, appearing for three seasons in Oscar Barrett's open-air productions at the Crystal Palace and in pantomime at Covent Garden. She then teamed with Flo Penley doing a dancing act on the leading London halls, including the Canterbury, Paragon, and Middlesex. Daisy made her stage debut at the age of 13 at the Kilburn Town Hall, doing a combined song and dance act, plus a skipping-rope routine. Veni and Daisy teamed as 'The Sisters Fortescue' in 1892.

Olive Fox *see* **Clarkson Rose**

Will Fox, comedian who styled himself 'The First of the Trick Playing Piano Acts'. Born in Baltimore, USA, in 1858, he made his first appearance in Louisville, Kentucky, in 1896 and in England at the Palace Theatre, London, where he appeared for 21 consecutive weeks in 1896. He remained in England for many years and toured Australia, South Africa, and most of Europe, with his burlesques of Paderewski, billing himself 'Will Fox—Paddywhiski'. He died in London on 2 August 1927.

Boy Foy, juggler, born in Glasgow in 1919. He was the son of Jack Melville of the comedy juggling act 'The Melvilles' with which he worked from his early youth. Made his first solo appearance at the Islington Empire in 1933, juggling while riding a unicycle with such skill that he was soon booked for the London Palladium and the Holborn Empire. He appeared in the Royal Variety Performance of 1935 and toured the USA the following year.

Tom Foy, dialect comedian who, although famed as 'The Yorkshire Lad', was born in Manchester of Irish parents in 1879. During his early career he gained experience in many branches of variety. After serving an apprenticeship as a signwriter, he set up in business in Halifax, training in his spare time as an acrobat at nearby Schroggs Park. He soon tired of sign-writing and joined a travelling circus as a scenic artist and clown, and made his first music-hall appearance in Manchester as a lightning cartoonist. He then worked a song-and-dance act, joined a Wild West show as a black-faced comedian, and then returned to variety as an Irish comedian with such a convincing accent that when he appeared in Ireland the local press rejoiced that he was 'not a stage Irishman, but a thorough Irishman with a brogue you could cut with a knife'. While appearing in pantomime for Pitt Hardacre at the Gaiety Theatre, Manchester, he met Eugene Stratton (qv) who urged him to go to London and arranged a trial turn at the Oxford. He was soon established in

Tom Foy and his donkey, 1904

TOM FOY AND HIS DONKEY.

Hana. Photo London

the West End, presenting broad Yorkshire comedy sketches, 'A Yorkshire Lad in London' and 'Tom Foy and His Donkey' (in which he used a live donkey), and as a solo act with his own whimsical style of North Country humour, 'All through t'black horse', 'Ah'm disguised', etc. In pantomime he was a popular dame, but his real pantomime speciality was the role of Idle Jack, in which he made his last pantomime appearance in the London Opera House in 1916–17. He collapsed while playing the Argyle, Birkenhead, on 23 July 1917 and died a few weeks later at the age of 38.

Harry Fragson, Anglo-French comedian and songs-at-the-piano act, born Leon Vince Philip Pott, at Richmond, Surrey, on 10 July 1896. Early success as an amateur entertainer at local smoking concerts encouraged him to try the music halls, and in about 1885 he auditioned at the Middlesex. A comedian singing at the piano was then a novelty, too much so for the management of the Middlesex, who firmly pointed out that with a good orchestra in the pit they were not interested in anyone with a piano on the stage.

Fragson went to Paris and largely because of the charm of his self-taught French, spoken with a distinct cockney accent, became a popular café concert singer. Graduating to the music halls and grand revue, for ten years he ranked with the greatest French comedians of the day, Polin, Mayol, Dranen and Paulus, while remaining virtually unknown in

Harry Fragson, 1910

"OH DEAR, I FEEL SO QUEER."

England. The deaths of Dan Leno and Herbert Campbell in 1904 deprived the Theatre Royal, Drury Lane, of its two greatest pantomime comedians, so when during the spring of 1905 Arthur Collins saw Fragson in a Folies Bergère revue, he booked him to play Dandigny, a 'Frenchified' Dandini, in *Cinderella* at Drury Lane the following Christmas. The song hit of the show was 'Whispers of Love' sung by Fragson and the American Cinderella, May de Sousa, and an 'Entente Cordiale' duet of 'The Two Coachers' sung by Fragson as a Paris cabman and Harry Randall (qv), the driver of a London 'growler'. At Christmas 1906 Fragson returned to the Lane as the Envoy to the Empress in *Sinbad*, and the following year played Mlle Lisette, the French governess in *Babes in the Wood*.

Between pantomime engagements Fragson appeared at the music halls of London and Paris singing at a grand piano with a French accent, which was as popular in London as the reverse was in Paris. He claimed to have a repertoire of over 300 songs, which included 'La Petite Femme du Metro', 'When Sister Mary Went to Gay Paree', 'John Bull's Budget', 'Billy Brown', and his most famous 'Hullo, Hullo, Who's Your Lady Friend'. Although perhaps lacking in popular appeal, he had a large and loyal following which grew into almost a cult. Billy Boardman, the manager of the Paris Alhambra and later the Brighton Hippodrome, had plenty of opportunities of watching Fragson in action, and wrote in 1935:

> There was something inscrutable and at the same time magnetic in Fragson's personality, something which drew as well as repelled. He was horribly alert, watchful, self-possessed. His restless, eager eyes seemed to be everywhere, his hard, unwinking gaze on everyone. There was something mocking in the way in which he proclaimed himself 'your most humble and obedient servant'. There was irony in the perfunctory bow and inquiring glance with which he greeted you when he strode out from the wings. There was defiance in the voice as he darted to the piano and, sitting himself sideways, announced, 'A humorous song entitled "The Other Department, Please"'.

Poor Harry came to a sad end at the age of 44. For some years his father had lived in retirement at Fragson's apartment on the Rue Lafayette, Paris, but failing health and growing senility were becoming increasingly evident. He grew insanely jealous of Harry's friends, their relationship becoming stretched to breaking point by Fragson's engagement in June 1913 to Paulette Frank, a 24-year-old dancer from Marseilles. Fragson made what was to be his last appearance in England at the Brighton Hippodrome on 27 December 1913, opening the following week at the Alhambra, Paris. Returning to his flat on 31 December he was confronted by his father who in a fit of insanity shot him in the head. He fell mortally wounded and died soon after. His body was buried in Montmartre Cemetery, the funeral being attended by an estimated 20,000 people. His father, Victor Potts, was found unfit to plead and committed to an asylum, where he died the following year.

George Franklin, comedian and comedy magician, born on 29 July 1887. He made his first variety appearance at Barnard's Palace, Chatham, in 1904 and in London at Collins Music Hall, Islington, in 1906. He toured the UK in variety, appeared in concert party, and as principal comedian in Harry Day revues. After serving in the First World War, he teamed with Tom Buffery as 'Buff and Franklin'. Later he presented a comedy illusion act billed as 'The Great Herman'.

Ronald Frankau, comedian and performer of songs-at-the-piano act. Born in London on 22 February 1894, he began his career as a chorus boy at Daly's in 1911, and joined the army in 1914. After the war he worked in repertory and concert party, and between 1920 and 1932 toured the UK and South and East Africa with his own concert party and revue company. His career covered most forms of light entertainment, pantomime, revue, radio and variety but he was perhaps at his best as a hotel and night-club cabaret artiste, doing a sophisticated song-and-patter act with Monte Crick at the piano. With Monte Crick, who later played Dan Archer in the long-running BBC radio series 'The Archers', Frankau wrote all his own material, which he sang in a style sounding like a cross between Max Miller and Noël Coward, with a touch of the 'repellent' Harry Fragson:

> Once a fella asked a young thing,
>   To become more than a friend.
> She said, 'P'raps', she said 'no', but she did.
> Then later on, he begged the girl
>   to go for a weekend.
> She said 'P'raps', she said 'no', but she did.
> And if anything should happen, darling,
>   after our affair,
> Something perhaps that merits the world's
>   unfriendly stare,
> Do you think that you could kill yourself?
>   he asked her with an air.
> She said 'P'raps', she said 'no', but she did.

A regular broadcaster from 1927, he made his first record for Parlophone in 1930, and later recorded for HMV. In 1930 he teamed with Tommy Handley (qv) as the radio double act 'North and South'. As Mr North the Liverpudlian Handley made an amusing contrast to the old Etonian drollery of Frankau's Mr South. This developed into the famous radio partnership of 'Mr Murgatroyd and Mr Winterbottom'. During the war he wrote and produced his own West End revues, *Beyond Compere* at the Duchess Theatre in 1940, and *The Nineteen Naughty One* at the Prince of Wales the following year. In 1942 he wrote the film script for George Formby's *Much Too Shy*, directed by Marcel Varnel. He starred in *Sauce Tartare* at the Cambridge Theatre, London in 1949 and died at the age of 57 in 1951.

Franklyn and York, comedy singing and dancing duo. Bill Franklyn, born in Boston on 9 December 1902, came to London with his parents in 1906. His first appearance was as a light comedian at the Alexandra, Hull, in 1920. His wife, Trudy York, was born in Hobart, Tasmania, in 1912 and made her first appearance as a singer and dancer at the Regent Theatre, Grimesthorpe, in 1926, and in London at the Bedford, Camden Town, in 1928. Franklyn and York teamed in 1936, presenting a comedy singing and dancing act in revue, variety and pantomime.

The Frantz Family, British acrobatic troupe formed by Richard Frantz, his three sisters and brother-in-law in 1890. They first appeared in Bordeaux, followed by engagements in Paris, Lisbon, Madrid and Barcelona, making their London debut at the Empire, Leicester Square, on 13 June 1891. After 14 months at the Empire they toured the USA in 1892. After further London appearances and tours of the UK they returned to America to star at Koster and Bial's Music Hall, New York. A feature of their act which set them apart from many similar ones was that they abandoned the traditional tights or leotards and performed their acrobatics in full evening dress.

Jean Fredericks, female impersonator. Born in Montreal, Canada, he made his first stage appearance as Buttercup in *HMS Pinafore* in Detroit, USA, in 1948, and in London in *A Man about the House* at the Scala Theatre in 1963. As a female impersonator he appeared in variety shows and is

Ronald Frankau, 1930

famed for his drag recitals, his voice ranging from butch soprano to camp baritone. A popular personality, he spends most of his time holding 'gay' balls in London.

Freddie Frinton, comedian famed for his 'drunk' routines and later as the hen-pecked husband of the television domestic comedy series 'Meet the Wife'. Born Frederick Hargate in Grimsby, 17 January 1911, he made his first appearance at the Theatre Royal, Sheffield, in 1931, and in 1935 worked in concert party at Cleethorpes with Jimmy Slater's 'Supper Follies'. Later he toured his own road show and appeared with Ernest Binn's Northern Concert Party. His London debut was at the East Ham Palace in 1935, and in 1940 he toured with George Lacey's revue *Lights Up*. During army service he appeared with George Black's famous forces show *Stars in Battledress* and after the war toured with George and Alfred Black's revues *Strike a New Note* (1946), *Strike It Again* (1947) and *Sky High* (1949). Between variety, revue and summer shows he worked each Christmas as a dame in pantomime. During the 1950s and 1960s he became well-known as a television character comedian, notably for his co-starring part in BBC television's 'Meet the Wife' with Thora Hird. He died on 17 October 1968.

Will Fyffe, one of the best-known Scottish comedians and character actors to appear on the variety stage. Born in Dundee on 16 February 1885, he played a wide range of juvenile roles as a member of his father's stock company, from his first, the traditional part of Little Willie in *East Lynne*, to Little Eva in *Uncle Tom's Cabin*. For years he toured in fit-up productions of Shakespeare and melodrama, barnstorming through Scotland and the North of England,

Above: Will Fyffe (photo, Rank Films)

Below: Jean Fredericks

gaining so much experience that at 15 he was regularly playing the ancient Polonius in *Hamlet*. When a number of Scottish character sketches he had written and submitted to Harry Lauder and Neil Kenyon were turned down, he decided to work them himself, and after touring as a comedian with the revue *Bo, Bo*, turned to the variety stage.

He made his first music-hall appearance in London at the Middlesex in 1916, but it was not until he appeared at the London Palladium in 1921 that he became, after 30 years on the stage, an overnight success as a music-hall comedian. During his two weeks at the top of the bill, Fyffe received variety and pantomime bookings for the next six years, and appeared in the Royal Variety Performance of 1922. He produced many fine character studies: a Highland railway guard, an old shepherd, a poacher, a ship's engineer singing 'Sailing up the Clyde', 'Dr McGregor' with his wee black bag, and the Glasgow working man singing the song without which his act was never considered complete, 'I Belong to Glasgow'. One of his most popular characters was the village idiot Daft Sandy, described by James Agate as a 'masterpiece of tragi-comedy'. Poor Sandy has been befriended since a boy by the gamekeeper Jim McGregor, who gave him shoes and stockings and never called him 'daft'. Now McGregor is dead and Sandy has drawn his precious life savings of £17 to give to his old friend's widow. Agate wrote:

He is not to be allowed to go to the funeral lest he should

make the villagers laugh! Fyffe has a sob here of which Garrick would have been proud. I use the great name to give this piece of acting its scale. Let there be no mistake. I do not say that Will Fyffe is as great an actor as Garrick, but I do say that the older actor could not have bettered that mingling of pathos and grotesquerie. If one may use the word 'genius' of a performance of our time, here is genius.

A popular member of the variety profession, he became a member of the Grand Order of Water Rats in 1928 and served as King Rat six years later. He made four Royal Variety appearances, in 1922, 1925, 1932, and 1937. In 1932 he appeared in 'Earl Carrol's Vanities' in New York and toured the USA in vaudeville and revue with great success. During the 1930s he was a regular broadcaster and between 1930 and 1950 appeared in many films. For his work during the Second World War he was awarded the CBE. In 1946 he was to appear in the film *Bonnie Prince Charlie* but an ear infection forced him to give up the part. An ear operation was a success but left him suffering from recurrent dizzy spells. While staying at the Rusacks Hotel, St Andrews, in December 1947 he suffered an attack of dizziness and fell to his death from his bedroom window.

G

Gaston and Andree, adagio dancers and gymnasts, well-known in variety during the 1930s. Before the First World War, Gaston worked under the name of Jimmy Wood, doing a double gymnastic act with a former member of the Cragg's acrobatic troupe, billed as 'Jimmy Wood and Arthur Cragg—Art in Athletics'. After the war he formed another act on the same lines with a girl partner and toured the world, appearing in 1926 on an 'All English' bill at the Palace Theatre, New York. In 1928 he teamed with Rosemary Andree and together they were the first to introduce adagio dancing to variety, topping bills throughout the UK and touring their own variety show. They appeared in the Royal Variety Performance at the London Palladium on 22 May 1933. Gaston died on 16 November 1966 and Rosemary Andree on 20 April 1974.

Geraldo, band-leader of variety and broadcasting fame. Born Gerald Bright in London in August 1904, the son of an East End tailor, he began his musical career playing a piano at a cinema in the Old Kent Road. During the 1920s he worked as a solo accordionist and pianist at Blackpool, later forming his Gaucho Tango Band, which appeared at the Savoy Hotel in August 1930. In August 1932 he made his variety debut at the Shepherd's Bush Empire, and on 22 May 1933 appeared in the Royal Variety Performance at the London Palladium. During the war he toured his band for ENSA and made many broadcasts. After the war he returned to variety and cabaret, at one time with Eve Boswell as his vocalist. Although always debonair and looking very much the top bandleader, he never lost his East End 'Blimey Bill' accent. When a BBC producer suggested he should take elocution lessons he was amazed at the suggestion, 'But I 'ave', he replied. During the dance-band slump of the 1960s he became a television executive, but with the revival of the big band sound, again took up his baton. He died while on holiday in Switzerland on 4 May 1974.

Gertie Gitana, charming singer of 'Nellie Dean' in the days when the song was as sweet as its singer and had not yet become a pub crawler's anthem. Born in Longport in 1888, she became a member of 'Tomlinson's Royal Gipsy Children' at the age of four. She made her solo music-hall

Gaston and Andree, 1935

debut at the Tivoli, Barrow-in-Furness, in 1896 as 'Little Gitana' and first appeared as 'Gertie Gitana—Dainty Comedienne' in 1900. She was one of the very few variety artistes to succeed at the Lyceum during its brief period as a music hall under the management of Thomas Barrasford in 1905–06, which led to her big chance as a deputy turn at the Holborn Empire. During the next 30 years she topped bills at all the principal London and provincial halls singing 'Nellie Dean', 'Silver Bell', 'When the Harvest Moon is Shining', and the plaintive ballad, 'Never Mind':

> Though your heart be full of pain, never mind,
> Though your face should lose its smile,
>   never mind,
> For there's sunshine after rain,
> And gladness follows pain
> You'll be happy once again, never mind.

In 1928 she married dancer Don Ross, who became an agent in 1933. She retired in 1938 but made a very successful comeback with Don Ross's *Thanks for the Memory* in 1948, appearing with the company in November that year in the Royal Variety Performance at the London Palladium. She died on 5 January 1957.

Shaun Glenville, Irish comedian and celebrated pantomime dame. Born in Dublin on 16 May 1884, two weeks later he was carried, in true theatrical tradition, on to the stage of the Theatre Royal, Birmingham, in Dion Boucicault's *Arrah-Na-Pogue*. He gained early acting experience in plays produced at a small theatre run by his mother, Mary Glenville Brown, which later became famous as the Abbey Theatre, Dublin. Receiving singing and dancing instruction from champion clog-dancer James Harvey, he made his first variety appearance in England in 1906, working the Liverpool halls in Irish character sketches, and made his London debut at the Holborn Empire in 1907. As Shaun Glenville Luck he toured England and America with the 'Six Brothers Luck', and later worked with Fred Karno's company. As a single turn in variety he toured the halls singing Irish comedy songs, 'Something in the Irish After All', 'Mickey Rooney's Ragtime Band', 'He's a Credit to Old Ireland Now', etc. He worked with success in musical comedy and revue, and was one of the greatest pantomime dames, usually appearing with his wife, the most famous of all modern principal boys, Dorothy Ward. They starred in pantomime for Howard and Wyndham, Robert Arthur, and for 19 years under the management of Julian Wylie. He died on 28 December 1968.

Above: Gertie Gitana, 'Sweet Nellie Dean'

Below: Shaun Glenville *(photo, Fielding of Leeds)*

Charles Godfrey, 1880

Charles Godfrey, music-hall sketch artist and descriptive vocalist, born Paul Lacey in London on 26 April 1851. His early stage experience came from playing melodramatic parts at the 'Old Blood Tub', the Bower Saloon in Stangate Street, Lambeth, and at the Pavilion, Mile End Road. His switch to music hall was inspired by Alfred Raynor, a member of Henry Irving's company who saw him playing at the Elephant and Castle Theatre, and being highly amused by his histrionics, advised him to try the halls. It was good advice well taken. Godfrey made his first music-hall appearance at Day's, Birmingham, on 7 June 1875, and through the agency of Maurice de Frece appeared at the

Royal Holborn soon after. He was then working as a Lion Comique, strolling on to the stage wearing a velvet suit, top hat, and carrying a silver topped cane in the fashion of George du Maurier's Postlethwaite drawings in *Punch*. His best songs of the period were 'The Masher King' and the rollicking tipsy serenade 'Hi-Tiddly-Hi-Ti!' In a more dramatic mood he sang 'Across the Bridge' and 'The Lost Daughter', two melancholy stories of suicide, linked in sentiment with the earlier days of Sam Cowell's 'Ratcatcher's Daughter'.

Music hall's greatest exponent of the dramatic song scene, he is best remembered for his patriotic sketches, 'On

Harry Gordon, 1929

Guard—A Story of Balaclava', and 'The 7th Royal Fusiliers—A Story of Inkerman'. 'On Guard' with Godfrey as a dejected old soldier, a neglected veteran of Balaclava, never failed to move the audience to thunderous applause. Its sequel, 'The 7th Royal Fusiliers', showed the old veteran now happy as a Chelsea Pensioner, telling his grandchildren the historic story of the Battle of Inkerman:

Oh, fighting with the 7th Royal Fusiliers!
Famous Fusiliers, Gallant Fusiliers.
Through deadly Russian shot and Cossack spears,
We carved our way to glory.

Wearing the appropriate uniform—correct, he insisted, in every detail—he appeared as Nelson, Wellington, Drake and General Gordon. Against tableaux of Trafalgar, Waterloo, Khartoum and the Spanish Main, with music, cannon fire,

and much flag waving, Godfrey reminded his audience of the nation's glory. In the days when it really did seem that the sun would never set on the British Empire, he earned £5,000 a year presenting three different songs, of three different heroes, at three different halls nightly. In a lighter mood, another song success was 'After the Ball', but for Godfrey the ball was over far too soon. Described rather sweepingly as 'the most popular entertainer of the 19th century' his popularity contributed to his early death. Because of overwork and a little too much of the 'Hi-Tiddly', his health was broken by the age of 45. In 1898 Harry Rickards (qv) arranged a tour of Australia in the hope that a long sea voyage would improve his condition. However, Australian hospitality further weakened it. While trying to fulfil an engagement in Birmingham, where his music-hall career had begun 25 years earlier, he died at the age of 48 on 28 March 1900.

Jimmy Gold *see* **Naughton and Gold**

Harry Gordon, Scots comedian of concert party, variety and pantomime. Born in Aberdeen on 11 July 1893, he first appeared with Monty's Pierrots at Stonehaven in 1912, later forming his own concert-party entertainment, 'Winners', which he toured between 1922 and 1927. Although he first appeared in London at the Palladium in October 1929, he worked mainly in Scotland, pioneering resident shows in variety theatres, notably at the Pavilion, Aberdeen, where 'Harry Gordon's Entertainers' were an attraction for 16 years (1924–40), and from there he made over 100 broadcasts. Between 1943 and 1948 he appeared each summer at the King's Theatres, Edinburgh and Glasgow, presenting a wide range of character studies, which he claimed numbered over 300, both as a single turn and partnered by Jack Holden. One of Scotland's favourite pantomime artistes, he appeared as principal comedian in four Julian Wylie pantomimes between 1929 and 1932, and played for eleven consecutive Christmases (1937–1948) for Tom Arnold at the Alhambra, Glasgow, co-starring in seven of these productions with Will Fyffe (qv).

El Granadas and Peter, rope-spinning speciality, formed by Cecil and Linda Granada. Cecil Granada, born Cecil Prentice, in West Hartlepool in August 1903, made his first stage appearance at the age of five singing in a Gus Lavaine pantomime at the Theatre Royal, Crook, Co Durham. He spent most of his childhood touring with his parents 'Les Zeimers', a music-hall and circus acrobatic act, and first presented his own rope-spinning routine in 1914. After making his London debut at the Theatre Royal, Stratford East, in 1921, he worked with a number of partners, and in 1926 joined 'The Daimlers', a comedy and acrobatic cycling act. Reverting to rope spinning and whip manipulating, in 1927 he formed a double act with his wife, a one-time member of the 'Sixteen Royal Scots' cycling act. Appearing first as 'La Rope and Lady' and from 1929 as 'El Granadas', they were joined in 1943 by their son Peter Prentice and changed their billing to 'El Granadas and Peter'. Peter first appeared at the Empire, Nottingham. The family took part in the Royal Variety Performance at the London Palladium on 4 November 1946. In 1949 the act also included Peter's wife, Dorothy. Cecil Granada died on 26 June 1971.

Rudi Grasl, novelty impressionist, born in Austria on 18 February 1906. First appeared at the Coliseum Theatre, Vienna, in October 1926, and after tours of Europe made his London debut at the Holborn Empire in September 1934. Subsequently he made many variety tours of the UK and appeared in cabaret at leading London hotels. In 1936 he appeared for a season with Clifford Fischer's 'Folies d'Amour' at the International Casino, New York, followed by a vaudeville tour of the USA.

Eddie Gray, popular red-nosed comedian famed for his grotesque false moustache, droll mixture of cockney English and 'fractured' French, and his billing, '"Monsewer" Eddie Gray'. He was born Edward Earl Gray in Pimlico, London, in 1898 and, like his fellow comedians W.C. Fields and Teddy Knox, began his career as a straight juggler, working from the age of nine with a juvenile juggling troupe touring the USA and Near and Far East. He is said to have picked up his ludicrous French while working with the troupe in Paris, later using it to comic advantage as a single act, combining juggling with comedy patter. During the 1920s he toured with Harry Lauder's variety company, and in 1930 appeared with comedy double Nervo and Knox (qv) in *Chelsea Follies* at the Victoria Palace. This led in 1932 to George Black's *Crazy Week* at the London Palladium, with Nervo and Knox, Eddie Gray, Naughton and Gold (qv), and husband-and-wife comedy act, Caryll and Mundy. Joined in March 1933 by Flanagan and Allen (qv), the *Crazy Week* developed into *Crazy Months* and eventually grew into the famous 'Crazy Gang' shows, with which Gray appeared on and off until the war. When the Gang re-formed for *Together Again* at the Victoria Palace in March 1947, Gray was fully booked as a single act in variety, but appeared with Bud Flanagan, Naughton and Gold, and Nervo and Knox, in the Royal Variety Performance at the London Palladium on 1 November 1948. He rejoined the Gang at the Victoria Palace in 1956, and remained a member until the last show, *Young in Heart*, brought the career of the Crazy Gang to an end on 19 May 1962. He continued to appear in variety, summer shows, and pantomime until his death in 1969.

George Gray, music-hall sketch artist, renowned as 'The Fighting Parson'. He began his career on the legitimate stage, appearing with the Kendals in London in 1893 and on a 70-week tour of the USA in 1894–5. Returning to England in 1895 he toured in burlesque and each Christmas played dame

George Gray, 'The Fighting Parson'

in pantomime. In March 1900 he was given a trial turn at the Tivoli Music Hall, London, singing 'London and Paris', a song he had written to music by Herman Fink. Tivoli manager George Adney Payne was not impressed and refused to book him. His first engagement for a regular variety bill came from Harry Lundy at the Alhambra, Blackpool, followed by 15 weeks at the London Pavilion.

Turning from singing to dramatic monologues, in November 1901 he revived Charles Godfrey's lurid sketch 'The Night Alarm' at the Paragon, Mile End. Considered to have been old-fashioned even when played by Godfrey during the 1880s, it was ridiculously melodramatic and featured a burning building, a real fire engine, a maiden in distress, and two songs. The East End audience loved it and it ran for months. Encouraged by the popularity of 'The Night Alarm', Gray wrote his own sketch, 'The Road to Ruin', first produced at the Royal Holborn on 14 August 1902. It was based on Frith's painting illustrating the evils of drink and gambling, and written around an incredibly sentimental ballad by Paul Pelham, with the chorus

> Don't forget your mother, take the advice
> she gives.
> Try to be her comfort and joy,
> She thinks the world of her boy.
> Don't forget her words, be honest, straight
> and true.
> For as you act to your mother, my boy,
> So heaven will deal with you.

Billed as a 'Dream Drama', it told of the slow sinking into the 'slough of despond', of an old sot, saved at the last moment by a vision of his future life, six scenes depicting DTs, madness and suicide. This sketch, spectacular with a cast of 50, was an immediate success and ran for eight weeks at the Royal, followed by other London halls. Gray's greatest success was 'The Fighting Parson', first produced at the Royal Holborn on 5 January 1903. Staged in five scenes, its climax was a realistic churchyard fight between Gray as a sporting parson and a sinner slow to repent. He presented many good sketches during his career, but like John Lawson (qv) and 'Humanity', George Gray became synonymous with 'The Fighting Parson'. He retired from the stage in 1913.

Larry Grayson, comedian famed for his audacious mixture of high camp and hypochondria. Born in Warwickshire on 31 August 'some time during the 1920s', he was brought up by foster parents in Nuneaton and began his career by singing comedy songs at local clubs at five shillings a performance. He later toured with Harry Leslie's 'Tomorrow's Stars', but for him tomorrow was a long time coming. During the late 1940s he worked a drag act and then toured the South as a stand-up comedian, appearing in London at the Metropolitan, Edgware Road, and at the Finsbury Park and Chiswick Empires. Those were the dying days of variety and Grayson played odd variety dates on bills between weeks of bingo and all-in wrestling, and often only just ahead of the bulldozer. By the 1960s he was back playing clubs in the Midlands and even if he had given up any dreams of stardom he was getting regular work and enjoying home life at Nuneaton.

Things changed drastically in 1969 when agent Peter Dulay persuaded him to return to London for a week's variety at the Theatre Royal, Stratford East. His twee style of camp gossip went down so well at the famous East End theatre that he remained on the bill for seven weeks. On 2 April 1970 he opened in *Birds of a Feather*, Paul Raymond's all-male 'revue spectacular' at the Royalty Theatre, Kingsway. Billed

Larry Grayson *(photo, courtesy ATV)*

as 'England's Comedy Sensation', in contrast to female impersonators Rickie Renee, Les Les, Terry Durham, and French drag fire-eater Laurence Daury (who did his act to the Grand March from *Aida*), Grayson's limp-wristed comedy seemed quite butch. Unlike the show itself, which soon closed, he got good press notices which led to a successful summer season on a bill with Hetty King at Brighton, variety at the London Palladium, pantomime at Christmas 1970 with Dora Bryan in *Goldilocks and the Three Bears* at the Theatre Royal, Brighton, and a cabaret season at Danny La Rue's club in Hanover Square.

In January 1972 he was booked for his first television spot on ATV's 'Saturday Variety' programme, and although more a mince-around comic than a stand-up comedian his outrageously camp innuendoes went over well on television. His act differed little from the one he had been working around the Midlands clubs for over ten years but now he was hailed as the show business phenomenon of the 1970s. In the music-hall tradition that goes back to Leno's Mrs Kelly, Grayson populates his act with imaginary characters so vivid that you expect them to walk on from the wings at any moment. There is his special friend Everard, Self-Raising Fred from the 'Friend in Hand', and Slack Alice and Apricot Lil, two factory workers just sacked from a jam works for pinching fruit. Shooting to the top with what has been described as a 'skilful amalgam of complaint and calculated insult', his first four minute television spot developed into his own 16-week, 45-minute show 'Shut that Door'. In 1973 he was chosen by the Variety Club of Great Britain as the Show Business Personality of the Year, and in May appeared before the Queen at the Royal Variety Gala held at the London Palladium in aid of the Olympics Fund.

That summer he appeared at the Winter Gardens, Margate, in *Grayson's Scandals*, which was such a success that a second edition was presented in 1974 at the ABC Theatre, Blackpool. In September 1974 he starred in the ITV spectacular 'Larry Grayson's Hour of Stars', and on 15 October *Grayson's Scandals* opened for a season at the London Palladium.

Harry Green, Jewish comedian, born in New York on 1 April 1892. He first appeared as a monologist at the Opera House, New Jersey, in January 1905. Later he toured in variety with a partner as 'Ross and Green', presenting Jewish comedy sketches based on the 'Potash and Perlmutter' stories. His first London appearance was at the Empire in the revue *Merry-Go-Round* in 1914, and he returned in August 1920 to appear in his famous sketch 'The Cherry Tree' at the London Coliseum. After variety and revue tours of the USA, Australia and South Africa, he appeared at the Palladium in 1932 and after the war in the revue *Fifty-Fifty* at the Strand Theatre. On 6 September 1948 he again presented 'The Cherry Tree' at the London Casino.

Griff, Harry Hadden Griffiths, juggler and comedian. He started his professional life as an office boy, appearing during his 'off-time' as a ventriloquist and making his stage debut with Terry's Amateur Burlesque Society in a production of *Aladdin* at the Bijou Opera House, Liverpool. He made his first music-hall appearance as a part of the double comic patter and juggling act billed as 'Evalo and Roisso, The Turk and Clown', and made his solo debut at the Middlesex Music Hall in 1896. He died on 14 April 1945.

Fred Griffiths, 'The Brothers Griffiths'. Born Frederick George Delaney on the island of Corfu, where his father was serving as a British Army bandmaster, in 1856. At the age of five he was apprenticed to the celebrated all-round circus performer William Frederick Matthews, with whom he made his first stage appearance in the pantomime *Hi-Diddle-Diddle* at the Effingham Theatre, Mile End, London, in 1861. For 16 years he remained with the Matthews family, gaining valuable, if often hard experience, touring the UK, Europe, the USA, and Russia in both music hall and circus entertainment, appearing in the USA in 1871 with Barnum's first three-ring circus. In 1877 Fred Griffiths left Matthews and with his brother Joe Griffiths, who had served a similar apprenticeship with Hanlon-Lee's Company, formed the 'Brothers Griffiths' act. Billed as 'The Safe Men on a Silver Bar and Magical Hatters', they presented a skilful juggling, grotesque gymnastics and acrobatic knockabout comedy routine. They later added a series of pantomime animal impersonations, including their famous 'Blondin Donkey', which they first introduced into their act at the Royal Holborn in 1885. It became such a popular feature that they were commanded to perform for Edward, Prince of Wales, and his family at Marlborough House in February 1886. Other early successes included a comedy lion-taming skit and a burlesque of the 'Sandow and Samson' strong man act. After the death of Joe Griffiths at 49 on 13 May 1901 Fred was joined by his son, known as Fred Griffiths Junior, and together they carried on as the 'Brothers Griffiths'. Assisted by Lutie Griffiths, Fred Junior's sister, they introduced 'Pogo the Performing Horse' and featured it in the Royal Variety Performance at the London Coliseum in December 1923. They were widely considered to have been the world's finest exponents of the art of pantomime animals. Their Daisy the Cow in *Jack and the Beanstalk* was a classic example. It had a pathos of its own which excited both laughter and tears from young and old. They were also masters of the harlequinade, now an almost forgotten pantomime tradition. The 'Brothers Griffiths' played the halls for a total of 60 years, until Fred Griffiths Senior retired at the age of 81 in 1937. He died on 11 July 1940.

Yvette Guilbert, great French diseuse, born in Paris on 20 January 1865. She made her stage debut in January 1886 in Alexandre Dumas' *La Reine Margot* at the Théâtre de Bouffes-du-Nord, Paris, and her first music-hall appearance at the Casino, Lyons, in September 1889. In Paris she appeared at the Eldorado Music Hall on the Boulevard de Strasbourg, totally without success, but slowly gained popularity at café concerts, notably at the Eden on the Boulevard Sebastopol. In 1890 she was engaged by Charles Zidler for his new dance hall, the Moulin Rouge, and in 1891 was a great hit at the Divan Japonais, a small hall on the Rue des Martyrs.

She had a wide range of songs from the low comedy repertoire of the Paris streets to those written by Xanrof (Leon Xanrof was the *nom de plume* of Leon Forneau). At the Japonais, a favourite meeting-place of the intellectual elite of Montmartre, Guilbert added to her repertoire the stark realism of Aristide Bruant and the ironic verse of the notorious Jean Lorrain. In September 1892 she scored a tremendous success at the Concert Parisien on the Faubourg Saint Denis, singing the most dramatic song of her career, 'Ma Tête' by Gaston Secretan. This gruesome song of an Apache murderer condemned to death by guillotine was in

Yvette Guilbert, Empire Theatre, London, 1894

The Brothers Griffiths and Lutie, in *Humpty Dumpty*, 1906–7

the tradition of 'Sam Hall', sung by W. G. Ross (qv) in London during the 1850s, and earned her the title of 'The Sarah Bernhardt of the Café Concert'.

She made her first appearance in London at the Empire, Leicester Square, on 9 May 1894 and was described by GBS in the *World* as 'one of the best singers and pantomimists in Europe'. Although cordially received she was far too rare a bird for her generally non-French-speaking audience. A return engagement at the Empire in December 1894 met with more general acclaim, due mainly to the success of her burlesque in English of Cissie Loftus (qv) singing 'Linger Longer Loo'. Loftus had for some months been doing a realistic impersonation of Guilbert at the Palace, and the audience at the Empire were quick to appreciate the justice of Yvette's parody and the improvement in her English since her London debut six months before. She returned to the Empire each year for four consecutive years and appeared with success at other London halls. She only made one tour of the UK, and one which she quickly regretted. As she put it

in her autobiography, published in 1928, 'to be howled down is called in slang "to get the bird". Well, I got an aviary-full.'

Her first appearance in the USA was at Hammerstein's Olympia, New York, on 16 December 1895. She was still singing her earthy songs of the Paris streets, and the New York press complained of her 'indecency'. Popular as these were in Paris, she decided to change her style and by 1900 her repertoire of 'boulevard indecencies' was gone, replaced by the songs of old France. In 1905 she gave a recital with Albert Chevalier (qv) at the Duke of York's Theatre, London, she singing 'La Chanson de France', and Chevalier the cockney carols of Whitechapel and the Old Kent Road. In 1906 they made a 27,000 mile tour of the USA and in 1908 she returned to America to appear for Charles Frohman and the following year for David Belasco at $2,500 per week. In 1909 she was engaged by Sir Alfred Butt for the Palace Theatre, London, and was rather put out at having to compete for star billing with Consul, a much-publicised chimpanzee.

She opened a theatre school in New York in 1915 which she ran until 1922. In June 1928 she returned to London for a series of recitals at the Arts Theatre Club, and in 1935 appeared in concert at the Wigmore Hall. In 1940 she retired to Aix-en-Provence, where she died on 3 February 1944. After the war her body was taken back to Paris and on a day of official national mourning it was re-interred in the cemetery of Père Lachaise.

H

Tony Hancock, the comic genius of the 1950s. Born in Small Heath, Birmingham, on 12 May 1924, he made his first appearance as 'Anthony Hancock, The Confidential Comic', at the Theatre Royal, Bournemouth in 1940. The following year he broadcast in a BBC talent show, reciting the monologue 'The Night the Opera Caught Fire'. Joining the RAF in 1942, he failed an ENSA audition (he dried up and never got beyond 'Ladies and Gentlemen') and 'rode along on the crest of a wave' with a unit of Ralph Reader's 'Gang Show'. After demob in November 1946 he toured with Reader's ex-RAF show *Wings*, played an Ugly Sister at Oxford in 1947, and appeared at the Windmill Theatre, London, in 1948. During the summer of 1949 he appeared with B. C. Hilliam's 'Flotsam's Follies' at Bognor Regis and later that year worked in variety for Moss at the Empress, Brixton, the Chelsea Palace and the Chiswick Empire.

Not a good stand-up comedian, Hancock kept his variety turn basically the same throughout his career, impersonating impersonators doing impersonations, Charles Laughton as the Hunchback of Notre Dame and Captain Bligh, Robert Newton as Long John Silver, and Henry Irving as Mathias in *The Bells*. In 1950 he broadcast in the very successful Sunday evening 'Variety Bandbox' and at Christmas appeared with the young Julie Andrews in pantomime at Nottingham. In 1951 he broadcast in Derek Roy's 'Happy go Lucky' and was engaged to tutor Archie Andrews in the hit show 'Educating Archie'. Written by Eric Sykes, Hancock's catch phrase 'flippin' kid' became the rage and shot him straight up the popularity pole. At Christmas that year he appeared at the Prince of Wales Theatre each morning and afternoon in a stage version of 'Educating Archie' and in the evening in Val Parnell's twice-nightly revue *Peep Show*. Early the following year he toured as leading comedian in a variety show topped by American singer Nat King Cole, and on 13 August 1952 opened at the Adelphi Theatre in Jack Hylton's revue *London Laughs*. On 3 November 1952 he took part in his first Royal Variety Performance at the London Palladium. Following the success of *London Laughs* he was booked to star in *Talk of the Town* which, after a summer season at Blackpool, opened at the Adelphi on 17 November 1954.

On 2 November 1954 'Hancock's Half Hour' went on the air for the first time and by 6 July 1956, when the show transferred to television, Anthony Aloysius St John Hancock of 23 Railway Cuttings, East Cheam, was a national celebrity. In 1957 and again in 1959 Hancock was voted Comedian of the Year, and in 1959 the award for the best television writers of the year went to Galton and Simpson for their scripts for 'Hancock's Half Hour'. For the last 'Hancock's Half Hour' series in 1961 Tony moved from East Cheam to a bedsitter in Earl's Court where, without his old side-kick, Sid James, he produced 'The Blood Donor', 'The Bedsitter' and 'The Radio Ham', all classic Hancock. The down-to-earth cockney Sid James had been an excellent foil to the pretentious and ridiculous Hancock character, but the success of the series proved that Tony could work without him. His first step towards professional suicide came in 1961 when he broke with Galton and Simpson. They went on to even greater success but Hancock never worked for the BBC again on a regular basis, although they did continue to screen frequent repeats, including 'The Best of Hancock' in 1975.

His first film *The Rebel* was released in 1961 and his second, *The Punch and Judy Man*, in 1962. Neither was a great success. In 1963 he worked for ITV on a new series written by Dr Who's creator, Terry Nation, but it never came up to the standard of the previous BBC series. He topped the bill of ITV's popular variety show 'Sunday Night at the London Palladium' in November 1964, and in June 1965 worked a not too happy cabaret season at the 'Talk of the Town' at the old London Hippodrome. A classic example of the tragic clown, Hancock concealed deep-rooted feelings of melancholy beneath the public mask of comedy, which led to heavy drinking and frequent need of psychiatric help. On 22 September 1966 he gave a solo performance at the London Festival Hall. Recorded by the BBC, its transmission showed that he was only the merest shadow of the great comedian he once was. A second ITV series in 1967 did nothing to restore his reputation. In 1968 he went to Australia to work on a series of 13 television programmes for Sydney's Channel Seven. The series, about a pompous and disgruntled 'pommie' immigrant, seemed well suited to Hancock's comedy line. Between drinking bouts and drying out he

Tony Hancock, 1956

managed to complete three episodes, but on 24 June 1968 he returned from the TV studios to his flat in the Sydney suburb of Bellevue Hill and committed suicide by taking an overdose of drugs washed down by vodka. 'Alas, poor Yorick!' This was a sad end to the brilliant career of a comedian still remembered by many with affection.

Tommy Handley, comedian whose wartime radio programme 'ITMA' ('It's That Man Again') made him the most popular comedian in the history of radio. Born in Liverpool in 1894, he made his first appearance in the chorus at Daly's Theatre in 1917, followed by a tour of *Maid of the Mountains*. After wartime service, mostly as a member of an army concert party, he toured with a fit-up variety show, and a touring company in the musical *Shanghai*. He worked with a concert party run by Jack Hylton at Bognor Regis in the summer of 1919, and later that year teamed with Jack as the comedy double act of 'Handley and Hylton'. They made their variety debut at the Bedford, Camden Town, in October 1919, but the act was short-lived and soon afterwards Handley was engaged for a musical burlesque, 'Seasoned to Taste'. Written by Con West with music by Jack Hylton, it opened at the Metropolitan, Edgware Road, on 1 December 1919, with Dorothy Frostick and Bobby Howes. In the summer of 1920 Hardley and Bobby Howes joined a concert party run by Tom Walls and Leslie Henson at Llandrindod Wells, North Wales. At the suggestion of Leslie Henson, Tommy read a sketch which had been popular with the troops in France during the war, but had never been given a public performance. Entitled 'The Disorderly Room', it was written by Eric Blore, later famous in English butler roles in Hollywood films. A musical skit on an army court martial, the dialogue set to the tunes of songs popular during the First World War, it was such a success during the summer in Wales that Handley decided to tour it as a music-hall sketch. Making its first appearance on a variety bill at the Shepherd's Bush Empire in 1921, it was soon an established favourite at all the leading halls, including the Alhambra, Coliseum and Holborn Empire. It was included in the Royal Variety Performance at the London Coliseum on 13 December 1923 and remained Handley's standby for over 20 years.

Between variety dates he appeared in revue, and made many recordings singing comedy songs. At Christmas 1923 he played in *Dick Whittington* at the London Palladium, followed in 1924 by the Palladium revue *The Whirl of the World*, with Nellie Wallace, Billy Merson and Nervo and Knox. Written by Albert de Courville and Edgar Wallace with music by Frederick Chappell, it ran for 53 weeks. Tommy Handley made his first studio broadcast from Savoy Hill in 1925. His homely and amusingly expressive voice impressed the BBC who were quick to realise his value to an industry as yet without stars. His first successful radio show, 'Radio Radiance' (1925), was followed by 'Inaninn' (In-an-Inn), 'Handley's Manoeuvres' 'Tommy Tours', and 'Hot Pot'. His famous radio comedy partnership with Ronald Frankau (qv) dates from 1930 when they teamed for the act 'North and South', which later developed into the famous double act 'Murgatroyd and Winterbottom'. Another notable radio and stage role during the 1930s was the Headmaster of St Basil's School in Harry S. Pepper's 'The White Coons'. 'ITMA' was first broadcast on 12 July 1939 and soon became the most popular programme of the war, making Tommy Handley a household name. In 1947 he made a rare trip abroad to broadcast in the 'We the People' series from the Hammerstein Theatre, New York. The last 'ITMA' (number 309) went on the air on 6 January 1949. Directly after the repeat broadcast at 5.30 pm on Sunday 9 January, the BBC

Tommy Handley, front right, Blackpool, 1930

news reader announced that Tommy Handley had died that afternoon at the age of 52.

The Harmonica Rascals, comedy harmonica act formed by Borrah Minevitch. Born in Russia, Minevitch went as a youth to the USA, making his debut with Hugo Rosenfeld's Orchestra at the Rialto, New York, in 1925 and later the same year as a straight solo harmonica player at the London Hippodrome. On his return to the USA he toured in vaudeville and appeared in 'Puzzles of 1926' with Elsie Janis. Forming his own comedy harmonic group billed as 'Borrah Minevitch Harmonica Rascals', he came to England in 1929 for a season at the London Palladium, followed by a cabaret engagement at the Casino de Paris, and a nine-month variety tour of the Moss Empires. After long periods on the bill at the Palace Theatre, New York, they returned to London in 1934 to appear at the Prince of Wales Theatre and tour in variety. When Minevitch retired in 1939 the lead was taken by Johnny Puleo, who joined the act in 1928, and from then on the act billed as 'The Harmonica Rascals, with Johnny Puleo'. It appeared in the Royal Variety Performances of 1947 and 1949.

The Harmony Four, American burlesque musical act, formed by T. C. Bergeron in 1898. Bergeron played a grand piano dressed like a corpulent 'Uncle Sam', E.M. Barrett played the violin, Alexander Ferguson sang tenor, and Edward Hughes was the comedian. The act first appeared in England at the London Pavilion in 1905 and later the same year at Barrasford's Alhambra, Paris.

Will Hay, comedian famous as the bogus schoolmaster of the Fourth Form of St Michael's. Born in December 1888, he made his stage debut at the age of eight with his family's concert party. Following three seasons with Dane's Minstrel Troupe on the Isle of Man, he made his solo music-hall debut as a mimic at the Empire, Hull, in 1908. During the 1920s he worked with Fred Karno, and later returned to the halls with a patter and school song act, performed in academic gown, pince-nez and mortarboard. This led to his billing as 'The Schoolmaster Comedian' and his St Michael's School sketches. By 1925 he was established as a top-of-the-bill variety act. In 1928 he took space in the press announcing:

St Michael's
School for Boys. No age limit.
All subjects mis-taught
Pleasantly situated overlooking
  Charing Cross Road
Playing Fields at Stage Lane, Edgware
Headmaster: Will Hay
For Prospectus, terms, etc, apply to
  School Governor, Julius Darewski.

He appeared in the Royal Variety Performance at the Alhambra in 1925, the Coliseum in 1928, and the Palladium in 1930. During the 1930s he starred in a series of Ealing and Gainsborough films which left little time for variety. In 1938 a second St Michael's sketch company was formed with Will Hay Junior, touring in his father's headmaster role. In private life Will Hay was far from the ignorant charlatan of his stage and screen character. A keen astronomer, he built an observatory near the Watford Way, Mill Hill. He was made a Fellow of the Royal Astronomical Society for his discovery of a white spot on Saturn, and in 1935 published a book on astronomy, *Through my Telescope*. He served as King Rat of the Grand Order of Water Rats in 1928 and in 1945 became vice-president of the Variety Artistes Federation. After the war, in which he served with ENSA, he returned to variety, taking part in the Royal Variety Show of 1945. Forced by ill health to retire in 1947, he died on 18 April 1949.

Hayman and Franklin *See p. 85.*

Dick Henderson, popular Yorkshire comedian, born in Hull on 20 March 1891. As a youth he served in the navy, appearing in ship's concerts as comic and singer. After his naval service, he toured Ireland with a concert party, and in 1916 made his first music-hall appearance as a solo comedian at the Imperial Theatre, Canning Town. As a rotund Yorkshire dialect comedian, wearing a bowler several sizes too small (the theory being that it presented a more difficult target for egg-throwers), he was one of the most popular variety comedians between the wars. He had a good line in domestic patter involving sweethearts and wives, and songs ranging from the emotional ballad 'Pal of My Cradle Days', to his greatest hits 'Tiptoe Through the Tulips' and 'Little White Rose'.

Dickie Henderson, light comedian. The son of singing Yorkshire comedian Dick Henderson (qv), he was born in London on 30 October 1922. In the early 1930s he went to Hollywood where his father was filming and at the age of ten appeared in Frank Lloyd's film version of *Cavalcade*. Returning to England he made his first variety stage appearance with his father's act at the Hippodrome, Ilford, in November 1937. After the war he toured for Tom Arnold, and in June 1948 opened at the Savoy Theatre in the revue 'A La Carte', followed in September 1949 with a Folies Bergère show at the London Hippodrome. From then on his career went from success to success and with his famous routine of

Dick Henderson

the crooning drunk tottering bleary-eyed on a bar stool, topped variety bills and starred in cabaret all over the UK and the USA. He has had his own shows at the London Palladium, and made countless television appearances. On 18 November 1957 he made his first Royal Variety appearance, and since then seems to have appeared at more royal shows than the Queen.

May Henderson, black-faced comedienne. Born in 1885, she made early appearances with her father, Billy Henderson, a comedian and clog dancer, and with the 'Henderson and Stanley Trio'. She made her first solo appearance in 1897 at Newcastle and in 1901 turned to black make-up and coon songs, billed as 'The Dusky Queen'. She died on 27 September 1937.

Carl Hertz, illusionist, born in San Francisco on 14 May 1859. He made his first appearance at Platt's Music Hall, San Francisco, in 1878 and came to England in 1884 to play at the Folly Theatre, Manchester, in August, and in London on 17 November 1884, appearing on the same night at the Royal Holborn, Canterbury, and Collins Music Halls. One of the finest variety magicians, he was the first to present Bautier de Kolta's famous illusions 'The Vanishing Lady' and 'The Flying Birdcage'. Appearing regularly in variety in England and Europe for 40 years, he also toured Africa and Australia, venturing as far east as China. While playing at the Coventry Hippodrome he died on 20 March 1924.

Will Hay, 1928

Hamilton Hill, Australian baritone, popular in England during the early 1900s as a singer of patriotic songs. He established a firm place in the history of music hall by being the original singer of the most famous song of the Boer War, 'Good Bye Dolly Gray'. Other songs included 'Bluebell', 'I Want to be a Soldier', 'A Little Boy Called Tap', and 'Don't Cry Sister Jane'.

Jenny Hill, one of the first female stars of the early music hall. Born in Paddington, London, in 1851, her father was a cab-minder at a rank close to the Marylebone Theatre, where at the age of seven she made her stage debut as a pantomime goose at sixpence a performance. In 1868 she married an acrobat, working with his act until her daughter was born and her husband abandoned her. She was given an audition by Emile Loible at the London Pavilion with immediate success, becoming a great favourite in London billed as 'The Vital Spark'. Essentially an artiste of the people, with what Harold Scot called an 'intense instinct of class consciousness', she excelled in character songs of costers and factory girls, singing 'The Coffee Shop Girl', 'Maggie Murphy's Home', 'I'm a Woman of Very Few Words' and 'What Cheer 'Arry'. She danced well, did male impersonations of coster boys and street vendors, and was a

Left: Hamilton Hill, 'Good Bye Dolly Gray'

Below: Jenny Hill, 1879

popular principal boy in pantomime. Although she was the first performer to be termed 'comedienne', pathos was as much a part of her act as comedy, turning laughter to tears with her melodramatic songs, 'The Little Stowaway', 'The City Waif', and 'Masks and Faces'. She was one of the first established British music-hall stars to appear in the USA, at Tony Pastor's in New York. In 1878 she was engaged by John Hollingshead to appear in H. J. Byron's burlesque 'Jack the Giant Killer' at the Gaiety. In 1869 she played Nan in a revival of John Baldwin Buckstone's *Good For Nothing Nan* at the Grecian. Although her legitimate ventures were not very successful, John Hollingshead held her in high esteem and wrote in his book of reminiscences, 'Jenny Hill was without exception one of the greatest female geniuses who ever appeared on the music hall stage'. During the 1890s ill health forced her retirement, but in 1895 she accepted an invitation from Luscombe Searella to visit South Africa. On her arrival in Johannesburg all she could do was make a brief appearance in a wheelchair: she was quite unable to sing. She returned to England and died on 28 June 1896 at the age of 45.

Violet and Daisy Hilton, Siamese twins, joined at the waist. Born in Brighton in 1906, they toured America as a circus and sideshow attraction and later presented a song, dance and instrumental act. They toured the UK in variety and appeared in London at the Holborn Empire and London Palladium in 1933. They died in the USA in 1969.

A. B. Hollingsworth, comic singer who made his first appearance at Wilton's Music Hall in 1853 and scored such a success singing 'The Man with the Carpet Bag' that he remained on the bill for five years. He went on to further success at the Canterbury and other leading halls, and when Charles Morton opened the Oxford Music Hall on 26 March

1861, Hollingsworth was one of his first star attractions. In June 1863 he suffered a partial paralysis and lost his sight. He continued to appear at benefits organised on his behalf, being led onto the stage by a small boy. He died on 10 October 1865.

Percy Honri, musical entertainer of music hall and revue, famed for his 'Concordia' and 'Concert-in-a-Turn'. Born Percy Henry Thompson at Thorpe Mandeville near Banbury on 24 June 1874, he came from a music-hall family and made his debut as 'Little Percy Thompson', a five-year-old clog dancer at the Odd Fellows' Hall, Great Bridge, on 29 September 1879. Later he toured with his father, then working a burnt-cork double act with Albert Virto as 'Virto and Thompson—The Musical Savages'. They appeared in 1883 at the Folies Bergère where in error Percy 'Henry' was billed as 'Percy Honri'. The name stuck, and he appeared as a solo turn as 'Percy Honri, The Wonderful Infantine Tenor'. In 1884 Albert Virto left the act and Percy teamed with his mother and father as 'The Thompson Trio'. After appearing before the Duke of Cambridge at the Cavalry Theatre, Aldershot, on 17 April 1890, they changed their billing to 'Royal Thompson Trio', and in 1893 made a vaudeville tour of the USA for Tony Pastor. In 1898 Percy turned solo and toured the Orpheum circuit of the USA, working a concertina and singing act. On his return to England he made his first London solo appearance at the London Pavilion on 22 May 1899. During the early 1900s he was the first to introduce bioscope back projection into his variety act, and with his famous 'Concordia' was the pioneer of touring revue. From 1906 he toured his own company of between 50 and 100 artistes, scoring a great success in 1913 with his elaborately staged 'Tango' revue *What About It*, consisting of a series of spectacular musical, singing and dancing episodes. After the First World War he reverted to a solo variety act until in 1935 he was joined by his daughter and as 'Mary and Percy Honri—A Concert-in-a-Turn' worked in variety, summer season and revue until his retirement in 1951. He died on 24 September 1953. The family tradition is still carried on by his grandson, Peter Honri, who in 1973 wrote the history of his family, *Working the Halls*.

Houdini, world famous escapologist born Ehrich Weiss in Budapest, Hungary, on 24 March 1874. His father, Rabbi Mayer Samuel Weiss, emigrated with his family to the USA soon after Ehrich's birth and settled in Appleton, Wisconsin. In 1888 the Weisses moved to 305 East 69th Street, New York, where Rabbi Weiss died on 5 October 1892.

In 1891 Ehrich added an extra syllable to the name of his great French idol Robert Houdin, and appeared at Huber's Dime Museum on 14th Street as Harry Houdini. Soon afterwards he teamed with his brother Theo, working the old roped and locked trunk trick escape, originated by J. N. Maskelyne in 1865. During the next few years they toured the Midwest and in 1893 appeared at the Chicago World Fair. The following year they worked theatre dates in New York, and Houdini introduced his 20-second escape, from a padlocked barrel. While appearing at Coney Island he met Beatrice Rahner, one half of the song-and-dance act 'The Floral Sisters'. They were married on 22 June 1894 and a few weeks later she replaced Theo in the act. Theo went solo, appearing at first as Professor Houdini. This conflict of names was later resolved by Theo working first as 'Hardin' and then as 'Hardeen'. When Houdini later became so famous that he was unable to take up all the bookings offered, Theo often played the smaller dates under his brother's name. In February 1895 'The Great Houdini' appeared at Tony Pastor's Music Hall, sharing the top of the bill with Bessie Bonehill. During a tour of Canada in 1896 he made his

A.B. Hollingsworth, 1861

Percy Honri *(photo, Walter Bird)*

first escape from a regulation straightjacket, loaned by an insane asylum at St John's, New Brunswick. By 1899 ways of freeing himself from all forms of official restraint, from handcuffs to prison cells, were a regular feature of his publicity on the Orpheum and Keith vaudeville circuits.

He made his first London appearance at the Alhambra in July 1900 and lived up to his billing of 'The Handcuff King' by escaping from regulation cuffs fitted by Scotland Yard. Following a tour of Europe, he returned to the Alhambra in December, and in February 1901 made his first provincial variety appearance at the Palace Theatre, Bradford. During the next 25 years he made frequent visits to England and in May 1911 was elected first president of the Magicians' Club of London, an office he held for 15 years.

The name Houdini became synonymous with escapology, and it seemed that nothing could hold him. In November 1908 he was thrown handcuffed into the Mississippi by the New Orleans police and was free again in 30 seconds. While appearing at the Paris Alhambra in April 1901 he caused a sensation by diving fully manacled from the wall of the Morgue into the Seine. At the Euston Palace, London, in 1908, he freed himself in 14 minutes from an 8 cwt burglar-proof safe supplied by a local tradesman who overlooked the fact that it was designed to keep burglars out, not Houdini in. At the Holborn Empire in December 1910 he was placed in handcuffs in an airtight galvanised iron can, which was then filled with water and locked with six padlocks. Three minutes later he was free. His most spectacular stage escape was from the luridly billed 'Water Torture Cell', which concluded his act from 1912. With his feet stuck into a sliding panel which secured his ankles like stocks, Houdini was lowered head first into a glass tank of water. It was then sealed by padlocks supplied by the audience which were clamped through hasps on the outside of the tank. While assistants stood by with firemen's axes raised, the curtains were drawn and three minutes later Houdini appeared, wet but free.

As an illusionist he 'walked' through brick walls, and made a fully grown elephant vanish from a wooden case placed in the centre of the brightly lit stage of the New York Hippodrome. His escapes fell into three groups: he freed himself from ropes and chains by tensing his muscles while being tied or chained. Once out of sight of the audience, he relaxed, which gave him enough slack to free himself. He got out of boxes, milk churns, coffins and so on, and from locked restraint—handcuffs, prison cells, safes etc.—by using lock-picking wires which he concealed on his person, sometimes in the most intimate places. He was an expert on all types of locks, and was also a great showman, making even a simple escape seem sensational. While appearing for the week of 18 October 1926 at the Palace Theatre, Montreal, he entertained in his dressing room three students from McGill University. Houdini was then over 50, but very proud of his fine physique, essential to his act, and foolishly invited one of the boys to punch him in the stomach. The blow came before he had time to brace himself, and his abdomen was injured. The next week at Detroit a doctor diagnosed appendicitis, but Houdini insisted on carrying on with that evening's performance at the Garrick Theatre. The Water Torture Cell routine proved too much of a strain and he collapsed after making his final escape. The ruptured appendix was removed, but peritonitis developed and he died on 31 October 1926.

The Houston Sisters, born in Scotland, Renee and Billie Gribbens first appeared in Northern concert party and variety in 1920. In 1924 they were booked to appear at the Pavilion Theatre, Glasgow, in Tommy Lorne's revue *Froth*,

The Houston Sisters, 1926

which led to a Glasgow pantomime engagement the following Christmas, and their London variety debut in 1925. Their precocious boy and girl act was soon an established attraction of the leading London and provincial halls, and was included in the Royal Variety Performance at the Alhambra on 27 May 1926. When Billie retired from the stage in 1936, Renee worked a new double act with her husband Donald Stewart, appearing together in the Royal Variety Show of 1938. She went on to considerable success as an actress of both stage and screen, and is well known as a member of the BBC radio hen party 'Petticoat Line'.

Frankie Howerd, star comedian of low comedy and high camp. Born Francis Alexander Howerd in York in 1921, his early ambitions for a stage career came to nothing. With a nervous stammer, later his stock-in-trade, he failed a RADA audition and was turned down by Carroll Levis (qv) on four occasions. After leaving the army in April 1946 he appeared at the 'Stage Door Canteen' and was booked for the variety road show *For The Fun Of It*, starring Donald Peers. He made his professional stage debut with the show at the Empire, Sheffield, on 19 July 1946, competing for bottom of the bill with Max Bygraves. Now with enough experience to at least make his stammers and ooo's and arrr's seem like part of his act, he attended a BBC audition and was engaged as resident comedian for the top Sunday night radio show 'Variety Bandbox'. Assisted at the piano by Madame Blanchie Moore, the silent stooge and butt for Howerd's humour—'No don't mock. Poor soul, she might be one of your own'—he topped the bill at variety theatres when only the year before he had worked at the bottom. He toured as principal comedian in Bernard Delfont's revue *Ta Ra Rah Boom de Ay*, worked a summer season on Blackpool's central pier in 1949, and at Christmas appeared in Tom Arnold's pantomime *Puss In Boots* at the Empire, Liverpool. In the autumn of 1950 he starred with Binnie Hale and Nat Jackley in *Out of this World* at the Palladium, making his first Royal Variety appearance on 13 November the same year. 1951 marked his fourth year in 'Variety Bandbox' and his first BBC television series. At Christmas 1952 he returned to the London Palladium as Idle Jack in *Dick Whittington*. On 24 September 1953 he opened at the Prince of Wales Theatre in the Folies Bergère revue *Pardon My French* which ran for 18 months (758 performances). At Christmas 1955 he played Lord Fancourt Babberley in *Charley's Aunt* at the Globe Theatre and in 1957 was acclaimed for his performance as Bottom in *A Midsummer Night's Dream* at the Old Vic.

After more than 10 years of success Howerd's career turned sour. In October 1958 he appeared in his first musical *Mr Venus*, which flopped badly. Variety dates were hard to get and for the first time in years he found himself out of work. During 1961 he only worked for three months but, hardened by the experience, a new Howerd emerged. In 1962 he appeared in cabaret at the Establishment, the famous club in Greek Street founded in the wake of the successful revue *Beyond the Fringe* and the haunt of the *Private Eye* set. Frankie had no interest in politics and satire was not his line, so he just stood there and sent the audience up. They loved it, and Frankie was back at the top. In October 1963 he opened at the Strand Theatre as star of the American musical *A Funny Thing Happened On the Way to the Forum*. As the slave Pseudolus, Howerd brought to the role created in New York by Zero Mostel all the traditional comedy of a music-hall red-nosed comic. He got rave press notices and the show ran for 762 performances. In 1966 he scored a personal triumph in the Royal Variety Performance and the following year returned to the Prince of Wales in the revue *Way Out in Piccadilly*. He recorded the first of the successful 'Up Pompeii' series in 1969, inspired by his performance in *A Funny Thing Happened on the Way to the Forum*. The film version of *Up Pompeii* was shown in London in March 1971. Although, as Howerd himself put it 'not a great masterpiece of cultural art', it was good box office and was followed by *Up the Chastity Belt* and *Up the Front*. At Christmas 1973 he returned to the London Palladium playing Simple Simon in *Jack and the Beanstalk*. His front-cloth solo spot was vintage Howerd; only Madame Blanchie Moore was missing.

Roy Hudd, comedian, born in Croydon, Surrey, on 16 May 1933. After National Service in the RAF, he formed a double comedy act with Eddy Cunningham with whom he made his first appearance at the Nuffield Centre in 1958. On 27 October 1958 they appeared in a television programme 'Bid For Fame' and made their first variety stage appearance at the Metropolitan Music Hall, Edgware Road, on 17 November. Turning solo in late 1958, Roy Hudd took part in the television programme 'Tell it to the Marines' and appeared in pantomime for Emile Littler. The turning point in his career came in 1963 when he was engaged by Ned Sherrin for his now famous satirical television programme 'Not So Much a Programme, More a Way of Life'. The following year he was given his own BBC show 'Hudd' which was shown on television weekly for six weeks and was followed in 1966 by the TV mime film 'The Maladjusted Busker', which won the Press Prize at that year's Montreux Festival. Other television shows followed including 'The Illustrated Weekly Hudd' and the ITV 'Roy Hudd Show'. With a great personal love of music hall, Roy Hudd often includes in his stage and television acts tributes to some of the comedy greats, including George Formby and Max Miller. In 1968 he got rave notices for his portrayal of Dan Leno in the BBC television adaptation of 'Dan Leno His Book'. His West End debut as Jim Busby in *The Giveaway* at the Garrick Theatre in April 1969 did nothing to further his career but in April 1970 he appeared as principal comedian at the Palace Theatre in Danny La Rue's show *Danny at the Palace*. Although his solo spot was well reviewed by the press, he was rather

Roy Hudd, 1970

overshadowed by his somewhat larger than life 'leading lady' and has yet to realize his full comedy potential.

Alec Hurley, coster comedian born in 1871. He made his debut at the Parthenon Music Hall in 1882, singing Irish songs. He was then only 11 and in his own words was a 'bloody frost'. After a few years as a fair-booth boxer he returned to the halls in 1891, scoring a hit at the Gaiety Music Hall, Portsmouth, singing 'The Strongest Man in the World'. Billed as 'The Coster King', he achieved fame as a cockney comedian, presenting his act with more realism and less histrionics than the more famous Albert Chevalier. With a good tenor voice and a hearty manner, he sang earthy cockney songs, the most famous being 'The Lambeth Walk', written by E. W. Rogers. (This is not to be confused with Noël Gay's 'Lambeth Walk' written in 1937 for Lupino Lane in 'Me and My Girl', although it was inspired by Hurley's successful original.) Other Hurley songs included 'My London Country Lane', 'Toy' and 'I Ain't Nobody in Particular'.

Hurley toured Australia with Marie Loyd in 1901, opening in May at Harry Rickard's Opera House, Melbourne. They had been close friends since 1896 and finally married on 27 October 1906. The costers' courtship lasted 10 years, but the costers' honeymoon was soon over. Divorce proceedings were started in 1911 but they were still legally man and wife when Hurley died at Jack Straw's Castle, Hampstead, at the age of 42 on 6 December 1913.

Millie Hylton, born in 1868, one of a famous family of musical-comedy sisters. Adelaide Astor, Letty Lind, Fanny Dango and the incongruously stage-named Lydia Flopp.

Millie began her career in pantomime in 1883 and after a period at the Gaiety made her music-hall debut as a male impersonator in 1888. By the 1890s male impersonation was the vogue both on the halls and as a popular feature at the Gaiety burlesques. With Fanny Robina and Bessie Bonehill, Millie Hylton led the field, giving vigorous larger-than-life impersonations of buxom swells and butch mashers which by 1900 had been totally outmoded by the more natural style and elegance of Vesta Tilley (qv). Her songs included 'The Rowdy Dowdy Boys', 'The Last of the Dandies' and 'Dear Old Boys'. She died in 1920 at the age of 52.

Hayman and Franklin, American Jewish dialect comedians. Joe Hayman originally worked with his brother Jack as 'Hayman and Hayman'. In 1899 he married Mildred Franklin, a burlesque comedienne, and together they presented a Jewish comedy act. With the help of Harry Houdini (qv) they were booked to tour England for Thomas Barrasford in 1904. They spent most of the rest of their career in this country, becoming popular at the halls in London's East End, Leeds and Manchester. Joe Hayman was an early recording artiste with 'Abe Levi's Wedding Day', 'Cohen on the Telephone', and other sketches.

J

Nat Jackley, born in Sunderland on 16 July 1909. He first appeared with 'Eight Lancashire Lads' at the Hippodrome, Chesterfield, in 1920. In 1927 he teamed with his sister Joy, and together they made their first London appearance with a piano comedy routine at the Alhambra in 1928. Turning solo in 1931 he toured in variety and revue for Tom Arnold. In 1942 he appeared at the Palladium in George Black's *Best Bib and Tucker*, and in 1946 in *High Time* at the same theatre. He took part in the Royal Variety Performance of 4 November 1946.

Ellis Jackson, musical comedian, born in the USA on 29 April 1891. From an early age he worked a double act with his father as 'The Musical Jacksons', making his first appearance in 1897, and in London at the Palace, Hammersmith, in 1907. Later he appeared with a musical trio, toured a solo act in vaudeville and variety, and for five years did a double turn with Jack Blake as 'Jackson and Blake'. During the 1920s he played with a jazz band in London, toured with Nervo and Knox's road show, 'Young Bloods of Variety', and in 1930 joined Billy Cotton's band. He retired in 1950.

Joe Jackson, comedy tramp cyclist, born in Vienna in 1878. In 1894 he won the cycling championship of Austria and in 1896 worked a solo act touring the music halls of Europe. He first appeared in London in 1898, working a six-week season at the Westminster Royal Aquarium, and later as a Christmas attraction at the Crystal Palace. Originally he presented a straight cycling act, but during a tour of the USA he added comedy which went over well. Adopting a tramp make-up and costume he played his first important engagement as a cycling comedian at Hammerstein's Theatre, New York, and his 'Stealing a Bicycle' became a classic comedy mime routine. In 1913 he returned to London for a four-week season at the Palace Theatre, remaining on the bill for a total of 22 weeks. In 1935 he played the London Coliseum, Palladium and Holborn Empire, appearing in October in the Royal Variety Performance at the Palladium. In 1930 he was joined in his act by his son, with whom he appeared at the Coliseum in 1936. Joe Jackson died on 14 May 1942, but his act was carried on by Joe Jackson Junior, who appeared as a solo act in London in 1948.

Daisy James, comedienne who, as Daisy Martin, made her first appearance singing and performing a skipping-rope

Opposite: Millie Hylton, 1891

Left: Joe Hayman, 'Yours in Yiddish', 1910

Right: Nat Jackley, 1942

routine at the Kilburn Town Hall, and as Daisy James, at the Standard Music Hall in 1895. Her first song successes were 'Her Eyes That Shine Like Diamonds', 'My Fellow's a Hero', 'Mine's a Better One Than Yours', 'Young Men Specially Invited', 'There's a Good Time Coming By and By'; and dressed as Ophelia, she sang 'Oh Hamlet What Have You Done To Me'. She died on 7 January 1940.

Jimmy James, character comedian, born James Casey at Stockton-on-Tees in 1892. His father worked in the Northern and Midland halls as a clog dancer, introducing Jimmy into the act in 1904. Billed as 'Terry the Blue-Eyed Irish Boy' he did a song and dance act, but his career took on a sporting flavour when he joined Will Netta's juvenile singing troupe 'Jockeys', and later toured with Phil Rees's 'Stable Lads' and Clara Coverdale's 'Ten to One, On'. Forming his own sketch company he toured 'The Spare Room', a character study of a bridegroom who got drunk at the reception and found himself locked out on his wedding night. While playing at a hall in Sunderland in 1929 he was seen by an agent for George Black and booked to appear at the London Palladium. After the unexpected failure of Lucan and McShane (qv) at the Palladium in 1943, George Black engaged him to appear with Max Miller in a record-breaking

Jimmy James, 1930

variety bill which ran for five and a half months. Again at the Palladium in January 1948, it was only James's able support of Mickey Rooney that saved the show from complete disaster. (Originally booked for three weeks Rooney was replaced by Sid Field after only two.)

Famed in variety for his drunk routines, he was essentially a visual comic, with cigarette-smoking facial contortions. For years his act relied on three routines: Drunk, Chipster and Shoebox. With these he was assisted by two stooges, the gormless Hutton Conyers and Bretton Woods. Conyers—'Here you are putting it around that I'm barmy'.—was originally played by James's brother-in-law Jack Darby, later by his son, Cass James, and between 1956 and 1959 by Roy Castle. Bretton Woods was played by James's nephew, Jack Casey. On 2 November 1953 James gave his famous 'Chipster Lecture' on the art and occupational hazards of chipping potatoes, in the Royal Variety Performance at the London Coliseum. His later years were a fight against ill health and insolvency. He continued to tour in variety, at that time supporting the latest rock-and-roll act, and to appear on television, co-starring at one time as Bernard Bresslaw's boxing manager in the BBC series 'Meet the Champ'. His last West End stage appearance was at the Comedy Theatre in January 1964 in Daniel Farson's abortive revival of old-time music hall 'Nights at the Comedy'. He suffered a heart attack later that year and died in 1965.

George Jessel, famous vaudevillian born in New York on 3 April 1898. He first appeared at the Imperial Theatre, New York, in 1912, working a singing trio with Jack Weiner and Walter Winchell as 'Leonard, Lawrence and McKinley—The Imperial Trio'. Jessel and Winchell then joined Eddie Cantor and others in Gus Edwards's 'School Days', Cantor and Jessel later touring in vaudeville as a double act. With Lou Edwards, Jessel made his first appearance at the Victoria Palace, London, on 1 July 1916, as 'Two Patches from a Crazy Quilt'. Following a variety tour of the UK they returned to London to appear at the London Music Hall, Shoreditch. On his return to the USA, he toured in vaudeville with his 'Hello Momma' monologue act, appeared for the Shuberts in their 'Passing Shows' at the Winter Garden, starred in George Jessel's *Trouble of 1919*, and as *The Jazz Singer* on Broadway. In 1930 he again teamed with Eddie Cantor to break all records at the Palace Theatre, New York, and in 1941 starred with Sophie Tucker in *The High Kickers*, a musical by Jerry Ross and Harry Ruby. Later he directed many Hollywood films, and died in 1969.

Jewel and Warriss, leading comedy double act of the 1940s and 1950s. Their early careers as light comedians ran on similar lines. Jimmy Jewel, born in Sheffield on 4 December 1909, worked with his father, a well-known and popular Yorkshire comedian, from the age of 10. His first London

Jewel and Warriss, 1950

appearance was at the Bedford Music Hall, Camden Town, in 1925; he then worked as a single turn between 1928 and 1934. His cousin, Ben Warriss, was born in Sheffield on 29 May 1909, making his first stage appearance on 19 October 1919 at the Hippodrome, Stockport. From the age of 10 to 14 he toured in revue, making his London debut at the Bedford, Camden Town, in 1920. He later broadcast from Savoy Hill in the 'Ridgeway Parade' programme, and worked a black-faced act on tour, and in London at the Piccadilly Theatre with the Alexander and Mose Minstrel Show.

Jewel and Warriss teamed in 1934 to appear in revue for J. D. Robertson. In 1937 they toured Australia, and as a double variety act toured the UK for Moss Empires. When Moss later refused to increase their terms to £35 a week they terminated their contract. Later that year Jewel and Warriss scored a great success on a variety bill in Glasgow, and Moss Empires had second thoughts, giving them a new contract on their own terms which had now jumped to £100 a week. This was the turning point of their career, and they soon established themselves as the leading double act of variety, revue and pantomime. They headlined in two shows at the London Palladium, *Gangway* (1943) and *High Time* (1946), appeared in the Royal Variety Performance of 1946, visited the USA in 1948, and later toured the UK with their own road show. Between 1942 and 1948 they starred in five pantomimes for Howard and Wyndham at the Opera House, Blackpool. Their hit radio show 'Up the Pole' made them popular with millions, and their many television and variety shows kept them on top throughout the 1950s. By the mid-1960s their cross-talking patter act, which had changed little in 25 years, was rather old hat. Engagements came mainly from the new-style Northern clubs, and then some of the old ones. Finally, after 34 years, the Jewel and Warriss partnership came to an end in 1967.

Jimmy Jewel started a new career as a character actor, notably as Eli Pledge in ITV's successful comedy show 'Nearest and Dearest' in which he co-starred with Hylda Baker, and as Tommy Butler, a retired railway worker, in ITV's 'Spring and Autumn', first screened in July 1973. In 1975 he appeared with the National Theatre Company at the Old Vic in a highly successful comedy drama *The Comedians* which, early in 1976, transferred to the West End. Ben Warriss spends much of his time looking after his business interests and working for charity as an active member of the Grand Order of Water Rats. In 1972 he did a 20-week summer season at the Winter Gardens Pavilion, Blackpool, acting as Chairman with Barney Colehan's stage production of the BBC television success 'The Good Old Days', starring Tessie O'Shea.

K

The Kafka, Stanley and Mae Four, American aerial and tight-wire walkers. Paul Kafka and Charles Stanley both spent their early youth with various circuses, teaming as a double high-wire act in 1916. Following vaudeville and circus tours of the USA, Canada and South America, they made their first appearance in England in 1922. On their return to America in 1924 Stanley married ex-Ziegfeld girl Florence Mae, and as 'Kafka, Stanley and Mae', appeared with the Ringling-Barnum Circus, and toured the leading vaudeville circuits. Following appearances at the London Palladium in 1927, they toured Europe, New Zealand, Australia and South Africa, returning to London in 1930. In July 1932 Italian Tony del Borelle joined the act and as the 'Kafka, Stanley and Mae Four' they appeared in the Royal Variety Performance of 1934.

Fred Karno, showman whose slapstick sketch company made his name synonymous with the absurd. Born Frederick Westcott in Exeter on 26 March 1886, he made his first music-hall appearance at the Crown and Cushion, a free-and-easy, in Nottingham in 1882, as Leanaro, the 'lady' acrobat of the acrobatic duo 'Olvene and Leanaro'. Turning solo, he did a circus act on the horizontal bar and double trapeze, working 20 shows a day, also acting in sketches, and as a ringmaster and a clown. Using the name of Alto, in 1888 he teamed with Robert Aubney and another partner as the acrobatic trio 'Zulia, Aubney and Alto'. Following a successful season at the Scotia Music Hall, Glasgow, they toured Europe appearing with Oscar Carre's Circus in Cologne, Flayen's Circus in Rotterdam, Van Haarlem's in Amsterdam, and in variety at the Eden Theatre, Brussels. Back in London he teamed with Ted Tysall and Bob Sewell, and was engaged by Maurice de Frece to deputise for an acrobatic act, 'The Three Carnos', at the Metropolitan, Edgware Road. Whatever the abilities of the original Carnos, Fred and his partners went over well as knockabout acrobats. Billed as 'The Three Karnos', they were held over for a month at the Metropolitan, followed by a season at the Westminster Royal Aquarium. In 1894 they appeared for a week at Barnard's Music Hall, Portsmouth, on a bill topped by Jem Mace, the boxer. At the last moment Mace was taken ill and Fred Karno and comedian Tom Leamore agreed to fill his spot in the old pantomime sketch 'Love in a Tub'. It went over well and some months later Karno repeated it at the Gaiety Music Hall, Birmingham, and the Fred Karno sketch company was born.

'Hilarity', the first original Karno sketch, was followed in 1895 by 'Jail Birds', 'Early Birds' and 'The New Woman's Club', the last ending with Fred as 'dame' doing his old trapeze routine from a chandelier hanging from the centre of the stage. The early sketches were produced at the Paragon, Mile End, but by 1897 he was an established music-hall attraction, fully booked until 1899. By the early 1900s Karno had five companies on the road, operating from the so-called 'Fred Karno Fun Factory' in Camberwell, London. Billed as 'Fred Karno's Speechless Comedians', his early sketches were pure pantomime. His first spoken production 'His Majesty's Guests', with book by Dan Leno's old script writer Herbert Darnley and music by Dudley Powell, was presented as the Christmas attraction at the Palace Theatre, Manchester, in 1901. It gave Fred Kitchen (qv), one of Karno's greatest comedians, his first big chance, jumping from a small part as a page boy to a triumph as principal comedian. The sketch was such a success that it was rebooked for Manchester the following year and a shorter version toured the music halls as 'The Dandy Thieves'.

Many great comedians worked for Karno, including Billy Bennett, Syd Walker, Max Miller, Charlie Chaplin, Sandy Powell, Bobby Howes, and Flanagan and Allen, but none is more closely associated with him than Fred Kitchen. About 1912 Karno produced a Jewish comedy sketch 'Moses and Son', which created for Kitchen the character of Perkins, who over the years turned up on many sketches and introduced Kitchen's famous catch phrase 'Meredith, we're in.' Karno's most famous sketch, 'Mumming Birds', was first presented at the Star Music Hall, Bermondsey, in 1904. Originally entitled 'Twice Nightly', the name was changed to 'Mumming Birds' to avoid confusion when it played once-nightly variety. When in 1905 one of Karno's troupes performed the sketch at Hammerstein's Variety Theatre, New York, the name was changed again to 'A Night in an English Music Hall'. Originally booked in New York for an eight-week season, it ran on and off for over nine years, with a second company touring the smaller vaudeville theatres.

ISLINGTON EMPIRE

(Adjoining the Royal Agricultural Hall Upper Street, N.)

Lessee and Proprietor ... ... WALTER GIBBONS.
Manager ... ... WILL SPEARMAN.

TWICE NIGHTLY at 6.45 & 9.10
MONDAY, MAY 9th, 1904

The First Appearance in London of the greatest production put upon any Stage.

FRED KARNO'S

Celebrated Company of Comedians,
Including

FRED KITCHEN,
COSSIE NOEL and
Band OF FIRST REGIMENT Caucasian Guards

Supported by the most Powerful Company ever seen at any Vaudeville Theatre. First Time on the Variety Stage, Introducing a New and Original Musical Comedy Extravaganza, in Three Episodes, Entitled—

SATURDAY TO MONDAY

Written by FRED KARNO, CHAS. BALDWIN, and FRED KITCHEN.
Music Composed by DUDLEY POWELL.

Fred Karno, 1882

Fred Karno took over the lease of Taggs Island in the Thames near Hampton Court in 1920 and built his famous 'Karsino' at a cost of £70,000. It opened with the usual Karno publicity on Sunday, 20 May 1913, and closed with Karno's bankruptcy in 1926. By the First World War Fred Karno was a household name for the farcical and absurd. The phrase 'Fred Karno's Army' became a familiar journalese, supplying the troops with one of their most popular marching songs, sung to the hymn tune 'The Church's One Foundation':

We are Fred Karno's army,
A jolly lot are we,
Fred Karno is our captain,
Charles Chaplin our OC
And when we get to Berlin,
The Kaiser he will say,
Hoch, Hoch, Mein Gott,
What a jolly fine lot,
Are the boys of Company A.

After the war Karno collaborated with Harry Gratton in producing the *1922 Revue*, which toured the Moss Empires. Another successful Karno show of the period was *The Love Match*, a mixture of comedy and melodrama with Billy Danvers and Jean Alliston (Mrs Tommy Handley), supported by a pack of 20 foxhounds, live rabbits, ferrets, four thoroughbred greys and a 'talking' horse. With the crash of Karsino, Fred again toured the variety theatres with 'Mumming Birds'. It appeared in Paris, and was the Christmas attraction at the Crystal Palace, London in 1928. In 1932 he produced 'Karno's Crazy Comics' which later that year formed the basis of George Black's 'Crazy Show' at the London Palladium. The revue *Real Life*, which was to be Karno's last stage production, opened at Leicester on 26

December 1935, followed by a tour of the Moss Empires. In 1935 Karno formed his own film company which screened its one and only film *Don't Rush Me* on 3 January 1936. Produced by Norman Lee and starring Robb Wilton, it was well received by the critics but failed at the box office. It was the end of Fred Karno. He retired to Lilliput in Dorset where he ran a wine shop until his death on 18 September 1941.

Danny Kaye, comedian and singer, born David Daniel Kaminski, New York, on 18 January 1913. He first entertained at summer camps in the Catskill Mountains. Following a variety tour of the Far East, he worked as stooge for comedian and dancer Nick Long, with whom he made his first London appearance in cabaret at the Dorchester Hotel in 1938. Back in New York in 1939 he appeared in Max Liebmann and Sylvia Fine's *Straw Hat Revue*. While appearing at La Martinique night club he was seen by Moss Hart, who was so impressed by his unique delivery of comedy songs that he wrote a special part for Kaye into Kurt Weill's musical *Lady In The Dark*. Starring Gertrude Lawrence and Victor Mature, it opened at the Alvin Theatre on 23 January 1941 and the unknown Kaye scored a tremendous hit with the tongue-twisting song 'Tchaikovsky'. When *Lady In The Dark* closed after 388 performances, Kaye starred in Cole Porter's *Let's Face It*, which opened at the Imperial Theatre on 29 October 1941. Kaye's hit of the show was 'Melody in Four F', interpolated into Porter's score by Danny's wife, Sylvia Fine. After a series of successful films, Kaye made his London variety debut at the London Palladium in February 1948 and was hailed as the greatest personal success in the history of variety for 30 years. On 1 November 1948 he appeared in the Royal Variety Performance and in April 1949 returned for his second triumphant variety season at the London Palladium.

During the next 20 years he made films in Hollywood, played Noah on Broadway in Richard Rogers's musical 'Two By Two', and travelled the world to appear in charity concerts which to date have raised 4½ million dollars for UNICEF. Although not featuring in variety in Britain since an engagement at the Palladium in 1955, he has appeared in various TV shows including playing Mr Darling—Captain Hook, in a specially made TV musical version of 'Peter Pan', with music and lyrics by Leslie Bricusse and Anthony Newley, first screened on 29 February 1976.

Irving Kaye, whistling violinist, born Isidor Kalusky in Kimberley, South Africa. Coming to London, he made his first variety appearance with a tango band at the Victoria Palace in September 1932. Later he worked in variety with a partner as 'Kaye and Edna', and whistling to his own violin, accompaniment, made his solo debut at the Players' Theatre, 'Late Joys', Covent Garden, on 25 May 1938. He toured in musical comedy in singing comedy roles, Blinky Bill in *Belle of New York*, etc., and broadcast in 'Band Waggon', 'Workers' Playtime' and 'Variety Bandbox'.

Annette Kellerman, the original 'Million Dollar Mermaid', born in Sydney, Australia, in 1888. She came to England at the age of 18 to play the London Hippodrome with her swimming and diving act and went on to the USA in 1907, making her American bow at the White City Amusement Park, Chicago, playing 55 shows a week. At Boston she caused a sensation with her tight-fitting bathing costume, and seen by B. F. Keith was booked to tour in vaudeville, making her first New York appearance at Proctor's Fifth Avenue Music Hall. Billed as 'The Diving Venus', she was in the 'Big Show of 1917' at the New York Hippodrome.

The Esther Williams of her day, she made a series of

Danny Kaye, London Palladium, 1948

successful swimming films, the first, *Neptune's Daughter of the Gods*, dating from 1916. She retired during the 1930s but in 1952 was the subject of the MGM film *The Million Dollar Mermaid* with Esther Williams swimming the title role. She died in Southport, Australia, on 5 November 1975.

Marie Kendall, music-hall comedienne and popular principal boy. Born in London in 1873, she made her first appearance at the age of five, billed as 'Baby Chester', at the Pavilion, Mile End, and for the next 10 years played pathetic, tear-jerking child roles in melodrama. At 15 she played principal boy to John 'Humanity' Lawson's (qv) Abanazer in a touring production of *Aladdin*. Another notable pantomime appearance of her early career was Dandini in *Cinderella* at the Pavilion, Mile End, with Alice and Gracie Lloyd as principal boy and girl. She had her first success in variety in 1894, appearing for 16 consecutive weeks at the Bedford Music Hall, Camden Town, singing 'I'm One of the Girls', a 'masher' song written by Charles Deane as the feminist reply to his own current hit, 'I'm One of the Boys'. Marie made the song the hit of London and was booked to appear the following Christmas at the Britannia Theatre, Hoxton. At the Bedford she earned 30 shillings a week as principal boy, at the Britannia £15 a week and, as George Foster later wrote in *The Spice of Life*, 'In two years Marie Kendall worked her salary up to £100 a week. She was the first and only woman who appeared at seven halls each night in London for over a month.' She had many good songs to her credit, including 'Oh, Said the Judge', 'Three Boys', 'Why Don't You Marry the Girl?' and 'Did Your First Wife Ever Do That?', but her greatest success was 'Just Like the Ivy', which she sang throughout the UK, America, Australia (52 weeks in 1925) and South Africa. One of the original stars of the 'Vintage Variety Company', which began a long tour at the London, Shoreditch, in March 1931, she appeared in the Royal Variety

Marie Kendall, 1905

Performance at the London Palladium in 1932. She retired in 1939 but continued to make occasional nostalgic appearances until a few years before her death in 1964 at the ripe old age of 91.

Neil Kenyon, comedian and Scottish character actor, born in 1873. He graduated to the halls by way of the old Scottish fit-up companies, making his first London appearance at the Pavilion in 1904. As a character comedian he is remembered for broad dialect monologues. 'The Stationmaster of Dunrobin', 'The Postie of Dunrobin', and 'The Poet of Dunrobin', and for the songs 'The Ne'er dae Weel', 'The Caddie' and 'The Elder of the Kirk', which were a wee bit dour for Southern tastes. During the 1914–18 war he introduced a number of patriotic monologues into his act, notably 'The Men Who Paved the Way', a tribute to the men of Mons. He retired from the variety stage in 1928, dying at his home in Park Avenue, Golders Green, on 1 June 1946.

Joe Keppel *See* **Wilson, Keppel and Betty**

Bobbie Kimber, ventriloquist and female impersonator. Born Robert Kimberley in Birmingham on 27 May 1918. He began his career as a straight ventriloquist in the style of Johnson Clark, making his debut at the Theatre Royal, West Bromwich, in 1935. He first presented his act in drag during a concert party season at Weston-super-Mare in 1937, and in

Neil Kenyon, 'The Postie of Dunrobin'

Bobbie Kimber with Augustus Peabody

London for the first time as a 'woman ventriloquist' at the Prince of Wales Theatre in 1939. After army service he appeared as an Ugly Sister in Jack Hylton's *Cinderella* at the Adelphi Theatre, London, and with his doll, Augustus Peabody, played the main variety theatres and appeared on television and radio. So convincing was his female impersonation that both James Agate and Hannen Swaffer wrote him up as a woman. In 1947 he became the first female impersonator to appear in a Royal Variety Performance, and was on the bill at the London Palladium during the famous Danny Kaye season. He has now retired from professional stage work but made a rare appearance at the British Music Hall Society's 'Cavalcade of Drag', held at the Horseshoe Hotel, Tottenham Court Road, in April 1969.

Hetty King, male impersonator, born in 1883. She first appeared at the London, Shoreditch, in 1897. Working as a male impersonator from 1905, she topped bills all over the world as a debonair man-about-town, and as the soldiers and sailors of both world wars. Singing her two greatest songs, 'All the Nice Girls Love a Sailor' and 'Piccadilly', she continued working in variety and summer shows with remarkable verve and vitality until shortly before her death at the age of 89 on 28 September 1972.

Pat Kirkwood, vocalist of variety, musical comedy, revue and pantomime. Born in Manchester on 24 February 1921, she first appeared in variety as 'The Schoolgirl Songstress' at the Argyle, Birkenhead on 20 April 1936. One of the finest principal boys, her first London appearance was as Dandini in *Cinderella* at the Princes Theatre in 1937. In 1939 she appeared in *Black Velvet* at the London Hippodrome, followed by revues at the Palladium. Acted in a number of Hollywood films, in which her screen roles have included Vesta Tilley and Marie Lloyd.

Fred Kitchen, popular sketch comedian and one of the greatest stars of Fred Karno's company (qv). Born in 1872, he was the son of Richard H. Kitchen, a one-time Shakespearean actor with whom Fred made his first appearance at the 'Old Blood Tub', as the Bower Saloon in Lambeth was popularly known. One of the earliest of 'Fred Karno's Speechless Comedians', in 1901 he appeared as principal comic in 'His Majesty's Guest' at the Palace Theatre, Manchester, going on to fame as Perkins in 'Moses and Son', 'Mumming Birds' and 'The Baliffs', which introduced his famous catch phrase 'Meredith, we're in'. Later he appeared on the halls in a variety of characters, notably Private Potts, and presented a series of mock-serious lectures, 'How to cook a sausage', etc. He died in 1950.

R. G. Knowles, Richard George Knowles, the self-styled 'Very Peculiar American Comedian'. Born in Hamilton, Ontario, Canada, on 7 October 1858, he was brought up in the USA and made his first professional stage appearance in Chicago in 1878, playing continuous vaudeville from 2pm until midnight. After developing his own 'very peculiar' style of comedy, which amounted to a verbal assault on the audience, he was booked by William Mitchell to appear at the Olympic Vaudeville Theatre, then the leading variety house of Chicago. Describing his comedy style in his autobiography, *A Modern Columbus*, Knowles wrote:

> I told a joke, and if the audience laughed at it I ridiculed them for being entertained with such consummate ease. If they did not laugh I jeered at their lack of appreciation and inability to observe real humour. When their mirth was not spontaneous I feigned anger at their dilatoriness. Did they anticipate me, I was equally annoyed because they were too quick. Summing up, I pointed out that if they did not laugh, well, they were losing money, on the other hand, if they indulged too hilariously, they were getting more than they were entitled to get so I invited them to go to the box office and pay up the difference.

In 1886 he appeared at Charles Cole's Parlour Opera House, Bridgeport, Connecticut. In 1887 he toured with the Austin Australian Novelty Company, run by the Austin sisters, an English trapeze act, and the following year appeared with Haverly's Minstrels at the Grand Opera House, Wallack's Theatre and Niblo's Gardens, New York. He first appeared in England at the Trocadero Music Hall, London, on 13 June 1891, at the bottom of a bill topped by Fanny Leslie with George Beauchamp and Charles Chaplin Senior. Also making her London debut on that bill was Knowles's wife, Winifred E. Johnson, a coon singer and 'past mistress of the banjo'. He was not exactly an instant success, as the audience was slow to take to Knowles's brash American drollery, but after ten minutes of 'enthusiastic silence' he managed to break the ice and left the stage to applause. His stage appearance was as individual and distinctive as his quick-fire repartee he played the halls in a crushed top hat, long shabby black frock-coat, high winged collar and bow-tie, big boots and white trousers. His singing voice has been compared to the caw of a crow but as all comedians sang, sing he did. His most successful song was 'Girly, Girly', written by Jerry Cohan of the American vaudeville act 'Jerry Cohan and his Six Irish Coleens', the father of George M. Cohan. After his first Trocadero

Hetty King, 1926

Fred Kitchen, 1922

93

R.G. Knowles, 'The Very Peculiar American Comedian'

engagement, which lasted a total of 68 weeks, he appeared at the Empire, Leicester Square, on Easter Monday 1892 and broke all records for a solo act by remaining on the bill, except for a week at Brighton, for 73 consecutive weeks. Even this marathon was exceeded later when he played the Tivoli, London, for two years and ten months. Knowles made his home in England, and over the next 25 years became very much a part of British music hall, although he never changed his original American style of comedy. He toured extensively throughout the UK, Australia, New Zealand, South Africa, and Ceylon, as well as making appearances in the USA and Canada. He died in England on 1 January 1919.

Jimmy Knox *See* **Nervo and Knox**

Harry Korris, comedian, well-known on radio and in variety with Bobbie Vincent and Cecil Fredericks as 'The Hippodrome Trio'. Born in Douglas, Isle of Man, on 6 October 1891, he began his career with a pierrot troupe in 1901. From 1931 to 1939 he appeared on Blackpool South Pier with 'Arcadia Follies', which broadcast regularly. During the war he became well-known in the BBC's 'Happidrome' programme, and later toured the variety theatres with a stage version of the show.

L

The Great Lafayette, magician and illusionist, born Sigmund Neuberger in Germany in 1872. He was brought up in the USA and during the California gold rush of the 1890s ran a tented dance hall and presented a crude form of music-hall entertainment. By permission of the United States Congress, he changed his name to 'The Great Lafayette' and made his first appearance in England in 1892. By 1900 he had established his magic show as a number one music-hall attraction, touring with 40 artistes, and a menagerie of animals including a lion, which appeared in his spectacular illusion 'The Lion's Bride'. Early in 1911 he signed a contract to appear the following Christmas at the London Coliseum at £1,000 a week and after announcing that he was fully booked for the next ten years, left London to tour the UK.

In May 1911 he opened at the Empire, Edinburgh, built in 1891 by Sir Edward Moss as the first of a chain of Moss Empires. The theatre was then being prepared for the first Royal Command Variety Performance, planned for the Coronation visit to Scotland of King George V in July 1911. During the second house on 9 May 1911, while 'The Lion's Bride' was in progress, a great burst of flame rose from the stage. So startling was its suddenness that the audience thought at first it was part of the illusion. One of Lafayette's negro attendants threw himself on the blaze in an attempt to stop it spreading, but the harem setting of hanging tapestries and oriental trimmings was soon a blazing inferno. The safety curtain was quickly lowered, and although the roof was soon burning, the fire was confined backstage and the audience left without loss of life. Alas, The Great Lafayette and eight members of his company died in the blaze. His show passed to his great friend Lalla Selbini of the 'Selbini Bicycle Troupe' (qv). After the loss of the Empire, Edinburgh, the first Royal Variety Performance was held at the Palace Theatre, London.

Lew Lake and Bob Morris, sketch artistes famous as 'Nobbler and Jerry, the Bloomsbury Burglars'. Bob Morris,

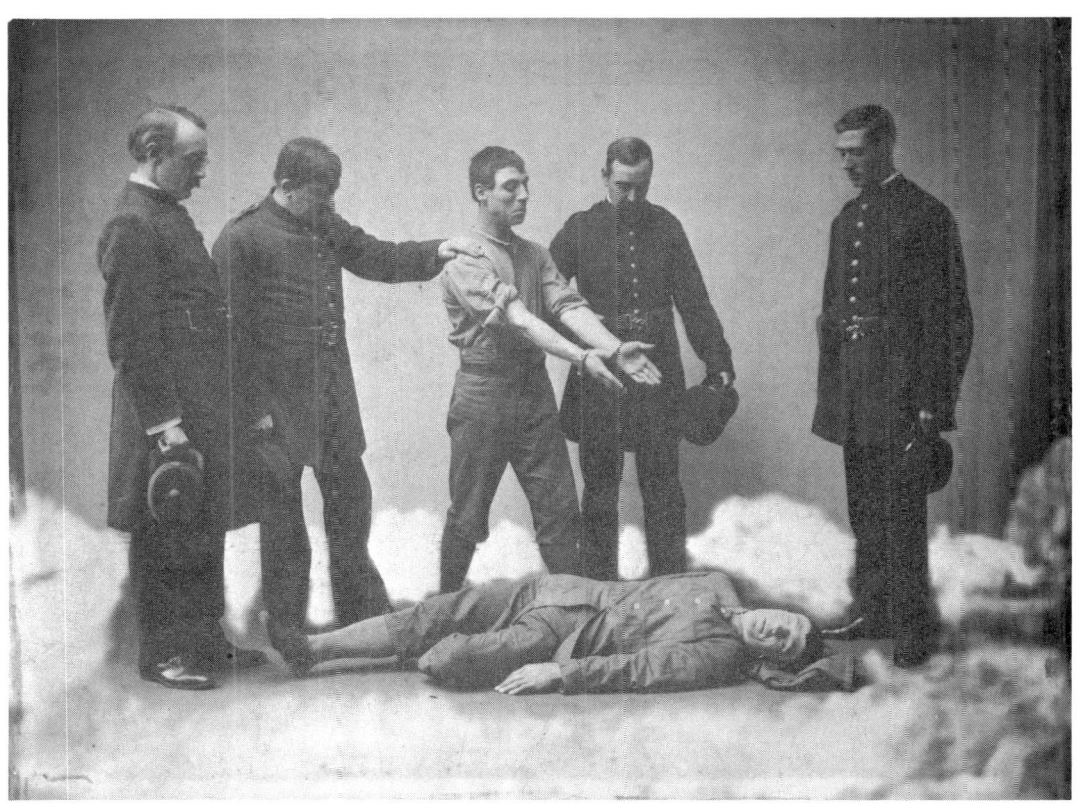

Lew Lake and Bob Morris, the end of 'Nobbler and Jerry, the Bloomsbury Burglars'

Danny La Rue, 1970

born 1866, and Lew Lake, born 1874, began their careers together, running a fairground boxing booth and going on to the halls as 'Nobbler and Jerry' in about 1902. On the slapstick lines of the later 'Keystone Cops', their 'Bloomsbury Burglars' sketch became a popular music-hall attraction with an exciting chase and rooftop fight, which added the phrase 'stick it Jerry' to the language, and for some unknown reason made 'Jerry' the nickname for the Germans of both wars. Lew Lake died in 1939 and Bob Morris in 1945. In 1941 Lew Lake's son of the same name became the manager of Collins Music Hall, Islington, where for over 20 years an oil painting by George Lazar of 'Nobbler and Jerry' hung over the bar.

Lana, female impersonator, born Alan Kemp on 5 February 1938. He first appeared at the '50' Club, Soho, in 1957, and the following year played at the famous Paris night club, Carrousel. During the next nine years he appeared in 37 different countries, and on his return to England in 1968 performed in major clubs up and down the country. In 1969 he appeared in summer season at the Tower Theatre, Yarmouth, and was such a success that he was rebooked to appear in his own show the following year. He toured the west coast of America in 1974.

Danny La Rue, female impersonator, born Daniel Patrick Carroll in Cork in July 1928. For him the die was cast early: while still at school he appeared as Juliet in *Romeo and Juliet*. He never aimed as high again, but although lacking the skill of Barbette, the finesse of Julian Eltinge, or the voice of Bert Errol, he succeeded in becoming the most successful and widely accepted female impersonator in the history of British variety.

At 17 he joined the navy, spending most of his three years' service as a member of the ship's concert party. He then toured for the next eight years as a chorus boy in revue, worked with drag shows such as *Forces in Petticoats*, and appeared in pantomime. While playing at the Irving Theatre, London, during 1958, he was seen by Charles Landeau and booked for cabaret at the fashionable Churchill's Club. From there he went to even greater success at Winston's, and then opened his own club in Hanover Square. With a small company—including the smallest of them all, Ronnie Corbett—he presented a host of outrageously brassy females, burlesquing the rather aggressive women of the period, epitomised by the stalwart of the Conservative Party, Lady Cynthia Grope. In 1966 he reached his widest audience to date with the pre-London tour of Ned Sherrin's musical *Come Spy With Me*, which went on to break all box office records for its 12 months' run at the Whitehall Theatre. At Christmas 1967 he starred with his long-time Ugly Sister, Alan Haynes, in *Queen Passionella and the Sleeping Beauty*, at the Golders Green Hippodrome. It was a great success, and no fault of Danny's that the pantomime closed the theatre (it is now a BBC television studio). He made his first record in 1968, singing the old Randolph Sutton favourite 'On Mother Kelly's Doorstep'.

The theatrical cliché 'record breaking' was now automatically applied to the billing of Danny La Rue, and when in 1968 *Queen Passionella* was re-staged at the Saville Theatre, London, it ran for six months, the longest run in the history of West End pantomime. On 19 November 1969 he took part in the Royal Variety Performance from the London Palladium and if not the first female impersonator to appear in a Royal Show, as widely stated at the time, he was certainly the most glamorous. That year he was voted by the Variety Club as Show Business Personality of 1969. He appeared as 'Charley's Aunt' on BBC television early in

George Lashwood, 1904

1970, and on 9 April that year opened in *Danny La Rue at the Palace*. The show ran for two years and took over a million pounds at the box office. At Christmas 1972 he played his 16th pantomime, *Queen of Hearts*, at the Palace Theatre, Manchester, and in December 1973 returned to the West End in the *Danny La Rue Show* at the Prince of Wales Theatre. Although fond of treating the press and public to an 'Oh what a butch boy am I' routine and threatening to give up drag, he is likely to remain a 'show business phenomenon' for just as long as he hangs on to his 'bristols'. He again appeared in drag at Christmas 1975 in the pantomime *Queen Danniella* at the London Casino.

George Lashwood, comedian and descriptive vocalist. Born in 1863, he made his first provincial stage appearance in 1883 and his London debut at the Middlesex Music Hall in 1889. A distinguished looking man who always dressed in the height of fashion, he was known by the splendid title 'The Beau Brummell of the Halls'. He had a very successful career introducing many popular songs, often of a patriotic nature in the style of Charles Godfrey. These included 'The Death and Glory Boys', 'The Gallant Twenty-First', 'Where are the Lads from the Village Tonight?', and 'Motherland'. In a more romantic mood were 'Dear Mr Admiral', Riding on Top of the Car', 'I've been out with Charlie Brown', 'Sea-Sea-Sea', and the best remembered 'After the Ball' and 'In the Twi-Twi-Twilight'. Lashwood retired from the stage after the First World War to farm in Worcestershire, and died on 20 January 1942.

Sir Harry Lauder, 'The Laird of the Halls', born Portobello, Scotland, on 4 August 1870. After 10 years down the pit of Allenton Colliery, he made his first professional appearance with a concert party in 1892, later touring in variety for Moss and Thornton. In 1896 he toured with Donald Munro's Northern Concert Party, and then teamed with violinist Mackenzie Murdock to form their own variety company as 'The Lauder-Murdock Concert Party'.

He made his first appearance in England at Denis J.

PHILCO SERIES 3445 B   MR. HARRY LAUDER.

Laurel and Hardy, London Palladium, 1947

Clark's famous variety theatre, the Argyle, Birkenhead, on 13 June 1896, not as a Scottish singer but as an Irish comedian. So successful was his Hibernian performance that the Liverpool-Irish audience clamoured for more. But when Clark pestered Lauder to go on again during the second half, he had to admit that he had exhausted his Irish repertoire. However, he agreed to take a chance with his usual act, and as an Irish comedian singing Scottish songs was an even greater success. Encouraged by this he decided to venture further south but was warned that success in Liverpool was one thing but London meant 'sudden death' to Scottish comics. On 18 March 1900 Lauder watched Dan Leno's act at the Empire, Glasgow, and on the theory that if Leno could earn £100 a week singing cockney songs in Glasgow, he could get £20 singing Scottish songs in London, he took the plunge. A week later he made his first London appearance as an 'extra turn' at Gatti's, Westminster Bridge Road, and was an overnight success. The next morning he was besieged by variety agents offering contracts, many of which he signed at terms he later regretted. By the time he left London he was booked for over six years' work. Setting up his home in Tooting, he appeared at up to four London halls a night for seven months of each year.

The greatest songs of his career include 'I Love a Lassie', first sung in pantomime at the Theatre Royal, Glasgow, in 1905, 'Roamin' in the Gloamin' 'Stop Your Ticklin' Jock', and 'Keep Right on to the End of the Road'. The most internationally celebrated of all British music-hall stars, he made his first appearance in America at the New York Theatre, Times Square, in November 1907, and for the next 30 years remained one of vaudeville's greatest box-office attractions. Under the management of William Morris, the famous agent for Klew and Erlinger who later formed his own 'American Music Hall' circuit, Lauder made 22 tours of the USA, lasting from five weeks to a year in duration. In February 1914 he made his first tour of Australia, appearing for a month at the Theatre Royal, Sydney, followed by another month's standing-room-only business in Melbourne. The start of the Great War in August 1914 cast a shadow over the tour but he went on to New Zealand and made another nationwide tour of the USA. Back in London in 1916 he starred with Ethel Levey in the revue *Three Cheers* at the Shaftesbury Theatre, and when the show closed Lauder enlisted for active service. Then aged 47 he was turned down by the War Office, which agreed instead that he should entertain the troops at the front line. For months he gave up to six concerts a day, singing at each 10 to 15 of his old songs. When the USA entered the war in 1917 he braved the Atlantic U-boats to return to New York for a war fund-raising concert which became known as 'Harry Lauder's Million Pound Fund'. For his outstanding contribution to the war effort he was knighted by George V in April 1919. Later that year he returned to Australia via the USA and in 1920 toured South Africa. He visited the Far East in 1925. After an absence from London of three years he topped the bill at the London Palladium in December 1930. Following an engagement at the Alhambra in October 1934, he made his last tour of the UK and retired in 1935. During the Second World War Sir Harry again entertained the troops and was President of the Scottish Regional Committee of ENSA. He died on 26 February 1950.

Stan Laurel of Laurel and Hardy, comedian famed as the timid partner of Oliver Hardy. Born Stanley Jefferson in Ulverston, Lancashire, on 16 June 1890. His father, Arthur Jefferson, took over the Scotia Music Hall, Glasgow, which was then being run as the Metropole Theatre, in 1901. There he staged melodrama of the most lurid kind, and there Stan Laurel made his first stage appearance in 1906. The following year he joined Fred Karno (qv), making his first London appearance at the Hackney Empire in 1908. He had his greatest success in the sketch 'Jimmy the Fearless', playing the name part originally offered by Karno to Charlie Chaplin, who turned it down. Laurel went to America with the Karno company in 1910 and in 1913 went into vaudeville, working as a solo comedian until 1918, when he went to Hollywood to make films for Universal, Vitograph, and Hal Roach. He worked with Oliver Hardy from 1925, making the first film of their famous partnership, *Putting the Pants on Philip*, in 1927. Between 1941 and 1945 Laurel and Hardy travelled over 200,000 miles entertaining American and British troops, and after the war made a world tour of personal appearances. They opened at the London Palladium on 10 March 1947, followed by a variety tour of Great Britain. They made their last film, *Atoll K*, in 1951. Oliver Hardy died in 1957 and Stan Laurel in 1965.

Jay Laurier, grotesque music-hall comedian and actor. Born in Birmingham on 31 May 1879, he first appeared at the Public Hall, Abertillery, in 1896 in a production of *The Arabian Nights*, and soon became a popular eccentric solo comic in variety. He was well-known for his red wig and

John 'Humanity' Lawson, 1904

Layton and Johnstone, 1925

costume made from Tate and Lyle sugar sacks, and for the songs 'I'm Always Doing Something Silly' and 'Ring-O-Roses'. Leaving the variety stage during the 1920s, in 1925 he appeared in *Cleopatra* at Daly's and played Doolittle in *Pygmalion* at the Old Vic in 1936. He played in Shakespeare at Stratford in 1938, but continued to appear in pantomime as a popular dame until his retirement after the Second World War. He went to live in South Africa and died at his home in Durban in 1969 at the age of 90.

John Lawson, sketch artist, born in 1867. After an early career as an actor and then acrobat, he made his music-hall debut in 1896, scoring a sensational success with the sketch 'Humanity', and for the rest of his career was billed as 'Humanity' Lawson. In the sketch Lawson played Jacob Silveni, a Jew with an unfaithful Gentile wife. He fought a duel with his wife's lover, in which everything breakable on the stage was smashed, and ended with a melodramatic fight on a staircase. Silveni tried to strangle his foe with a pair of tongs, and as the staircase collapsed they both fell dead on to the stage. 'Humanity' was followed on bills by the musical monologue 'Only a Jew', and later he presented 'The Monkey's Paw', 'The Shield of David', 'The King of Palestine' and 'Dizzy', in which Lawson played Benjamin Disraeli. He died in 1920 at the age of 53.

Layton and Johnstone, American entertainers at the piano, famous in variety and radio during the 1920s and 1930s. Turner Layton made his first stage appearance at the Times Square Theatre, New York, in 1920, and made his first recording for the famous 'Black Swan' label in 1921. While working in the New York publishing office of W. C. Handy, he met Clarence Johnstone and they appeared together as society entertainers in 1922. Coming to England in 1923 they worked the London night clubs where they were seen by Elsie Janis, and booked for their first London stage appearance in *Elsie Janis at Home*, which opened at the Queen's Theatre on 2 June 1924. Although only a small show with just curtains, lamps, flowers and a piano, it became the rage of London, due mainly to Layton and Johnstone's popularity with the Prince of Wales. Becoming a top-of-the-bill variety and cabaret attraction, and leading radio and recording artistes, Johnstone and Layton lasted as partners until 1935, when Johnstone returned to the USA and Layton reverted to a solo act. He has lived in London ever since. He is also the composer of many popular songs, including 'After You've Gone', 'Way Down Yonder in New Orleans', 'Down By The River', and 'Southland'.

Alice Leamar, serio-comedienne, born in London. She made her first appearance at the age of ten at the People's Palace, Leeds, working a double dancing act with a partner as 'Alice and Eugenie'. In 1892 she appeared in pantomime at Drury Lane and the following year toured Australia and New Zealand for George Edwardes, singing and dancing Lottie Collins's (qv) success 'Ta-ra-ra-boom-de-ay'. In 1895 she went to South Africa to appear in Cape Town and Johannesburg with Luscombe Searelle's Variety Company, followed by two years in Australia touring for Harry Rickards and Williamson and Musgrove. Returning to London in 1898 she became well-known in variety singing 'Her Golden Hair Was Hanging Down Her Back' by Felix McGlennon.

Tom Leamore, comedian, born 1866. He first appeared on the halls in 1884, making his London debut the following year as a 'trial turn' at the Star, Bermondsey. Another novice on the bill was Marie Lloyd doing a song and dance routine. They were both engaged by manager Jonny Hart at 15 shillings each for the week. Soon afterwards, while appearing at the Hammersmith Palace, Leamore was seen by variety agent Hugh J. Didcott and booked to appear at the Trocadero. From then on he never looked back, becoming one of the most successful character comedians of the late 1890s, singing his famous song of the not-so-swell 'swell', 'Percy from Pimlico'. He was one of the 'Veterans of Variety' during the mid-1930s and died on 6 September 1939.

Lily Lena, serio-comedienne, born in 1877. She was a cousin of Marie Lloyd and from the death of her mother in 1887 was brought up as a member of the Wood family. She made her first appearance in 1893 working a double act with Rosie Lloyd, appearing in pantomime and at the smaller London halls. She made her solo debut at the London, Shoreditch, in September 1896. The songs included 'Don't I Wish It Was Me', 'You Can't Be Sure You've Married the Man, Till You've Been on Honeymoon' and 'The White Silk Dress'.

Arthur Lennard, comic singer, born Plumstead, London, in 1867. He first appeared in London at the Royal Holborn in December 1887. With a good tenor voice his range covered topical songs, parody and ballads. His song 'Skylark', of the latter category, told of a 'little child who invoked a soaring bird and entreated it, should it happen to notice Mother among the angels,' to 'ask her to come back to earth to poor Daddy and me'. Good Victorian stuff which contrasted with his 'Little Golden Hair' parody of Alice Leamar's (qv) 'Her Golden Hair was Hanging Down Her Back'. This told the sad story of Bertie, who on his wedding night discovered that his wife was not quite intact, and beauty was not even skin deep:

> Her pearly teeth were in a glass upon the mantelpiece,
> Her eyebrows too had given her the sack,
> Her bald head made Bertie stare,
> By the bedside stood a chair,
> And her golden hair was hanging down the back.

His career spanned 30 years of variety and pantomime; he retired from the stage in December 1916.

Above: Tom Leamore, 'Percy from Pimlico', 1887

Below: Arthur Lennard, 1913

Dan Leno, 'The King's Jester', 1901

Dan Leno, the greatest comedian in the history of music hall. Born George Galvin in London on 20 December 1860, he was the son of variety performers who appeared as 'Mr and Mrs Johnny Wild—Singing and Acting Duettists'. His first appearance, at the Cosmothica Music Hall, Bell Street, Paddington, in 1864, was as 'Little George, the Infant Wonder, Contortionist and Posturer'. During the next 20 years he ran through a long list of pretentious billings before becoming 'The One and Only Dan Leno'.

His father died in 1864 and his mother later married William Grant, who worked the halls under the name of Leno. By 1867 Dan was appearing with his brother Jack as 'The Great Little Lenos'. In 1869 he worked solo at the Britannia Theatre, Hoxton, billed as 'The First Appearance of the Great Little Leno—The Quintessence of Irish Comedians'. Later he appeared with the Leno troupe as 'Dan Patrick Leno, Descriptive and Irish Character Vocalist'. At the Princesses Music Hall, Leeds, in 1880, he became 'The Champion Clog Dancer of the World', and for the next five years featured a clog dance in his act. In 1883 he married Lydia Reynolds, a singer who had joined the family act in 1880, and together they worked the halls, appearing as separate solo turns on the same bill.

Leno made his first London appearance as a solo comedian and clog dancer at the Forester's Music Hall, Mile End, on 5 October 1885. He sang 'Going to Buy Milk for the Twins', followed by a character song entitled 'When Rafferty Raffled His Watch'. Both went over well but his clog dance, which had been so popular in the North, was a disaster in London and was soon dropped from his act. Soon after his East End debut he appeared at the Middlesex Music Hall, Drury Lane, and was seen by George Conquest who engaged him to play dame in *Jack and the Beanstalk* at the Surrey Theatre at Christmas 1886. He and his wife were booked at a joint salary of £20 per week, and were such a success that Dan was re-engaged to play dame, and Lydia Reynolds principal boy, in *Sinbad the Sailor* the following year. Between pantomimes he appeared in variety and was soon topping bills at the main London halls, considered the number-one box-office attraction for the rest of his life. The first of the new revues, *Atlanta* by George B. Hawtrey, opened at the Strand Theatre on 17 November 1888, but although it had a strong cast which included Alma Stanley, Minnie Cunningham and Tom Squire, was not at first a success. Late in November Leno was engaged to strengthen the comedy line and succeeded in increasing its popularity very considerably, but as he was under contract to Sir Augustus Harris to appear that Christmas at Drury Lane, he left the cast and business slumped again.

The Drury Lane pantomime of 1888, *Babes in the Wood*, was the first of 15 consecutive pantomimes at Drury Lane, which earned him a legendary place in the history of the Theatre Royal. W. Macqueen Pope, the official historian of the Theatre Royal, wrote in *The Melodies Linger On:*

> There was only one Dan Leno he never had a rival, and will never have a successor. He stands in the mighty frieze of Drury Lane alongside and equal with all of its great ones, the peer of Hart, Mohun, Betterton, Cibber, Wilkes, Macklin, Quin, Edmund Kean, Macready, John Philip Kemble, and even the mighty Garrick himself. There is no statue to him there and no plaque, but almost everybody who enters remembers that this was where Dan Leno played.

No great singer, Dan's songs were really rambling monologues introducing a legion of brilliant character impersonations, a railway guard, shopwalker, recruiting sergeant, fireman, Beefeater, huntsman, or just telling the audience of a visit to the races, or the latest gossip of the mythical Mrs Kelly. 'You remember Mrs Kelly!' Only five foot three, he had an expressive face with high eyebrows which always seemed to be arched in surprise. He had a wide range of facial expressions and although he did not use these indiscriminately, he was able to convulse his audience with a look. A great favourite wherever he appeared, he spent months on the bill of the London Pavilion.

He made his first appearance in America at Oscar Hammerstein's Music Hall, New York, on 12 April 1897. Faced with the intimidating billing of 'Dan Leno, the funniest man on earth', he was only a moderate success. In 1898 Leno toured in the name part of Milton Bode's burlesque *Orlando Dando*, a revue written to show off the full range of Dan's comedy. A great success, the following year he again toured with Bode's *Mr Wix of Wickham*. By 1900 Dan Leno had appeared on the stage almost daily for 36 years, and he was still under 40. For such a conscientious artiste this represented a terrible mental and physical strain. On 26 November 1901 he was commanded by Edward VII to appear at Sandringham, the first royal command of his reign. In recognition of his talents the King presented him with a diamond cravat pin in the form of the royal cypher; and by popular acclaim he was then dubbed 'The King's Jester'. He suffered a mental breakdown in 1903 but recovered sufficiently to appear at Christmas in *Humpty Dumpty* at Drury Lane. He seemed to be his old self, scoring his usual success in the role of the Queen to Herbert Campbell's (qv) King. The following year he had a relapse and died at the age of 43 on 31 October 1904.

It was long believed that *Dan Leno Hys Book* was written by Leno in 1899. But after a BBC television adaptation of the book in January 1968 with Roy Hudd (qv) appearing as Leno, it was learned that it had really been ghosted by T. C. Elder, who then aged 99 was living in Reigate, Surrey.

Leo the Ventriloquist, 1888

Leo, American ventriloquist who started his career as an Indian Club swinger and juggler at dime shows, rodeos, and in 1874 toured Australia and New Zealand with Cooper and Bailey's Circus. Turning to ventriloquism he made his first appearance in England at the Oxford Music Hall, London, in 1879, but it was not until 1888, when he returned to appear as a Christmas attraction at the Canterbury, that he met with any real success. After engagements at the Empire and Royal Holborn he appeared at the Folies Bergère, Paris, in 1890, and made Paris his home.

Leotard, aerial performer credited with being the creator of the flying trapeze. Born in Toulouse, France, in 1842, he received early training from his father and by the age of 18 was the premier aerialist of the Cirque Franconi, Paris. As soon as he made his first London appearance at the Alhambra on 26 May 1861 he became the rage, returning

Leotard, the original 'Daring Young Man on the Flying Trapeze', 1861

with equal success in 1866 and 1868. As George Leybourne sang:

> He'd fly through the air with the greatest
>   of ease,
> A daring young man on the flying trapeze,
> His movements were graceful,
> All girls he could please,
> And my love he purloined away.

Leotard was paid £180 a week for his 1868 season at the Alhambra, and later appeared at other music halls and pleasure-gardens in London before his return to France in 1869. He died of smallpox in 1870 at the age of 28.

Fanny Leslie, serio-comic and burlesque artiste. Born in England in 1857, she spent the early years of her life in America where she made her first stage appearance in 1872. Coming to London the following year she scored her first music-hall success at the Oxford, singing 'Buy a Box of Lights, Sir'. After 18 months on the London and provincial halls she returned to the USA to tour with Lydia Thompson's **Burlesque Company.** Back in London she married music-hall and theatre manager Walter Gooch, and under his management appeared in 1879 at the Princesses Theatre in the famous temperance play *Drink*, Charles Reade's adaptation of Zola's *L'Assommoir*. During the next 10 years this self-styled 'Queen of Burlesque' appeared mainly on the muscial comedy stage as a member of George Edwardes's Gaiety Company, and as principal boy in pantomime. In 1881 she played Robinson Crusoe at Drury Lane, returning to the Theatre Royal in 1884 to play Dick Whittington. She made her variety comeback in 1891 on the bill of a benefit matinee given for Charles Morton on his retirement from the Alhambra. Singing 'Dancing Up To Date' she went over well with the largely theatrical audience and this resulted in a variety contract for the Trocadero, Canterbury, and Oxford, and an engagement from Sir Augustus Harris to appear at Christmas in *Humpty Dumpty* at Drury Lane with Little Tich as Humpty Dumpty, Marie Lloyd as Princess Allfair and Herbert Campbell and Dan Leno as the King and Queen. She remained a popular serio and male impersonator throughout the 1890s, singing 'masher' and jolly 'boy' songs. She lived for many years in obscure retirement, dying in 1935.

Alfred Lester, revue, musical comedy and variety artiste, remembered on the halls as the lugubrious comedian with the woeful expression. Born in Nottingham on 25 October 1872, his father was a touring actor, and he made the traditional first appearance as Little Willy in *East Lynne*. His first music-hall appearance was at the Palace in London in 1905 and, after three years at the Gaiety, he scored a great personal hit in 1909 as Peter Doody in *The Arcadians* at the Shaftesbury. Between 1911 and 1916 he appeared mainly in variety, becoming popular with the sketches 'The Scene-Shifter's Lament', 'Longshoreman Bill', 'A Restaurant Episode', 'The Amateur Hairdresser' and 'The Village Fire Brigade'. 'The Scene-Shifter's Lament', with Lester as the cockney scene-shifter suggesting in melancholy tones how to brighten up *Hamlet*, was a music-hall classic. At the first Royal Command Variety Performance at the Palace Theatre in 1912 Lester appeared with 'The Village Fire Brigade'. At the Alhambra in 1916 he starred with George Robey and Violet Loraine in 'The Bing Boys are Here', and although the hit song of the show was Robey and Loraine's famous duet 'If You Were The Only Girl In The World', Lester as Oliver Bing had a great success with his song of the shirker 'Send Out My Brother, My Sister and My Mother, but for Gawd's Sake Don't Send Me'. He died on 6 May 1925.

Harry and Burton Lester, of 'Harry Lester and his Hayseeds', hillbilly singing and comedy act. Brothers born in Fort Worth, Texas, their father John Lester was well known for a variety of show-business ventures from barnstorming with a dramatic repertory company to touring with his own Wild West show. Turning to vaudeville, John, Harry and Burton Lester toured the USA as a single trio, and in August 1914 appeared in Australia. After a further tour of South Africa they made their first London appearance at the Victoria Palace on 20 December 1915. Making their home in Britain, they became well known for a succession of novel speciality acts, including pioneer, jazz and ragtime bands, 'The Frisco Five', 'The Cowboy Syncopators', 'The Upside Down Band', 'The Round Up', and 'The Hollywood Band' and 'Movie Girls'. Introducing their 'Hayseeds' act during the 1940s they appeared in the Royal Variety Performance at

Harry and Burton Lester *(photo. S. Georges, London)*

Alfred Lester, 'Longshoreman Bill', 1908

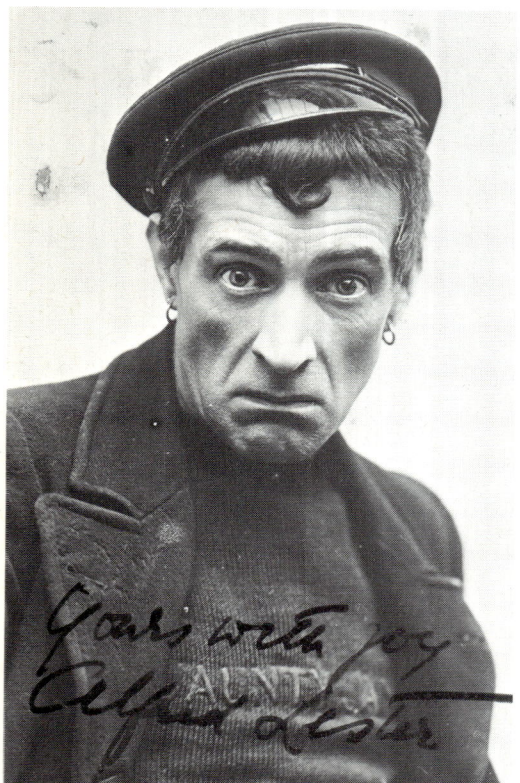

the London Palladium in 1946. 'Harry Lester and his Hayseeds', followed in 1949 by 'Your Country Cousins', remained popular in variety, pantomime and radio throughout the 1950s.

Letine, leader of an acrobatic bicycle act well known on the music halls of the 1880s. Born George Gorin in 1853, he formed the act with his wife and daughters; they appeared as 'The Wonderful Letine Troupe' at all the leading London halls. In 1887 the act was joined by Beatrice Curragh, a young girl who ran away from home to tour with Letine, but was forced by ill-health to leave the troupe in August 1888. She died of consumption in December that year and her death had a tragic sequel. Her father, Nathaniel Curragh, became obsessed with the idea that his daughter had died because of ill treatment by Letine, and in 1889 brought a private action against him. The charge was completely without foundation and dismissed by the court. In June Letine was appearing in London at the Paragon, Mile End, and later the same evening at the Canterbury. On the evening of Friday 21 June 1889 the troupe travelled from the East End to Lambeth in a carriage, arriving at Westminster Bridge Road at 10.45 pm. As Letine was getting out of the carriage at the Canterbury stage door, Curragh sprang from the shadows of the nearby railway arch and plunged a dagger deep into Letine's stomach. Crossing the road, he drew a revolver and shot himself in the mouth. Both were taken to nearby St Thomas's Hospital, where Letine died two hours later. Curragh recovered and in August 1889 appeared at the Central Criminal court charged with murder, but was found unfit to plead on the grounds of insanity.

Florence Levey, dancer who made her first appearance in the chorus of Augustus Harris's pantomime *Bluebeard* at the Crystal Palace in 1883, followed by the ballet *The Palace of Pearl* at the Empire and *Alice in Wonderland* at the Prince of Wales. In 1888 she became a member of George Edwardes's Gaiety Burlesque Company and toured the USA and Australia. Her first music-hall appearance as a solo speciality dancer was in 1892.

Carroll Levis, Canadian impresario and compere, famous in this country during the 1940s and 1950s for his radio and touring 'Discovery' shows. He was born in Toronto on 15 March 1910, the son of a murdered policeman. At the age of 15, he was considerably overweight and looked much older than his years. So he managed to get a job as assistant cinema manager at the Empress Theatre, Vancouver, and later acted as compere at its cine-variety shows. In 1927 he toured in small-time vaudeville, first as a comic lead and then billed as 'The Great Richelieu. Magician, Eminent Hypnotist and Necromancer'. This led in 1928 to engagements with a Canadian radio station, analysing listeners' dreams on a programme called 'Arvella The Dream Girl'. During one of these broadcasts he found himself running under time and impetuously invited any member of the studio audience to fill the gap. A schoolboy got up and sang 'Margie', and the 'Carroll Levis Discovery Show' was born.

When he came to England at the age of 25 his hair was already silver and he weighed 23 stone. He made his first broadcast as an actor in February 1936. Encouraged by Eric Maschwitz, then Head of BBC Variety, to tour his Discovery Show, he made his London stage debut at the Gaumont Palace, Lewisham, in July 1936, and his first BBC variety date followed on 8 September. With his own variety company of star discoveries, he toured the music halls and cinemas, inviting the 'good people' of this and that town to 'step this way for the chance of a lifetime'. With the

Carroll Levis, 1938

inducement of small money prizes, and for the best, a chance of broadcasting on the BBC's 'Amateur Hour', they stepped forward in thousands.

During the war he toured extensively, entertaining the troops with his 'Stars from the Services' shows. He suffered a serious mental breakdown in 1947 and returned to Canada while during the next three years his shows continued to tour the UK with Carroll doubled by his brother, Cyril Levis. He made his comeback at the Shepherd's Bush Empire on 23 January 1950, and was soon back on top both on radio, introduced by his famous signature tune 'Stardust', and with his three road shows, 'Carroll Levis and his Discoveries', 'Teenage Discoveries' and 'The Show Stoppers'. Unlike his great rival Hughie Green, he did not go over well on television. His exuberant, larger-than-life personality, which for years had helped to fill the largest of the Empires and Gaumont Palaces, seemed patronising and insincere when confined to the small screen. He spent the last 15 years of his life working behind the scenes, and died in Scotland on 18 October 1968 at the age of 58.

George Leybourne, one of the greatest of the early music-hall performers whose flamboyant style of dress and swaggering songs founded the tradition of the 'Lion Comique'. Born Joe Saunders in 1842, in the early 1860s he gave up his trade as a mechanic for the more convivial life of the music halls and free-and-easies of the Midlands. With his handsome appearance and fine voice he soon became a firm favourite in Leeds, Manchester, Liverpool and Birmingham and made his first London appearances at the Gilbert Music Hall, Whitechapel, and the Raglan, Theobalds Road, Holborn, in 1864.

George Leybourne, the first 'Lion Comique', 1870

While playing Collins Music Hall, Islington, in 1865 he met Albert Lee, who composed 'Chang the Chinese Giant' for him. It was a topical song which Leybourne sang walking around the halls on stilts. The following year they collaborated on 'Champagne Charlie', which after a try out at the Scotia Music Hall, Glasgow, Leybourne sang with historic success at the Canterbury. When William Holland took over the management of the hall from Charles Morton in 1868 Leybourne was soon established as his star attraction. Holland, the self-styled 'people's caterer', and Leybourne the 'heavy swell par excellence', were well-matched. Holland paid him a record salary of £30 a week, dressed him immaculately as a man-about-town, gave him a carriage-and-four, and told him that in public he must drink nothing but champagne. George was happy to oblige, and making it clear in this greatest of all 'commercials' that 'Moet's vintage only, satisfied the champagne swell', he sang:

Whoever drinks at my expense,
Are treated all the same,
From Dukes and Lords to cabman down
I make them drink champagne

He remained at the Canterbury for over a year and then pushed his salary up to £120 a week at the Oxford and Royal Music Hall, Holborn. Other drinking songs followed the success of 'Champagne Charlie' and, spurred on by commercial handouts and the friendly rivalry of Alfred Vance, he sang his way through the wine list from 'Cool Burgundy Ben' to 'John Barleycorn'.

He had many other good songs, often up-to-the-minute topical ones, such as 'Zazal! Zazal!', about a female human cannon ball then all the rage at London's pleasure gardens, and 'Up in a Balloon' which dates from the siege of Paris in 1870. 'The Daring Young Man On The Flying Trapeze' marked Leotard's Alhambra season of 1868. The first of the 'mashers' to be billed as 'Lion Comique', he was so dubbed by J. J. Poole, the one-time musical director of the Metropolitan, Edgware Road, and later manager of the South London Music Hall and London Pavilion.

One of the brightest stars to shine during the golden age of music hall, he lived the life of 'Champagne Charlie' too well and too long, failing to adjust to the changing tastes of the 1880s. When his popularity declined he managed and chaired a number of smaller halls, later working a double act with his daughter, Florrie Leybourne (later Mrs Albert Chevalier). His last engagement was at the Queen's, Poplar, a few months before his death on 15 September 1884 at the age of 44.

Marie Leyton, speciality dancer. She made her first London appearance in 1890 as a performer in a pas de quatre, danced by the 'Sisters Leyton'. Shortly afterwards she travelled to the USA, appearing in *Cinderella* at the Academy of Arts, New York, in 1892. The star of the show, Loie Fuller, caused a sensation with her famous serpentine dance. This dance Marie Leyton adapted for her own use, performing it for the first time at Engle's Pavilion, Clark Street, Chicago. On her return to London in 1894 she introduced the routine into variety, appearing for over a year at the Tivoli. Loie Fuller later had her own success with the dance in London and Paris.

The Six Lias, German acrobatic act, originally three brothers and their three sisters. The leader, Carl Lias, began his career with the Austrian Circus Kuhlmogan; he was later joined by his two brothers, Arthur and Walter, and with them toured on the flying trapeze and slack wire and as acrobatic clowns. Turning to variety they were joined by their sisters and as 'The Six Lias' were soon established as a leading continental music-hall attraction, appearing at the Wintergarten, Berlin, the Cirque d'Hiver, Paris, and the Ronacher, Vienna. When war broke out in August 1914 they were appearing in Russia and were interned until 1919. When the three sisters married they were replaced by three male acrobats, and the now all-male 'Six Lias' made their first appearance in England at the Argyle Birkenhead, in 1927. In 1930 they returned to Britain and at Christmas 1933 presented their act during the pantomime season at the Lyceum, London. In 1934 they appeared in George Black's *Crazy Show* at the Palladium, and the following year appeared for Black in *Round About Regent Street*. The scene in which they featured was included in the Royal Variety Performance of 1935.

Liberace, 'The Rhinestone Rubinstein'. Flamboyant piano virtuoso, born plain Wladziu Valentino Liberace, in West Allis, Wisconsin, in 1919. Even before he appeared in Britain he built up a following of millions through the transmission by the BBC of his American television shows. So his popularity was already tremendous when he came to London to take part in the Royal Variety Performance of 1956. At the last moment the show was cancelled because of the Suez crisis, but Liberace remained to top the bill at the London Palladium, give concerts at the Albert Hall and Festival Hall, play cabaret engagements at the Café de Paris, and make a provincial variety tour. With his grand piano, silver candelabra and outrageous wardrobe, he has since made many visits to this country and appeared in three Royal Variety shows, the last in 1971. Even in today's pop scene of megalomaniac excess and high camp, he remains one of America's top showmen.

Liberace, 1956

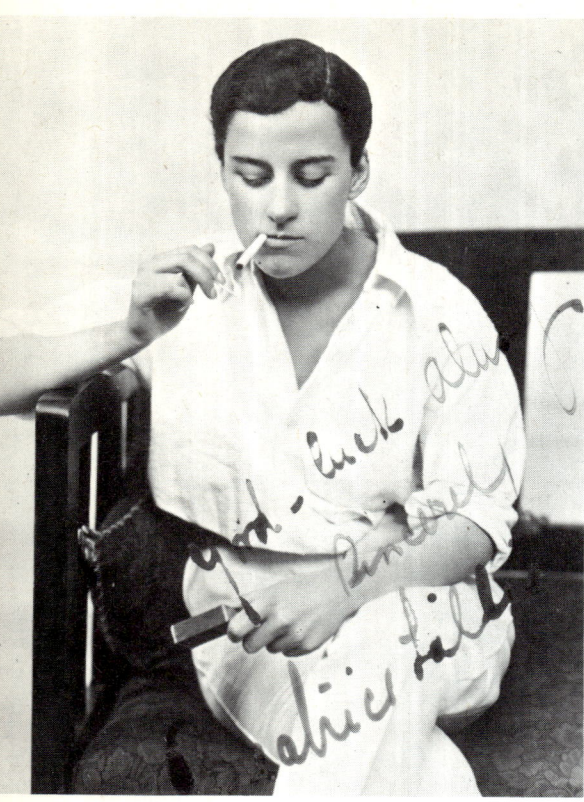

Beatrice Lillie, 1916

Beatrice Lillie, queen of cabaret and Charlot revues. Born in Canada in 1899, she first appeared with her mother and sister as 'The Lillie Trio, High Class Entertainers' and later did a solo turn billed as 'Serio Comic Singer with a Refined Repertoire'. Coming to England just before the First World War, she made her London variety debut at the Camberwell Palace. Not having made a great success as 'Canada's Own Sweetheart of Song', she then worked a 'boy' act in variety and revue. In 1917 she appeared in revue for Andre Charlot at the Vaudeville Theatre, playing a Canadian soldier. This 'fly season' came to an end in 1919, and on developing her own very distinctive style of comedy she was soon established as the leading revue comedienne of London and New York. However, she continued to make occasional variety appearances and to work in West End cabaret. She now lives in retirement in New York.

Sam Linfield, born Sam Clifton in Birmingham, 1898. The son of Joe Boganny, he began his career with his father's famous 'Lunatic Bakers', making his first London appearance at the Paragon Music Hall, Mile End, in 1906. Later he worked with his uncle, Jack Clifton, who toured the 'Five X-Rays and Six Ceylons'. Turning solo as a knockabout comedian, he toured the UK and USA with his 'No Man's Land', 'Boot Villa', and 'HMS Lively' acts.

Harry Liston, dialect comedian born in Manchester in September 1843. Making his first music-hall appearance at the Scotia, Glasgow, in July 1863, he soon afterwards devised a two-hour one-man show which, billed as 'The Stage-Struck Hero', toured throughout the northern counties. His first London appearances were for J. J. Poole at the Cambridge and Metropolitan on 12 June 1865, and were followed by a two-month engagement at the Alhambra. In February 1866 he became a member of Arthur Lloyd's 'Comical Company' and the following year formed his own concert party, 'Merry Moments', which toured the provinces for many years. A great favourite at the Oxford Music Hall during its early days, his best songs included 'Nobody's Child', 'The Convict', 'The Heavy Swell of the Sea', 'The Tin Pot Band' and his greatest hit 'When Johnny Comes Marching Home'. He died on 8 April 1929.

Victor Liston, a very popular comic singer during the early days of music hall, who made his first appearance at the age of 17 at the Bower Saloon, London, in 1855. A singing engagement followed shortly afterwards at Parker's Music Hall, Sheffield, and within a few years he was appearing regularly at the Cider Cellars, Dr Johnson's Tavern, The Coal Hole, and Evans Song and Supper Room. Billed as 'The Robson of the Halls', he scored his greatest success with the song 'Shabby Genteel', which he sang at the Philharmonic Hall, Islington, for seven months in 1868, followed by further success at the Metropolitan, Collins Music Hall, and a five-month tour of the USA. Composed by Henry S. Leigh, 'Shabby Genteel' was in the popular Victorian 'poor but honest' tradition. Its chorus ran:

Too proud to beg, too honest to steal,
I know what it is to be wanting a meal
My tatters and rags, I try to conceal
I'm one of the shabby genteel.

In later years he became the manager of the Bon Accord in Aberdeen, as well as small halls in Gloucester and Cheltenham. He died 11 July 1913.

Little Tich, famous music-hall comedian, born Harry Relph, at Cudham, Kent, on 21 July 1867. As a boy of 13 he played a tin whistle at the Rosherville Gardens, Gravesend, and in 1881 appeared as a burnt-cork comedian at Barnard's Music Hall, Chatham. With the Juvenile Christy Minstrels he appeared at the Royal Victoria Hall and Coffee Tavern (later known as the Old Vic) then run by Emma Cons, secretary of Coffee Music Hall Co Ltd. Relph was then billing himself as 'The Great Little Mackney' but when E.W. Mackney objected he changed to 'Little Tich' (because, it is said, of his likeness to Arthur Orton, the Tichborne claimant). His first solo London music hall appearance was at Forester's Music Hall on 3 November 1884. He made his pantomime debut the following year in Glasgow. He was still working a black-faced act, a feature of his turn being his big boot dance. These boots were longer than he was tall, but he managed to dance in them with great skill and dexterity, suddenly shooting into the air and remaining on his toes as if on a pair of stilts.

He went to America in 1887, and for three seasons toured the USA with Tony Pastor's Vaudeville Troupe, and with the Chicago Opera House Company. After Christmas pantomime at the Palace Theatre, Manchester, in 1889, he returned to New York for a further season in 1890. Back in London he appeared at the Gaiety Theatre in the role of Quasimodo in the burlesque *Miss Esmerelda*. With the billing 'One Tich of Nature makes the Whole World Grin' he became a great favourite at the London Pavilion, Tivoli and Oxford, and was as popular in Paris at the Olympia and Alhambra as he was in London. Between 1891 and 1894 he appeared each Christmas with Marie Lloyd, Dan Leno and Herbert Campbell in pantomime at Drury Lane. He was in the farce *Lord Tom Noddy* at the Garrick Theatre in 1896 and appeared as principal comedian in *Giddy Ostend* which opened at the London Hippodrome in 1900. In variety he was one of the select band of comedians led by Leno who gave each of his characters, no matter how eccentric, the touch of realism that distinguishes true burlesque. His 'Gas Inspector', 'Sergeant Major', 'Park Keeper', 'Ballerina', and the fiery Spanish señorita, 'Little Miss Serpentine', were characterisations of great comic genius.

A member of the Grand Order of Water Rats, he was King Rat in 1906 and in recognition of his services to the French music hall he was made an Officer of the Académie Française in 1910. His last appearance took place at the London Alhambra on 13 November 1927. He died at his home in Hendon, North London, on 10 February 1928.

Little Tony, diminutive comedian, well-known to music-hall audiences of the 1890s. Born in Liverpool in 1875 he made his first stage appearance aged four at the Liverpool Amphitheatre. By the age of 15 he was only four feet tall and, joining Newsome's Circus, toured the UK billed as 'The Smallest Clown in the World'. He later teamed with Chang, a Chinese giant, and as a double act worked in circus and variety. Turning solo in 1895 he remained a popular music-hall turn until his death at the age of 41 on 23 February 1918.

Arthur Lloyd, comic vocalist and sketch artiste who pioneered touring concert party entertainment. Born in Edinburgh in 1840, he gained early stage experience with a local stock company and as a singer of comic songs at the Whitebait Tavern, Glasgow. In 1856 he joined Newcombe's company at the Theatre Royal, Plymouth, and during the following three seasons supported many prominent guest artistes, including Charlotte Cushman and Ira Aldridge. He made his first London music-hall appearance at the Sun, Knightsbridge, in October 1862, followed by a 12-month engagement at the Canterbury. He achieved a great personal

Arthur Lloyd, 'The German Band', 1864

Little Tich

triumph at the London Pavilion and did much to establish the hall opened the year before by Loible and Sonnenhammer.

He was a singer of 'swell' songs, a contemporary of Leybourne and Vance, and his greatest successes were 'Not For Joseph', 'The German Band', 'The Organ Grinder', 'Pretty Lips, Sweeter Than Cherry or Plum' and 'Immenskoff'. He and Harry Liston formed a concert party in 1866 which toured as 'Two Hours of Fun with Arthur Lloyd and his Comical Company'. He took a three-year lease on the Queen's Theatre, Dublin, in 1874, presenting variety and dramatic sketches, and in 1878 returned to London and further success at the Pavilion. In 1883 he introduced dialogue sketches into his act, appearing with his wife, Kitty King; he then wrote a four-act drama entitled *Bally Voyan*, which was performed in Newcastle in 1887. On the death of his wife in 1892 his son and daughter joined the act, touring the USA for 40 weeks in 1893 with the vaudeville sketch 'Our Party'. Known as 'The last of the "Lion Comiques"', he died on 20 July 1904.

Marie Lloyd, comedienne who shares with Dan Leno the supreme place in the history of music hall. Born Matilda Alice Victoria Wood, in Hoxton, London, on 12 February 1870, she made her first appearance as an extra Saturday night turn at the Grecian Assembly Rooms, part of the famous Eagle Tavern in the City Road, on 9 May 1885. She was then 15 years old and used the name Bella Delmare. Her two songs 'My Soldier Laddie' and 'Time is Flying' went over well enough to be booked by Charles Leach to appear later that same night at the Rosemary Branch in nearby Shepperton Street, Islington.

She appeared as 'Marie Lloyd' on the regular bill at the Eagle in June 1885, 'Marie' because she liked the name, and 'Lloyd' after *Lloyd's Weekly News*. Soon afterwards she played Sebright's Music Hall, Hackney, and in August appeared for John Hart at the Star, Bermondsey, singing 'The Boy I Love is up in the Gallery', a song pinched from Nelly Power. (Strangely, this song is always associated with Marie Lloyd but in fact she stopped using it very early in her career, after being ticked off by Nelly Power.) From then on her rise to fame was meteoric. Early in 1891 she played variety dates in Ireland, and by the end of that year was appearing at four and five London halls a night, earning £100 a week. A great favourite at the Middlesex, Pavilion, and Tivoli, she spent most of 1891 on the bill of the Oxford, scoring a tremendous success with the song 'Oh Jeremiah Don't You Go To Sea'. Still only 18, she made a speciality of cheeky girl songs such as 'She'd Never Had Her Ticket Punched Before'. This and others established a reputation for 'blueness' which persisted through the rest of her career. 'Johnny Jones', another early song, ran:

What's that for, eh! Oh tell me Ma.
If you won't tell me, I'll ask Pa.
But Ma said, Oh it's nothing, hold your row.
Well, I've asked Johnny Jones see,
So I know now!.

Other songs of the period included 'Twiggy Vous', 'Wink the Other Eye', and 'Oh Mister Porter', all composed by George Le Brun.

At Christmas 1891 she appeared as principal girl at the Theatre Royal, Drury Lane, in the first of three pantomimes for Sir Augustus Harris in which she co-starred with Dan Leno, Herbert Campbell and Little Tich. In 1896 she toured South Africa for Hyman and Alexander, and in 1901 appeared with coster comedian Alec Hurley (qv) at Harry Rickards' Opera House, Melbourne. Her New York debut was not a great success. Although she was later to shock the USA, she disappointed audiences on her first visit by not being as 'blue' as she had been painted. In Berlin she topped the bill at the Winter Garden, and her success in Paris inspired 'The Coster in Paris', one of the very few songs she recorded. In November 1902 she topped the anniversary bill of 103 artists at the Middlesex, billed simply as 'Our Marie'. Max Beerbohm rated her with Queen Victoria and Florence Nightingale as one of the three most memorable women of the age, and Sarah Bernhardt dubbed her 'The Bernhardt of the Music Halls'.

For the sake of clarity Marie has to be an exception to my rule of avoiding details of artistes' private lives. Much has been written about her exclusion from the first Royal Command Performance held at the Palace Theatre in 1912. The only surprise was that anybody really expected her to be included. On professional merit and popularity alone she should have been top of the bill, but by the official moral standards of the time she was clearly unacceptable. She was divorced by her first husband, Percy Courtney, in 1904 on the grounds of her adultery with Alec Hurley. Incapable of hypocrisy or deceit she had been openly living with Hurley since 1900 and continued to do so for over a year after her divorce became absolute in May 1905. They married in October 1906 but in 1911 began divorce proceedings. At the time of the Royal Command, Marie was living with jockey Bernard Dillon, who had won the Derby on Linberg in 1910 but had his racing licence revoked in 1911. If she were alive today she would be singing 'I Did it My Way', but however talented, generous and honest she may have been, her way was not the way to a royal command.

She was engaged to tour the USA and Canada for six months in 1913 at a salary of £150 a week. The fact that she and Dillon crossed the Atlantic as man and wife incurred the censure of the US Department of Immigration, and on their arrival at New York they were refused entry and detained on Ellis Island. An order for their deportation on the grounds of moral turpitude was issued, but at the last moment Washington agreed that they could stay on £600 bail, on condition that they did not cohabit. Alec Hurley died in December 1913 and on 21 February 1914 Marie and Dillon married at the British Consulate at Portland, Oregon. They returned to England in June 1914 and during the war she sang at military hospitals and topped fund-raising variety bills. When the time came for the second (and last) Royal Command Performance, held at the Coliseum on 28 July 1919 to celebrate the end of the war, she was again ignored. Although her popularity never declined and her top-of-the-bill status was never challenged, her later career was not happy. She was 18 years older than Dillon and the marriage was not a success. She was still earning up to £600 a week singing the best character songs of her career, 'Don't Dilly Dally' ('My Old Man Said Follow the Van'), 'A Little of What You Fancy' and 'One of the Ruins that Cromwell Knocked About a Bit', but by 1920 her health was broken. Her 50th birthday passed while she was on the bill of the Bedford, Camden Town, and was marked by a public tribute. The stage was filled with flowers and the other performers presented her with a huge bouquet with a bottle of champagne swinging from it. But 1920 was a bad year for Marie, with her personal life once more mercilessly exposed. When she braced herself to make her entrance and tottered down to the footlights to sing 'One of the Ruins' the audience knew it was not Cromwell who had been doing the knocking about. The song ended her act for the last time at Edmonton on Wednesday 4 October 1922. As the curtain fell she collapsed in the wings and died three days later at her home in Golders Green. She was 52.

Marie Lloyd, 'The Queen of the Halls'

The Lloyd Family: Alice, Daisy, Rosie and Marie Lloyd Junior, 1933

The Lloyd Family, act formed by three of Marie Lloyd's sisters, Alice, Daisy, and Rosie, and later joined by her daughter, Marie Lloyd Junior. Alice Lloyd was born on 20 October 1873. Marie's success firmly stamped the Wood family with the name 'Lloyd' and Alice, with another sister, Gracie, made her first appearance at Forester's Music Hall in 1888 as 'The Lloyd Sisters'. When Gracie married jockey George Hyman and gave up the stage Alice turned solo. On 16 January 1905 she married Tom McNaughton of 'The Two McNaughtons' cross-talking act. Soon after they went to the USA and made their debut at the Colonial Theatre, New York, where Alice Lloyd was an overnight success and for the next 25 years was almost as popular in the USA as her sister was in this country. Though their home was in the USA, Alice Lloyd and her husband made occasional visits to London, Alice appearing as Dandini at the Lyceum in 1918.

Daisy Wood, born 15 September 1877, stuck to the name of Wood, unlike her sisters. She made her first appearance at the South London Palace in 1891 and was a great favourite in variety. One of the most popular pincipal boys of the North, she was billed at one time as 'Lancashire's Own Principal Boy'.

Rosie Lloyd, born 5 June 1879, began her career with Bella Orchard as one of the 'Sisters Lloyd'. When Bella married boxer Dick Burge, Rosie turned solo and was regarded by some as having the best voice and stage presence of any in the famous family.

Marie Lloyd Junior was born Marie Courtney and first appeared as a child while touring South Africa with her mother and Alec Hurley in 1896. After her mother's death in 1922 she went on the halls doing Marie Lloyd's act. During the 1960s she toured with Don Ross's *Thanks for the Memory* show.

Tom McNaughton died in 1923 and after touring Australia and Canada in 1924 Alice Lloyd returned to England. Rosie, Daisy and Alice then combined their considerable talents into an act billed 'The Lloyd Family' singing songs which they and Marie had made famous. They were later joined by Marie Lloyd Junior. Rosie Lloyd died in 1944, Alice in 1949, Daisy in 1961, and Marie Lloyd Junior on 26 December 1967.

Cissie Loftus, actress and music-hall artiste whose extraordinary powers of mimicry were only equalled many years later by Florence Desmond (qv). Born in Scotland in 1876, she was given a convent school education, but after playing Ariel in a school production of *The Tempest* became so stage struck that at the age of 15 she followed her mother, Marie Loftus, on to the halls, making her first London appearance at the Oxford in 1893. Her fine impersonations of well-known actresses immediately established her as a star attraction. She was particularly successful at the Palace Theatre with her brilliant study of the great French diseuse Yvette Guilbert (qv). After a season in musical comedy at the Gaiety Theatre, she returned to the music hall and in 1894 appeared in vaudeville at the Lyceum, New York. In 1896 she eloped with Justin Huntly McCarthy, the novelist son of the leader of the Irish Party in the House of Commons. The marriage was short lived. In 1898 she appeared with Martin Harvey in *The Children of the King* at the Court Theatre, London. The following year she returned to the USA to tour in vaudeville, later appearing in comedy at the Empire Theatre, New York, under the management of Charles Frohman. Sir Henry Irving saw Cissie Loftus perform on 21 October 1901 during his seventh tour of the USA at the Knickerbocker Theatre, New York, and was so impressed that he engaged her to appear with him in the parts that Ellen Terry had grown too old to play. In April 1902 she appeared

Cissie Loftus, 1902

Marie Loftus, 1905

as Marguerite in *Faust* which opened Irving's 25th and final season at the Lyceum. She later toured with Irving at a salary of £100 a week, half of what she could have earned on the halls.

She appeared as Peter Pan at the Duke of York's Theatre, London, in 1905 and later that year was a successful Nora in *A Doll's House*. In 1906 she toured with the variety sketch 'The Diamond Express' and appeared in the Royal Command Variety Performance at the Palace Theatre in 1912. During the next 20 years she oscillated between the legitimate stage and the music halls of both England and America, dying in the USA on 12 July 1943.

Marie Loftus, music-hall singer and pantomime principal boy. Born in Scotland in 1857, she made her first appearance as a music-hall singer in Glasgow in 1874 and in London at the Oxford in 1877. A handsome woman, always beautifully dressed, with a dramatic stage presence, she was one of the first women to top music-hall bills in Britain, and to tour with success in South Africa and the USA. A sort of female counterpart of Harry Clifton, she was a singer of motto songs, including 'To Err is Human, To Forgive, Divine', 'That's Love', 'The Things You Can't Buy With Gold', and 'One Touch of Nature Makes the Whole World Akin'. A popular principal boy of the 1880s and 1890s, she appeared as Little Bo Peep at Drury Lane at Christmas 1892 with what must have been the strongest music-hall cast ever to make its 'vulgarising incursion into pantomime'. It included Marie Lloyd, Dan Leno, Herbert Campbell, Ada Blanche, Arthur Williams and Little Tich. After many years of retirement she died in 1940. She was the mother of Cissie Loftus.

Norman Long, 'A Song, a Smile, and a Piano'. Born in Deal, Kent, on 26 March 1893. He first appeared with Charles Heslop's Brownies at the Winter Garden, Bournemouth, in March 1914. Other concert party shows followed and he made his variety debut at the Lewisham Hippodrome in December 1919. A regular broadcaster from 1922, he made a Royal Variety appearance at the Victoria Palace in 1927. Retired from the stage after the war, he continued to make occasional broadcasts until his death in 1950.

Long and Sharp, Sam Long and Dolly Sharp, American comedy singing act. After touring in vaudeville with Foster's Variety Company, Vadio Sisters, Fields and Hanson, and Barnum and Bailey's Concert Company, they made their first appearance in England at the London, Shoreditch, in December 1897.

Tommy Lorne, Scottish music hall, revue and pantomime comedian. Born Hugh Gallagher Corcoran, near Glasgow, on 7 December 1890. As a boy he joined a local minstrel troupe, 'The Port Dundas Court Juvenile Minstrels', making his first music-hall appearance in a George Formby Senior talent competition at the Queen's Theatre, Glasgow. Later he worked a step-dancing act with a partner at the Bijou Picture House, Cowcaddens, and made his solo debut at the Tivoli, Anderston, in 1904. Working with a partner as 'Wallace and Lorne', he secured a number of good bookings at smaller Glasgow halls and his first date outside Scotland at the Buffalo Theatre, Ashington. Billed as 'Champion Dancers of the World', they did a burlesque sand dance, and for the next three-and-a-half years played the towns of Northumberland, followed by a 52 week variety tour of Wales. Wallace and Lorne split when they joined the army in 1916 and on his discharge in January 1920 Lorne was given a four-and-a-half year contract as principal comedian in Harry McKelvie's revue and pantomime company. At Christmas 1920 he

Ernie Lotinga, 1941

appeared in pantomime at the Princess Theatre, Glasgow, with such success that he was retained as principal comedian for the next three pantomimes. Now established as one of the most popular of Scottish comedians, he toured the halls of Scotland and the north of England in eccentric clown-like make-up, kilt, Glengarry bonnet, high collar with a bootlace for a tie, a very short jacket, tartan garters, long white gloves, and boots several sizes too large for his already big feet.

He made his first London appearance at the Chelsea Palace in 1924, but Northern bookings did not allow for many appearances that far south of the border. Although he was made good offers to appear in pantomime in London, and admitted to an ambition to do so, he was always forced to refuse. In 1924 he made a record-breaking tour of Scotland with the revue *Froth*. When the show played the Pavilion, Glasgow, it was joined by the local sisters Renee and Billie Gribbens, better known as the 'Houston Sisters' (qv). His earlier pantomime roles were restricted to principal comedian roles, Buttons, Baron, etc., but he was reluctant to play dame. When he finally did so at the King's Theatre, Edinburgh, in 1928 he scored the greatest hit of his successful pantomime career. His work was greatly admired by both Harry Lauder and Will Fyffe; the latter, on introducing him to theatre managers Howard and Wyndham said, 'I'll be finished with you shortly and I want you to meet my successor.' Praise indeed from Scotland's greatest comedian, but Fyffe outlived Lorne by a good few years. Tommy died on 17 April 1935 at the age of 45.

Ernie Lotinga, comedian born in Sunderland in 1876. He first worked as a comic vocalist at smoking concerts, making his music-hall debut under the name of Dan Roy at the Tivoli, Dover, in 1898. In 1899 he became one of the 'Six Brothers

Luck', remaining with the act until 1909. He appeared in New York in 1909 and on his return formed his own sketch and revue company, becoming well known in the character of Jimmy Josser, both on the variety stage and in films from 1929. He was also a fine pantomime artiste who excelled in his own special type of dame role. After the Second World War he continued to tour his own revues, dying in 1951 at the age of 75.

Lucan and McShane, comedy double act, famed as 'Old Mother Riley and Her Daughter Kitty'. Arthur Lucan, born Arthur Towle in Boston, Lancashire, in 1887 began his career with the 'Musical Clifftons' Concert Party', with which he appeared for seven years. While touring Ireland with a comedy sketch and variety company in 1912 he played his first dame, an old Irish washerwoman by the name of Mrs O'Flinn. In 1913 he married Kitty McShane, a 16-year-old girl from Dublin and they toured Ireland with a mother-and-daughter act which eventually developed into the famous 'Old Mother Riley' routine. On their return to England they appeared with success at the Argyle, Birkenhead, and following a tour of the UK were booked by J. C. Williamson for a ten-week season in Melbourne, followed by a tour of Australia and New Zealand. Back in England they starred for three years with the touring revue *Irish Follies*, followed by *Jazz Parade* and *Paris 1930*. In 1931 they scored a great success with their 'Matchseller' act, which took them to the London Palladium, and the equally successful 'Bridget's Night Out' was produced for the first time at the Holborn Empire in April 1934. From then on they topped bills at all the major halls and appeared in the Royal Variety Performance at the London Palladium in 1934. In 1937 they made the first of 14 'Old Mother Riley' films, which with their touring stage shows, radio and pantomime appearances, established them as one of the greatest variety attractions of the 1930s and 1940s. In September 1941 Columbia Records issued an interesting recording of Arthur Lucan singing Sam Cowell's song of the 1860s, 'Villikins and his Dinah'.

Unfortunately their married life was not too harmonious, and their slapstick, arm-waving histrionics were not confined to the stage and screen. In 1952 Lucan made his last film, *Old Mother Riley Meets the Vampire*, starring Bela Lugosi but not Kitty McShane, and for the next four years he toured in variety without his wife. During a tour of 'Old Mother Riley Goes to Paris', Arthur Lucan died in the wings of the Tivoli Theatre, Hull, on 17 May 1954. After his death Kitty McShane resumed her original stage role, touring with Lucan's understudy and film double, Roy Roland. But the days in which Lucan and McShane rated £1,000 a week were over, and after a few years McShane retired. She died on 24 March 1964.

Ben Lyon and Bebe Daniels, celebrated husband-and-wife comedy act, remembered for their wartime radio series 'Hi Gang'. Ben Lyon, born in Atlanta, Georgia, on 6 February

Lucan and McShane, 'Old Mother Riley and Her Daughter Kitty', 1943

1901 began his career in 'stock', making his first appearance at Providence, Rhode Island, in 1919. The following year he toured with Jeanne Eagels. He then went into films, playing many lead roles in Hollywood productions between 1923 and 1935. Bebe Daniels, born in Texas on 14 January 1901, first appeared on the stage at the age of four, making her film debut the following year. She played opposite many of the great screen lovers, including Valentino.

Bebe and Ben came to England in 1936, Bebe to work in films and Ben to make his London stage debut at the Palladium on 29 June 1936. Variety tours followed, until December 1939, when they appeared together in the revue *Haw Haw* at the Holborn Empire, and in December 1941 in *Gangway* at the London Palladium. But their greatest success and popularity came through radio: their first broadcast was with Vic Oliver in 'Hi Gang' (1939–41), followed by 'Stars and Stripes in Great Britain' (1941–43). Ben joined the US Army Air Force in 1942, eventually gaining the rank of Lieutenant-Colonel with the USO Special Services, while Bebe made extensive tours with ENSA, both as a solo artiste and with the 'Hi Gang' show. In November 1943 she appeared as Hattie Maloney in *Panama Hattie* at the Piccadilly Theatre, touring the same part the following year. Returning to the USA in 1945, Ben Lyon became a film executive and in 1948 was the first to recognise the star potential of the legendary Marilyn Monroe. Their return to England in 1949 was marked by a new series of 'Hi Gang' shows, and though not as successful as before, the Lyons made their home in this country and became firm radio favourites during the 1950s with a new-style domestic comedy series, 'Life with the Lyons', in which their son and daughter, Richard and Barbara Lyon, also appeared. After a long illness Bebe Daniels died on 16 March 1971, and the following year Ben Lyon returned to the USA.

M

Macari and his Dutch Serenaders, act formed by Anthony Macari. Born in Liverpool in 1896 Macari began his career as a boy accordionist at the Alhambra Theatre, Belfast, in 1907, appearing in London at the Canterbury Music Hall in 1911. He worked for 15 years with a partner as the double accordion act 'The Macari Brothers', and from 1931 with his 'Dutch Serenaders' stage band.

G. H. Macdermott, singer famous for the song 'By Jingo' which he sang at the London Pavilion in 1877, thereby adding the word 'jingoism' to the English language. Born Gilbert Hastings Farrel in 1845, he spent some years at sea before appearing as actor and stage manager of the Grecian Theatre under the name of Gilbert Hastings. In 1872 he appeared at the Britannia Theatre as Grewgious in his own adaptation of *Edwin Drood*. At the Grecian he sang 'If Ever There Was A Damned Scamp' in a burlesque by Henry Pettitt, which led to his first appearance on the halls about 1874. His greatest success, 'By Jingo' by G. H. Hunt, dates from the Russian-Turkish wars When the Russians threatened Constantinople in 1877 British public opinion was very pro-Turkish and the Tory Government of the day carried a vote of credit for £6 million to support Turkey and oppose Russian imperialism in the Near East. Macdermott, billed as 'The Great Macdermott', sang:

> We don't want to fight, but by jingo if we do,
> We've got the ships, we've got the men and got the money too.
> We've fought the Bear before, and while we're Britons true,
> The Russians shall not have Constantinople.

He sang other topical songs, including 'True Blues, Stand By Your Guns' and 'Charlie Dilke Upset the Milk' which dates from the notorious Charles Wentworth Dilke divorce case of 1885, but it is for 'By Jingo' that Macdermott is remembered. He was also the singer of 'Dear Old Pals'. Later in his career he became a variety agent and music-hall manager, dying on 8 May 1901.

Owen McGiveney, quick-change and dramatic sketch actor, famed on the halls for his characters from Dickens. Born in Preston, Lancashire, in 1884, he started his stage career as a straight actor at the Theatre Royal, Preston, in 1906. After summer seasons with various concert parties of the north he appeared in variety as a quick-change artiste specialising in characters from Dickens, making his first London appearance at the Camberwell Palace on 2 August 1910. Bransby Williams (qv) had already cornered the British music-hall market in this kind of act, and it was not until he went to America that he achieved star billing. In 1913 he toured the USA for Martin Beck and on 5 May that year

G.H. Macdermott, 'By Jingo', 1877

shared the top of the bill at the Palace, New York, with W. C. Fields and Sarah Bernhardt. This was the first of many star engagements at the Palace, and in 1943 McGiveney made his home permanently in the USA.

Sandy MacGregor, singer, born John White in Glasgow in 1893. He first appeared at the Grand Theatre, Glasgow, in 1908 and in London the following year at the South London Palace. He toured in variety for Moss and Stoll and throughout the USA on the Keith Albee and William Morris vaudeville circuits.

E. W. Machney, black-faced comedian, born in London in 1825. He first appeared in pantomime in 1834. While appearing at Evans Song and Supper Rooms he was seen by Charles Morton and booked for the Canterbury. Billed as 'The Great Machney—The Negro Delineator' he was paid £25 a week as the music hall's first 'coon' singer. Playing a banjo and wearing rags he presented a rather grotesque caricature of an American plantation negro singing 'Sally Come Up', 'Dixie' and 'The Whole Hog or None'. He died on 26 March 1909.

Ernest Mack, character comedian born Ernest Stone. He began his career as a straight actor touring with fit-up productions of drama and pantomime. His first London appearance, at the West London Theatre in 1904, was followed by a tour of the USA with one of Fred Karno's companies in 1906. He appeared in 1907 at the Palace Theatre, Manchester, in 'The Football Match', one of Karno's most successful sketches, remaining with Karno until 1912. During the First World War he went into management, touring musical comedy and revue. In 1934 he teamed with Frank Murphy, appearing in variety as 'Murphy and Mack—The Major's Reflection', until Murphy's death in 1944.

Tex McLeod, American cowboy comedian, well-known in Great Britain in variety and revue. Born in Texas on 11 November 1899, he made his first appearance in New York cabaret in 1917 and later toured as a roper and rider with rodeos and 'Buffalo Bill's Wild West Show'. His first London appearance was at the Victoria Palace on 16 June 1919 and in 1921 he was featured in C. B. Cochran's *League of Notions* starring the Dolly Sisters at the New Oxford Theatre. In 1927 he appeared with Maurice Chevalier in *White Birds* at His Majesty's Theatre. During the 1930s and 1940s he headlined in variety and toured his own revues. He died in 1973.

Will Mahoney, vaudeville comedian, born in Helena, Montana, on 5 February 1896. Beginning his career in vaudeville as a singer and dancer, he returned to comedy and became famous for his 'falling down' routine and his dance on a xylophone. First appeared in England at the London Palladium in 1926 and during the next 10 years made frequent variety tours of the UK. He was one of the few American stars to play in traditional Christmas pantomime, appearing at the Palace Theatre, Manchester, in 1934. He took part in the Royal Variety Performance at the London Palladium in 1935. During the war he toured his own variety company in Australia.

The Three Manley Brothers, musical comedians, born in Copenhagen: Wilhelm Manley in 1897, Charles in 1901 and Aage in 1906. The two elder brothers first appeared at the White Star, Copenhagen, in 1916. Joined by Aage in 1922 they presented an eccentric dancing speciality act, and with the help of impresario Alexandroff (late of the 'Great Alexandroff Troupe') they toured Europe for the next 15 years in variety, circus and revue. Their first English appearance was at the Belle Vue Circus, Manchester, in 1931, and in London at the Victoria Palace on 8 February 1932.

Margery Manners, singer and popular principal boy. Born in Coventry on 18 March 1926, from the age of eight she sang at concerts and clubs of the Midlands. At 12 she was doing summer shows with 'Billy Merrin and His Commanders' and at 14 she toured with Big Bill Campbell's Western shows. After the war, spent touring for ENSA, she established herself as one of the most popular of modern principal boys, working for top managements in London and the provinces. During the 1960s and 1970s she made almost annual tours of South Africa.

'Skeets' Martin, 'mimetic comedian', born in Liverpool on 21 January 1886. After serving as a bugler in the Boer War, he made his first stage appearance at the Westminster Theatre, Liverpool, in 1906 and in London at the Shoreditch in 1910. A good middle-of-the-bill comedian, he toured the UK in variety and became a well-known radio comic. During the Second World War he was very active with ENSA concert parties.

Paul Martinetti, probably the finest pantomimist to appear on the music-hall stage. Born in the USA on 22 January 1851, he came from a famous French family of mime artistes; his father, grandfather and great-grandfather were all prominent pantomimists. He made his debut in America at the age of six, and in London in *The Magic Flute* at the Princesses' Theatre, Oxford Street, on 30 September 1876. At this same theatre in February 1877 he played for the first time in the role of Jacques Strop in *Robert Macaire*, a part he was later to introduce to the halls. His first appearance in a music hall was at Lusby's, Mile End Road, on 2 April 1877, as a member of a comic ballet company, and soon afterwards he formed his own pantomime troupe in partnership with his brother Alfred Martinetti. He became one of music-hall's biggest attractions, and for over thirty years presented a series of melodramatic sketches, notably 'The Remorse', 'A Duel in the Snow', 'A Terrible Night', 'After the Ball', 'Paris by Night', 'The Village Schoolmaster', and his famous lurid version of 'Robert Macaire'. A popular member of the variety profession, he was a King Rat in the Grand Order of Water Rats. He retired just before the First World War and died in Algiers on 26 December 1924.

Fred Mason, 'The Whistling Coster'. Born in Brooklyn, New York, on 2 November 1865, he was the son of a well-known American theatrical manager who came to England with his family in 1866 and bought an interest in the National Standard and City of London Theatres. At the Standard baby Fred was carried on stage in the traditional harlequinade by the clown Joey Jones and at Christmas 1872 played one of the 'Babes in the Wood'. About 1880 Mason Senior took a variety company on a three-year tour of Australia and New Zealand and on his return Fred Mason made his London music-hall debut as a comic singer and 'extempore vocalist' at the Sun, Knightsbridge. Joined later by two American instrumentalists, he formed the trio 'Mason, Myers and Davis', and toured the halls as a musical knockabout act. When his partners returned to the USA he turned solo, billed as 'England's Greatest Whistling Comedian', and worked for eight months with the Livermore Minstrels and a year and a half as principal comedian of the married to Lottie Collins, qv). One of the finest principal boys, famed for her lovely legs and amazingly fine deportment, Clarice Mayne appeared in five pantomimes at the London Palladium and three at the London Hippodrome. When Tate died on 5 February 1922, Clarice Mayne turned solo, working in variety at home and on tours of the USA and South Africa. She also played in revue and straight plays until she gave up the stage in 1942. She lived the rest of her life in domestic retirement with her second husband, Teddy Knox of the double act 'Nervo and Knox' (qv). She died in 1966.

Sam Mayo, comedian and comic singer, born Waterloo Road, Lambeth, in 1881. His father ran a second-hand clothes' shop in the Cut, close to the Old Vic and the so-called 'Poverty Corner'. He made his first public appearance at a Sunday morning concert presented by Barry Ono at the Victoria Club in Blackfriars Road, followed by a lodge meeting of the 'Sons of the Phoenix' in the New Cut, Lambeth. His first real music-hall appearance was at the Alhambra, Sandgate, in 1898 and he soon became popular as a comedian. He dressed in a sort of dressing-gown and motoring cap and sang comic songs with a lugubrious expression. Billed as 'The Immobile One' he sang songs at the piano, including 'The Widow', 'She Cost me Seven and Sixpence', 'Baby, Baby', and 'I've Only Come Down for the

Paul Martinetti, 'After the Ball'

Clarice Mayne as Prince Charming

Bohee Minstrels. In 1889 he was awarded a silver belt by Lord Lonsdale for entertaining the National Sporting Club by whistling selections from *Il Trovatore* in 10 different ways. Returning to variety, billed as 'The Whistling Coster', he was a favourite at the Middlesex, singing and whistling 'Woa Polly', 'Down Petticoat Lane', and 'Four Pots a Shilling'. For the last he wrote the words to the music of R. J. MacDermott, and it later became one of Kate Carney's (qv) most famous songs. Fred Mason died on 29 December 1895 at the age of 30.

Clarice Mayne, famous music-hall singer and principal boy. She first appeared in variety with her husband, J. W. Tate, at the Oxford Music Hall on 13 June 1908, and for many years was popular as 'Clarice Mayne and That'. In 1912 they were chosen to appear in the first Royal Command Performance from the Palace Theatre singing 'I'm Longing For Someone to Love Me'.

With 'That' at the piano she introduced many good songs, mostly written by Tate, including 'Put On Your Tat-Ta Little Girlie', 'Ev'ry Little While', 'I Was a Good Little Girl Till I Met You', and her greatest success, 'Joshua'. Tate also wrote extensively for musical comedy, including some of the best numbers in *Maid of the Mountains*, which were sung by his stepdaughter, Josie Collins (he was previously

Day'. He also toured his own revues and was popular in pantomime. He died on 31 March 1938.

G. S. Melvin, character comedian famous for his 'dame' variety act. Born in Aberdeen on 20 February 1886, his father was also in the profession and at the age of five he made his first appearance at the Alhambra, Aberdeen, doing a parody of his father's act, while Melvin Senior changed for his next number. Later he worked with his father as a member of the 'Garden and Melvin Quintet' before turning solo and appearing for a number of years as an Irish comedian, using the name Hugh Donovan. Reverting to his own name, he made his first London variety appearance at Sadlers Wells, and while playing the Palace Theatre was seen by the American agent Martin Beck, who booked him for a tour of the Orpheum vaudeville circuit in 1908. A clever artiste, he appealed to both broad and subtle tastes in comedy; he was a great quick-change artist and a burlesque comedian, and as a soft-shoe dancer was only surpassed on the variety stage by Eugene Stratton. His music-hall characters ranged from a Victorian dandy to a Clydeside stoker. During the 1920s he developed his own very distinctive style of female impersonation, sending up the hearty girl guides and other devotees of open air activities. Pushing a bicycle and wearing a beret, well-stuffed blouse, shorts, gloves, anklesocks and plimsolls, with red nose, spectacles, pearl necklace and a kiss curl, he sang 'I Like to Jump Upon a Bike'. Discarding the bike for a haversack, his greatest success was 'I'm Happy When I'm Hiking', which became the hikers' marching song of the 1930s. He made three tours of the USA, in 1908, 1912 and 1924, and visited South Africa in 1916. As well as in variety he was popular in pantomime, performing in two at Drury Lane, as well as in revue and musical comedy. He was drowned in a flooded reach of the Thames near his home at Kingswood Creek in December 1946.

G S. Melvin, 1930

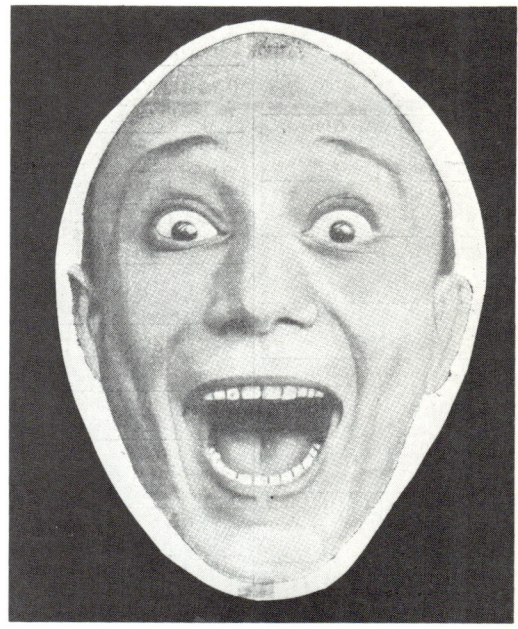

Sam Mayo, 'The Immobile One'

Billy Merson, comedian of variety, pantomime, revue and musical comedy, composer and singer of 'The Spaniard that Blighted my Life'. Born William Henry Thompson in Nottingham in 1881, he started his working career with the National Telephone Company, appearing in the evenings with Bernard Whiteman, with whom he played the smalls of Birmingham as 'Whiteman and Thompson—Irish Comedians and Trapeze performers'. After changing their billing to 'Snakella and Travella' they made their first professional appearance in Nuneaton on 26 December 1901 in a fit-up production of *Sinbad the Sailor*. In April 1902 they joined Alexander's Australian Circus, touring Ireland as 'Eccentric Equilibrists and Gymnasts', with Thompson also billed as 'Ping Pong, Australia's Greatest Clown'. Seven months later 'Snakella and Travella' returned to England, touring the northern halls and appearing in *Robinson Crusoe* at the Carlton Theatre, Saltly, Yorkshire, at Christmas 1902 and *Aladdin* at Portsmouth the following year. Thompson and Whiteman again changed their names to 'Keith and Merson' in 1904, but the partnership came to an end in 1908 and Thompson appeared as a single turn at the New Cross and Shepherd's Bush Empire, billed for the first time as 'Billy Merson'.

In February 1909 he made his West End solo debut on a bill at the Oxford which included Little Tich, Joe Elvin, Victoria Monks and Harry Tate. Shortly afterwards he appeared at the Royal Holborn, Tivoli and London Pavilion singing 'The Spaniard that Blighted my Life'. He played his first revue in 1912, joining the cast of Albert de Courville's *Hullo Ragtime* at the London Hippodrome. Between variety and pantomime engagements he appeared in *Hullo Tango*, also at the Hippodrome, *Look Who's Here* at the London Opera House, *The Whirlygig* and *Brighter London* at the Palace, and *The Whirl of the World* at the Palladium. He replaced Stanley Lupino in *Hullo America* at the Palace Theatre in December 1918. Starring Elsie Janis, the show also marked the first London appearance of Maurice

Billy Merson, 'The Spaniard that Blighted my Life'

Chevalier, who 30 years later recalled Merson in his autobiography *The Man in the Straw Hat* (1950): 'Bill Merson was not only very funny, but he was fast on his feet as well and had a good baritone voice. At home our comedians are usually funny but they are almost always awkward, and their voices are apt to be impossible. But this man had everything.'

He appeared in 1925 as the original Hard Boiled Herman in *Rose Marie* at Drury Lane, but after an unsuccessful attempt at actor-management returned to the halls. Dressed in eccentric costume, make-up, and ginger wig, he revived his old act of 25 years before, singing 'On the Good Ship Yacki Huki Doola', 'Wi Ki Walla-Wallu-Ooh-By-By' (they don't write songs like that anymore), 'Desdemonia' and the famous story of his rivalry with Alfonso Sapgoni, the Spaniard that blighted his life. When Al Jolson sang this song, Merson took him to court for copyright infringement, but lost the case on a technicality. He died on 25 June 1947.

Max Miller, the one and only 'Cheeky Chappie', who carried the low comedy tradition of music hall into the 1950s and, although not always so highly rated, is posthumously regarded as one of variety's greatest comedians. Born Thomas Henry Sargent in Brighton in 1895, he began his working life as a motor mechanic. A keen fan of G.H. Elliott (qv), he devised a routine based on the 'Chocolate Coloured Coon's' which he played at amateur concerts in the Brighton area in 1914. After war service with an Indian army concert party he got his first professional engagement as a light comedian and dancer with Jack Sheppard's Entertainers, and in 1921 toured with Ernest Binn's Northern Concert Party. His first London appearance was at the Shoreditch Music Hall in 1922, but it was not until 1924 that, billed for the first time as 'The Cheeky Chappie', he first made an impact as a single turn. While appearing at the Holborn Empire in 1925 he was seen by Tom Arnold and booked to tour as principal comedian in *Piccadilly*. With his outrageously vulgar, loudly coloured suits, baggy plus-fours, kipper tie, white trilby hat with an upturned brim, and huge diamond ring flashing as he strummed his banjo, he soon became one of London's favourite top-of-the-bills at the Palladium and Finsbury Park, Shepherd's Bush and Holborn Empires. On stage he impudently displayed his famous gag books, one white and the other blue, into which his jokes were segregated, the clean from the dirty. However, as his reputation grew, even the 'white' ones got decidedly 'bluer'. The master of timing and double entendre, his audience always met him halfway in anticipation of his punch line, only leaving Max to complain with mock innocence, 'It's people like you who get me a bad name.' Although the self-assured egoist with libido high and flying, Max was something of a contradiction. His garish silk clothes, his flat pink make-up, camp gestures and asides made him seem almost effeminate. Yet at the same time the audience was left in no doubt as to the masculinity of his tastes:

I like the girls who do,
I like the girls who don't,
I hate the girl who says she will,
And then she says she won't.
But the girl I like the best,
And I think you'll say I'm right,
Is the girl who says she never does,
But looks as though she might.

He took part in his first Royal Variety Show in 1931, appearing again in 1937 and 1950. Told to tone down his material, the irrepressible 'Cheekie Chappie' strolled onto the Palladium stage for the Coronation Year show of 1937 in a red, white and blue coat with matching silk plus fours, remarking to his immaculately dressed audience, 'I know how to dress for these occasions, nice and quiet!' After a few typical Miller jokes he audaciously cocked his head at the royal box and cracked 'All clean stuff, lady, no rubbish'. No wonder the *Daily Express* described him as 'Exquisitely vulgar, loud, earthy and blue'. He opened at the Holborn Empire on 27 August 1940 with Vera Lynn in *Apple Sauce*. The run was interrupted after only a few weeks by the Blitz, which eventually destroyed the Holborn Empire, but on 5 March 1941 it reopened at the London Palladium and ran for 462 performances.

After years of revue, in August 1943 the Palladium under George Black reverted to variety with a bill headed by Max

Max Miller, 1942

Miller, with Anne Shelton, Maurice Colleano and Billy Cotton. Max was such a success that after the unexpectedly short run of Lucan and McShane he was re-booked to top the bill for 20 weeks, the longest run of a variety star in the history of that theatre. Max enjoyed his greatest popularity during the war and although gaining the reputation for being the 'bluest' comedian in London, he was just what the doctor ordered to chase away wartime 'blues'. He returned to the Palladium in 1953 but with the decline of variety semi-retired to his home in Brighton, where unlike the philandering Max of the halls, he had lived happily married for over 40 years. Fortunately one of his last regular variety engagements at the Metropolitan Music Hall, Edgware Road, (30 November 1957) was recorded. He was generally considered to have been the original of Archie Rice, the seedy salacious music-hall comedian of John Osborne's *The Entertainer*, and when asked what he thought of the unflattering simile, replied with dignity, 'I consider it a compliment to be insulted by Sir Laurence Olivier'. Max Miller died on 7 May 1963.

Florence Mills, American Negro singer described by C. B. Cochran as 'one of the greatest artistes that ever walked onto a stage'. Born in 1901, at 17 she worked as a club singer and later toured the Keith vaudeville circuit with 'The Tennessee Ten', which included her husband, dancer Ulysses 'Slow Kid' Thompson. Singing 'I'm Craving for that Kind of Love' at Baron Wilkins's Night Club in New York's Harlem in 1921, she was heard by its composer Noble Sissle of the double act 'Sissle and Blake' (qv) and engaged to replace Gertrude Saunders in their smash hit all-Negro revue *Shuffle Along*. Only a tiny girl, she was described by Sissle as 'Dresden china that turned into a stick of dynamite', and like Josephine Baker and Paul Robeson, stepped from the show to international stardom. In 1922 she left *Shuffle Along* to star in the Plantation Club floor show, and in 1923 appeared in 'The Plantation Revue' in C. B. Cochran's *Dover Street to Dixie* at the London Pavilion. After London variety appearances she returned to the USA, establishing herself as one of the first great Negro artistes of vaudeville. She starred on Broadway in 1926 in Lew Leslie's *Blackbirds*, opening with the show at the London Pavilion on 11 September the same year. Her greatest song success was 'Bye Bye, Blackbird', but the world said 'bye, bye' to this little blackbird far too soon. She died on 1 November 1927 at the age of 26.

Florence Mills, 'Bye Bye, Blackbird', 1926

Nat Mills and Bobbie, popular husband-and-wife double comedy act. Nat Mills began his career in pantomime with Andrew Melville's company at the Holloway Empire. Turning solo he worked in working men's clubs in London and made his variety debut as an impressionist at the Bedford Music Hall, Camden Town. He then teamed with Bobbie, who started her career as a child actress and went on to tour as Mamie in *The Belle of New York*, and they made their first appearance together as a double novelty comedy act at the Woolwich Empire. They became popular with their distinctive comedy style, in which Nat did all the talking in a long-suffering tone and the lugubrious Bobbie bleated 'yes' and 'no' in reply, spending six months of each year playing the leading London halls. Their popularity was not confined to this country. Early in their career they toured South Africa and in August 1930 made their first visit to the USA, opening at the 58th Street Theatre, going on to appear at the Palace, and doing a year's vaudeville tour. They went to Australia in 1931, playing 22 weeks for J. C. Williamson. They made their first broadcast in 1938 and during the war years became

Nat Mills and Bobbie, 1928

well-known radio comedians, introducing Nat's famous frustrated catch phrase 'Well, let's get on with it'. They toured and broadcast for ENSA and on 4 November 1946 appeared in the Royal Variety Performance. When Bobbie died on 20 January 1955, Nat Mills retired from the stage but continued to work behind the scenes of show business and remains a respected member of the Grand Order of Water Rats.

Clement Minns, ventriloquist and magician, born in Ilford, Essex, in 1893. He began as a boy ventriloquist billed locally as 'The World's Youngest Ventriloquist'. His first variety appearance was at the Royal West London Theatre, Church Street, Edgware Road, in 1913. Later he worked in variety with his wife and son, presenting his magical ventriloquist act from 1920. He appeared at St George's Hall for the Maskelynes for 25 seasons.

Mistinguett, queen of the French music hall, born Jeanne Bourgeois at Enghien, near Paris, on 5 August 1875. Her first appearance was made at the Casino de Paris in 1895, singing 'La Mome du Casino'. Later the same year, billed as 'Miss Tinquette', she played the Trianon Concert Hall, Paris. From 1897 to 1907 she appeared at the Eldorado Music Hall on the Boulevard de Strasbourg, rising gradually from virtually a child vamp, standing by the footlights with her black stockings rolled halfway down her calves, singing the songs of the street urchin, to one of the Eldorado's greatest attractions. She was adored not only by the working-class audiences, but also by the fashionable intelligentsia, which included the sculptor Rodin, Oscar Wilde and the young Jean Cocteau. Her popularity was comparable to that in England of Marie Lloyd, but her Eldorado repertoire never rose above café-concert songs and low comedy routines. Temporarily leaving the music hall, she appeared in Feydeau's *La Dame de Chez Maxim's*, directed by the author in Brussels in 1907, followed by light comedy, operetta and more farce with the Folies Dramatiques. At the Bouffes Parisiennes in 1908 she was a great success in the sketch 'La Mome Flora', appropriately enough, for as a child she herself sold flowers outside the Casino at Engheim.

She made her London debut in 1909, playing a week's variety engagement at the Palace Theatre. Although her performance went almost without notice, in those days when a 'glimpse of stocking was something shocking' one critic commented that she 'showed her legs with rather more generosity than was consistent with normal standards of decorum'. Returning to Paris and the music hall, in 1911 she appeared at the Moulin Rouge in *La Revue de la Femme*, in which she and Max Dearly created the famous apache dance 'Valse Chaloupée'. Later the same year she joined the Paris Varieties, appearing in a successful revival of *La Vie Parisienne*. In 1911, as she put it, 'I joined forces with the two great loves of my life—Grande Revue and Maurice Chevalier'. Chevalier (qv) was then only 22 and still little more than a red-nosed comedian, described at his first appearance at the Folies Bergère by *Figaro* as a 'great gangling lout'. Mistinguett claims the credit for cultivating the gangling lout into the most internationally famous of all the French music-hall artistes. Their dancing partnership and personal relationship lasted for nearly 10 years, until Chevalier's success led to professional jealousy. At the Casino de Paris in 1920 she introduced the song with which she is most closely associated, 'Mon Homme' (the English version, 'My Man', was introduced in the Ziegfeld Follies of 1921 by Fanny Brice). The 1920s were spent in a series of Mistinguett revues at the Moulin Rouge, Scala and Casino de Paris.

She went to New York in 1924 to appear in the Ziegfeld Follies but when the contract fell through made her debut with the Shubert Brothers. After a world tour, in 1931 she opened in *Paris qui Brille*, at the Casino de Paris, followed by further visits to the USA and tours of North Africa and Europe. During the war she continued to appear in occupied Paris at the Etoile Palace, Casino, and Alhambra. After an absence of nearly 40 years she returned to England to make what is regarded as her London debut at the Casino on 8 December 1947. She was then over 70 and, nervous of facing a London audience after so long, dried up while singing, of all songs, 'Mon Homme'. She described her experience in her autobiography, *Mistinguett, Queen of the Paris Night* (published in England in 1954): 'It hardly seems possible—a song I had been singing steadily for the last 20 years. My hands flew to my face in an involuntary gesture of horror. And I began to cry before a dismayed and speechless audience. I left the stage and took refuge in the wings.' Pulling herself together she went on again, but dried up in the same spot and once again left the stage in tears. Bernard Delfont, who was presenting the show, was ready to bring down the curtain but she bravely went on again and sang the song without a hitch. She closed to generous applause and the rest of the two-week engagement went well, but she wisely refused an offer to make a variety tour of the Moss Empires. She made her last appearance at the ABC Music Hall, Paris, in September 1950 and died at the age of 81 at her villa at Antibes in January 1956.

Albert Modley, Yorkshire comedian, born in Barnsley on 3 March 1901. His father, known as 'Professor Modley, ran a gymnasium at Ilkley and in the early years of the 1900s staged gymnastic exhibitions, presenting among others strong man Eugene Sandow and George Hackenschmidt, the 'Russion Lion'. Albert Modley began his professional life as a railway porter at Bradford, working the local pubs as a comedian in his spare time. He first worked for Ernest Binn's Northern Concert Party at Morecambe, making his first stage appearance at the Hippodrome, Eastbourne, in February 1930 and in London at the London Music Hall, Shoreditch, in April the same year. Between 1931 and 1934 he appeared with the Arcadian Follies, working as Enoch in a double act with Harry Korris. One of the finest Yorkshire dialect comedians, he appeared in summer shows, variety and pantomime for Prince Littler, Francis Laidler, Tom Arnold and Lawrence Wright. From 1940 he toured his own show, 'On With the Modley', and after the war became popular on radio as resident comedian with 'Variety Bandbox'.

Victoria Monks, music-hall singer famed for the song 'Won't You Come Home Bill Bailey'. Born in Manchester on 1 November 1884, she made her first appearance under the name 'Little Victoria' in 1899 and in London at the Oxford Music Hall in 1903. Billed as 'John Bull's Girl', she soon became a great favourite, singing with gusto 'Sweet Saturday Night', 'Give My Regards to Leicester Square', 'Take Me Back to London Town', 'Call Round Any Old Time' and 'Bill Bailey'. Her last appearance was at the Croydon Empire on 17 January 1927, making her final plea to her wayward lover:

Won't you come home Bill Bailey, won't you
   come home,
I'll do the cooking, darling. I'll pay the rent.

After the first house she collapsed suffering from severe influenza and died of pneumonia on 26 January 1927 at the age of 43.

Mistinguett and Maurice Chevalier, about 1925

Victoria Monks, 1918

Harry Mooney, comedian, born Harry Goodchild in 1889. He made his first appearance at the Star, Bermondsey, in October 1924. As a partner in a double act, 'Murray and Mooney', he became well known in variety, appearing in the Royal Variety Performances of 1934 and 1938. Later he teamed with Victor King, and as 'Harry Mooney and Victor King' became a well-known radio act. He died on 28 September 1972.

Morecambe and Wise, comedy double act which carries on the cross-talking music-hall tradition of the 1890s. Eric Morecambe, born John Eric Bartholomew in Morecambe, Lancashire on 14 May 1926, first appeared as a 'gormless' comic in variety at the Empire, Nottingham, in 1939. Ernie Wise, born Ernest Wiseman in Leeds on 27 November 1925, appeared at the age of seven with his father, playing the local working-men's clubs as an amateur turn known as 'Carson and Kid'. His first professional appearance was at the Prince's Theatre, London, in January 1939. He teamed with Eric Morecambe in 1940, and with him appeared in a juvenile discoveries show *Youth Takes a Bow*, *Garrison Theatre* and, in 1943, *Strike a New Note*, George Black's revue starring Sid Field at the Prince of Wales Theatre, London. During the war Ernie served for three years in the Merchant Navy and Eric worked for a time with comedian Gus Morris, until he was drawn in the ballot to go down the mines as a 'Bevin Boy'. Teaming again after the war, they worked in variety, toured with low comedy 'tit and bum' road shows, appeared in pantomime for Prince Littler and broadcast in BBC radio variety shows. Their first television appearance for Ronnie Waldman in 1954 gave no hint of their later pre-eminent position in television comedy, but in 1960 they appeared in ITV's 'Sunday Night at the London

Mooney and King, 1935

Morecambe and Wise, 1952

Palladium'. This led to their own television series and the Royal Variety Performance at the Prince of Wales Theatre on 6 November 1961. They have since established themselves as the most popular comedy double act in the history of television.

Jane Moore and Billy Revel, comedy dance duo. Jane Moore was born in Brooklyn, New York and began her career in small-time vaudeville and burlesque, graduating to Broadway revues. In partnership with Sylvan Lee she appeared in the musical comedy *Naughty Riquette* with Mitza and Stanley Lupino, followed by *Lady Do*, which featured female impersonator Karyl Norman of 'Creole Fashion Plate' fame. Her first appearance in England was at the Gaiety in 1927 in *The Girl from Cook's*, and in 1928 she teamed with English dancer Billy Revel. After successful music hall appearances in Paris, they returned to England to work in cabaret and made their first London variety appearance as a double act at the London Palladium in August 1929. They appeared in the Royal Variety Performance of 1931.

Morris and Cowley, comedians, two brothers known as Harry Morris and Frank Cowley. Born Frank and Harry Birkenhead, they first appeared with another brother, their mother and two girls at the Palace Theatre, Oldbury, in September 1911. Billed as 'The Birkenhead Family' they toured the halls with the sketch 'Her Boy's Birthday' until the outbreak of war when all three brothers joined the army. After the war Frank and Harry formed a double act, working until 1923 as 'The Vesta Brothers'. Changing their stage name to 'Morris and Cowley' they became well known in variety and as radio comedians. During the 1940s they toured with their own shows, notably *The Squire's Party*.

Lily Morris, popular comedienne and singer. Born in London in 1884, at the age of 10 she appeared in pantomime at Drury Lane and later toured as a juvenile for Moss Empires. Becoming well known as a chorus singer with a big voice and personality to match, the songs 'In the Shade of the Old Apple Tree', 'Don't Have Any More Mrs Moore', and 'Why Am I Always the Bridesmaid' took her to the top of the bill and to the Royal Variety Performance on 24 February 1927. She came out of retirement in 1948 to replace Nellie Wallace on the *Thanks for the Memory* tour. She died in 1952.

George Mozart, comedian, born David Gillings in Yarmouth in 1864. From the age of fourteen he received musical training as a volunteer bandsman with the Prince of Wales Own Artillery and later played with local music-hall and theatre orchestras. His first professional appearance was as a clown with John Henry Cook's circus in Edinburgh. He later joined the Livermore Brothers Court Minstrels, first as musical director and violinist, and then as corner man. His London debut was as a black-faced minstrel at the Marylebone Music Hall in 1886. For the next year he worked with a partner as 'Engist and Orsa—Musical Clowns', and then teamed with Charles Warrington as the comedy and musical act 'Warrington and Gillings'. Changing their name to 'the Mozarts' they made their first London appearance at the Queen's, Poplar, in 1891. Other London bookings followed, including a season in 1893 with Charles Morritt's

Morris and Cowley, 1930

George Mozart, 1908

Lily Morris, 1925

magic and variety company at the Prince's Hall, Piccadilly, and a 12-month engagement for Charles Morton at the Palace. While playing in *Aladdin* at the Grand Theatre, Islington, in 1895, George Mozart was seen by Sir Augustus Harris who offered him a part as solo comedian in his next pantomime at Drury Lane. Harris died two weeks later, but the offer decided George to turn solo, appearing soon after at the Westminster Aquarium and the Canterbury.

He became one of the finest character comedians and pantomime artistes, topping bills at all the major halls for nearly 30 years notably with the one-man sketches 'A Soldier and a Maid' and 'The Family Album'. With his own variety company he toured the USA in 1907, appearing in New York at the Colonial, Hammerstein's and the Orpheum theatres. (On the same tour Marie Dressler was appearing in vaudeville with her burlesque of David Belasco's *Girl of the Golden West*.) He first appeared in revue in 1915, playing Queen Elizabeth in André Charlot's *Now is the Time* at the Alhambra. From the earliest days he had an interest in film-making and was one of the first directors of Hammer Productions. During the 1920s he was the landlord of the Green Man and French Horn in St Martin's Lane, London, but also continued to play London variety engagements, including a season in 1928 with Maskelyne's Mysteries at the St George's Hall. He died on 9 December 1947.

Will Murray, comedian whose famous music-hall sketch 'Casey's Court' was the nursery of many future star comedians. Born in Liverpool on 11 April 1877, he made his first stage appearance at the Haymarket Music Hall, Liverpool, in 1890, and in London at the Star, Bermondsey, in 1892. He produced the juvenile sketch 'Casey's Circus' in 1906 and later developed into 'Casey's Court'. It gave young Charlie Chaplin his first music-hall engagement, doing a burlesque of Dr Walford Bodie. Although Chaplin later described it as an 'awful show' he admitted it gave him a chance to develop as a comedian. During the long career of the sketch in which Will Murray was later joined by his son and grandson, it introduced many comedians to variety: Stanley Lupino, Jack Edge, George Doonan, Robbie Vincent, Dave Morris and Tommy Trinder among them.

'My Fancy' (Mrs E. Bawn), dancer, born in St Louis, USA, in 1878. She made early appearances with a juvenile troupe, later teaming with another girl working a trapeze and acrobatic act as 'The Mucumber Sisters'. She made her first appearance in London as a solo dancer at the London Pavilion in 1894, and as 'My Fancy' played a long engagement at the Oxford in 1895. Billed as 'The Finest Sand Dancer in the World', she appeared at the principal variety theatres of Europe and America, including the bill that opened Hammerstein's Olympia, New York, in 1896. She died in February 1933.

N

Jolly John Nash, the original laughing comedian. Born in 1830, he spent his early years mining ore and smelting iron in the Forest of Dean. By way of smoking concerts and the free-and-easies of the Midlands, where he was known as 'The Laughing Blacksmith', he arrived in London some time in the late 1850s. With his bluff, hearty appearance and fine physique which quivered and shook as he sang his laughing songs, he was soon a great favourite at Masonic meetings and London song-and-supper rooms. When the South London Music Hall opened in December 1860, 'Jolly' John was one of its first star attractions, billed above George Leybourne as 'Jolly John Nash—The Merry Son of Momus of Side-splitting Notoriety'. In 1861 he was one of the first comedians to appear on the bill of Charles Morton's New Oxford Music Hall, singing 'Sister Mary Walked Like That' (he had a special line in funny walks), 'The Little Fat Grey Man', and 'I Couldn't Help Laughing It Tickled Me So'. He went on to star for long periods at Weston's, and in 1866 was engaged as Chairman of the Strand Musick Hall, in an attempt to save it from its previous policy of 'refined sentiment and classic art'. Even so, the music-hall public preferred its music without a 'k' and the hall was forced to close in 1868 (the Gaiety Theatre was built on the site later that year). With Arthur Lloyd he was the first music-hall performer to appear before royalty when he was engaged by William Holland to sing at a stag party given by the Earl of Carrington for the Prince of Wales. The young Prince took a great liking to Jolly John singing 'The Merry Topper', 'I'm Not Inquisitive' and a comic walking song, 'Rackity Jack', and from then on made a point of seeing Nash wherever he appeared, thus ensuring him the best possible bookings. He played several instruments in his act, closing with a tune played on a solid silver cornet presented to him by the Prince. The royal favour came to an abrupt end when Nash got a bit too jolly and slapped His Royal Highness on the back.

Nash toured the USA in 1874, one of the first British music-hall performers to do so, and returned to appear with success in New York in 1876. In 1877 he presented his own one-man show 'Be Merry and Wise' at the Egyptian Hall, London, followed by a year's tour of the UK with his own company performing comedy and opera. With his *All for Fun* variety show he returned to the USA in October 1886 and made an 18-month tour from New York to San Francisco. In later years he had a great success with the song 'Ho, Ho, Ho—Hee, Hee, Hee', still remembered as 'Little Brown Jug'. He outlived his great contemporaries, George Leybourne and Vance, by many years, dying on 13 October 1901.

Naughton and Gold, double comedy act of variety and 'Crazy Gang' fame. Both were born in Glasgow, Charlie Naughton in 1887 and Jimmy Gold in 1886. They began their stage careers together at the Glasgow Hippodrome on 10 July 1908 and in London at the Empress, Brixton, two weeks later. With their comedy act of the British working man 'Turn It Around the Other Way', they toured in variety and appeared in pantomime throughout the UK. For the week of 30 November 1931 they appeared at the London Palladium in the first of George Black's *Crazy Weeks*, which eventually developed into the 'Crazy Gang' shows at the Palladium and Victoria Palace (see also Bud Flanagan). Jimmy Gold died in 1967 aged 81, and Charlie Naughton on 11 February 1976 at the age of 89.

Navarre, Australian impressionist, born Alexander Wright. He first appeared in variety in England with American 'silent' comedian and xylophonist, Fred 'Pansy' Sanborn, later working a solo comedy act as André Navarre. In 1935 he became an impressionist, quickly making a name in variety, cabaret and radio, not only in London and the UK but also in Denmark, Sweden and Norway. He was killed by enemy action on 14 October 1940.

Nellie Navette, serio-comedienne and dancer. Made her debut at the age of 11 in military spectaculars at the Canterbury entitled 'The Fall of Pevna' and 'Trafalgar'. Trained as a dancer, she appeared in pantomime at the Surrey and as principal dancer at the Canterbury, Elephant and Castle Theatre, Philharmonic in Islington, Pavilion, and Crystal Palace. She first worked a solo turn at the York

Pavilion, Southampton, in April 1888, and in June the same year appeared at the Cambridge Music Hall, London. A popular principal boy, she appeared in pantomime at the Prince of Wales Theatre, Liverpool, in 1888, and at the Theatre Royal, Manchester, in 1889 and 1890. She was frequently seen at the London Pavilion from 1890, singing 'English Lady Cricketers', a burlesque which distinguished her from the many minor serio-comediennes of the day.

Nazzaro, impressionist, born Erminio Nazzaro in Naples on 20 April 1912. With a large repertoire of animal, bird, and mechanical sound impressions he first appeared at Bologna, Italy, in 1939. After the war he toured the world with his act, making his first appearance in England at the Palace, Leicester, in August 1949. His London debut at the Golders Green Hippodrome on 5 September 1949 was followed by an appearance at the Palladium. He featured a 'Jekyll and Hyde' impression in his act, of which *The Performer* commented, 'Nazzaro has the unique ability to control the flow of the blood to his head and face and is thus able to perform this amazing and somewhat macabre impression.'

Frederic Neiman, ventriloquist, born in 1860. At the age of 17 he toured for nine months with a company presenting a panorama of the Russian-Turkish war. Billed as 'Neiman—The Youngest Ventriloquist in the World', he made his first music-hall appearance at the Star, Liverpool, in 1878. He developed ventriloquism to a standard previously unsurpassed in scale and originality. At Lusby's and the Canterbury in 1883 he presented a nigger minstrel troupe of seven dolls, and his 'Ventriloquial Parliament', with dolls caricaturing the leading politicians of the day, was first presented at the Royal Aquarium, Westminster, in 1886. He left England in 1887 for a two-year tour of the USA, appearing at the White House, Washington, before President

Above: Jolly John Nash, 1870

Below: Naughton and Gold, 1911

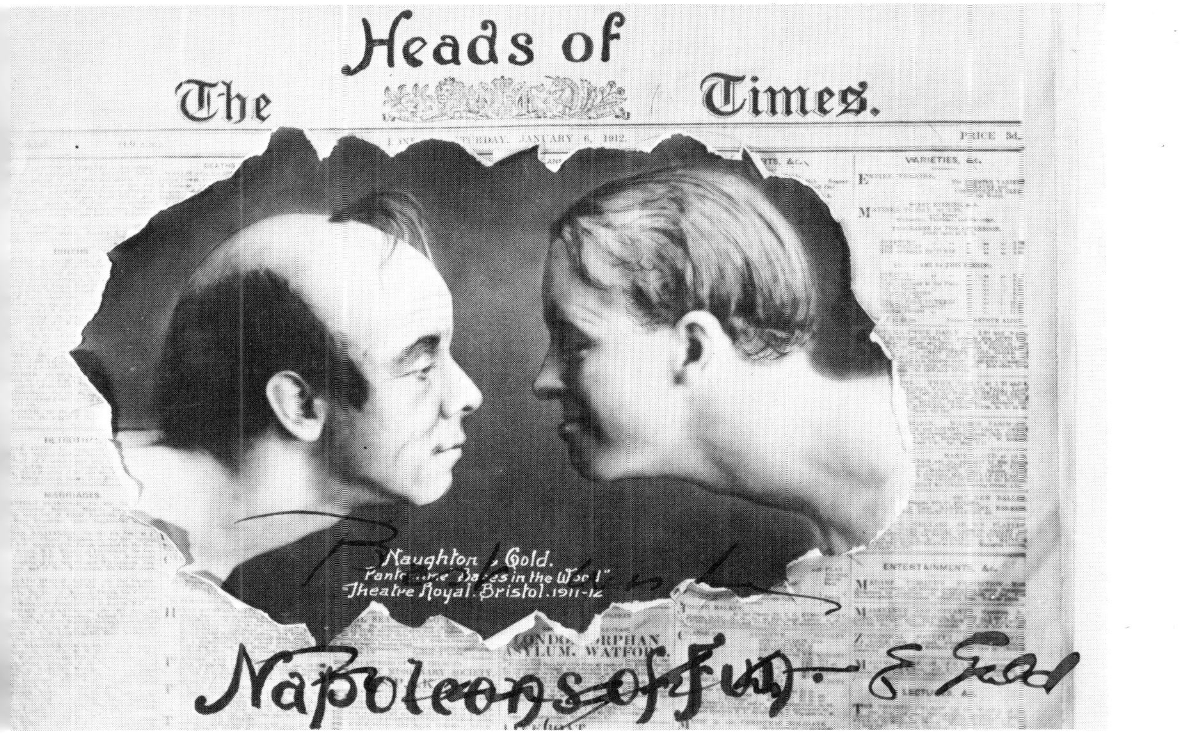

Grover Cleveland in 1888. On his return to England he toured with the Livermore Brothers Court Minstrels, and on 24 May 1890 presented his 'Ventriloquial Minstrels' at the opening of the Tivoli Music Hall, London. He later became a **variety agent and died on Christmas Day, 1910 at the age of 50.**

Nervo and Knox, comedy double act famous in variety and pantomime and as members of the 'Crazy Gang'. Jimmy Nervo, born James Holloway in 1897, was the son of George **Holloway of the 'Brothers Holloway'** circus acrobatic act. He began his career as a juggler and acrobat at the Bedford, Camden Town, in 1912 and later worked for two years with Fred Karno (qv). Teddy Knox, born in 1896, began his career as a juvenile in variety, billed as 'Chinko the Boy Juggler', and then worked with his brothers as 'The Cromwells', and as part of the double act 'Chinko and Kaufman'. Nervo and Knox teamed in 1919, appearing as gymnasts and knock-about comedians in variety and touring in revue for Albert de Courville. In 1923 they presented their 'Fantastic Frolics' on an all-British variety bill at the Palace Theatre, New York, followed by a season in the Ziegfeld Follies. While appearing in their own touring revue *Young Bloods of Variety* at the Empire, Nottingham, they were seen by Val Parnell, then booking manager for George Black and the GTC. *Young Bloods* was a crazy affair with several variety acts getting hilariously involved with each other's turns. The idea appealed to Parnell and finding himself with three comedy acts, Nervo and Knox, Naughton and Gold (qv), and Caryll and Mundy, on the same bill at the Palladium for the week of 30 November 1931, decided to try it himself. This original 'Crazy Week' developed into crazy months, and eventually into George Black's 'Crazy Shows'. With time off for revue and pantomime, Nervo and Knox appeared in the 'Crazy Gang' shows at the Palladium between 1932 and 1940 and from 1947 to 1962 at the Victoria Palace (see also Bud Flanagan). Teddy Knox died at his home in Salcombe, Devon, in December 1974 and Jimmy Nervo on 5 December 1975.

Noni, musical clown who, before his variety appearances in England, toured the circuses of Europe, playing his act in French, Italian, Spanish and German. Hailed by the press as the 'successor to Grock', he appeared on the London halls with an acrobatic, juggling and musical act with his wife, trick cyclist Dolly Victoria. With his son Horace he was a great success at the Royal Variety Performance at the London **Coliseum in March 1928.** At the end of his turn he advanced to the footlights and plaintively said to the conductor, 'What, no flowers?' Queen Mary was amused at the remark and gave **Harry Marlow** a posy from her own bouquet to present to Noni. In a less sensation-hungry age the incident had good news value and Noni charmingly billed himself as 'The Clown to whom the Queen sent a flower'.

O

Talbot O'Farrell, comedian and Irish tenor. Although the leading stage Irishman of his day, he was born William Parrot in the north of England in 1878 and sang at Northern clubs and small halls from the age of 10. After army service during the Boer War, he appeared with Alder and Sutton's Pierrots at New Brighton. Billed as 'Jock McIver, Scottish Comedian and Vocalist', he made his first London variety **appearance at the Metropolitan, Edgware Road, in 1902.** After years struggling as a Scottish singer he switched to Irish songs and as Talbot O'Farrell never looked back. He evolved a new type of 'Paddy', replacing the traditional knee breeches, shamrock and shillelagh with immaculate black

Nervo and Knox, 1926

Above: Noni and Horace, 1928

Below: Talbot O'Farrell, 1948

coat, check trousers, waistcoat, white gloves, spats and grey silk topper, and was dubbed by Archibald Haddon 'The Irishman from Savile Row'. He became immensely popular in London, holding the record for headlining appearances at the Victoria Palace; he appeared in the Royal Variety Performance at the Alhambra in 1925.

He spent long periods in the USA and on several occasions made successful variety tours of Canada, Australia and South Africa. One of the first established stars of variety to broadcast, his humour was sophisticated and his voice melodious. His songs however were highly charged with sentiment—as in, for example, 'That Old Fashioned Mother of Mine' and 'The Lisp of a Baby's Prayer'. In April 1939 he appeared on an old-time bill at the Holborn Empire with Hetty King, Albert Whelan, Harry Tate, Ada Reeve, Alice Lloyd, G. H. Elliott and Wilkie Bard. Originally billed as *Stars Who Made the Holborn Empire* it later toured as *Their Names Made Variety*. He again toured in 1948 with the very successful *Thanks for the Memory*, appearing with the company in the Royal Variety Performance in November 1948. He died in 1952.

Joe O'Gorman, comedian, born in Dublin, 24 May 1863. In his youth he gained a local reputation as a comic singer and dancer and at 16 came to England, making his first London appearance with partner Horace Wheatly in 1879. When this act broke up he worked the smalls as a single turn, teaming with Joe Tennyson in 1881. As 'Tennyson and O'Gorman' they became one of the leading cross-talking comedy acts, developing the original minstrel troupe 'question and answers' comedy technique into a more even contest between comic and feed, and establishing a comedy tradition still maintained by such acts as Morecambe and Wise. The partnership came to an end in 1901 and Joe O'Gorman again worked solo (Joe Tennyson died in 1926). He joined Wal Pink in 1914 to produce the revue *Irish and Proud Of It*, followed over the years by *Shamrock Time*, *Irish Aristocracy* and *As Irish As Ever*.

In 1891 he became one of the first members of the Grand Order of Water Rats, serving as King Rat in 1898 and again in 1901. On 8 February 1906 he became member number one of the Variety Artistes Federation, which he founded with Wal Pink, Fred Russell and W. H. Clemart. As chairman of the VAF, in 1907 he led the historic music-hall strike, which led to improvement in conditions for artistes, mainly in regard to their contracts. After years of retirement, Joe made a comeback in 1933, appearing with a veterans' company at the Hackney, Shepherd's Bush and Chiswick Empires, dying in harness at the age of 74 on 1 August 1937. His two sons, Joe and Dave O'Gorman, kept up the family tradition as 'The O'Gorman Brothers', a popular act in variety and radio between the wars.

Vic Oliver, comedian and musician, born Viktor Oliver Samek at Voslau, near Bada, Austria, on 8 July 1898. During the First World War he served as a cavalry officer and personal adjutant to Prince René Bourbon Parma. The defeat of the Central Powers and the revolution that followed the death of Emperor Franz Josef, drastically changed the old Viennese way of life and Samek left Austria for France on a forged Romanian passport. At Rouen he worked as a jazz drummer with a band playing in an 'American' bar, billed as 'Harry Brown, the American Jazz Drummer', and he later played with the band for six months at the Casino at Le Havre.

He went to America in December 1922, where during the next six months he did everything from touring vaudeville as a pianist to an indifferent tenor, to playing 'A Pretty Girl is Like a Melody' over and over again in a New York brothel. He joined a jazz combination, 'The Nine Knights of Jazz', in 1923. The following year he formed a double act with violinist Margaret Crangle and dressed in turban and Eastern robes billed himself as 'The Continental Wizard' or 'The Piano-Playing Baron'. Their act, played perfectly straight, got the 'bird' in every third-rate theatre they visited. The double act eventually broke up and in 1927 Oliver was appointed conductor and compere of the first travelling radio show, touring the theatres with a variety company and a portable transmitter with a range of about 20 miles. The following year Oliver and Crangle teamed again, now as musical comedians, playing their first important New York date at Proctor's 125th Street Theatre in 1929. Although *Variety* whimsically commented that 'Mr Oliver looks more like a piano tuner than a comic. As for his violin playing, he is not half as funny as Fritz Kreisler,' within a year they had reached the Mecca of American vaudeville, the Palace Theatre, New York.

Oliver and Crangle made their first appearance in England at the London Palladium in 1931 on a bill topped by Layton and Johnson (qv). Val Parnell retained them for a further week at the Palladium, followed by a week at the Empire, Glasgow, and the Hippodrome, Brighton. Parnell declined his option for a further eight weeks, and they returned to the USA where the act broke up. As a solo comedian who

Vic Oliver, 1936

interrupted his comic patter to play the violin Oliver was in great demand, and he was soon back at the Palace, and touring the other Keith vaudeville theatres of the USA. He returned to London in 1933 to play the Palladium and Holborn Empire, with such success that by 1935 he was appearing at the top of the Palladium bill, and sharing with Max Miller the record for appearances at the Holborn Empire. Gaining a reputation as a sophisticated if rather risqué cabaret artiste, in 1936 he appeared as principal comedian in C. B. Cochran's revue *Follow the Sun* at the Adelphi Theatre. One of the 'Cochran's Young Ladies' in the show was Sarah Churchill, daughter of Winston Churchill. At the end of the run Oliver returned to New York to star in the revue *It's The Tops* and in a blaze of publicity was joined by Sarah Churchill. They were married on Christmas Day 1936.

Oliver opened in 1939 at the London Hippodrome in George Black's revue *Black and Blue*. The run of the show was cut short by the outbreak of war but in October he was back at the Hippodrome in *Black Velvet*, which ran for 16 months, followed by *Get A Load of This* and *The Night and the Music* at the Coliseum. During the war he became a well-known radio comedian, appearing with Bebe Daniels and Ben Lyon (qv) in 'Hi Gang', and 'Bebe, Ben and Vic'. His own radio shows followed, 'Oliver Twist', 'Oliver Again', 'Yankee Doodle Do', and in 1944, 'Vic Oliver Introduces'. In the last he conducted his own orchestra, formed from professional orchestral players, and known as the British Concert Orchestra. After 26 weeks on the air Vic and the orchestra went on tour under the management of Harold Fielding and after concerts at the Albert Hall toured the UK. He appeared in the Royal Variety Performance at the London Coliseum in 1945 and at the London Palladium in

1952. He starred in *Starlight Roof* in 1947, Robert Nesbitt's revue at the London Hippodrome, and in 1948 appeared in Emile Littler's *Latin Quarter* at the London Casino. He remained a popular comedian in variety, revue, pantomime and on radio and television until his death on 15 August 1964.

Olsen and Johnson, crazy comics of 'Hellzapoppin' fame. Ole Olsen, born in Indiana, USA, on 6 November 1892, began his career as a solo act in vaudeville in 1914. He was not a great success, and the following year teamed with Chic Johnson, born in Chicago on 5 March 1891, with whom he made his bow as a violin-and-piano duo in a Chicago café. Turning to crazy comedy routines they were described by Bernard Sobel as 'Comic nuts, who were kings of cacophony, unconventionality and conviviality'. They appeared in the Ziegfeld Follies of 1922 and following a tour of Australia visited England but were prevented from making a planned variety tour by the sudden illness of Olsen. Back in the USA they appeared in *Monkey Business of 1926* and *Atrocities of 1932*. In 1933 they replaced Jack Haley and Sid Silvers as two confidence tricksters in the musical *Take a Chance*, which starred Ethel Merman and ran for a total of 243 performances at the Apollo Theatre, New York. The greatest success of their career came in September 1938 when they opened in their own free-for-all vaudeville revue *Hellzapoppin* at the 46th Street Theatre, New York. Very much on the lines of George Black's Palladium 'Crazy Gang' shows, it lived up to its billing of a 'screamlined revue designed for laughing' and set a record for the longest Broadway run to date of 1,404 performances. It was followed in December 1941 by *Sons of Fun* (742 performances), and in 1944 by *Laffing Room Only* (233 performances), both at the Winter Garden, New York. They made their first London appearance with an abridged version of *Hellzapoppin*, which played a six-week variety season at the Casino in February-March 1948, followed during April-May with a full-length version at the Princes Theatre. Johnson died on 25 February 1962 and Olsen on 26 January 1963.

Omar, Arab acrobatic dancer, born in Morocco in 1904. His father, Sheik Abdullah Ben Omar, ran a folklore and acrobatic dance troupe with which Omar went to America at the age of seven. He teamed in 1919 with a Frenchman and an Irishman as a comedy acrobatic trio, which toured the Keith-Albee vaudeville circuit. Turning solo in 1922 he appeared in Earl Carrol's *Scrap Book Revue*, remaining with the show until May 1931. Following appearances in February 1933 at the UFA-Palast, Hamburg, and Scala, Berlin, he made his first appearance in England in cabaret at the Savoy Hotel, London, on 3 April. Variety engagements followed at the London Palladium and Holborn Empire, where he aroused great interest with his exotic dervish dance, which he performed in that year's Royal Variety Performance at the Palladium.

Beryl Orde, impressionist, born in Liverpool on 9 November 1914. She first appeared at the Argyle Theatre, Birkenhead, in 1923 and in London at the Century Theatre, Notting Hill Gate, in 1928. Appearing in variety, revue, concert party and pantomime, she became very well known as a radio artiste in 'Variety Bandbox', 'Worker's Playtime', and so on. She died on 10 September 1966.

Navan O'Reilly, ventriloquist, born Tom Franks in Ireland on 21 December 1869. He began his career playing concert halls in Ireland in 1887 and made his first music-hall appearance in England at the Queens Park Hippodrome, Manchester, in 1909. The same year he made his London debut at the Canterbury and became well-known in London and provincial halls for his 'talking dog' act. He also toured his own road shows, 'O'Reilly's Vaudevillians' and 'Hammer and Tongs', in which he appeared in the USA and Canada in 1911–13.

Tessie O'Shea, exuberant comedienne with a personality as big as her billing of 'Two Ton Tessie'. Born in Cardiff, Wales, on 13 March 1914, from the age of eight she sang comedy songs at local hospitals and charity shows with Billy Barnes's Concert Party. Coming to London with Barnes in 1925 she was seen by agents for Stoll and booked for her first solo appearance at the Hippodrome, Bristol, in March 1926, and in London at the Chiswick Empire the following June. Other dates followed, including the London, Shoreditch, on a bill topped by Ella Shields, and a tour of the Macnaughton houses. As a girl she modelled her performance on Lilly Morris of 'Don't Have Any More, Mrs Moore' fame, but soon developed her own boisterous 'laugh and grow fat' style of comedy, singing to her own banjulele accompaniment. Although still very low on the bill, she appeared for George Black at the London Palladium and toured the UK in variety, becoming a great favourite at the Argyle, Birkenhead, and in summer season at Blackpool.

During the war she became a well-known radio comedienne, and entertained both on the air and on tour for ENSA. Early in 1944 she shared the top of the London Palladium bill with Max Miller and in April 1946 returned to

Tessie O'Shea, 1973

star in Val Parnell's first revue *High Time*, making her entrance on the back of a pregnant elephant. Unfortunately the delicate state of Mrs Jumbo's health was not realised until the night she took exception to 'Two-Ton Tessie' and threw her to the stage. She was out of the show for three months, returning in time to take part in the Royal Variety Performance on 4 November 1946. In 1949 she and Billy Cotton toured the road show 'Tess and Bill', and in November that year appeared with the show for a season at the Victoria Palace. During the 1950s her career settled down to the routine of summer shows, cabaret, radio and television spots. She also appeared in productions of *Sailor Beware* and *Romanoff and Juliet*, and in the films *The Blue Lamp* (1948) and *The Shiralee* (1957).

Her career took an entirely new turn when on 8 December 1963 she opened at the Broadway Theatre, New York in Noël Coward's musical *The Girl Who Came To Supper*, based on Terence Rattigan's successful play *The Sleeping Prince*. Tessie appeared as Ada Cockle, selling fish and chips to the crowds lining the route of George V's coronation procession. She scored a great personal triumph, singing 'Don't Take Our Charlie For the Army', and leading a chorus of 'pearlies' in 'London's a Little Bit of All Right' and 'Saturday Night at the Rose and Crown'. Tessie became the toast of New York, appearing on American television chat shows, and guest-starring in leading comedy spectaculars. She returned to the USA in 1966 to star as Beth Morgan in *A Time for Singing*, a musical adaptation of Richard Llewellyn's novel *How Green Was My Valley*. Also starring Ivor Emmanuel, Laurence Naismith and Shani Wallis, it opened at the Broadway Theatre, New York, on 21 May 1966. Somewhat overshadowed by the success of *Mame* which opened at the Winter Gardens three days later, it closed after 41 performances. Tessie remains one of the most popular comediennes of variety, summer shows and television.

MR. WALTER PASSMORE.

Walter Passmore, 1903

P

Gaston Palmer, comedy juggler, born in Marseilles on 4 March 1890. His father was George Palmer, an equestrian juggler from Bradford who married Adele Rancy, whose father ran the well-known French 'Circus Rancy'. Gaston appeared with the circus from the age of five, making his stage debut with his father, brother and two sisters at the Casino, Lyons, in 1902 as 'The Five Pirroscoffs'. Going to the USA, he made his first solo appearance at the Broadway Theatre, New Jersey, in October 1914, followed by tours of the Keith vaudeville circuit. His London debut was at the Coliseum on 17 May 1920, followed by UK variety tours. He appeared in the Royal Variety Performance on 22 May 1930.

Walter Passmore, actor, comedian and comic vocalist. Born in London on 10 May 1867 he made his first stage appearance in pantomime in Sunderland in 1881, and in London at the Savoy Theatre on 3 May 1893. During his 10 years with the Savoy company he worked mainly in Gilbert and Sullivan operetta, playing Tarara in the original production of *Utopia Ltd* in 1893, and Rudolph in *The Grand Duke* in 1896. Although the great days of the Savoy Opera were almost over, he was very successful in the revivals of the 1890s, playing many of the low comedy parts created by George Grossmith. A fine dancer and broad comedian, he was popular in pantomime, appearing in three of Arthur Collins's productions at Drury Lane: as Baroness De Bluff in *Cinderella* in 1905–06, the name part in *Sinbad* in 1906–07, and Reggie, one of the 'Babes in the Wood' in 1907–08. At Christmas 1910 he appeared in *Chick in the Wood* at the London Hippodrome, followed by variety dates at various London halls. He later toured the variety theatres with a comedy sketch company in *Queer Fish, The Soldier's Mess, Sweet William* and *Ducks and Quacks*. He retired to run a tobacconist's shop in Golders Green until his death on 29 August 1946.

Gilbert Payne, comedian, born in Leeds on 30 December 1877. He first appeared at the Princess Palace, Leeds, in 1893 and toured the halls with his own sketches, 'Checked Again' and 'Bingle's Bungle', making his first London appearance at the Empire, Shoreditch, in October 1910. Later he toured as principal comedian in his own revues and appeared regularly in Christmas pantomime and summer shows.

Bob and Alf Pearson, 'My Brother and I', entertainers at the piano, popular in variety and on the air since the early 1930s. Brothers born in Sunderland, Robert in August 1907 and Alfred in June 1910, they first appeared with a local concert party and in 1929 won a talent competition sponsored by Columbia Records, and later that year made their first broadcast from Savoy Hill. Their professional stage debut was 24 December 1929 at the Empire, Gateshead, and in London at the Coliseum on 21 June 1930. Their work in

Bob and Alf Pearson, 'My Brother and I'

cabaret, variety, summer shows and frequent broadcasts has kept them to the fore, both in this country and on world tours ever since.

Donald Peers, variety's number-one singing star of the 1950s. Born in Ammanford, Wales, on 10 July 1908, at 16 he toured the army barracks of London, Aldershot, Catterick and points north, not as a singer but as a painter with a company under contract to the War Office. The job did however lead to his first success as a vocalist, competing in a talent contest organised by Fred Karno at Aldershot and singing with a dance band at Catterick Camp. His first professional stage appearance was on 20 September 1927 with the 'Tons of Fun' Concert party at the New Theatre, Lowestoft. His first broadcast, singing 'In a Shady Nook' (better known later by its second line, 'By a Babbling Brook'), was from the BBC 2LO studios on 17 December 1927. During 1928 he toured with Clifton Shaw's Concert Party as 'Smiling Donald Peers and his Ukulele', and at Christmas he sang in the chorus and acted as understudy to principal boy Randolph Sutton (qv) in the pantomime *Babes in the Wood* at the Grand Theatre, Plymouth. His first London appearance was with Sutton's touring revue *Spare Time* at the Bedford, Camden Town, in August 1929.

In 1933 he tasted his first success in variety supporting good bills at number one and number two theatres. The turning point of his career came in April that year when John Sharman booked him for his radio programme 'Music Hall'. *Daily Express* critic Collie Knox gave him a rave review which helped greatly in promoting his variety prospects, and led to his first record for HMV. He spent the war serving with the RASC and broadcasting from the BBC's wartime studios at Bangor. In 1949 his radio show 'The Cavalier of Song', broadcast live from the Kilburn Empire, established him as Britain's number one heart-throb. On a tremendous wave of popularity, perhaps only equalled by the Beatlemania of the 1960s, he headlined all over the country and for several years was the biggest name in variety. On 9 May 1949 he gave a solo concert at the Royal Albert Hall, but while appearing in Blackpool that summer had to undergo a throat operation which put him out of action for six months. Returning to radio on 8 February 1950, he was soon back on top, appearing in August as the star attraction at the Palladium, and in that year's Royal Variety Performance. Besides 'By a **Babbling Brook**', his famous signature tune, his song hits included 'Powder Your Face With Sunshine', 'Lavender Blue', and 'Far Away Places', which in this country alone sold a total of ten million copies. At the height of his success he earned £50,000 a year, but as he prophetically wrote in 1950, 'What goes up, must come down', and after a few years at the top his career was hit by rock and roll. Although never expecting to gain his previous phenomenal popularity, he toured Australia with success and on his return worked the Northern clubs. In 1969 he made a comeback with a song, 'Please Don't Go', which reached number four in the national hit parade. While touring Australia in 1971 he injured his back and was for a time confined to a wheelchair, but on his return home made one more bid for fame, with a song ironically entitled 'Give Me One More Chance'. He died in Brighton on 9 August 1973.

H. G. Pelissier, musician and pierrot who founded the famous Pelissier's Follies which appeared in the West End and toured the music halls with a series of burlesques and revues. Of Franco-Prussian descent he was born Harry Gabriel Pelissier in London in 1874. Musically educated in England and France, by the age of 15 he was composing songs for Jessie Bond of the D'Oyly Carte Savoy Company.

His first solo stage appearance was as an 'early turn' at the Marylebone Music Hall, singing his own song 'Mein Faderland', and he was greeted by catcalls and a cry from the gallery of 'When are they going ter burn yer?' As an entertainer at the piano in the style of George Grossmith Senior, he met with greater success and in 1895 joined 'The Follies Pierrot Troupe' at Worthing. Originally an amateur company formed by the Baddeley Brothers (tennis players of the day) to raise money for charities, it was then being run by Sharington Chinn. Pierrots were fast replacing the nigger minstrels as the popular form of seaside entertainment, and in 1896 Pelissier purchased the show from Chinn. By reducing

Donald Peers, 1938

the company from ten to six and adopting the motto 'excelsior', he set out to produce a slicker, more sophisticated production than the usual seaside show. Pelissier saw his troupe not just as seasonal entertainment but as an all-year-round touring show appearing at theatres and music halls of the major towns and cities.

Pelissier's Follies were engaged to support a recital given by Albert Chevalier (qv) at the Queen's Hall, London in 1898. Engagements at the Alhambra followed, and in January 1904 Pelissier's Follies—that is, Marjorie Napier, Ethel Allandale, Dan Everard, Lewis Sydney, Gwennie Mars and H. G. himself, appeared on the variety bill of the

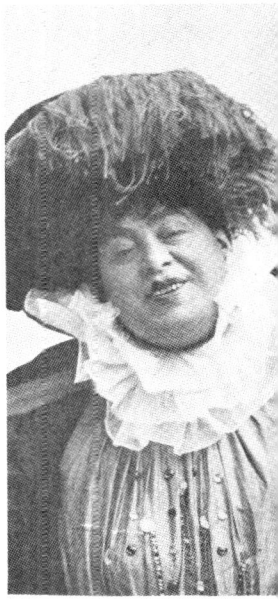

H.G. Pelissier as himself (left) and as two characters from his music-hall burlesque: 'The Coster Comedian' (centre) and 'The Charming Serio', 1907

Palace Theatre. The Follies' first appearance on a regular variety bill was at the Tivoli Music Hall, London, in October 1904, presenting skits on musical comedy and Wagnerian opera. The following December they returned to the Palace with a burlesque of *Hamlet* and were commanded to appear at Sandringham to entertain a party given for Queen Alexandra's birthday. The Follies appeared for a six-week season at the Midland Theatre, Manchester, in 1906 and proved their ability to sustain a complete evening's entertainment instead of just a 30-minute spot on a music hall bill. Pelissier presented the first of his 'potted' plays at the New Royalty Theatre, London in April 1907. Entitled 'Baffles—A Peter Pan-tomime', it was a combined skit of *Raffles* and *Peter Pan*. A few months later the company returned to the Royalty with a music-hall burlesque starring Douglas Maclaren as 'George Robeville, the refined Humorist', Morris Harvey as 'Mr Grandsby Bilious in his Drawing Room Entertainment—What the Dickens', Dan Everard and Effie Cook as 'Colonel Swanky D. Codder and Miss A. Lotta Bulls in their sensational Wild West Kilburn Shooting Act' and Pelissier as 'Miss May de Colte, the Charming Serio'.

While still in her early teens actress Fay Compton made her stage debut with the Follies and later married Pelissier. The perfect example of the expression 'laugh and grow fat', Pelissier's rotundity was his undoing. He died in 1913 at the age of 39.

The Peters Sisters, heavyweight negro singing trio, born Mattye, Anne and Virginia Peters in Santa Monica, California. They first appeared at the Club Trocadero, Hollywood, in 1935 and in London at the Palladium in 1938. During the war they made films for 20th Century Fox and between 1945 and 1950 made several variety tours of the UK. Very popular on the continent, they were a great success at the Paris Olympia in 1958.

The Two Petries, American child act, Willie and Alfy Petrie, appearing in vaudeville as 'Singing and Dancing Comedians and Plantation Cane Dancers'. They made their first appearance at Kingham, Kansas, in 1891 and in New York at Tony Pastor's Music Hall. Coming to London in 1893, their odd mixture of comedy was no a success. They went over better at the Star Music Hall, Dublin, in 1894, and the following year played four months in Liverpool.

Sam Picton, comedian and tenor, born in 1359. He made his music-hall debut in 1876 singing 'Going Through the Mill', 'Rose, Shamrock and Thistle', and a parody of 'The Man Who Broke the Bank at Monte Carlo'. He died while playing Thornton's Theatre of Varieties, South Shields, at the age of 34 in 1893.

The Piddingtons, Sidney and Lesley Piddington, Australian mind-reading act which caused a sensation on stage and radio during the late 1940s. Sidney Piddington, born in Sydney, Australia, on 14 May 1918, first devised his act while a prisoner-of-war of the Japanese at Changi Camp, Singapore. After the war he returned home to Australia and married Lesley Pope, with whom he toured and broadcast in 1947. The couple toured Australia in variety with comedian Will Mahoney, and came to England in 1949 to broadcast in a series of programmes for the BBC. Following their tremendous success on the air, the Piddingtons made their first London variety appearance at the top of the bill at the London Palladium in September 1949. After an even more impressive second radio series, which included Sidney in an airplane 'reading' the mind of Lesley in a BBC studio, they toured the UK in variety.

Jack Pleasants, 'shy' Yorkshire comedian, born in Bradford on 17 August 1874. After graduating from singing at Band of Hope and smoking concerts, he entered a talent contest held at the Scarborough Hotel, Leeds, which led to his first music-hall engagements at the City of Varieties in 1884. His first London appearance was at the Bedford, Camden Town, in January 1901 followed by a booking at the Gaiety Music Hall, Chatham. Not a great success, he returned to provincial variety and worked as a comic singer with a circus. In 1907 he appeared with George Mozart in the pantomime *Goody*

Jack Pleasants

Two Shoes at the Theatre Royal, Bradford, and was a great home-town success. From then on his career improved, and as a shy and awkward Yorkshire goon, billed as 'The Bashful Limit', he established himself as one of the most popular of the Northern dialect comedians. Wearing eccentric make-up and costume, a black frock-coat, trousers, bowler hat, and holding a large marguerite, he sang 'Norman the Mormon', 'Feeding the Ducks in the Park', 'I'm a Dada', 'Rocking the Baby to Sleep', 'The Bad Lad of the Drama', 'Watching the Trains Go By', 'I'm Twenty-one Today', and 'I'm Shy, Mary Ellen, I'm Shy'. He died while appearing in pantomime in Bradford on 26 December 1923 at the age of 49.

Alec Pleon, comedian, born St Pancras, London, on 26 April 1911. He first appeared at the Empire, Mile End, in 1923. With his grotesque comedy routine and billing of 'Funny Face', he toured the UK in variety and revue for Moss and Stoll, and made several tours of Australia and South Africa.

Gillie Potter, variety comedian famous as radio's 'Squire of Hogsnorton', opening his act with the greeting 'Good evening England, this is Gillie Potter speaking to you in basic English'. Born in 1887, he made his first London stage appearance in 1908, 'walking on' as a cowboy in Lewis Waller's *The White Man* at the Lyric, and later with H. Hamilton Stewart in *Sherlock Holmes*, playing a variety of parts including Dr Watson. In musical comedy he worked as an eccentric dancer with a tour of *The Gay Gordons*, and in 1913 co-starred with Connie Emerald (Mrs Stanley Lupino) in concert party. Following a pantomime engagement at Exeter he was booked by Oswald Stoll to tour in variety and during the run of *The Bing Boys* at the Alhambra in 1916–17 acted as understudy to George Robey. Returning to variety with a comedy monologue act he was the outstanding success of the Royal Variety Performance of 1930. *The Times* wrote of his performance:

> The programme offered lovers of the music hall a choice entertainment. Every turn was that of a 'star' certain to shed radiance on the evening. All shone but Mr Gillie Potter contrived to shine a little brighter than the rest. His patter was of the stuff on which laughter in the music hall had always thriven and delivered with an air of suave gravity that would have become the chairman of the board of directors declaring a dividend. It had an immediate and immense success which clearly extended to the royal box.

With his rather schoolmasterish voice and air of superiority, not all would agree that this was the comedy on which the music hall had thrived. However, with Harrovian straw boater and rimless glasses, dressed in Oxford bags, boots and blazer, and carrying an umbrella, he remained a popular variety and radio patter comedian until the mid-1950s. He died on 4 March 1975.

Sandy Powell, comedian, born Rotherham, Yorkshire, in 1900. His mother, Lillie La Main, toured a marionette show and from an early age Sandy assisted her in the act. His first solo appearance was as a boy soprano in 1907 and when his voice broke he switched to giving impressions and toured as a comedian in juvenile revues. He made his London debut at the Palace, Bow, in 1915, and later that year appeared at the London Hippodrome in Harry Day's *Business as Usual*, playing one of the boys in Harry Tate's sketch, 'Fortifying the Garden'.

He and his mother worked a double variety act in 1916, billed as 'Lillie and Sandy', and while playing the Dewsbury Empire were seen by a Stoll talent scout and booked for the Shepherd's Bush Empire. Lillie La Main eventually dropped out of the act as Sandy developed as a solo comedian, but she was not to be forgotten. Sandy's 'Can you hear me, Mother?' became the first radio catch phrase and one of the most famous of variety. At 16 he played his first principal comedian role, in pantomime at the Rotunda, Liverpool, and at 18 repeated this success at the Princess Theatre, Glasgow. From 1921 he appeared on the halls with a series of comedy sketches, over 40 of which he recorded. 'The Lost Policeman' sold over half a million copies, and his total output of gramophone records has been estimated at seven million. His first Royal Variety appearance was at the London Palladium in 1935, assisted by Jimmy Fletcher and Roy Jeffries in 'The Test Match'. He made two short films of his most popular sketches in 1930 ('The Lost Policeman' and 'Sandy the Fireman') and later starred in eight feature films, *The Third String* (1932), *Can You Hear Me Mother?* (1934), *Leave It To Me* (1935), *It's a Grand Old World* (1935), *I've Got a Horse* (1938), *All at Sea* (1939), *Home From Home* (1939), and *Cup Tie Honeymoon* (1948). He has been a radio comedian since 1928, and with his variety act, pantomime, and from 1932 'The Sandy Powell Road Show', he has remained a popular and respected performer for over 40 years. He still appears in old-time music-hall shows, works summer seasons, and performs on television. He made a successful Royal Variety appearance in 1970, assisted by his wife Kay White, when he presented his hilariously funny ventriloquist burlesque. He was awarded the MBE in 1975.

Above: Arthur Prince and Jim, 'Naval Occasions', 1912

Below: Sandy Powell, 'Can you hear me, Mother?'

Arthur Prince, leading music-hall ventriloquist, born in London on 17 November 1881. His first appearance was in 1897 when at the age of 16 he joined a concert party at Llandrindod Wells. After four seasons as a beach entertainer, billed as 'The Court Magician and Ventriloquist' he made his London debut at the South London Palace in 1902. From the earliest days ventriloquists were popular with music-hall audiences, and dressed in a white naval uniform with his famous doll 'Jim' as a cheeky Able Seaman, Prince rapidly came to the fore as a performer. He appeared in the first Royal Command Performance at the Palace Theatre in 1912 and toured the world with his act 'Naval Occasions'. He was the first to use the ventriloquist routine of drinking a glass of water while his doll chattered on, and shared with Fred Russell the distinction of being music-hall's greatest ventriloquist. He died on 14 April 1948.

R

Alan Randall, singing comedian and musical entertainer on piano, drums, trombone, trumpet, banjo and ukulele. Born in Bedworth, Warwickshire, he made his first solo variety appearance at the Windmill Theatre, London, in 1960. Eight months at the Windmill were followed in 1961 by his first summer season at the ABC Yarmouth, which led to club and variety dates, touring the leading variety theatres of the UK, Australia, South Africa, the USA and Canada. Considered to be the natural successor to George Formby (qv), singing and playing the ukulele, his resemblance to the great George is uncanny. Although he claims that this is not a deliberate impersonation, he does include many of Formby's songs in his repertoire, and in February 1969 issued an LP in tribute, 'I Remember George'. With Ray Seaton he wrote the biography *George Formby* (1974).

Alan Randall, 'I Remember George'

Harry Randall, leading music-hall comedian and one of the greatest pantomime dames. Born in High Holborn, London,

Harry Randall, 'What! Me Afraid of Men'

on 22 March 1860, he made his first stage appearance at the age of 11 in a pantomime at the Princesses' Theatre, Oxford Street. His first professional appearance was at Deacon's Music Hall, Islington, in 1884. He was such an immediate success that a few weeks later he was given equal billing with Charles Godfrey at the Middlesex, and was booked for 18 months at the Oxford and London Pavilion.

Specialising in character comedy songs, he scored his earliest success with 'The Ghost of John James Benjamin Binns', first sung at the Oxford Music Hall, Brighton, in 1885. Other included 'Exchange and Mart', 'Love by One Who Knows', 'Drink by One Who's Had Some', 'Men by One Who Loathes 'Em', 'Our Happy Little Home' and 'It Ain't All Lavender'. Like all comic singers of the day, he had a good stock of topical songs, the most successful being 'Who Killed Cock Warren?' First sung at the London Pavilion in 1888, it expressed the dissatisfaction felt about the efforts of the Chief of the Metropolitan Police, Sir Charles Warren, to catch Jack the Ripper. The Prince of Wales made a special visit to the Alhambra to hear Randall sing the song and Warren was eventually forced to resign.

At Christmas 1885 Randall appeared in his first pantomime, playing Will Atkins in *Robinson Crusoe* at the Theatre Royal, Birmingham. Vesta Tilley was on home ground as principal boy, and the following year he played the same theatre with Jenny Hill (qv) in the name part of *Goody Two Shoes*. His first London pantomime was *Dick Whittington* at the Grand Theatre, Islington, in 1891. Over the next ten years he appeared in almost every pantomime at the Grand, becoming as popular in North London as Dan Leno was at Drury Lane. At Christmas 1892 he played Ali Baba in *The Naughty Forty Thieves* with Tom Costello (qv) as his wife, Cogia Baba, and in 1893 appeared as Mother Hubbard. This, his first dame role, was such a success that the following year he appeared as Mrs Crusoe, in the absurdly named pantomime *Robinson Crusoe, or the Harlequin Good Man Friday Who Kept the House Tidy, and Sweet Polly Perkins of Wapping Old Stairs*.

From his earliest days on the halls Randall had been an admirer of the great Dan Leno, and over the years this admiration developed into a fond friendship. Early in 1903 Leno suffered the first of his mental breakdowns and as the months went by it seemed to Arthur Collins of Drury Lane that after 15 consecutive years as dame he would have to be replaced that Christmas. Harry Randall was the obvious choice and was engaged to play Little Mary in *Humpty Dumpty* with Herbert Campbell as Queen Spritely. At the last moment Dan was released from hospital and welcomed back to the Lane, taking the part of the Queen while a new role as King was written in for Campbell. Some expressed doubts about the wisdom of having both Leno and Randall playing dames as they were so much alike. However, though they resembled each other in appearance, in comedy style they were distinctly different, and in their double comedy spots, the kitchen scene and the traditional sketch, the 'Tree of Truth', were the hits of the show. The following Christmas Randall was back at Drury Lane, but alas without his two old friends Leno and Campbell, whose sudden deaths in October and July 1904 marked the end of an era of Drury Lane pantomime. The pantomime was *The White Cat* with Randall as Fairy Asbestos, a lady who had spent 40 years in the back row of the chorus and made her entrance from the wings on a flying wire. Of his performance the *Morning Post* wrote: 'The part bears traces of having been originally designed for Mr Dan Leno. Mr Randall is no Leno, but neither was Mr Leno a Randall and in a vast house like Drury Lane we do not know that the robust comedian is not also more effective.' His last pantomime was *Jack and the Beanstalk* at Drury Lane in 1910, but by then he was showing signs of a nervous disorder which on the death of his wife in 1913 resulted in a complete breakdown and his retirement from the stage. He died on 18 May 1932.

The Rao Brothers, Indian roller balancing acrobatic speciality. Brothers Babu and Shanker Rao were born in Post Mhaisal, Bombay, in 1913 and 1923 respectively. Babu first appeared in circus in 1925, being joined by his younger brother in 1928. They made their first appearance in England at Blackpool in 1936 and in London on a variety bill at the Palace, Walthamstow, on 1 January 1939. After a serious accident on stage Shanker Rao was forced to retire and returned to India in 1948. His brother turned solo and as 'Babu, Thrills and Fun on the Slack Wire' toured in variety for a number of years.

The Rastellis, family trampoline act led by Oreste Rastelli, born Bologna, Italy, on 31 January 1900. He began his career as a boy, billed as 'Voltige à la Richard', at the Casino de Paris on 1 August 1909. After appearing with his father's act in circus and variety, he formed his own act with his wife, son, and two other male acrobats. As 'The Rastellis' they made their first London appearance at the London Palladium in February 1929 and toured the UK for many years, working a trampoline act and as musical clowns billed as 'Chocolate and Co'.

Rawicz and Landauer, variety and radio double piano act. Both born in Austria, Maryan Rawicz and Walter Landauer met while on holiday in the Austrian Alps in 1928 and made their debut as concert piano duettists in Vienna in 1930. They came to England as refugees from Nazi anti-semitism and were first heard on the air in 1935. Cabaret and revue for C.B. Cochran were followed by variety tours. Although they never played down to their music hall audiences, they always hit the right low-highbrow note which kept them at the top of the bill for nearly 40 years. While playing at the Hippodrome, Eastbourne, in September 1969, Rawicz had a heart attack. He recovered enough to play again, but died at

Rawicz and Landauer, 1967

the age of 71 on 30 January 1970. Walter Landauer continued as a solo act.

Ted Ray, popular variety and radio comedian, born Charles Olden in Wigan in 1909. He played outside right for Liverpool AFC in 1925 and later joined Ainsdale FC. On giving up the idea of becoming a professional footballer, he teamed with friend Harry Wardle, working the local clubs and in cine-variety as 'Wardle and Olden', Wardle on the piano and Olden playing the violin. When his act broke up in 1927 Olden turned solo, appearing first as 'Hugh Neek' and then as 'Nedlo the Gypsy Violinist', working the music halls and cinemas of the Liverpool area and with Jason and Montgomery's touring revue 'On the Panel'. Ignoring his agent's advice of 'Play your fiddle, but don't talk, son', he introduced comedy patter into his act and although still billed as 'Nedlo', dropped the gypsy make-up and costume in favour of a black dinner-jacket, stuffed shirt and white bowler hat. This in turn was replaced by a more casual comedy style, just strolling onto the stage in an ordinary suit, an approach which was considered quite an innovation in the days when a music-hall comic relied on grotesque props ranging from a red nose to big boots.

With the help of Alf Thomas, a popular Northern comedian who billed himself as 'Mrs Thomas's Favourite Husband', Nedlo made his first London appearance at the London Music Hall, Shoreditch, in May 1930. Even with the first house on Monday, he went over well and by the end of the week had signed a year's contract with George Barclay, London's most important variety agent, who agreed to represent him providing he changed his name. He adopted that of the British winner of the US Open Golf Championship of 1920, and 'Ted Ray' appeared on a bill for the first time at the Hippodrome, Aldershot, a few weeks later. In March 1931 he 'died a death' as first turn at the Metropolitan, Edgware Road, but a few weeks later did better at the Victoria Palace on a bill topped by Hutch and Debroy Somers. Following a 12-week tour of South Africa, he toured with a variety show headed by G. H. Elliott (qv) and Gertie Gitana (qv) and on 25 July 1932 made his first appearance at the London Palladium. At the end of the week, Val Parnell gave him a contract for six return engagements and from then on he never looked back.

He worked the Moss Empires with his 'Fiddling and Fooling' act, slowly establishing himself as one of the best stand-up comedians in variety. In 1933 he again teamed with Gertie Gitana and G. H. Elliott to tour with the variety show 'George, Gertie and Ted'. He returned to South Africa in 1936 for the International Variety Association and on his return starred with Don Ross's touring show *Personality Parade*. He made his first broadcast in the BBC 'Music Hall' programme in 1939 but plans for Ray to star with Binnie Hale and Dave and Joe O'Gorman in the comedy series 'Just Fooling' never got beyond the first programme because of the outbreak of war.

By the end of the war he had been in show business nearly 20 years and although successful in variety, revue, summer shows and even pantomime (he played Widow Twankey in 1944), was not yet regarded as a really big name. Things changed almost overnight when in February 1948 he supported Danny Kaye's first London variety season at the Palladium. Kaye scored the greatest personal triumph in the history of the Palladium, but in the press backlash Ray was hailed as 'the man who carried the banner of British prestige in the face of this overwhelming example of what Hollywood could offer in high-powered comedy'. One newspaper even went as far as to pose the question 'Which is better, Kaye or Ray?' As Ray fairly states in *Raising the Laughs* (1952), any comparison was absurd, but the many who flocked to the Palladium in cheer Kaye also stopped to applaud Ray and this included the King and most of the royal family. When both Danny Kaye and Ted Ray appeared in the Royal Variety Performance on 1 November 1948 it was Ray who was the hit of the show and was requested to return to the Royal Variety in 1949.

His famous domestic BBC radio comedy series 'Ray's a Laugh' was first broadcast on 4 April 1949. Ted's radio wife was played by Australian Kitty Bluett, his brother-in-law, Nelson, was originally Fred Yule and later Kenneth Connor, and a variety of parts were played by Peter Sellers, then

Ted Ray

working as an impressionist. Music was supplied by Stanley Black and his Dance Orchestra, and by Bob and Alf Pearson of 'My Brother and I' fame. Although not as original as its rival 'Take It From Here', it had one radio innovation in the regular feature 'George, the man with the conscience', and remained a popular show for 12 years. In addition to his own show, Ted Ray broadcast for 70 consecutive weeks in 'Calling all Forces'. The last 'Ray's a Laugh' programme was broadcast on 13 January 1961, and since then Ted has appeared in numerous television and radio programmes, among them as resident comedian with Arthur Askey (qv) in 'Joker's Wild', in BBC radio's 'Does the Team Think', and ITV's 'New Faces'. An active member of the Grand Order of Water Rats, he served as King Rat in 1949–50. He was involved in a serious road accident in 1975 but happily recovered to appear again on 'New Faces' in January 1976.

Martha Raye, vaudeville and film comedienne, born in the USA on 27 August 1916. She first appeared with her parents, the vaudeville act 'Reed and Hooper', later teaming with five other girls as a singing and dancing act. As a solo act, and with partner Will Morrissey, she toured the leading vaudeville circuits. She starred in 1940 with Al Jolson in *Hold onto Your Hats* at the Shubert Theatre, New York, and during the war became famous in films as the little comedienne with the big mouth. She made her first appearance in London at the top of the London Palladium bill on 20 March 1948, and followed it by a variety tour of the UK.

Arthur Reece, comedian and ballad singer, the son of 'Jovial Joe Colverd', an early music-hall singer famed for his 'John Bull' characterisations. On giving up a civil service career, Reece turned to the halls as a descriptive vocalist in the style of Charles Godfrey, who gave him permission to sing any of his songs in towns where he himself was not working. The vogue for so-called 'dramatic scenes', led by Godfrey and George Lashwood (qv), reached its height during the Boer War, and the titles of some of Reece's songs give a good idea of the rather mawkish sentiments expressed by the patriotic songs of the time 'Good News from the War', 'A Mother's Gift to Her Country', 'Bury Her Picture With Me', 'Break the News to Mother' and 'The Boers Have Got My Daddy'. One of Reece's greatest hits was 'The Wedding Bells Shall Not Ring Out' which he sang for over a year at the Oxford, but he is best remembered as the singer of Felix McGlennon's 'Sons of the Sea':

> Sons of the sea, all British born,
> Sailing every ocean, laughing fear to scorn,
> They may build their ships my lads, and think
>   they know the game,
> But you can't beat the boys of the
>   bulldog breed,
> Who made old England's name.

He continued to work well into old age, appearing in the 1930s with Charles Austin's ciné-variety company and was featured in the 'Cavalcade of Variety' finale of the 1935 Royal Variety Performance at the London Palladium.

Ada Reeve, music-hall comedienne and star of musical comedy. She was born Adelaide Mary Isaacs in Jubilee Street, Mile End, on 3 March 1874 to parents of Dutch and French Jewish origin: her mother was a dancer known as 'Little Harriet Saunders' and her father an actor who worked under the name of Charles Reeves. Between 1878 and 1887 she appeared in juvenile roles in pantomime and melodrama at the Pavilion, Whitechapel, and the Britannia, Hoxton. Her first music-hall appearance was at Sebright's, Hackney, in 1886 and her West End debut was at the Hungerford Music Hall, Charing Cross, in 1888.

Ada went to America in 1893 to appear at Koster and Bial's Music Hall, New York, and on her return to London signed a three-year contract to appear in musical comedy for George Edwardes, making her Gaiety debut on 24 November 1894 in the title role of Bessie Brent in *The Shop Girl*. Because of a previous pantomime commitment she left the cast at the end of December to appear for J. Pitt Hardacre at the Comedy Theatre, Manchester, and Ellaline Terriss took over the role for the rest of the two-year run. Following her London success as Julie Bon-Bon in *The Gay Parisienne*, Reeve was engaged by Williamson and Musgrove to tour Australia with the show, opening at the Princess's Theatre, Melbourne, on 30 October 1897. At Christmas she played *Robin Hood* in Sydney and following a tour of *The Gay Parisienne* opened in August 1898 at the Opera House, Melbourne, at the top of a variety bill presented by Harry Rickards (qv).

On her return to London she appeared at the Comedy Theatre opposite Arthur Roberts in the musical play *Milord Sir Smith* and in 1899 played for six months at the Palace Theatre of Varieties under the management of Charles

Ada Reeve, 1915

Morton. For the next 10 years she was one of the leading soubrettes of musical comedy, notably as Lady Holyrood for the 13 month run of Leslie Stuart's *Florodora* in 1899–1900. She made the first of six tours of South Africa in 1906, appearing for ten weeks at the New Empire Theatre, Johannesburg, followed by six weeks in Cape Town. She toured the Orpheum vaudeville circuit of the USA and Canada in 1911 and in May 1914 was engaged by Hugh D. McIntosh to appear at the Tivoli Music Hall, Melbourne, a counter-attraction to Harry Lauder, then appearing for J. C. Williamson at the Theatre Royal. During the Great War she entertained troops both in the UK and abroad, introducing 'The Long, Long Trail', remembered as one of the best songs of the war. Although continuing to make tours of the USA and South Africa, and making occasional visits to London, she made her home in Australia between 1917 and 1935. Her greatest Australian success was the revue *Spangles*, with which she toured her own company and which ran for over 200 performances at the Palace Theatre, Melbourne, in 1922. She became a well-known broadcaster on Australian radio, both as a singer and a straight actress, and founded her own stage school.

On her return to England in 1936 she appeared in revue for C. B. Cochran, played at the Holborn Empire with *These Names Made Variety*, and in 1940 joined the cast of *Black Velvet* at the London Hippodrome. In 1943 she appeared with great success as the philosophical charwoman Mrs Batley in J. B. Priestley's *They Came to a City*. Between 1944 and 1952 she appeared in eight films and made her television debut in 1947 as Queen Victoria in Hugh Ross Williamson's play *Mr Gladstone*. She died at the age of 92 on 22 September 1966.

Ella Retford, singer and actress, born in Ireland. She began her career as a dancer in 1900, but later turned to music-hall 'coon' singing with 'Under the Honeymoon Tree'. During the First World War she had a great success with 'Hello There Little Tommy Atkins', and from 1915 she starred in revue. A popular principal boy, she made her last stage appearance in pantomime at the Palace Theatre, Newcastle, at Christmas 1949, after which she was forced by ill health to retire. She died on 29 June 1962.

Revnell and West, The Long and the Short of It'. One of the most successful female double comedy acts, well known in variety, pantomime and radio as 'Ethel and Gracie—The Cockney Kids' during the 1930s and 40s. They met as members of Wilfred Lewe's Concert Party and teamed to work for two seasons with another summer show known as the 'Margate Pedlars'. After a variety tour of South Africa, they spent most of 1928–29 with Tom Arnold's touring revue 'One Damn Thing After Another', and played a number of

Ella Retford, 1919

Revnell and West, 'The Long and the Short of It'

successful pantomimes for Julian Wylie. At Christmas 1940 they played the 'Babes in the Wood' at the Theatre Royal, Birmingham. Clarkson Rose played Nurse Merryweather and later wrote in his book, *With a Twinkle in My Eye* (1951): 'Ethel Revnell and Gracie West were the completely successful "Babes". Ethel Revnell, a supreme low comedy woman, was so much the gamin that one forgot her height and forgot that she was an adult—and Gracie was the ideal foil as the rather brow-beaten brother.' Billed as 'The Long and the Short of It' they were very popular in variety and radio for many years, introducing their famous Cockney Kids routine in 1935. *The Performer* wrote of their appearance at the Royal Variety Performance at the London Palladium on 15 November 1937:

> Some more robust humour came from Ethel Revnell and Gracie West, the 'long and short of it', whose contrast in sizes made their entrance one of the most effective on the programme. Attired in striking black stockings and black costumes they made a hit right away with their impressions of two cockneys on the spree, but this was transcended when they reappeared as the two cockney school children getting ready for a motor coach outing. How everyone in the Royal Box laughed when Ethel Revnell turning out the contents of her bag complete with purse of 'spending money', kept continually looking on her own level to find that her diminutive partner's head was a couple of feet below her own. Their exchange of secrets as to what presents they would buy everyone at home, their quarrel and nearly missing the charabanc were of the robust nature that typifies music hall characterisation at its best.

When ill health forced Gracie West's retirement, Ethel Revnell worked solo, appearing in the Royal Variety Performance at the London Coliseum on 2 November 1953.

Harry Richman, singer and pianist, born Cincinnati, Ohio, on 10 August 1895. Toured in vaudeville with a partner as 'Remington and Richman', and in 1922 became accompanist to Mae West and later to the Dolly Sisters. His first significant Broadway appearance was in the *George White Scandals of 1926* singing 'The Girl is You'. His first London

J.W. Rickaby, 'They Built Piccadilly For Me'

appearance at the London Palladium in July 1937 was followed by a variety tour of the UK singing among other successes 'The Birth of the Blues', another De Sylva, Brown and Henderson song from *Scandals of 1926*. Returning to London he topped the bill in a variety season at the Casino in July 1948, singing 'Magnolia', 'Shake Hands with a Millionaire' and 'Putting on the Ritz'.

J. W. Rickaby, fine character comedian born in Manchester in 1870. He started his career as a straight actor and singer, but when times were hard turned to comic singing and character impersonations, making his first music-hall appearance in Hull in 1904. Among his early songs were 'PC 49', 'The Ragtime Navy', 'What Ho She Bumps', 'Just as the Sun Goes Down', 'Hokey Pokey', 'Major Worthington', and his most successful 'Silk-Hat Tony', which is perhaps better remembered as 'They Built Piccadilly For Me'. In the true tradition of the music hall, this song was out of the same stable as 'Shabby Genteel', 'I Live in Trafalgar Square' and 'Burlington Bertie'. Dressed in a shabby frock-coat, battered topper, old boots, trousers, spats and fingerless gloves, Rickaby sang:

I'm silk-hat Tony, I'm not only broke but I'm bent,
I stroll the West gaily, you'll see me there daily,
From Burlington Arcade up to the Old Bailey,
Though I haven't a fraction,
I have this satisfaction,
They built Piccadilly for me.

He died on 1 October 1929.

Harry Rickards, comic singer who fled to Australia to avoid his creditors and there established a circuit of variety theatres employing the best music-hall performers from England. Born in London in 1841, he was originally a mechanic in the Woolwich Dockyard, graduating to the Oxford Music Hall during the 1860s by way of the small halls of the East End. A singer in the tradition of the 'Lion Comique', he is associated with the songs 'Strolling in the Burlington', 'Oxford Joe', 'Lardy Dardy Do', and 'Captain Jinks of the Horse Marines'.

Harry Rickards, 1865

Another song success, written by G. W. Hunt, was 'Cerulea the Beautiful' which like many music-hall songs before and since, did nothing to promote the Queen's English:

Cerulea was beautiful,
Cerulea was fair,
She lived with her grandma,
In Gooseberry Square,
She was once my unkydoodleum,
But now alas she,
Play kissy kissy with an officer,
In the artilleree.

Arthur Roberts, 'The Hansom Cabby', 1895

Rickards was at his best singing patriotic songs such as 'That's the Sort of Man We Want in England Here Today' by Vincent Davies and John S. Haydon. However, his patriotism allowed the 'dig' at Queen Victoria's prolonged mourning at Windsor, in Harrington and Le Brun's 'In England Now':

> In England, in England,
> In England the ruler of the sea,
> We sing 'God Save the Queen',
> Though she's very seldom seen,
> In England the Land of the Free.

Although only a minor artiste, Rickards did quite well on the halls and bought a half share in the Swiss Cottage, a public house in Hackney with a concert and music hall on the floor above the bar. He soon ran into serious financial problems and did a moonlight flit to Sydney, where he established music-hall entertainment on London lines. He died a rich man on 13 October 1911.

Jack Riskit, gymnast and wire-walker who presented a novel speciality act known as the 'Dental Riskit'. Born John Evans in Manchester on 8 August 1879, he made his first stage appearance at Barnard's Music Hall, Chatham, in 1898. Soon afterwards he went to South Africa as a wire-walker and comic singer, and in 1902 opened for Harry Rickards at the Opera House, Melbourne, doing a drag wire act billed as 'The Girl on the Slack Wire'. This was followed by a tour of Australia, playing the Rickards's Tivoli theatres and Fulbar's variety circuit. On his return to London in 1909, he appeared at the Oxford Music Hall in July that year. Billed as 'Dental Riskit' he toured in variety with a partner and in 1914 went back to Australia. Later he toured South America, North Africa and Spain with his own variety company. While appearing at a charity show in West Bromwich during the Second World War, he fell from the slack wire and spent several months recovering. Forced to give up active stage work he went into theatre management.

Roberto and Halla, magic speciality act from Holland. Roberto was born in Rotterdam on 16 February 1936 and Hella on 4 May 1939. Roberto first appeared as a boy in Amsterdam in August 1947 and with Hella in January 1961. Their first appearance in England was at La Strada Club, Sunderland, in 1966.

Arthur Roberts, music-hall comedian and first star of musical comedy, described by George Graves as 'the greatest genius of the English comic tradition'. Born in Westbourne Grove, London, in 1852, at the age of 15 he worked as a busker on Yarmouth Sands. His first regular variety appearance was at Crowder's Music Hall, Greenwich, in 1871, singing 'If Mary Jane Would Only Marry Me' and performing a character monologue 'The Broken Down Tragedian'. For the next few years he played the smaller halls of London and the provinces, eventually appearing with success at the Oxford singing 'If I Was Only Long Enough, a Soldier I Would Be'. Although his material was considered to be decidedly 'blue', he was soon firmly established at the top of the bill.

During the decade before Leno and Robey, Roberts was music hall's foremost comedian but unlike most comics of the day, was neither red-nosed nor shabby. He was instead the immaculate man-about-town, and as such became the beau ideal of the halls. During the late 1870s he worked in variety and pantomime with James Fawn of 'If You Want to Know the Time Ask a Policeman' fame. Between 1880 and 1883 they appeared together in three pantomimes at Drury Lane. Although innocuous by today's standards, such songs as Roberts's 'I'm Living with Mother Now' were in the 1880s very near the knuckle (an expression said to have been coined by Roberts):

> Stand me a cab fare, duckie,
> Do now, there's a dear,
> Or buy me a hot potato,
> For I'm feeling awfully queer.
> Your eyes look dreadful wicked,
> But kissing I couldn't allow,
> I might have done so a few months ago,
> But I'm living with mother now.

After running into trouble with the Middlesex Licensing Authority in 1883 Roberts left the music halls to tour with Emily Duncan's company, playing Ravina in *The Miller and his Men*. For the next 20 years he was regarded with Fred Leslie as the leading burlesque comedian, largely responsible for the revival of flagging interest in opera bouffe, and as Captain Coddington in the musical farce *In Town*. First produced by George Edwardes at the Prince of Wales Theatre on 15 October 1891, *In Town* introduced a new form of entertainment which was described by *The Times* as 'a curious medley of songs, dance and nonsense'; it is now regarded as the first musical comedy. Thanks to Roberts's personal popularity, plus a galaxy of female beauty, *In Town* ran for a total of 295 performances. His greatest musical comedy success was as The Hansom Cabby, the leading part in *Gentleman Joe* by Basil Hood at the Prince of Wales Theatre in 1895. He returned to variety in 1904, delighting the audience of the Empire, Leicester Square, singing 'Some Girls Do, and Some Girls Don't'. He later toured the halls with sketches 'The Girl Who Lost Her Honeymoon' and 'The Girl Who Took the Wrong Tow Path'.

One of Roberts's greatest admirers was C. B. Cochran, who described him as 'a very great comedian and one of the quickest and most brilliant extemporaneous wits I have known'. When after the First World War Roberts found engagements harder to come by Cochran offered him £20 a week for life if he would appear in any of his shows which required his services, and he became a permanent member of Cochran's revue company at the London Pavilion. In 1926 he toured with *Veterans of Variety* and in 1927 published a book of reminiscences, *Fifty Years of Spoof*. He died in 1933.

George Robey, distinguished music hall comedian, known as 'The Prime Minister of Mirth'. Born George Wade at Herne Hill, London on 20 September 1869, at the age of 11 he went to live in Germany, where his father worked as a civil engineer. Soon he was speaking fluent German, and on leaving school in Dresden went to study science at Leipzig University, but soon transferred his studies to Cambridge. Although Max Beerbohm later remarked, 'I consider Mr George Robey to be the one brilliant man that Cambridge has produced during the last 25 years,' his university career was short-lived. A change in his family's fortunes forced him to leave the university and earn a living as a clerk-of-works on the construction of Birmingham's first cable tramway.

After appearing as a comic singer at smoking concerts in Birmingham he made his first London appearance on 28 April 1891, at the Horns Assembly Rooms, Kennington, singing 'He Was Never Used to Luxuries' and 'Where Did You Get That Hat?'. His West End debut followed at the Oxford Music Hall on 6 June 1891, and he was signed on for a year's contract as 'George Robey—The Coming Man!'. He did not take long to arrive and within the year was top of the bill, a position he did not relinquish for the rest of his long career. Described by James Agate as 'the greatest artiste of his kind since Leno', he created dozens of comedy characters, among them, 'Clarence, the Last of the Dandies', 'The Pro's Landlady', 'The Prehistoric Man', 'The Mayor of Mudcumdyke', 'The German Musician' and 'Daisy Dillwater, District Nurse'. When not in character he appeared in simple black semi-clerical costume, bowler hat, thin swish cane and arching his famous black eyebrows. The king of red-nosed comics, he was often accused of being vulgar, although he always insisted that it was honest vulgarity, 'the perfect antidote to hypocrisy'. He needed no introduction, his entrance invariably being greeted by roars of laughter. With an air of outraged dignity he would raise his hand 'like an archdeacon reproving a choir', and command his audience to 'desist', reminding them that he had not come there to be laughed at. He appeared in both Command Performances, the first in 1912 and the other in 1919.

The finest of pantomime dames, he played his first pantomime at the Alhambra, Brighton, in 1892. For years his Widow Twankey and Dame Trot so delighted the audiences of the main provincial cities that he only found time to appear in one London pantomime, *Jack and the Beanstalk* at the Hippodrome in 1921.

Robey made his first appearance in revue in April 1916, in the phenomenally successful *The Bing Boys are Here* at the Alhambra. Thousands who would never have gone to the music-halls to see him as 'Daisy Dillwater' flocked to see him as Lucifer Bing, singing 'If You Were The Only Girl in the World' to Violet Loraine's 'If You Were The Only Boy'. It ran for 378 performances and was seen by 600,000 people during its nine-month run. He opened on 31 January 1917 in Albert de Courville's *Zig Zag* at the London Hippodrome. It ran for 648 performances, after which he was engaged by Oswald Stoll to play again Lucifer Bing in *The Bing Boys on Broadway*. During the First World War he entertained the troops and raised an estimated £500,000 for the Red Cross. He was awarded the CBE for his war work in 1919.

The Bing Boys revue marked a turning point in Robey's career: although he remained basically a music-hall performer his work in revue was just an extension of his variety act. *The Bing Boys on Broadway* was followed in 1919 by *Joy Bells* at the Hippodrome, *Johnny Jones* and *Robey en Casserole* at the Alhambra in 1920 and 1921, and *Round in Fifty* at the Hippodrome in March 1922. In 1926 Robey toured his own road show *Bits and Pieces*, which after playing the Moss Empires opened at the Princes Theatre, Shaftesbury Avenue, on 26 December. Originally booked as a six-week Christmas attraction, it was such a success that it ran for six months, and then toured South Africa in 1927, Canada in 1928 and returned to South Africa in 1929.

Robey turned to operetta at the age of 62, appearing for C.B. Cochran as King Menelaus in *Helen*, A.P. Herbert's adaptation of Offenbach's *La Belle Hélène*. Directed by Max Reinhardt, with Evelyn Laye as Helen and Bruce Carfax as Paris, it opened at the Adelphi Theatre in January 1932. When Sir Oswald Stoll built his film studio at Cricklewood Robey was one of his first stars, playing, among other roles, Sancho Panza to Jerrold Robertshaw's Don Quixote. In 1932 he was again cast as Sancho Panza in a sound version produced by Pabst, with the great Russian actor and singer Fedor Chaliapin as Don Quixote. He scored the most remarkable success of his incredibly versatile career on 28 February 1935 when he opened at His Majesty's Theatre, London, as Falstaff in *Henry IV Part I*. His was the perfect Falstaff, as bawdy and robust a squire as Shakespeare intended. As W.A. Darlington put it, 'I do not know which to wonder at more, the way in which Robey fits Falstaff, or the way in which Falstaff fits Robey.' He never again played a Shakespearean role on the stage, but in 1944 appeared as the dying Falstaff, the scene from *Henry IV* which Laurence Olivier interpolated into his film version of *Henry V*. A great admirer of Robey, Lord Olivier wrote of him in a letter to the present author dated 19 January 1971:

> One of his particular gifts was a whiplash diction that would hit the back of the pit with a smack, of course, in the same conditions as any other performer until recent years, without any amplification. This quality, added to those of his countenance and his wonderful comic gift, gave Sydney Carroll the extremely bright idea of presenting him as Falstaff, in which he gave a truly remarkable performance. Having seen his performance it needed no great stretch of imagination on my part to cast him for the little bowdlerized scene in *Henry V*.

Robey appeared in September 1936 in the musical comedy *Certainly Sir* at the Hippodrome. It was not a success, and later that year he starred in *Laughter over London*, a music-hall revue at the Victoria Palace. In December 1937 he took part in *Les Folies de Paris et Londres* at the Prince of Wales Theatre. A non-stop revue which played from noon until midnight, Robey at the age of 68 appeared 16 times daily.

He made his first broadcast in 1936 in 'The Spice of Life' programme and in 1937 was appointed a member of the BBC General Advisory Council. He made his television debut in 1938. In June 1939 he left England for a variety tour of Australia, opening at the Tivoli Theatre, Melbourne, in July. The tour was intended to include New Zealand and South Africa but had to be curtailed because war broke out. Returning to London in October 1939, he spent the war years in fund-raising activities and service entertaining, and in 1942 he made his last pantomime appearance, as Mrs Crusoe at the Bristol Hippodrome.

In 1938 he married Blanche Littler, the sister of impresarios Prince and Emile Littler, and at 80 he toured with her revue *Touch Wood and Whistle*. He toured again in July 1951 with Hetty King and Dolly Harmer in Bernard Delfont's *Do You Remember?*. In June 1952 he added a touch of nostalgia to the all-star posthumous tribute to Sid Field (q.v.) at the London Palladium. Dressed for almost the last time in his little bowler with eyebrows at the arch, he sang 'I Stopped, I Looked and I Listened' and 'If You Were the Only Girl in the World'. In recognition of his years of service to all branches of the theatre he was given a knighthood by the Queen in the New Year Honours List of 1954. Never had the accolade rested on more popular shoulders, but the honour came too late. Sir George died on 29 November 1954 at the age of 85.

Bill Robinson, American dancer and comedian, one of America's best-known negro vaudeville performers. The grandson of a slave, he was born on 25 May 1878 at Richmond, Virginia. He began his career with small-time minstrel shows, developing an amazing talent as a tap dancer and exponent of the then current dance craze, the cake walk. His vaudeville debut was in Chicago in 1897, when he appeared with his wife, Fanny Clay, as 'Robinson and Clay'. Later he teamed with male partners as 'Butler and Robinson' and 'Cooper and Robinson'. Turning solo in 1900, he was seen by an agent for E. F. Albee who booked him for an extensive tour of the Albee vaudeville circuit, performing his intricate 'up-and-down-stairs' dance and doing comedy impressions. Billed as 'Bojangles' Robinson, he was soon considered to be the greatest tap dancer in the world, and one of the most successful vaudeville headliners, frequently

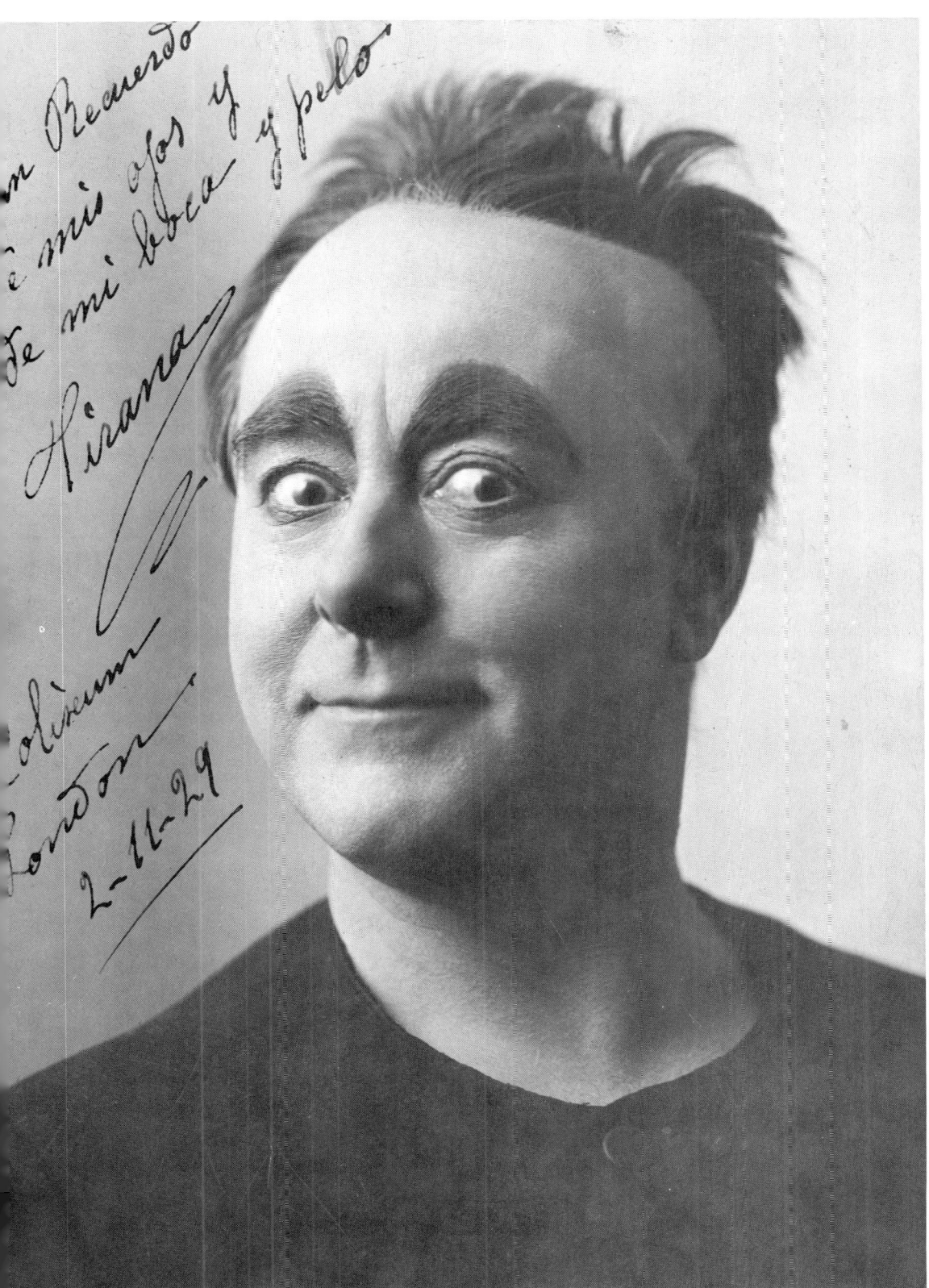

George Robey, 1929

playing the New York Palace and other top houses throughout the USA.

His first London appearance was at the Alhambra in 1903 and he returned to star in 1913. On his last visit he topped the bill at the Brighton Hippodrome for the week of 12 July 1926, followed by engagements at the Holborn Empire and Victoria Palace, London.

On Broadway he appeared in a number of very successful revues, including Lew Leslie's *Blackbirds of 1928* and *Brown Buddies* in 1930. *Blackbirds* was the first of a successful run of all-negro revues, billed by Leslie as the 'World's Funniest and Fastest Revues—Glorifying the American Negro', in something of a send-up of the Ziegfeld Follies, which were described as 'Glorifying the American Girl'! Robinson scored a great hit with his song-and-dance number 'Doing the New Low Down', and returned to the *Blackbirds* show in 1933. In 1939 he played in *Hot Mikado* at the Broadhurst Theatre, and his last Broadway show was *Memphis Bound* in 1945.

In films he co-starred with Shirley Temple in *The Little Colonel*, while other screen appearances included *One Mile From Heaven* and *Up the River*. As mayor of Harlem he contributed freely to both black and white charities and was for many years President of the Negro Artists' Guild. When he died on 25 November 1949 his body lay in state in New York while hundreds of thousands of people filed past. The funeral procession went down Broadway into Times Square, stopping briefly outside the Palace Theatre, where below neon lights proclaiming 'Eight Big Vaudeville Acts and Feature Picture' hung a banner with the simple message 'So Long, Bill Robinson'. At the graveside pall-bearers included Joe Louis, Cole Porter, Irving Berlin, Bob Hope, Alfred Lunt, Louis B. Mayer, Darryl Zanuck and Jimmy Durante.

Frederick Robson, celebrated actor who has a place in the early history of the music hall as the original singer of E. L. Blanchard's narrative song 'Villikins and his Dinah'. Born Thomas Robson Brownbill in Margate in 1821, he made his first stage appearance at a private theatre in Catherine Street, London, as Simm Mealbag in the drama *Grace Huntly*. He was a member of the Grecian Theatre from 1844 to 1849, appearing in Shakespeare plays, singing comic cockney songs and performing acrobatics in the saloon attached to the main theatre. In 1850 he went to Dublin and on his return in 1852 joined William Farren's company at the Olympic Theatre, London.

Affectionately known as the 'Great Little Robson', he was a great success in Talford's burlesque of *Macbeth*, and became the mainstay of the Olympic. His most popular part was Jim Baggs in *The Wandering Minstrel* in which he revived 'Villikins and his Dinah'. He originally sang the song at the Grecian when the play was presented by Thomas Rouse, but it was not until the Olympic revival of 1853 that it achieved its great vogue. He was an ugly little man with a very unstable personality, of whom Henry Barton Baker supplied a vivid and startling description in his *History of the London Stage—Its Famous Players 1576–1903* (1904):

Who that saw him when in the full possession of his powers can ever forget that strange looking little man, with the small body and the big head, who played upon his audience as though they had been the keys of a piano, now convulsing them with laughter as he perpetrated some outrageous drollery, now lashing them into awe-struck silence with an electrical burst of passion or pathos, or holding them midway between terror and laughter as he performed some weirdly grotesque dance? The impression he made at such moments was that of a man over-wrought by excitement to the verge of madness: the wild gleaming eyes, the nervous twitchings of the marvellously plastic features, the utter abandon to the feeling of the moment, whether it were tragic or grotesque, the instantaneous transition from the tragedian to the clown, which was no stage trick but an inspiration, an irrepressible impulse, were all so creepy, so uncanny as to suggest incipient insanity. He was morbidly timid and nervous, he could never realise the great position he had attained, and was ever haunted by a fear that his fall would be as sudden as his rise; success had a delirious effect on him, and to deaden his stage fright, which he could never overcome, he resorted to stimulants—with the usual result. Robson had been famous scarcely seven years when his powers began to fail, and his terror of facing the audience became so great that while waiting for his cue he would gnaw his arms until they bled, and cry out piteously, 'I dare not go on, I dare not!' until the prompter had at times absolutely to thrust him before the footlights.

Other of Robson's successes included the name part in *The Yellow Dwarf* and a parody of Charles Kean in *The Corsican Brothers*. In 1857 he took over the management of the Olympic in partnership with William Emden. The Robson tradition was carried on by Sam Cowell (q.v.), who sang 'Villikins' at the song-and-supper rooms and music halls, and was greatly influenced by Robson's style and Shakespearean burlesques. Frederick Robson died in 1864 at the age of 43, 'a victim of intemperance', as the *Oxford Companion to the Theatre* put it.

Alfred Rodes and his eighteen Tziganes. Alfred Rodes was born in the Argentine in 1905, and as a child prodigy gave his first violin concert in Paris at the age of eight, billed as 'l'enfant Paganini'. He formed a string band of Romanian and Hungarian gypsies in 1930, which made its London debut on the bill of the Royal Variety Performance on 11 May 1931, followed by a very successful season at the London Palladium.

Rogers and Starr, Michael Rogers and Roy Starr, comedy double act who have established themselves as the most popular pair in drag. They first met in 'intimate revue' at the Irving Theatre, a club in Leicester Square which was so small it was difficult to do anything without being intimate. Finding their comedy style compatible—they at least made each other laugh—they teamed as female impersonators in 1955 and worked a semi-pro cabaret act. With the help of Jack Lawrence they went on to present their own shows at the St George's Hall, part of the old YMCA in Tottenham Court Road, and at the Chepstow Theatre, Notting Hill Gate. An extremely successful series of late night revues at the Hampstead Theatre Club brought them to the notice of a wider public. They appeared as the Ugly Sisters at the Odeon, Golders Green, and in October 1972 were booked by Harold Fielding for their first professional revue, *Hulla Baloo* at the Criterion Theatre. Set in a public lavatory and mixing the high camp of Rogers and Starr with the buffoonery of Jimmy Edwards, it was not a great success. On 7 May 1974 they opened at the Arts Theatre Club in *Off the Peg*, Gordon Deighton's all-male revue inspired by the sensational Paris drag show La Grande Eugène. Later that year they appeared in Max Bygraves's hugely successful show, *Swingalongamax*, at the Victoria Palace. In 1976 Michael Rogers decided to make his home in the USA, and Rogers and Starr made their last appearance together at the Theatre Royal, Stratford, on 29 February.

Will Rogers, American vaudeville comedian and droll raconteur. Born in Oolagun, part of the Indian territory of

Rogers and Starr, 1969

Oklahoma, on 4 November 1879, he was part Red Indian and worked as a cowboy from the age of 14, later going to the Argentine as a rancher. He went broke in Buenos Aires in 1902 and he worked his passage to Durban with the intention of fighting in the Boer War. The war ended almost before he arrived and he was forced to work as a farm hand and mule driver. At Ladysmith he joined Texas Jack's Wild West Circus, doing Western-style rope tricks billed as 'The Cherokee Kid'. From South Africa he toured Australia and New Zealand and on his return to the USA joined Zack Mulhall's Wild West Show, making his first appearance in New York at Madison Square Garden soon afterwards.

He turned to vaudeville with a girl partner and a pony and later developed a droll comedy solo act, casually spinning a rope and caustically commenting in a lazy drawl on current affairs. Billed as 'The World's Number One Wisecracker', he became one of the most popular variety headliners and greatest stars of the Palace Theatre, New York, making frequent appearances in London. His first major Broadway success was rather incongruously doing his lariat routine in Karl Hoschna's operetta *Wall Street Girl*, which opened at the George M. Cohan Theatre on 15 April 1912. The show was not a success and only ran for 56 performances, but Rogers went on to appear in Florenz Ziegfeld's *Midnight Follies* at the Amsterdam Roof, and from 1917 onwards was one of the greatest comedians of the Ziegfeld Follies.

The friend of kings and presidents, this self-styled 'poet lariat' refused to take himself seriously. Nonchalantly twirling his rope, he quipped with a lazy smile, 'Yep, spinnin' a rope's a lot of fun, providen your neck ain't in it,' 'There's no such thing as a big rope trick, rope tricks is all little,' and 'The only amazing thing about these rope tricks is that a grown man should be doin' them and that grown people pay to watch him'. His dry comments on world events ranged from the love life of the Prince of Wales to the latest doings of Dopey, his pot-bellied pony. Described by Eddie Cantor as 'The Policeman of America', his wit was kindly but very much to the point. For years he wrote a column in the *New*

York Times which was syndicated throughout the USA.

His last Follies show was in July 1925, after which he spent most of his time making films and working on radio. He took off with air ace Wiley Post on a flight to Moscow on 16 August 1935. Their light aircraft crashed in Alaska and both were killed. President Franklin D. Roosevelt paid him a last tribute: 'His humour and comments were always kind. His was no biting sarcasm that hurt the highest or lowest of his fellow citizens. When he wanted people to laugh out loud he used the methods of pure fun, and when he wanted to make a point for the good of mankind he used the kind of gentle irony that left no scars behind it.'

Rolo and Lady, trapeze act formed by Fred Greenhalgh, born in Rochdale in 1872. During the 1920s he worked in variety with partner Lillian Black, billed as 'Rolo and Lady—The Ape and the Maid'. While appearing at the Palace, Wellingborough, on 28 December 1927 he swung over the audience without the usual safety rope securing his foot to the trapeze. He crashed into the stalls, killing himself and fracturing the thigh of the girl on whose lap he landed.

Clarkson Rose, celebrated variety comedian and one of pantomime's finest dames, who for over 40 years presented the famous seaside summer show, *Twinkle*. Born in Dudley, Worcestershire, on 8 December 1890, he began his professional life as a bank clerk with the National Provincial at Shrewsbury, entertaining in his spare time at smoking concerts as 'A. C. Rose—Comedian', and later forming his own concert party of eight, known locally as 'The Pengwern Pierrots'.

His first London stage appearance was a walk-on in Beerbohm Tree's production of *Julius Caesar* at His Majesty's Theatre. He joined the Liverpool Repertory Company in 1911 and between seasons toured with Estelle Stead's Shakespearean troupe. During the summer of 1914 he worked with 'The Moonbeams', a concert party run by L.M. Musgrove of Seaford. Because of the outbreak of war the Liverpool Repertory did not open that autumn and Rose was one of a splinter group of actors who founded the Liverpool Commonwealth Company, and as Captain De Phoenix in *Trelawny of the Wells*, appeared at the Kingsway Theatre, London, in March 1915.

While in Westcliff-on-Sea for the summer of 1918 he met Olive Fox, an established concert entertainer at the piano in the style of Margaret Cooper. They married and formed a double act as 'Fox and Rose', a partnership which lasted 46 years. Their music-hall debut was at the Hippodrome, Rotherhithe, and through the agency of Bernard Sherek they were booked to tour the Stoll variety theatres and Moss Empires. Summer seasons for Wallis Arthur were followed by variety and pantomime, five for Fred Warden in Ireland. While Fox and Rose were appearing at the Bristol Hippodrome early in 1922 Olive Fox was taken ill and Rose went on alone. Such was his success that he was booked as a solo turn at the Alhambra, London, and went over well with both audience and critics.

When in 1921 Powis Pinder, the Isle of Wight entrepreneur, found himself without a show on Ryde Pier, Clarkson Rose presented his own six-handed pierrot revue and *Twinkle* was born. In variety he toured the UK for Stoll and Macnaughton and appeared regularly at the Alhambra and Coliseum. While playing an Alhambra date in 1927 he was seen by Philip Rodway and engaged to play his first pantomime dame at the Theatre Royal, Birmingham. Rodway's pantomimes were the finest since the days of Augustus Harris, and in *Robinson Crusoe* at Christmas 1927 Rose as Mrs Crusoe co-starred with Robb Wilton as Will

Clarkson Rose, 1968

Atkins. This combination was described by James Agate as the best he had seen since the days of Dan Leno and Herbert Campbell at Drury Lane. Rose appeared in the Royal Variety Performance at the London Coliseum on 1 March 1928, singing his Victorian dame song, 'The Girls of the Old Brigade'.

Twinkle, in its 12th year by 1933, was firmly established as the number-one summer show wherever it appeared. In March that year Rose and his wife left England to tour *Twinkle* in Australia for J. C. Williamson. Billed as a 'revusical gay-as-you-please show of nimbleness and nonsense—for laughing purposes only', it opened at the Theatre Royal, Sydney, on 15 April 1933 to rave notices. A month later it moved to His Majesty's Theatre, Brisbane, with such success that it went into a second edition, entitled *Happy Hours*. Rose joined forces with Ernest Rolls in June, the *Twinkle* company forming the basis of Rolls's spectacular revue *Tout Paris*, which after 11 weeks at Melbourne appeared at Adelaide and Brisbane. Rose was offered a two-year contract to tour Australia for the Tait Brothers, but he was booked to present *Twinkle* at Shanklin, Isle of Wight. Rose appeared in London at Christmas 1936, 1937, and 1938 as dame in pantomime for Walter and Frederick Melville at the Lyceum Theatre. During the war 'Clarkie' continued to 'twinkle' at Eastbourne, Torquay, Llandudno and on tour for ENSA. After the war he toured *Twinkle* around the London and provincial variety theatres.

For many years a member of the Grand Order of Water Rats, Rose was King Rat in 1958. During the 43 year history of *Twinkle*, Rose gave early chances to many future stars; at various times his leading men included Tommy Fields,

Ernest Arnley, Garry Peters, Chris Carlson, Terry Scott, Bobby Dennis and Norman Vaughan. He was always quick to spot talent and many leading ladies stepped from his famous chorus of 'Rosebuds'. After 35 years as leading lady of *Twinkle* Olive Fox retired in 1956. She died at her home in Eastbourne on 28 September 1964. Clarkson Rose's last pantomime was at Leicester at Christmas 1967. He planned to present the 46th year of *Twinkle* at Teignmouth the following summer but died on 23 April 1968.

Julian Rose, Jewish dialect comedian well known in variety for his Mr Levinsky character sketches, 'Mr Levinsky's Wedding', etc. Born in the USA in 1879, he began professional life as a bookkeeper for a telephone company in Philadelphia, at the same time developing a reputation at smoking concerts and lodge meetings as an amusing raconteur. Following success at the Philadelphia Turf Club and an amateur night at a local vaudeville theatre he made his professional debut in Boston with Tom Miaco's 'Night Owls Concert Party'. A few months later he appeared as a solo comedian at a Milwaukee vaudeville house, followed by tours of the so called 'aching heart' circuits. He first appeared in England in 1905 billed as 'Our Hebrew Friend'. After making his home in the UK he became and remained a popular variety act in London and on tour for over 30 years. He appeared in the Royal Variety Performance at the Palladium in 1933, dying at the age of 56 on 13 September 1935.

Tommy Rose, female impersonator and singer, born 27 September 1916. His first appearance was as a straight actor at the Cambridge Theatre, London, in 1931. During the war he served in the navy and turned to comedy on his discharge. He toured in 1946 with the service show *Tokyo Express*. He later teamed with Sonny Dawkes, appearing with him in pantomime as the Ugly Sisters, in *This was the Army* and other drag revues, and touring in variety as 'Dawkes and Rose'.

W. G. Ross, celebrated concert and supper-room singer of the 1840s and 1850s. He was compositor on a Glasgow newspaper until his success in local harmonic meetings encouraged him to go south and try his luck as a professional vocalist. His first appearance outside Scotland was at Sharple's Concert Rooms, Bolton, and in London at the notorious Cider Cellars in Maiden Lane. His earliest songs included 'The Lively Flea' (a parody of 'Ivy Green'), 'Mrs Johnson', 'Pat's Leather Breeches' 'Going Home with the Milk', and 'Jack Rag'. Although billed as a serio-comic vocalist, his greatest success, 'Sam Hall', a grisly ballad of a chimney-sweep condemned to death, was far from humorous. It told in dramatic terms of Sam Hall's crimes and his thoughts during his journey up Holborn Hill, his last drink at St Giles, and his public execution at Tyburn. Each verse ended with a foul oath and it says much for Ross's realistic and powerful performance that for nearly ten years the song brought huge crowds to the Cider Cellars, Coal Hole, Dr Johnson's Tavern and in 1847 to Vauxhall Gardens. The song's great vogue had declined by the late 1850s and Ross was never able to recapture his popularity with any other song. He turned briefly to the legitimate stage, appearing at the Theatre Royal, Haymarket, under the management of John Buckstone. He is thought to have had some acting experience before coming to London but his debut at the Haymarket in an Irish farce was not a success and he returned to the music halls and concert platform.

He toured the provinces with his own company, which included his daughter Lillian Ross. A bill for City Hall,

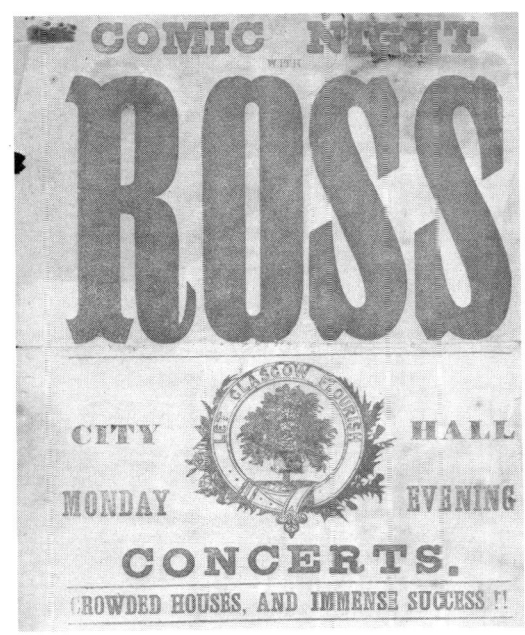

W.G. Ross tops the bill of the City Hall, Glasgow, March 1856

Below: W.G. Ross as 'Sam Hall'

Glasgow, for 3 March 1856 describes Ross as 'The greatest dramatic humorist of the day, who holds the highest place in the estimation of the London public, and who will appear in his newly conceived characters and costumes to represent an entirely new style of vocal performances'. These included a comic medley, 'The Musical Times We Live In', a new version of 'Billy Barlow' and a serio-comic song 'Hamlet Ye Dane', which according to the bills was written for Ross by John Lebern and which, with imitations of Charles Kean, he performed 'upwards of three hundred nights in London'.

Other Shakespearean burlesques included 'Othello, Ye Moore of Venice' and Ross concluded his performance with his 'Black Lecture on Phrenology'. He died in obscurity, the date unrecorded.

Derek Roy, light comedian, born in London. A broadcast on 'Henry Hall's Guest Night' in 1942 led to an engagement as vocalist and comedian with Geraldo and his Orchestra which lasted for two and a half years. He became resident comedian in 'Variety Bandbox' in 1946, hosting it on alternate weeks to Frankie Howerd (q.v.). The friendly rivalry between the two lasted with the show for three-and-a-half years and established both in their careers. At Christmas 1946 he toured the Rank Cinemas with his own production of *Cinderella*. An ideal Buttons he repeated his success in the role for top managements, including Emile Littler, Bertram Montague, S. H. Newsome and Bernard Delfont.

Following the popularity of 'Variety Bandbox' he topped variety bills, appeared in the Royal Variety Performance of 1948 and starred in his own radio show 'Happy Go Lucky'. Since then he has appeared with success in almost every branch of entertainment from front-cloth variety comic to slapstick farce. In revue he starred in *Light Up the Town* at the London Palladium in 1964, and made six consecutive tours of South Africa.

His exuberant comedy style has established him as one of the most popular and dependable of summer-show attractions and when not playing his celebrated Buttons, he is an excellent pantomime dame in the true tradition of Dan Leno.

Billy Russell, character comedian, born Adam George Brown, in Birmingham on 16 July 1893. His father was a scenic artist at the Theatre Royal, Birmingham, and he began his career as a 12-year-old juvenile with ex-lightweight champion Billy Ross, who was there working the halls with the sketch 'The Hot Member'. His first London appearance was with Ross at the Royal Albert Music Hall, Canning Town, in 1905 and he later toured with his father's and Tom Pritchard's combined variety and cinema show. Teaming with Gus Granville as 'Russell and Granville' they worked a comedy patter act, Russell also doing a solo turn on the same variety programme as 'Baroni—The Ambidextrous Cartoonist'. While serving with the South Staffs Regiment during the First World War he appeared in concert party as Bruce Barnsfarther's famous cartoon character 'Old Bill', presenting a stand-up comedy routine which after the war formed the basis of his celebrated navvy act 'On Behalf of the Working Classes'. Billed as 'The Son of Toil' he appeared in the Royal Variety Performance at the London Palladium in 1933 and again in 1947. He was popular in variety and with his own road show until the mid-1950s and later became a highly regarded character actor, appearing frequently on television and the West End stage. In October 1969 he appeared with great success in David Storey's play *The Contractor* at the Royal Court Theatre, repeating the role at the Fortune Theatre in April 1970. He continued to work literally to the end of his life, dying in a London TV studio on 25 November 1971.

Charles Russell, descriptive vocalist born in Barnsbury, North London, in 1866. At the age of 17 he formed a nigger minstrel troupe, 'Daly's Unrivalled Minstrels', and worked with a partner in a black-faced variety act. He appeared at Forrester's Music Hall and the Alexandra Palace in 1888 as one of the 'Brothers Eloe', presenting a comedy double trapeze act. His solo debut came in 1891 when he sang a patriotic ditty entitled 'John Bull' at Collins Music Hall,

Above: Derek Roy, 1975   Below: Billy Russell

Islington, and he soon built up a reputation as a descriptive vocalist in the style of Charles Godfrey (q.v.). With a small company of sketch artistes who supplied histrionic support to his songs he toured the halls during the 1890s and early 1900s. Songs included 'The Soldier's Letter', 'Gutter Hotel', and a typically jingoistic song of the period, 'On Duty'. He died on 24 October 1948.

Fred Russell, one of the most famous music-hall ventriloquists who did much to pioneer the modern style of comedy patter between vent and single doll. Born Thomas Frederick Parnell in London on 29 September 1862, he began his career as a journalist with the *Hackney and Kingsland Gazette*, becoming its senior reporter in 1885, and editor in 1894. He entertained as an amateur actor from 1879 and from 1886 worked as a semi-pro ventriloquist at drawing-room concerts, children's parties and as a seaside beach entertainer. His first music-hall appearance was at the Palace Theatre, London, on 6 March 1896. It was so successful that he gave up journalism and for the next 20 months made more than 400 appearances at the Palace under the management of Charles Morton. With his doll, the cheeky Coster Joe, he played every hall of note in London and the provinces during the next 40 years, also visiting America and New Zealand, and touring Australia and South Africa three times.

A highly regarded member of the variety profession, he was one of the founder members of the Variety Artistes Federation in 1906, becoming chairman in 1908. In 1906 he founded *The Performer*, the official news sheet of the VAF. It was run by committee until 1911 when it became a limited company with Russell acting as its managing director and chairman from 1915 to 1945. A Water Rat from 1898, he served as King Rat in 1903, 1914, 1929 and 1939, also serving as Preceptor of the Order for over 20 years. At the age of 70 he was still touring with Lew Lake's *Stars Who Never Fail to Shine*, and took part in the Royal Variety Performance at the Palladium in 1932 and again in 1952. Known as the 'Father of the Profession', he received the OBE in 1948. He died in 1957 at the age of 95.

Russell's son, Fred Russell Parnell, followed in his father's footsteps, appearing as a ventriloquist under the name of Russ Carr. He toured the world in variety, later becoming an agent. He died on 29 April 1973. Another son, Val Parnell, succeeded George Black as Managing Director of Moss Empires in 1945, controlling the London Palladium until his death on 24 September 1972. The Russell/Parnell family variety stage tradition is carried on by band leader Jack Parnell, grandson of Fred Russell.

S

Eugene Sandow, famous gymnast and music-hall strong man. Born in Konigsberg, Germany, on 10 April 1867. During the mid-1880s he toured the fairs and exhibitions of Europe, and made his first appearance in London at the Westminster Royal Aquarium on 29 October 1889. At the Aquarium he successfully challenged Samson, the leading strongman of the day, who billed himself 'The Most Powerful Man on Earth'. This led to challenges from Samson's 19-year-old apprentice Cyclops, from Ajax, the so-called 'Strongman of Paris', and the McCann Brothers, who worked as 'Hercules and Samson'. Sandow came out on top, and as 'The Strongest Man in the World', appeared at all the leading London halls. At the Royal Holborn he lifted with one hand a 312lb dumbell (the official record of the time was less than 250lb), and at the Tivoli in 1891 caused a sensation by lifting with one hand a live cart horse weighing 600lb. At

Above: Charles Russell, 'On Duty', 1898

Below: Eugene Sandow, 'The Modern Hercules and Perfect Man'

the time his vital statistics were given as: weight, 14 stone 3 pounds; inflated chest 50 inches; and 19¾ inches around the biceps.

He headlined at the Casino Theatre, New York, in 1893. This famous vaudeville house on 39th Street was run by Rudolph Aronson and Henry Abbey. Booked at $1,000 a week he was poorly presented and not a great success. However he was seen by the young Florenz Ziegfeld and engaged for the Trocadero Music Hall, Chicago, newly built by Ziegfeld's father for that year's Columbian Exposition and World Fair. For Sandow's opening in August 1893 Ziegfeld posted Chicago with enormous posters billing him as 'The Unprecedented Sensation of this Century—The Modern Hercules and the Perfect Man'. The Trocadero on Michigan Avenue and Munroe Street was a genuine music hall with food and drink served at tables during the performance. The Von Bulow Military Band from Hamburg played the Trocadero March specially composed by its musical director Fritz Scheel. Above the diners' heads Astarte performed 'Aerial Evolutions' on the flying trapeze, and the Ivanoffs' Imperial Dancing Troupe from St Petersburg, 'hoofed' on the stage. Discarding the woollen tights and leopard skins of the traditional music hall strong man, Sandow, in tight silk shorts and a golden laurel crown, his otherwise naked body covered with bronze make-up, stood in a single spotlight striking classical poses like a golden Apollo. With one hand he lifted his friend the pianist Martinus Sieveking, followed by his grand piano. As a finale he raised a giant dumbbell with a man sitting inside each of the balls. He was a sensation, and for weeks the society matrons of Chicago queued up to pay $300 each for the privilege of feeling his muscles. The money went to charity. Chicago was followed by a two-year tour of the USA. At San Francisco's Midwinter Fair of 1893 he fought a lion which, it was claimed, had eaten its keeper the week before. (The music hall on both sides of the Atlantic would have been struck dumb by today's Trade Descriptions Act.) The tour made $250,000 for Ziegfeld and 10 per cent for Sandow. On his return to England he topped bills throughout the UK and his name was used to advertise everything from corsets to cocoa. He retired from the stage in 1907 to popularise physical culture. Ironically, in 1925 he suffered a stroke while trying to lift his car out of a ditch and died at the age of 58.

Leslie Sarony, comedy vocalist, both as a solo act and with Leslie Holmes. Born Leslie Sarony-Frye at Surbiton, Surrey, in 1897, at 14 he joined the juvenile troupe 'Park's Eton Boys', making his first West End appearance in the revue *Escalade* at the London Hippodrome in 1911. Other revues followed and after the First World War he appeared in variety, singing his own comedy songs, 'Ain't It Grand to be Blooming Well Dead', 'Teas, Light Refreshments and Minerals', 'Lift up my Finger and Say "Tweet Tweet"', and others very much in the old music-hall tradition. In 1935 he met Leslie Holmes, a one-time dance-band drummer then working for the music publishers Campbell Connelly & Co. Soon afterwards they appeared together in variety as 'The Two Leslies' appearing in the Royal Variety Performance at the London Coliseum in 1938. The act split in 1946 when Holmes went to work as publicity manager of the *News of the World* and Sarony teamed for a time with Michael Cole. Later he reverted to solo comedy and has become well known as a television and stage character actor.

Albert Saveen, ventriloquist born in Southwark, London, in 1914. He gave up a career in the printing trade to make his first variety appearance at the Coliseum, Portsmouth, on 27 May 1940. After being invalided out of the Royal Artillery he

Scott and Whaley, 'Cuthbert and Pussyfoot', 1910

toured for Moss and GTC, becoming well known in variety with his dolls Daisy May and Andy the Spiv, billed as 'Daisy May with Saveen'.

Billy 'Uke' Scott, vocal and instrumental act. Born in Sunderland on 12 March 1923 he made his first appearance at the Empire, Newcastle, in 1936, and became well known in variety for his fast-playing versatility on the ukulele. His first London appearance was at the Chelsea Palace in 1939 and during the war he was a popular radio act.

Scott and Whaley, American negro cross-talking act of 'Cuthbert and Pussyfoot'. Harry Scott was born in Cleveland, Ohio, in 1879 and Eddie Whaley in Montgomery, Alabama, in 1886. Without having achieved any great success in America they made their first appearance in England at the Hippodrome, Sheffield, on 1 November 1909, and in London at the Empire, Leicester Square, on 8 January 1910. They arrived in England with bookings for only eight weeks, but were so successful they never returned to the USA and became British subjects. As 'Cuthbert and Pussyfoot' their cross-talking routine was very much in the bones-and-corner-man tradition of the nigger minstrels, and they also worked a songs-at-the-piano act. Whaley was vocalist and Scott a good jazz pianist. They were popular in variety for over 30 years and from 1933 were known on radio as the 'Kentucky Minstrels'. When the partnership broke up in 1946 Whaley teamed with Chris Gill, but Scott and Whaley appeared together again at the Queen's, Poplar, on 19 May 1947. Harry Scott died a month later and Whaley retired to Brighton where he ran a hotel until his death on 16 November 1961.

Malcolm Scott, dame comedian, famous in variety billed as 'The Woman Who Knows'. Born in 1872 he made his first appearance as a straight actor at the Theatre Royal, Margate, in 1886. As a pierrot with Adler and Sutton at Llandudno, he appeared as a female impersonator of a somewhat higher tone than the usual grotesque dames of the period. When Dan Leno suffered the first of his mental breakdowns in 1903 Scott was engaged as 'deputy' turn at the London Pavilion with such success that he was given a ten-year contract to appear for six months each year at the Palace and Pavilion. For 25 years he was popular in variety and pantomime, touring the UK, Australia, South Africa, Europe and the USA. His female roles were achieved without being either glamorous or grotesque and although his most famous role was Katherine Parr, 'The Woman Who Knows', other popular impersonations included 'The Gibson Girl', 'Nell

Gwyn', 'The Directoire Girl', 'Boadicea', 'Mrs John Bull' and 'Salome'. In every role his patter was as witty as it was impromptu. He died on 7 September 1929.

Harry Secombe, outsize comedian with a personality to match. Born in Swansea on 8 September 1921, he enlisted in the Royal Artillery at 17, gaining experience as an entertainer with an army concert party in Italy. After the war he made his first professional stage appearance in Vivian Van Damm's *Revuedeville* at the Windmill Theatre, the famous Soho theatre which was the first rung on the ladder of success for so many post-war comics. There Harry played a six-a-day comedy shaving routine, did impressions and sent up the Jeanette MacDonald—Nelson Eddy 'Sweetheart' duet. He subsequently broadcast in 'Variety Bandbox', 'Welsh Rarebit' and 'Educating Archie'. In 1951 he appeared with Peter Sellers, Michael Bentine and Spike Milligan in the radio show 'Crazy People', which as 'The Goon Show' developed into the comedy cult of the 1950s. The enormous success of the Goons led to star billing in the Palladium revues *Let Yourself Go, Rocking the Town* and *Large as Life*, which established him as one of the most popular and genuinely likable comedians in variety. His first Royal Variety appearances were at the Victoria Palace in 1951 and in 1957 he returned to the Royal Show as soloist with the Morriston Orpheus Choir. He has a good tenor voice which he distorts from bass to soprano, and appeared in the name part of the musical *Pickwick* at the Saville Theatre in 1963, and scored a great hit with the song 'If I Ruled the World'. As D'Artagnan he later fooled and sang himself hoarse in an attempt to make a success of the unsuccessful musical *The Four Musketeers* at the Theatre Royal, Drury Lane. In 1975 he opened at the Prince of Wales Theatre, London, in his first straight play, *The Plumber's Progress*, and made another Royal Variety appearance at the London Palladium, singing with Vera Lynn and the Rhos Male Voice Choir.

The Selbinis, troupe of acrobatic trick cyclists formed in 1884 by John Selbini. Born in Westfield, Massachusetts, in June 1855, Selbini was apprenticed to a circus and came to

Malcolm Scott, 'Mrs John Bull'

England during the 1860s. After a few years with Powel and Clarke's Circus, he became the pupil of George Corin, later known as 'Latine'. Gorin formed a troupe with Selbini, a girl known as Mademoiselle Kate, and another man by the name of Villion. Selbini and Villion later formed a double act, appearing in pantomime at Covent Garden in 1876, and for eight years were members of Hengler's Circus. When the partnership broke up Selbini, his wife and daughter Lalla formed a troupe and for the next five years toured the USA with Tony Pastor's vaudeville company and Boston Howard's Athenaeum Company. While appearing at the Folies Bergère, Paris, in June 1889 he heard the news of

The Selbini Troupe, 1890

Latine's murder and returned to London to appear at a benefit for his widow. This led to an 18-month engagement at the Canterbury under George Adney Payne and in 1894 he signed three-year contracts for the London Pavilion and Oxford Music Hall. During the next 10 years the family made seven tours of the UK for Moss and Thornton.

Lalla Selbini was the close friend of 'The Great Lafayette' (qv) and after his tragic death in 1911 inherited what was left of his show. She later worked a solo act in variety, billed as 'The Bathing Belle on the Bicycle'. She died in the USA on 14 February 1942.

J. W. Sharpe, supper-room tavern singer who appeared at the Vauxhall Gardens in 1847 and became a great favourite at Evans Song and Supper Room in the 1850s. His most popular songs were by John Lebern and included 'Who'll Buy My Images', 'Pity the Downfall of Poor Punch and Judy' and 'Cadger's Ball'. Although one of the greatest comic singers of the day, he died in Dover workhouse from exposure and semi-starvation in 1846 at the age of 35.

Buster Shaver with Olive, George and Richard, Lilliputian novelty dancing, singing and comedy act. Buster Shaver, born in New York on 7 February 1905, began his career in the chorus of *Irene* in 1922, followed by vaudeville with 10-year-old Olive and 15-year-old George Brassano, who had made their first appearance in the vaudeville miniature revue *Romeo and Juliet* in 1926. 'Buster Shaver with Olive and George' made their London debut at the Palladium on 4 September 1933, followed by a variety tour of the UK and Europe. On their return to the USA they worked in vaudeville, revue, and were featured in a number of films. In 1938 Richard Brassano, the 14-year-old midget brother of Olive and George, joined the act. After the war they returned to England to tour in variety, appearing at the London Casino and Palladium in 1947 and at Christmas played in *Babes in the Wood* at the Princes Theatre, London. On 1 November 1948 Buster Shaver and his Lilliputian trio took part in the Royal Variety Performance at the London Palladium, followed by their ninth variety tour of Great Britain.

Mark Sheridan, comic singer of such music hall classics as 'I Do Like to Be Beside the Seaside', and 'Who Were You With Last Night?'. Born Fred Shaw, at Hendon, County Durham, in 1867, he first appeared with a partner as 'The Sheridans', touring the halls of the north. In 1892 he went to Australia for Harry Rickards and as a solo turn appeared in London at the Standard Music Hall, Pimlico in 1895. Dressed eccentrically in high black top hat, tight frockcoat, and bell-bottomed trousers, he was soon established in the front rank of music-hall comedians.

A singer of great chorus songs, which he conducted with his baggy umbrella, he led 'Here We Are, Here We Are, Here We Are Again', 'We All Went Marching Home Again', 'All the Little Ducks Went Quack Quack', 'You Can Do a Lot of Things at the Seaside That You Can't Do in Town', and the popular if historically inaccurate 'Belgium Put the Kybosh on the Kaiser'. During the First World War he toured the music halls with his own burlesque company which included his wife, son and daughter. On 14 January 1918 his show opened at the Glasgow Coliseum with Sheridan playing the part of Napoleon in *Gay Paree, or a Royal Discourse*, a parody on the West End success *A Royal Divorce*. Having appeared in four Glasgow pantomimes he was well-known in the city and went over well. Sadly, Sheridan was suffering from acute depression and, imagining that his popularity was waning, shot himself in Kelvin Grove Park.

His son, born in 1890, also played in variety, mainly as part of the comedy duo 'Elva and Mark Sheridan'.

Ella Shields, born in Baltimore, Maryland, on 26 September 1879. Her first appearance was in Altoona, Pennsylvania, on 28 April 1898, and she toured extensively throughout the USA as a coon singer. As such she made her first London appearance at Forester's Music Hall on 10 October 1904, and the following Christmas appeared as principal girl in pantomime at the Pavilion, Mile End. Famous as a male impersonator, she first appeared in top hat and tails for the opening of the London Palladium on 26 December 1910. Even if she lacked the greatness of Vesta Tilley or the character range and power of Hetty King, she was a charming artiste, popular for many years on the British music halls singing 'If You Knew Susie', 'Adeline', 'You'll Stick to London Town', 'Show Me The Way to Go Home' and the most famous 'Burlington Bertie from Bow'. First sung at Newcastle in 1914, 'Burlington Bertie', written by Ella's husband William Hargreaves, takes its place in the long line of broken-down swell songs:

> I'm Burlington Bertie,
> I rise at ten-thirty and saunter along
>   like a toff,
> I walk down the Strand with my gloves
>   on my hand,
> Then I walk down again with them off,
> I'm all airs and graces, correct easy paces,
> Without food so long I've forgot where
>   my face is,

Mark Sheridan, 1910

Ella Shields, 'Burlington Bertie'

> I'm Bert, Bert, I haven't a shirt, but my people are well off, you know!
> Nearly ev'ry one knows me, from Smith to Lord Roseb'ry,
> I'm Burlington Bertie from Bow.

The song should not be confused with Vesta Tilley's 'Burlington Bertie—the boy with the Hyde Park drawl', although Hargreaves based his version on Tilley's original. Bertie may have lost his shirt and come from Bow, but Ella Shields sang of him dressed in immaculate top hat and tails, and with a slight American accent. She returned to the USA in 1929 but after years of obscurity made a comeback in 1947 by touring Australia. In November 1948 she was one of the *Thanks for the Memory* company, introducing a new generation to the drolleries of 'Burlington Bertie'. She was taken ill while appearing at a Morecambe holiday camp on 3 August 1952 and died three days later.

Mrs Shufflewick, creation of the well-loved drag comedian Rex Jamieson, famous as the not-so-refined little old lady 'broadminded to the point of obscenity', and bewildered at the strange things that can happen to a weak-willed and easily led woman. Originally a member of Ralph Reader's 'Gang Show', as Mrs Shufflewick Rex became so popular in variety, cabaret, radio and television that he is now never referred to by his real name. A polished artiste in the true music-hall tradition, a sort of cross between Arthur Lucan and Nellie Wallace, he combines the immaculate timing of the stand-up comedian with the low comedy of a pantomime dame. He appears regularly at the New Black Cap, a well known drag pub in Camden Town, where in addition to his twin set and fur routine, he does a hilariously funny ballerina and 'swinging nun' double act with fellow drag artiste Marc Fleming. In 1973 he made a live record of his act at the New Black Cap, 'A Drop of the Hard Stuff'.

Sissle and Blake, American negro musicians who appeared in London and on variety tours of the UK singing their own compositions, notably 'I'm Just Wild About Harry'. Noble Sissle was born in Indianapolis, Indiana, on 10 July 1889 and Eubie Black in Baltimore on 7 February 1883. They met as members of Joe Porter's Serenaders, a summer show band in River View Park, Baltimore, in 1915.

After the war, in which Sissle served as a lieutenant in France with James Reese Europ's all-negro 369th US Infantry 'Hell Fighters' Band', they teamed as a vaudeville act and in 1919 played the Palace Theatre, New York, billed as the 'Dixie Duo'. In Philadelphia in 1920 they met comedy dancing team Flournoy Miller and Aubrey Lyles, and decided to join forces in producing and starring in their own musical comedy show. The result was *Shuffle Along* with book by Miller and Lyles and music and lyrics by Sissle and Blake. After a tour of one-night stands the all-negro 'musical melange' opened at the 63rd Street Theatre on 23 May 1921. Well received by the press, the hit of the show was 'Love Will Find a Way', with 'I'm Just Wild About Harry' a close second. Gertrude Saunders, the leading lady, left the show a few months after it opened and was replaced by Florence Mills. After 14 months on Broadway, *Shuffle Along* played 15 weeks each in Chicago and Boston, followed by a national tour. Without Miller and Lyles, Sissle and Blake wrote *In Bamville*, which opened at the Lyceum Theatre, Rochester, on 10 March 1924 and after 24 weeks on the road opened as

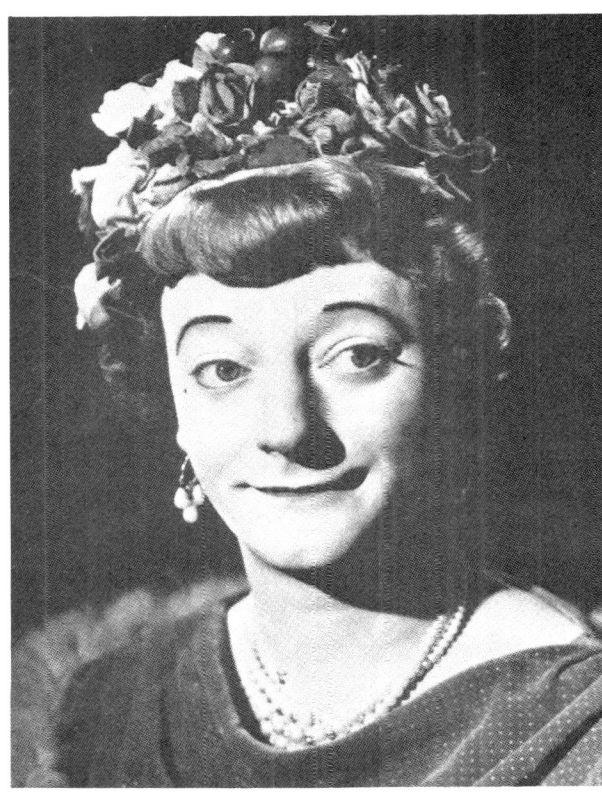

Mrs Shufflewick

The Chocolate Dandies at the Colonial Theatre, New York, on 1 September 1924. The female comedy lead of the show was Josephine Baker (q.v.), promoted from the touring chorus of *Shuffle Along*. Although getting even better reviews than their previous success it closed in May 1925 for a loss of $60,000. Billed as the 'American Ambassadors of Syncopation' Sissle and Blake made their London debut at the Holborn Empire in September 1925 and went on to star at the Coliseum and in the Piccadilly Cabaret. On 12 October 1925 they opened in twice-nightly variety at the Victoria Palace, sharing the top of the bill with fellow American Ethel Levey, and in February 1926 they appeared at the Alhambra with Little Tich. They contributed songs to C. B. Cochran's *1926 Revue*, which went over so well that Cochran invited them to write the score for his revue of 1927. Eubie Blake was anxious to return to the USA so Sissle reluctantly refused and Cochran's score was supplied by Rodgers and Hart.

After a tour of eight months in London and on tour of the UK they returned to tour the USA in vaudeville. The act broke up in 1927 and Sissle returned to London in 1928 to appear in variety with British pianist Harry Revel, who later wrote the song hit 'Did you Ever See a Dream Walking'. Later in 1928 Sissle formed his own orchestra to play at Les Ambassadeurs, Paris, which in 1929 came to London and toured the UK.

Later Sissle and Blake got together again for a number of unsuccessful revivals of *Shuffle Along*. They wrote many songs together and both ran their own 'society' orchestras. A great champion of negro rights, Noble Sissle was the first president of the Negro Actors' Guild, and on the death of Bill Robinson (qv) in 1949 was elected Mayor of Harlem. The revival in 1948 of 'I'm Just Wild About Harry' as the presidential campaign song of Harry S. Truman prompted interest in a new edition of *Shuffle Along*. It opened in New York on 8 May 1952 and closed four nights later.

Noble Sissle died on 17 December 1975 and Eubie Blake, aged 93, is living in New York.

Chung Ling Soo, illusionist, born William Ellsworth Robinson, in New York on 2 April 1861. Although the place of his birth has been frequently disputed, Robinson's First World War passport, in the collection of the magician The Great Levante, gives New York as his birthplace. During the 1880s he played the variety theatres of the eastern states of the USA billed as 'Robinson, the Man of Mystery'. In 1888 he became assistant and stage manager to Harry Keller and in 1893 to Alexander Herman. Both magicians used Robinson's original illusions in their acts and in return gave him the benefit of their vast experience of stage techniques and management. It was from Herman, known as 'Alexander the Great', that he learned the art of stage make-up which enabled him to double for Herman and which he used so effectively in his own act later on. On the death of Alexander Herman in 1896 his act was worked by his widow, Adelaide Herman, assisted by Robinson and managed by Herman's nephew Leon. In 1899 Robinson returned to vaudeville with his own company and in April that year as Mongolian magician Chung Ling Foo appeared with success at Keith's Variety Theatre, New York. His act was purely traditional Chinese conjuring, acrobats and juggling, but proved a great attraction. Robinson had long realised the value of exploiting the mysterious East and early in his career had billed himself as 'Achmed Ben Ali', 'Abdul Khan' and 'Nana Sahib'.

Chung Ling Foo's success prompted him to present a new 'Chinese' act, and as 'Hop Ling Soo' he opened at the Folies Bergère on 15 April 1900, and as 'Chung Ling Soo' at the Alhambra, London, on 14 May 1900. The Alhambra engagement lasted for three months, during which he

perfected his act to a standard which for nearly 20 years kept him at the top of variety bills, and established a legendary and bizarre place for him in the history of British music hall. His act was staged with all the oriental splendour of imperial China. It was announced that Soo's robes were those of his venerable ancestors and that the palanquin in which he was carried onto the stage by four attendants was the gift of the Dowager Empress of China, the instigator of the bloody Boxer uprising of 1900. He never spoke on stage, using a Chinese (actually a Korean) to address the audience. So perfect was his make-up and inscrutable his oriental manner that it was generally believed even by his fellow artistes that he really was Chinese. In 1904 Soo introduced the ill-famed bullet-catching routine into his act. It had been performed since the seventeenth century, but was justly viewed with grave misgivings by contemporary magicians because of its many fatalities. The trick consisted of an assistant firing a pistol or rifle at the illusionist, who appeared to catch the bullet on a china plate. For many years Chung Ling Soo 'defied death' twice nightly, building up the 'Living Target' illusion to a lavish stage spectacular, culminating in his 'execution' by a Boxer firing squad. During the second house at the Wood Green Empire on 23 March 1918, the routine went wrong. The mechanism in the rifle which should have retained the bullet in the muzzle failed to operate and Robinson fell fatally wounded. The bullet passed through his right lung and he died a few hours later at Wood Green Hospital.

Elsie Southgate (Lady Odin Pearse), violinist, born in 1890. At the age of ten she won a scholarship to the Royal Academy of Music, and made her first concert appearance with the Queen's Hall Orchestra under Sir Henry Wood in 1905. In addition to her concert work she had a successful career on the halls, making her variety debut at the London Pavilion in 1910. During the next 20 years she made frequent variety tours of the UK billed as 'Elsie Southgate, The Royal Violinist', and in 1926 toured the vaudeville theatres of the USA and Canada. She died in May 1946.

Stainless Stephen, comedian, born Arthur Clifford Baynes in Sheffield in 1892. His first stage appearance was at the Palace, Luton, in September 1921. He was then a full-time schoolmaster who could only appear in variety during the school holidays and was a star of radio long before his first London appearance at the Victoria Palace in July 1930. He gave up school mastering for a full-time variety and radio career about 1937, but never lost his scholarly air, and became famed for his highly original comic method of speaking the punctuation instead of using it. For example:
Somebody once said inverted commas comedians are born not made. Well slight pause to heighten egotistical effect comma let me tell you my dense public (innuendo) that I was born eighteen ninety something, owing to my female fan following the two final digits must be left to the imagination, especially as I may be offered a juvenile leadership on a television fashion programme. End of first paragraph and a fresh line. (From *Radio Variety*, edited by John Watt, published in 1939.)
His curious stage dress—dinner jacket, bowler hat, white bow tie, and a stainless-steel shirt front, contrasted with his 'egg-headed' humour. His topical comedy and inverted verbal punctuation was known to irritate as well as amuse, but he made several extensive tours for ENSA and appeared before the royal family at Buckingham Palace and Windsor Castle. He died on 13 January 1971.

Stanelli, musician and comedian, studied at the Royal College of Music under Sir Charles Stanford, but gave up his studies to make his first music-hall appearance at the Metropolitan in 1914. He worked a musical double act with a partner as 'Stanelli and Douglas', appearing in the Royal Variety Performance at the London Coliseum on 1 March 1928. Later he worked as a solo comedian in variety and on radio and teamed with another partner as 'Stanelli and Edgar'. Stanelli, real name Edward Stanley de Groot, has also conducted the London Symphony Orchestra and the Hallé Orchestra.

Jack Stanford, eccentric comedy dancer, born in Colchester on 26 June 1900. At 15 he appeared with a concert party and made his variety debut at the Empire, Swindon, in 1916. After army service during the First World War he made his first London appearance at the Canterbury Music Hall in January 1920. He scored his first real success in an Albert de

Stainless Stephen, 1930

Courville revue in Monte Carlo, which led to a year at the Folies Bergère, Paris, in a revue starring Joseph ne Baker. Later he toured the USA in vaudeville, starred at the Winter Garden, New York, and for six months was with Shubert's *Greenwich Village Follies*. Back in London he starred in cabaret at the Trocadero, and billed as 'the Dancing Fool' toured in variety for Stoll and GTC, appearing in the Royal Variety Performance on 11 May 1931. He appeared in C. B. Cochran's *The Year of Grace* at the Pavilion and in 1941 with Max Miller in *Apple Sauce* at the London Palladium.

Tommy Steele, cockney singer who developed from being a rock-and-roll teenage idol of the 1950s into an international star of variety and musical comedy. Born Thomas Hicks in Bermondsey, London, on 17 December 1936, he left school at 15 and in April 1952 went to sea with the Cunard Line, working between Southampton and New York. At ship's concerts he sang and did a comedy routine in the style of Norman Wisdom. Between ships in 1956 he took his guitar to London's Soho and while playing at the Two Eyes coffee bar was photographed by a freelance photographer, who sold the

Tommy Steele, 1957

prints to a Sunday newspaper. These were used to illustrate the growing rock-and-roll craze and led to Tommy's first record 'Rock With the Caveman', written by Tommy and his friend Lionel Bart, then a small-time jobbing printer. On 15 October 1956 he made his television debut in BBC's 'Off the Record' and on 5 November made his first stage appearance at the top of the bill at the Empire Theatre, Sunderland. On 21 January 1957 he began a two-week cabaret engagement at the Café de Paris, London, and in May worked his first London variety date at the Dominion, Tottenham Court Road. During February and March 1957 he worked on the film *The Tommy Steele Story*, a biographical picture intended to cash in on his tremendous popularity. Made on a shoestring of £20,000 it was phenomenally successful and grossed more than £500,000, and led to Tommy's dual role in *The Duke Wore Jeans*. Following a tour of Europe and Scandinavia, in October 1957, the BBC acknowledged his swift rise to fame with an hour-long programme aptly entitled 'The Golden Year'. To bring 1957 to a momentous close, on 18 November he appeared in the Royal Variety Performance at the London Palladium. In the spring of 1958 he toured South Africa and at Christmas played Buttons in Rodgers and Hammerstein's pantomime *Cinderella* at the London Coliseum. He made two further films in 1959, *Tommy the Toreador* and *Touch it*

Light and in February 1960 toured Australia. He made his legitimate stage debut on 8 November 1960 in the role of Tony Lumpkin in *She Stoops to Conquer* at the Old Vic.

Now no longer considered just a flash in the pop pan, his greatest success has been the comedy role of Kipps in the musical version of H. G. Wells's novel *Half a Sixpence*. The opening night at the Cambridge Theatre, London, on 31 March 1963 was an unqualified triumph for Tommy, with the critics unanimous in their praise of his achievement. Harold Hobson of the *Sunday Times* considered Tommy's performance the best he had ever seen in a musical. He made a second Royal Variety appearance on 4 November 1964 and on Christmas Day appeared as Richard Whittington Esq in a television pantomime, for which he wrote all the music and lyrics. After 20 months' run in London *Half a Sixpence* opened at the Broadhurst Theatre, New York, on 25 April 1965. Tommy Steele's performance, personality and personal charm captivated New York and he was hailed as 'Broadway's Cockney Star'. When the show closed the following spring he went to Hollywood to star with Greer Garson and Fred MacMurray in Walt Disney's film *The Happiest Millionaire* and in September 1966 returned to England to star in the film version of *Half a Sixpence*. He was back in Hollywood in 1967 to star with Fred Astaire and Petula Clark in the film version of the musical *Finian's Rainbow*. Although his reputation in America was based on his own great cockney personality, with typical Hollywood perversity he was cast as an Irishman in both films. In complete contrast to Irish butlers and leprechauns, in England he played Truffaldino in the classical Italian comedy *The Servant of Two Masters*, Feste in an all-star BBC television production of *Twelfth Night*, and at Christmas 1969 appeared as Dick Whittington at the London Palladium. In November 1974 he returned to the Palladium to star in Frank Loesser's musical *Hans Andersen*, bringing his own exuberance and style to the role originally created on the screen by Danny Kaye.

Lee Stevens, female impersonator, born Liverpool in 1931, he first appeared as a child variety singer at the Argyle Theatre, Birkenhead, in 1938. After two years' national service with the RAF he toured the music halls using the name 'Alan Avid' in 1951 and then joined *Soldiers in Skirts* and other all-male road shows. In 1955 he teamed with Gary Webb to present the drag act 'Avid and Webb', appearing as the Ugly Sisters in pantomime, and playing resident cabaret seasons at London's top night spots, the Stork, Starlight, Panama, and Gargoyle clubs. They also played variety dates, appearing on tours with Randolph Sutton and Dorothy Squires. After pantomime at Worthing in 1963 the double act split, Avid leaving the profession for a number of years. As Lee Stevens he made a comeback in January 1968, working a single act at London's Blue Angel Club. Later that year he worked a season at the Theatre Royal, Stratford East. This led to his television debut in 1969 and a part in the short-lived Paul Raymond revue *Birds of a Feather*, which opened at the Royalty Theatre, Kingsway, on 2 April 1970. Billed as 'The Bird with the Feathers', he remains a popular club variety act, appearing in 1973 with Mrs Shufflewick, Ford and Sheen and Marc Fleming in Jack Lawrence's *Gaiety Box Revue*. A great admirer of the late Alma Cogan, he sings her songs and wears her original stage costumes in his act, including a heavily jewelled and feathered dress made for her American television debut.

Eugene Stratton, 'the Dandy Coloured Coon', born Eugene Augustus Ruhlmann in Buffalo, New York, on 8 May 1861. Teamed at the age of ten with a partner as 'The Two

Eugene Stratton, 'The Dandy Coloured Coon'

Wesleys', he appeared at Dan Shelly's Saloon, Buffalo, in a burnt-cork sketch, 'The Big and the Little of It'. In 1876 he toured the USA and Canada with a black-faced sketch troupe known as 'The Four Arnolds', which in 1878 joined Haveley's Mustoden Minstrels. Under the management of Charles Frohman, Haveley's Minstrels came to England in 1880, opening at Her Majesty's Theatre, London, on 31 July 1881. When Haveley's returned to the USA, Stratton joined the Moore and Burgess Minstrels at the St James's Hall, Piccadilly, acting for 11 years as comedian, singer, dancer and principal tambourine man. A natural dancer with a wonderful sense of movement, he devised the troupe's song and dance numbers. Developing a powerful whistle, his first song success was 'The Whistling Coon' which he bought from veteran minstrel Sam Raeburn. He made his music-hall debut at the Royal Holborn in August 1892, performing a soft-shoe song-and-dance routine. Not a great success, he reverted to coon singing, giving a much more sophisticated and subtle performance than the usual plantation negro types favoured by the nigger minstrels of the period. His first song successes were 'I Lub a Lubbly Girl' by Brandon Thomas, and 'The Dandy Coloured Coon' by Morton and Le Brunn, but he is best remembered as the singer of the great songs of Leslie Stuart, the composer of *Florodora*. These included 'Little Dolly Day Dream', 'I May Be Crazy', 'My Little Octoroon' and 'Lily of Laguna'. He had neither a powerful nor an especially good voice, but he projected his songs by sheer artistry and natural acting ability. He stood on a stage lighted by a single spot, a slight figure in a black frock coat, silk top hat and bow tie. Seemingly oblivious of the audience, he sang softly at first, and slowly rising in pitch and volume, declared that Lily of Laguna was his lady love, or that Little Dolly Daydream was the pride of Idaho. In a different mood he presented a dramatic and pathetic picture of a negro horse-thief, who with pursuers close behind stops to make one last desperate plea to a girl who has spurned his love. As he sang 'I Must be Crazy but I Love You', the tension created by his quivering figure and hunted backward glances was quite electrifying. Towards the end of his song he would drift into a soft-shoe dance, full of delicate grace and accompanying himself with his powerful whistle. His dancing was perhaps the strongest feature of his performance. Sir Seymour Hicks eloquently described him as a dancer 'beautiful beyond words, who seemed to be a feather blown hither and thither by Leslie Stuart's melodies, which he taught the town to sing'. A member of the Grand Order of Water Rats from 1893, he was King Rat in 1896 and again in 1900. Ill health excluded him from a deserved place in the first Royal Command Variety Performance in 1912. He gave his last performance at the Queen's, Poplar, in 1914, dying on 15 September 1918.

Dan Sullivan, strong man who first appeared in London at the Imperial Theatre on 3 February 1892, swinging a 56lb weight from a chain held between his teeth. He closed his act by standing on a pedestal and lifting by means of a chain a 15 cwt elephant to a height of four inches off the stage. Billed as the 'Wonder of the Age', he appeared at other London halls, lifting by his teeth a live horse and a cart with four people seated in it.

Randolph Sutton, light comedian, born Bristol on 24 July 1888. At 17 he gave up his job as clerk and joined a seaside concert party. He made his first London appearance at the Pavilion in 1915, later touring his own road shows, and appearing as one of the first male principal boys in pantomime. Famed as the singer of 'On Mother Kelly's Doorstep', in 1948 he was one of the original members of Don Ross's *Thanks for the Memory* company, appearing with it in the Royal Variety Performance of 1948. He continued to appear in variety even at the age of 80, making his last appearance on a bill at St Albans a few days before his death on 28 February 1969.

Randolph Sutton, his last appearance at St Albans, 1969 (collection, Tony and David Oaks)

Harry Sydney, top of the bill at the Euston Music Hall, October 1857

Harry Sydney, topical vocalist, born in 1825. During his early career he appeared at the Colosseum Saloon in Albion Street, near Regent's Park, and later was a regular entertainer at Evans Song and Supper Rooms. When Charles Morton opened the Oxford Music Hall in 1861, Sydney was one of his first attractions, singing 'A Quiet Sort of Man', 'A Rolling Stone Gathers No Moss', and 'Let the World Jog Along'. He was a great friend of vocalist Sam Collins (qv), and when Collins took over the Lansdown Arms, Islington Green, in 1862, he became resident singer. On the death of Collins in 1865, Sydney took over the chairman's hammer and ran the hall for Sam's widow, later becoming the manager of Charles Morton's Philharmonic Hall, Islington, known locally as the 'Spittoon'. Sydney wrote the lyrics for his own songs, and was known in his time as a 'librettist'. He is now only remembered as the author of Sam Collins's epitaph in Kensal Green Cemetery:

A loving husband and a faithful friend,
Ever the first a helping hand to lend,
Farewell, good-natured, honest-hearted Sam,
Until we meet before the Great I Am.

No great literary masterpiece. The 'Great I Am' did not have long to wait. Harry Sydney died of Bright's Disease on 16 June 1870 aged 45.

T

Takio, animal and bird mimic. Billed as 'The Japanese Entertainer' he made his first London appearance at the Palladium in March 1917. He presented his act in an original way, standing on the stage before a screen onto which slides of birds and animals were projected with Takio supplying the appropriate bird calls and animal noises. He later made a successful tour of the Moss Empires.

Above: Harry Tate, 'Golfing' Below: Suzette Tarri

Suzette Tarri, comedienne and vocalist, born Hoxton, London, in 1881. She first appeared as a child violinist and later as a concert and oratorio contralto. Her variety debut was at the Walthamstow Palace, followed by a summer season at Ilfracombe in 1911. She was an early broadcaster for Ernest Longstaffe, and during the 1930s took part in pioneering television transmissions. In 1938 she appeared at the Metropolitan Music Hall, Edgware Road, and from then on was a popular comedienne both in variety and as radio's cockney charwoman 'Our Ada'. Famous for her song 'Red Sails in the Sunset', with which she finished her comedy patter routine, she recorded for Decca and Columbia, and made films for Pathe. She made her last stage appearance at the Theatre Royal, Portsmouth, in December 1954, and her final broadcast on Henry Hall's 'Guest Night' a week later. She died on 10 October 1955.

Harry Tate, comedian, born Ronald Macdonald Hutchison, in Scotland on 4 July 1872. He began professional life working for the sugar firm of Henry Tate and Sons, appearing in his spare time at smoking-room concerts. Early in 1895 he appeared as a mimic at the Camberwell Empire on a bill topped by Marie Lloyd, and as 'Harry Tate' made his West End debut at the Oxford on 13 April the same year. His earliest material consisted of two sketches, 'A Ward in Chancery' and 'Number Seven', featuring impersonations of

1848 A THE TILLER TROUPE. ROTARY PHOTO, E.C.
MISS NELLIE WHITING. MISS NELLIE TURNER.
MISS DAISY WOODWORTH. MISS MILLIE WILLIAMS.

Have you seen these girls? They are fine dancers.

Dan Leno, Eugene Stratton, George Robey, Charles Godfrey and Cissie Loftus. An early car owner, he realised the comic potential of the automobile and from small beginnings developed the sketch 'Motoring' into one of the most hilarious acts on the halls. His troupe included Tommy Tweedly as his son, an exasperating child in a top hat and Eton suit, who sat in the back of Harry's broken-down car making inane remarks like 'Isn't it amazing Papa' in a high falsetto voice, and every time the car seemed about to start, 'Good-by-ee'. 'Motoring' established Harry Tate as one of music hall's greats, and it was followed by 'Flying', 'Golfing', 'Billiards', 'Fishing' 'Selling a Car' and 'Broadcasting'. He appeared in both Royal Variety Command Performances in 1912 and 1919.

In 1913 he starred in *Hullo Tango* at the London Hippodrome and with the decline of music hall turned more and more to revue. In 1918 he returned to the Hippodrome in *Box of Tricks*, followed by *Push and Go, Business as Usual* and *Smith and Co.* His last appearance was in *All Clear* at the Theatre Royal, Brighton, in December 1939. He died on 14 February 1940 from injuries received during an air raid on Dundee.

Harry Tate, Junior, born Ronald Hutchison in London on 22 February 1902. He first appeared with his father, Harry Tate, at the London Hippodrome in 1917, and worked with his father's act until 1940. After Harry's death he continued in variety and revue with a similar act and toured the USA and Canada.

Tennyson and O'Gorman, cross-talking act. Joe Tennyson first appeared with a partner as 'Tennyson and Traynor', in 1878. About 1880 he worked with another comedian as 'Hartley and Devine' and in 1881 teamed with Joe O'Gorman. Billed at first as 'Devine and O'Gorman', Tennyson soon reverted to his real name, and as Tennyson and O'Gorman they toured the UK, USA and Australia. The double act broke up in 1901 and after a short period as a single act, Tennyson teamed with songwriter William Wallis, until Wallis retired in 1915. Joe O'Gorman worked a single turn and was active in forming the Variety Artistes Federation, being followed also to the halls by his sons, Joe and Dave O'Gorman, popular in variety and on radio as 'The O'Gorman Brothers'. Joe Tennyson died on 5 September 1926, and Joe O'Gorman on 1 August 1937.

Terry Thomas, moustached, gap-toothed, upper-crust comedian who in the earlier days of music hall would have been classed as a 'silly ass' comic. Born Thomas Terry Hoar-Stevens in Finchley, London, on 14 July 1914. He first appeared in cabaret at the Paradise Coconut Grove, London, in 1938, and made his stage debut at the Tivoli, Hull, in January 1939. During the war he toured for ENSA in *Cabaret Parade* and *Stars in Battledress*, and after army service broadcast and toured in variety for GTC. He opened on 11 October 1946 at the Prince of Wales Theatre, London, as second comedian in *Piccadilly Hayride* starring Sid Fields. During the 778 performances of the show Thomas scored a great hit with his 'Technical Hitch' routine, appearing as a disc-jockey who, when his gramophone fails, does impressions of the records he should have been playing. The routine was the basis of his variety act thereafter. He appeared in the Royal Variety Performance of 1946 and broadcast in his own shows, 'To Town with Terry' (1949). In 1953 he starred with George Formby and Billy Cotton in *Fun of the Fair* at the London Palladium. He appeared in the Boulting Brothers film *Private's Progress* in 1956. This led to parts in a highly successful series of comedy films made by both British and Hollywood studios, and established Terry Thomas as America's favourite British comedian.

John Tiller, dancing master who founded the famous Tiller Girls Dancing Troupe, first presented at the King's Theatre, Manchester, in 1890. The John Tiller schools supplied troupes of long-legged, high-kicking, precision dancers to the leading music halls of the UK and Europe. The Palace Tiller Girls appeared at the first Royal Command Variety Performance at the Palace Theatre, London, in 1912, and for many years a Tiller Troupe of 'Les Girls' were a resident attraction at the Folies Bergère, Paris. John Tiller died on 22 October 1925, but the Tiller Girls carried on his name as the chorus lines of variety, revue and pantomime, and became synonymous with shows at the London Palladium.

Vesta Tilley, the greatest of music hall's male impersonators. Born Matilda Alice Powles in Worcester in 1864, she made a precocious first appearance aged four at a music hall in Gloucester run by her father, known on the halls as Harry Ball (qv). He later moved to Nottingham to act as chairman at the St George's Music Hall, but as the popularity of his daughter grew he toured in variety as 'Harry Ball the Tramp Musician and the Great Little Tilley'. Tilley was then doing a standard song-and-impressions act but soon switched to top hat and tails. She wrote of her early days in *Recollections of Vesta Tilley* (1934): 'Young as I was I had, in song, run through the whole gamut of female characters, from baby songs to old maid's ditties, and I concluded that female costume was rather a drag. I felt that I could express myself better if I were dressed as a boy.'

Billed as 'The Pocket Sims Reeves' (after the famous tenor of that name) singing 'The Anchors Weighed', 'Pretty Jane' and 'Come Into The Garden Maud', she made her first appearance as a male impersonator at Day's Concert Hall, Birmingham, in 1869. Her London debut was at the Canterbury in 1874, and by 1880 she was appearing for at least three months of each year in the West End, billed as 'The London Idol'. Immaculately dressed in the height of fashion, in suits and military uniforms by the best Savile Row tailors, whether appearing as man-about-town, soldier, sailor, policeman or priest, her costumes could seldom be faulted. Before she first sang 'Six Days Leave' she spent an hour at Victoria Station watching troop trains arrive, and noting the way that 'Tommy' handled his pack when getting on and off the train. She had a wonderfully light and graceful touch and despite her masculine dress never gave an aggressively 'butch' performance. Even when smoking a cigar, singing 'The Bold Militia-man' or drilling with a regulation service rifle, she always managed to maintain her basic femininity. She appeared in the first Royal Command Performance in 1912 (when it was incorrectly reported that Queen Mary turned her back on Tilley's performance). She was the only male impersonator to appear in a Royal Variety show until Ella Shields appeared with the *Thanks for the Memory* company 36 years later.

During her long career her song successes include 'Mary and John' written by Sir Oswald Stoll, 'Following in Father's Footsteps', 'After the Ball', 'Algy—The Piccadilly Johnny with the Little Glass Eye', 'The Midnight Son', 'Burlington Bertie' and 'The Newmarket Coat'. She made her first appearance in America at Tony Pastor's Music Hall, New York, in 1898. The press were unanimous in their praise, and even arch critic Alan Dale who, although born in Birmingham had a formidable reputation for being very hard on visiting British music hall artistes, referred to her as the 'Irving of the Halls'.

She made several more visits to the USA, playing return

Vesta Tilley in military guise (left) and as man-about-town (right)

engagements at Pastor's, appearing between acts at the Chicago Opera House, and for six weeks sharing the top of the bill with Lillian Russell, at Weber and Field's Music Hall, New York. For Weber, Fields and de Frece, she toured the main cities of the northern states with 'The Vesta Tilley Vaudeville Company', which included veteran minstrel-man Lew Dockstader, Charles T. Aldrich, and the Cohan family. Back in New York she appeared at Daly's Theatre in the light opera *My Lady Molly* and then toured in *Algy*, a comedy based on her Piccadilly Johnny song. During the Great War she introduced many fine songs, 'Jolly Good Luck to the Girls Who Love a Soldier', 'London in France', 'A Bit of a Blighty One', 'The Girl I Left Behind Me', and the best of the lot 'The Army of Today's All Right':

It's all right, it's all right now,
There's no need to worry any more,
Who said the army wasn't strong,
Kitchener proved them wrong,
On the day he came along,
So let the band play and shout 'Hooray',
I'll show the Germans how to fight,
I joined the army yesterday,
So the army of today's all right.

This jingoistic ditty was responsible for so many enlistments that, like Lord Kitchener, she became known as 'England's Greatest Recruiting Sergeant'. In 1890 she married Walter de Frece, a music-hall and theatre proprietor, who was knighted in 1919 and became a member of Parliament for Ashton and later Blackpool. After 50 years on the stage Vesta Tilley decided that she would retire and start a new life as Lady de Frece. She began a farewell tour on 6 August 1919 and made her last professional music hall appearance at the London Coliseum on 5 June 1920. Her swan song was 'Jolly Good Luck to the Girl who Loved a Soldier', and after 17 curtain calls, Dame Ellen Terry came on to the stage and presented her with 'The People's Tribute to Vesta Tilley', a set of books containing the signatures of two million admirers. After 32 years of retirement, spent in England and the South of France, she died in Monte Carlo in 1952.

Arthur Tolcher, harmonica player, born in Bloxwich, Staffordshire, on 9 April 1922. At 14 he broadcast on a programme with Sandy Powell, making his first stage appearance at the Grand Theatre, Wolverhampton, in 1937, and in London at the Lewisham Hippodrome in 1938. He toured in variety as a solo act and with Jack Hylton's revues. During the war he appeared with the RAF *Gang Show*, and made many broadcasts

Sam Torr, comedian and singer, born in Nottingham in 1846. He made his first appearance at the Athenaeum,

Nottingham, and later gained a local reputation at Nottingham's first music hall built onto the Golden Ball Tavern, Coalport Lane. His London debut was at Harwood's Palace of Varieties, Pitfield Street, Hoxton, in 1870, appearing soon after at Weston's Music Hall singing 'The Same Old Game'. In 1882 he took over the Gladstone Vaults, Leicester, which he converted into the Gaiety Music Hall, announcing his intention of running the hall on 'high class lines catering for the better class society of the hosiery metropolis'. Like other 'high class' music hall ventures, the hall was not a success under Torr's management and in 1877 he returned to London. He had a great success with the song 'To Be There', a burlesque of the newly formed Salvation Army, and in 1889 sang a radical song which was almost lèse majesté:

> I am a Liberal, Radical, Conservative
>   And Tory,
> In fact to tell the truth, I am a little
>   bit of everything,
> Hip, Hip, Hooray! For Queen Victoria,
> Long may she live in glory,
> But oh, my! Shan't I be glad when the
>   Prince of Wales is King.

His greatest song was 'On the Back of Daddy Oh!', which made 'Daddy Oh!' as popular a Victorian expression as 'By Jingo'. He died in 1899.

Toto, circus and variety clown. Born Armando Novello in Switzerland, his father was an Italian who trained circus horses and ran a school for clowns which included his star pupil, Grock. Toto made his first appearance at the Cirque Nouveau, Paris, and later became a member of Albert Schumann's Circus in Berlin. He first appeared in variety on the vaudeville and burlesque circuits of the USA and as a clever mimic and acrobatic dancer made popular tours of the UK during the 1920s. He appeared in the Royal Variety Performance at the London Palladium on 22 May 1930. He died in the USA in December 1938.

Al Trahan, comedian, born in New Bedford, USA, in 1897, he worked a solo vaudeville act from 1912 and in partnership with singer Vesta Wallace appeared at the Alhambra, London, with a singing and piano comedy routine in 1912. On his return to the USA he toured a 'High Class Musical Burlesque' act with Lady Marie Duval. Later teaming with Lady Yukona Cameron, he returned to England and appeared at the London Palladium in February 1931. He took part in the Royal Variety Performance of 11 May that year, after which he appeared with great success at the Empire Music Hall, Paris.

Lieutenant Frank Travis, ventriloquist, born on 18 January 1854. After service with the Royal Artillery, he made his first London appearance at the Lord Raglan Music Hall, Theobalds Road, London, in 1879. For many years he was the leading music-hall ventriloquist, using as many as 13 figures in his act. He retired in 1905 and died on 28 June 1931.

Tommy Trinder, variety and revue comedian well known for his rather egoistic and caustic comedy style: 'Trinder's the name, you lucky people'. Born in Streatham, London, in 1909 he began his career as a boy vocalist at London working men's clubs, and made his first variety appearance at Collins Music Hall, Islington, in 1922. Billed as 'Red Nirt' (Trinder backwards) he worked for a while with Will Murray's

TOMMY TRINDER.

'Casey's Court', and toured in revue for Archie Pitt, Jimmy Hunter and Jack Sonn. After a tour of South Africa in 1931 he worked the smaller provincial halls, combining the older tradition of high speed delivery of Harry Champion with the verbal assault of R. G. Knowles. He was then working a 12-minute turn, usually second act on the first half, or first turn on the second, both thankless spots. He often complained that he never saw an audience sitting down. His first real success in variety was at the Birmingham Hippodrome in 1933 on a bill topped by Latin American screen lover Ramon Novarro. From then on his career improved and in 1939 he was engaged by George Black to appear in Jack Hylton's *Bandwaggon* at the London Palladium. Although this stage version of the popular radio series was not a great success Trinder made a hit and was booked by Black to substitute for Naughton and Gold in the Crazy Gang revue *Top of the World*. Its opening at the Palladium on 4 September 1940 coincided with the start of the Blitz, and on 8 September it was forced to close. Late in 194 he was back at the Palladium with Bebe Daniels and Ben Lyon in *Gangway*, which ran for 535 performances. This was followed by *Best Bib and Tucker*, which George Black built around Trinder's personal comedy style, appearing in one scene as Carmen Miranda singing 'No, No, No, Columbus, You've Discovered Enough Tonight' with Edmundo Ross and his band. Rather more in character, about this time he decided on a bit of self-advertisement, bill-posting prime London hoardings with a huge caricature of himself with the words, 'If it's laughter you're after, Trinder's the name, you lucky people.' He even had the foresight to have one printed in Yiddish and posted at Aldgate Station. Between Palladium revues and variety tours, he broadcast and made a number of films, including (in 1944) the part of George Leybourne in Alberto Cavalcanti's film *Champagne Charlie*. He opened at the Palladium on 3

October 1944 in *Happy and Glorious*, which ran for 987 performances, the longest run of any Palladium show, and happily marked the end of the war—and sadly the death of George Black on 4 March 1945.

Trinder was commanded in 1944 to appear at Windsor Castle to entertain King George VI and Queen Elizabeth. Reminded by Trinder that they had last met when he was Duke of York, the King commented that Trinder had done very well since those days. To which Tommy, never lost for words on or off stage, replied with audacious bravado, 'You haven't done so badly yourself, sir'. He appeared in the Royal Variety Performance at the London Coliseum on 5 November 1945 and at the Palladium on 3 November 1947. During 1946 he toured the world entertaining troops in Egypt, Syria, Ceylon, Burma, Malaya, Japan and Australia. On his return to London he again starred in revue at the Palladium, appropriately entitled 'Here, There and Everywhere', and at Christmas 1948 was a notable Buttons in *Cinderella*. Although he never again achieved the success he enjoyed during the 1940s, he remained a popular variety, pantomime and summer-show comedian, and toured the UK and Australia with his own road show. On Good Friday, 12 April 1963, he compered an all-star charity show in aid of the Variety Artistes Benevolent Fund, which was the last performance at the Metropolitan Music Hall, Edgware Road. The master of ad-lib, he is at his most spontaneous in cabaret, and as a member of the 'Does the Team Think?' radio show. He has a keen interest in football, serving for many years as Chairman of Fulham Football Club. He was awarded the CBE in 1975.

Sophie Tucker, American vaudeville artiste, well-known on the British music hall stage as the 'Last of the Red Hot Mommas'. Born Sophie Abuza, of Russian Jewish parents, in Boston on 13 January 1884, she gained early experience singing at her father's kosher restaurant, and made her first professional appearance at the Ratskeller in the German Village on 40th Street, then New York's Red Light district, in 1906. Following success at an amateur night at the 125th Street Theatre, she toured the small time vaudeville houses, billed as 'Sophie Tucker, The World Renowned Coon Shouter'. Working a black-faced act she made her first New York vaudeville appearance at the 116th Street Music Hall on 6 December 1907. While playing at Tony Pastor's early the following year, she was booked for an eight-month tour with the burlesque show 'Harry Emerson and the Gay Masqueraders'.

Late in 1908 she was seen by Marc Klew of Klew and Erlanger and engaged for the second production of the Ziegfeld Follies. She was still singing coon songs but had dropped the black-faced make-up, originally forced on her by an agent at her first trial engagement because he considered her too fat and ugly to go over straight. The Follies of 1909 opened at Atlantic City in June with Sophie singing 'It's Moving Day Way Down South' and doing a six-minute solo spot just before the finale, singing Irving Berlin's 'The Yiddisher Rag' and 'The Right Church but the Wrong Pew'. She stopped the show and Ziegfeld's $40,000 finale had to wait an extra six minutes for $100-a-week Sophie Tucker. The star of the show, Nora Bayes, objected to her stealing the limelight, and Sophie's solo turn was written out of the show. Soon after the Follies opened in New York on 22 June 1909, Nora Bayes left the cast and was replaced by Eva Tanguay, who took a fancy to Sophie's one remaining song, and she was out of a job. The turning point in her career came in 1910 when she appeared for William Morris at the American Music Hall, Chicago. As number four on an 18 act bill topped by Julian Eltinge and Pauline the Hypnotist, she sang two double entendre songs, 'But He Only Stayed Till Sunday' and 'I Just Couldn't Make My Feelings Behave'. She was the hit of the show.

Billed as the 'Mary Garden of Ragtime', she became a firm favourite in Chicago, playing eight- to ten-week seasons at Morris's American Music Hall, followed by weeks in cine variety for Balaban and Katz. A.J. Balaban and Sam Katz were the pioneers of the de luxe picture house of the USA and the first to present cinema stage shows on a large scale. The Circle Cinema on Chicago's West Side opened in September 1909 with Sophie Tucker and Minnie Palmer's 'Fun in High School' act. (Minnie Palmer made several music hall tours of Great Britain. Her 'High School' act included her five sons, later famous as the Marx Brothers.) In Chicago in 1911 Sophie Tucker met Shelton Brooks, the young negro songwriter of 'Dark Town Strutters' Ball', who supplied her with her signature tune, 'Some of these Days'. In spring that year she made her first appearance in musical comedy in *Merry Mary*, which opened and 'died' at the Whitney Opera House, Chicago. The following year she tried again in a supporting role in *Louisiana Lou*, starring Alexander Carr, which after a successful run at the La Salle Theatre, Chicago, made a nationwide tour. Back in vaudeville she formed a double act with comedy pianist Frank Westphal, and toured the Keith circuit, appearing at the Palace Theatre, New York, in 1914. She married Westphal, but when the marriage failed she worked for the next five years with a jazz quartet billed as 'Madame Sophie Tucker, the Queen of Jazz and the Four Kings of Syncopation'. In 1915 she sang the first song written by Sissle and Blake (qv), 'It's All Your Fault', and on 23 December appeared in cabaret at Reisenweber's Restaurant, New York, becoming the first established vaudeville headliner to star in cabaret. She changed her act in 1921, appearing with a pianist, violinist and negro dancer Ida Forsyne, but the following year switched to just piano accompaniment supplied by Eva Tanguay's ex-pianist Ted Shapiro, who remained with her for the rest of her career.

Her first London appearance was as an extra turn at the Stratford Empire in April 1922. Singing 'Dapper Dan', 'There's More Music in a Grand Baby than there is in a Baby Grand' and 'When They Get Too Wild for Everyone Else, They're Perfect for Me', she completely won over the East End audience. The following Sunday she appeared in a Jewish charity performance at the London Palladium, working her first regular variety engagement at the Finsbury Park Empire the following week. Hannen Swaffer described her as 'a big fat blonde genius with a dynamic personality and amazing vitality'. Following a provincial variety tour she joined George Robey and Barry Lupino on 17 May 1922 in the revue *Round in Fifty* at the London Hippodrome. Each night after the show she sang in the Midnight Hotel Follies Cabaret at the Metropole Hotel, and the climax to her first visit to London was at the Rivoli Theatre, Whitechapel, where for six matinees and six nights she sang herself hoarse, billed as 'America's Foremost Jewish Actress'. She returned to London in 1925, opening a ten-week cabaret season at the Kit Kat Club on 31 August, doubling in variety at the Coliseum, Alhambra and Holborn Empire. At the Palace, New York, in 1925, she introduced her famous 'tear jerker', 'My Yiddisher Momma', written for her by Jack Yellen and Lou Pollack. She sang it in good times and bad for the rest of her career being hissed off the stage by a gallery clique when she tried to sing it at the Empire, Paris, in 1928. During a visit to Vienna the same year she sang it in the streets at the request of a crowd of admirers, and nearly a million records of it were sold throughout the world. (When the Nazis banned the song and ordered all records smashed in Germany and Austria,

Sophie Tucker, 1922

Sophie wrote a letter of protest to Hitler; she never received a reply.)

Back in London in September 1930 she opened in Vivian Ellis's musical comedy *Follow a Star* at the Winter Garden. During the week of 7 May 1934 she topped the bill at the Holborn Empire, appeared in the Royal Variety Performance at the London Palladium, and opened an eight-week cabaret season at the Café de Paris. Her song successes of the period included 'Tall, Dark and Handsome', 'Louisville Lady', 'My People', 'River Stay Away From My Door', 'A Good Man is Hard to Find', 'I Picked a Pansy in the Garden of Love', and her famous standby, 'Life Begins at Forty'. Film work and the war kept her away from England for 12 years, until her postwar come-back in variety at the London Casino on 31 May 1948. From then on her visits were almost an annual event, appearing with Ted Shapiro in variety, cabaret, television and several Royal Variety Shows. Her last London cabaret appearance was at the 'Talk of the Town' cabaret-restaurant in 1964. She made her last visit to London in 1965 to appear in the Jack Hylton Memorial television show. On 13 October 1965 she opened in the New York Latin Quarter but two days later ill health forced her to call off the engagement. She died at 82 on 9 February 1966.

Joan Turner, actress, singer and comedienne, billed as 'The Girl with a Thousand Voices'. Born in Belfast on 24 November 1922, at 11 she appeared in a talent competition at a cinema in Peckham, London, doing impressions of Shirley Temple, Gracie Fields and Jessie Matthews. Her first stage appearance was at the Queen's, Poplar, on 7 August 1937 followed by several years touring in revue for Ernie Lotinga. In variety she first appeared at the Finsbury Park Empire and toured the UK for ENSA, putting her fine soprano voice to good use, singing operatic arias straight and giving comedy impressions of Judy Garland and Eartha Kitt. For four consecutive Christmases she played Aladdin for Lew and Leslie Grade. Becoming popular as a singing comedienne known as the 'Whacky Warbler', a sort of female Harry Secombe, her first television break came in 1950. She appeared with the Crazy Gang at the Victoria Palace, was a hit at the London Palladium, and sang with Eric Robinson and his Orchestra in the Royal Variety Performance at the Palladium on 1 November 1954. Two weeks later she opened with Jimmy Edwards and Tony Hancock in the revue *Talk of the Town* at the Adelphi Theatre, which ran for 656 performances. She has appeared at top night spots in London and New York, toured in her own two-hour one-woman show, and appeared in the straight plays *The Killing of Sister George* and *There is a Green Hill*. She has made a number of recordings, including 'The Joan Turner Workshop', and a studio cast recording of the musical *Mame*, in which she sings the part of Vera Charles to Beryl Reid's Mame.

V

The Great Vance, one of the most important of the early music-hall performers, the prototype of the coster comedians perfected later by Gus Elen and Albert Chevalier. Born Alfred Peck Stevens in London in 1839, he spent three restless years as a solicitor's clerk in Lincoln's Inn Fields before getting his first professional stage engagement with Edmund Falconer's Preston Theatre Company. During the late 1850s he ran a dancing school in Liverpool, and when that failed, toured his own variety company which was virtually a one-man show. Acting, singing and dancing his way from one 'free-and-easy' to the next 'penny gaff', he played up to 20 parts at each performance, equally at ease in male or female roles. Partnered by Paul Herring at Christmas 1859 he appeared in '"Punch and Judy", or Harlequin and the Fairy of the Crystal Caves' at the St James's Theatre, London. According to Harry Reynolds in *Minstrel Memories* (1928), Vance made his first music-hall appearance in 1860, working a double black-faced act with his brother, billed as 'Alfred G. and C. Vance—Negro Comedians'. His solo London music-hall debut was at the South London Palace in 1864 and he soon became popular singing broad cockney songs such as 'The Chickaleery Cove':

> I'm a Chickaleery bloke, with my one,
> two, three.
> Vitechapel was the willage I was born in.
> To catch me on the hop,
> Or on my tibby drop,
> You must vake up wery early in the morning.

Abandoning the stage cockney for the heavy swell of the 'Lion Comique', Vance's arrival on the music-hall scene coincided with that of George Leybourne (qv), and a friendly rivalry soon developed between the two. Flamboyantly dressed, a gaudy larger-than-life parody of a dashing man-about-town, combining cockney humour with mock gentility, Vance strutted and swaggered about the stage singing his swell songs 'Jolly Dogs', 'The Bon-Bon Beau', 'Toothpick and Crutch' and 'A la française', the last with the saucy verse:

> I kissed her in German, I loved her in Dutch,
> We courted in various ways,
> For foreigners tickled her fancy so much,
> 'Twas everything à la française.

When Vance sang 'Walking in the Zoo', Leybourne answered with 'Lounging in the Aq' (the Westminster Aquarium). While Leybourne was drawing crowds to the Canterbury to hear him sing 'Champagne Charlie', Charles Morton booked Vance for the Oxford to sing 'Cliquot, Cliquot! That's the Wine for Me'. Contemporary and later opinions differ as to which was the greater artiste. Harold Scott in *The Early Doors* (1946) held that George Leybourne shared with Marie Lloyd and Dan Leno the 'supreme place in music hall history'. W. Macqueen Pope wrote in *The Melodies Linger On* (1950): 'Leybourne had more than a tendency to "blueness", in fact one or two of his songs were so vulgar and suggestive that he had trouble with the authorities. Vance was not guiltless in that respect, but he was never so "blue" as Leybourne, and always put it over more delicately; he was certainly the greater of the two.'

Unlike Leybourne, Vance's greater versatility allowed him to survive the decline in the vogue of the Lion Comique. He turned to motto songs in the style of Harry Clifton, such as 'Act on the Square Boys', and comedy songs in character, 'Peter Potts the Peeler', and 'Come to your Martha', a bawdy burlesque of a bathing-machine woman. He then toured his own concert party, a style of entertainment originally devised by another of his contemporaries, Arthur Lloyd (qv). He remained popular literally to the end of his life, dropping dead to cheers on the stage of the Sun Music Hall, Knightsbridge, on Boxing Day 1888 at the age of 50.

Vasco, comedy musician. Born in 1871, as a boy soldier with the 15th Royal Hussars he received early musical training at the Army School of Music, Kneller Hall. After six years army service he toured South Africa with Luscombe Searelle's Opera Company, and as a musical clown made extensive tours with the Frank Fillis Circus. His first music hall appearance was at the Alhambra, Leicester Square, in

The Great Vance, 1864

1897, and from then on he was popular in variety billed as 'Vasco the Mad Musician'. During a career of 30 years he toured the world, making his last appearance at the Circo, Madrid, in April 1923. He died on 9 May 1925.

Frankie Vaughan, popular high-kicking variety and cabaret singer. Born Frank Ableson in Liverpool on 3 February 1928, he won a scholarship to the Lancaster College of Art and a place at Leeds University. Called up in 1945, he spent three-and-a-half years in the RAMC, and on his discharge in 1949 returned to Leeds University as a student teacher. Giving up teaching in favour of a career as a commercial artist, in 1950 he designed a stand for the Earl's Court Furniture Exhibition, the only highlight in an otherwise uneventful and short-lived career in this field. Before the war he had been a local success singing with dance bands at gigs in the Leeds area, so he decided to try his luck as a singer. With the help of agent Billy March of the Bernard Delfont Organisation he made his variety debut in May 1950, as a trial turn at the Kingston Empire on a bill topped by Jimmy Wheeler. Singing the Donald Peers hit 'Powder Your Face With Sunshine', he stopped the show. Two weeks later he appeared at the Hulme Hippodrome, Manchester, and soon afterwards toured with 'New Stars and Old Favourites'. One of the old favourites, Hetty King (qv), was impressed by Frankie's act and coached him in a top-hat-and-cane routine which from then on became a feature of his performance. Following an audition for Val Parnell at the London Hippodrome he was booked to tour the Moss Empires and in 1953 made his first recording, 'My Sweetie Went Away'. While appearing in Glasgow he found the sheet music of Fred Barnes's old hit 'Give Me The Moonlight', which he turned into a worldwide success, singing it at the top of the bill at the London Palladium. He made his first Royal Variety appearance at the London Coliseum; in 1959 he was a great hit in Las Vegas; and in January 1960 was seen on television in the BBC transmission of 'The Perry Como Music Hall'.

He made his first film, in 1956, starring with Arthur Askey in *Ramsbottom Rides Again* and in 1957–8 co-starred with Anna Neagle in *These Dangerous Years, Wonderful Things,* and *The Lady is a Square*. He went to Hollywood in 1960 to appear in *Let's Make Love* but was rather out-classed in the film by Yves Montand and Marilyn Monroe.

Vaughan was the first British artiste to win the Gold Microphone, the International Sound Industry's award to show business. Bing Crosby, Sammy Davis Junior, Frank Sinatra and Marlene Dietrich are the only other recipients. For outstanding work for the National Association of Boys' Clubs, to which he donated the royalties on the sale of one million records, he was awarded the OBE in 1965. At the age of 39 he became the youngest ever King Rat of the Grand

Order of Water Rats. In 1975 he made his ninth appearance at the Talk of the Town, London, and that year celebrated 25 years in show business, an occasion marked by pages of tributes in *The Stage*, including one from Prime Minister Harold Wilson.

Vesta Victoria, famous music-hall singer and comedienne, born in Leeds in 1874. The daughter of Joe Lawrence, an old-time black-faced artiste who billed himself as 'The Upside Down Comedian' and sang comic songs standing on his head. Her first stage appearance was at the age of four, singing with her father, and her professional debut was as 'Little Victoria' in 1883. Her first great success was in 1893 when the song 'Daddy wouldn't Buy me a Bow Wow' established her at the top of the bill both in the UK and the USA. In America she toured in vaudeville for a total of six years, singing her numbers with an audacious mixture of coy innocence and innocuous innuendo. 'Our Lodger's Such a Nice Young Man', her song hit of 1892, is a good example of her style:

> Our lodger's such a nice young man, such a
>   good young man is he.
> So good, so kind to all our family! He's never
>   going to leave us,
> Oh dear, oh dear, no!
> He's such a good goody goody man, Mamma told me so.
> He kissed Mamma and all of us, 'cos Papa was away.

Vesta Victoria was the prototype of the 'dumb blonde' whose path of true love never ran smooth. There was the young man she once took home to meet Mother, and later complained 'And now I have to call him Father'. When she was not having trouble with her own mother, it was with prospective mothers-in-law. She sang 'Poor John' with great success in 1907:

> John took me round to see his mother!
> His mother! His mother!
> And while he introduced us to each other,
> She weighed up everything that I had on,
> She put me through a cross-examination,
> I fairly boiled with aggravation,
> Then she shook her head, looked at me and said.
> Poor John! Poor John!

After 'Daddy wouldn't Buy me a Bow Wow', her best-remembered song was certainly 'Waiting at the Church' (1906), in which she suffered the cruellest indignity of all, being jilted at the very steps of the altar. Although at her best singing comedy songs, she had several successful straight ballads, notably the charming 'All in a Day' by Joseph Tabrar. She retired from the stage after the First World War, but made a comeback in 1929 to tour with Fred Collins's road show *Vaudeville Past and Present*. During 1931–2 she again toured with Wilkie Bard, Harry Champion, Florence Smithson and Fred Barnes in Lew Lake's *Stars Who Never Failed to Shine*. She appeared in the Royal Variety finale on 30 May 1932 at the London Palladium. She died in 1951.

W

Max Waldon, female impersonator and dancer. Born in Berne, Switzerland, he studied dancing with the Royal German Ballet, making his first appearance in the corps de ballet in Berlin in 1884. Coming to England in 1896 to tour the Stoll and Livermore variety theatres, he made his first

Vesta Victoria

London appearance at the Tivoli on 26 September 1898. The bill was topped by Dan Leno and G. H. Chirgwin, but *Encore* found space to write of Waldon's performance:

> On the stage there is a small decorated cabinet, and when the curtains are drawn aside a charming lady in Tyrolese costume is discovered. She trips lightly down the steps, yodels bewitchingly and does a graceful little dance, then disappears behind the screen. In a few seconds the curtains open again and a dainty Spanish maiden springs forth, sings a Castilian melody, dances the Cashuca, and in her turn gives way to a chic little specimen of the French soubrette, who warbles a chansonette and tastefully displays the dainty lingerie which appears to be the principal reason of the soubrette's existence. Then a premier danseuse emerges from the cabinet and pirouettes about the stage in a manner which would not have disgraced a Fanny Elessler or a Cerito. Anon she disappears and immediately afterwards Mr Max Waldon in ordinary evening dress steps forth.

This polished quick-change female impersonator remained a novel attraction in London and the provinces for a few years and went on to further success on the French music halls.

Syd Walker, born Sidney Kirkman in Salford, in 1887. Best remembered as a radio comedian but in his early days appeared on the halls as a single act and with partners as 'Crosby and Walker' and 'Walker and Lake'. After years of slapstick comedy with Fred Karno he jumped to national fame with the BBC radio programme 'Band Waggon', and later with his own show, 'Mr Walker Wants to Know'. Having lost all traces of his native Lancashire dialect he was regarded as a typical stage cockney, with his famous catch phrase 'What would you do, chums?', and his wartime song 'Any Rags, Bottles or Bones?'. While playing Idle Jack in *Dick Whittington* at the Grand Theatre, Croydon, in 1945, he was taken ill with an infected appendicitis and died on 13 January.

Max Wall, low comedian of high reputation. Born Maxwell George Lorimer in Brixton, London, on 12 March 1908. His father was the well-known comedian Jack Lorimer, and Max first appeared with a touring pantomime for Ellis Slack in 1922. Later he worked a dance act in cabaret, and made his first West End appearance as a speciality dancer in *The London Revue* at the Lyceum Theatre in 1925. He worked a variety double dancing act with Mary Lawson and in 1926 got his first speaking part in the musical *Merely Molly* starring Evelyn Laye at the Adelphi He was engaged by C. B. Cochran in May 1927 for *One Damn Thing After Another* at the London Pavilion, of which James Agate wrote, 'One of the best things in the show is the dancing of Max Wall who performs in a dinner-jacket many steps more appropriate to the coster's jersey.' Cabaret and variety in Britain and on the Continent led to his American debut in September 1932 in 'Earl Carrol's Vanities', in which he appeared for a year at

Max Wall, 1927

the Broadway Theatre, New York. Turning to full-time comedy he appeared in variety and revue, and at Christmas 1936 played Jack in *Mother Goose* at the London Hippodrome. Following more variety dates as a comedian and a tour with Larry Adler's road show, he opened in *Black and Blue* at the London Hippodrome in March 1939. He was invalided out of the RAF in 1943 and appeared with Bebe Daniels in the musical *Panama Hattie* at the Piccadilly Theatre. The show later toured the provinces and in January 1945 reopened in London at the Adelphi Theatre.

His dancing experience was put to good use in the ballet sketch 'Watch the Birdie' in the revue *Make it a Date* at the Duchess Theatre in 1946. The show also introduced Max's famous grotesque pianist Professor Wallofsky, whom in black tails, ballet tights and big boots, he developed into a music hall classic. During the 1950s bad publicity, prompted by his marital difficulties, damaged his career and for nearly ten years the top managements just did not want to know. His first step back was in 1966 when he appeared to critical acclaim in the title role in Jarry's play *Ubu Roi* at the Royal Court Theatre. He returned to the same theatre in 1972 in the leading part in Arnold Wesker's *The Old Ones*. In 1974, an eventful year for Max, he appeared in *Cockie*, a so-called musical tribute to C.B. Cochran at the Vaudeville Theatre. It was only his brilliant front-cloth comedy spot that saved the show from complete disaster. He opened on 9 September 1974 at the London Palladium on a bill topped by Ethel Merman, and after 50 years was hailed as an 'authentic music hall great'. On 2 December 1974 he opened at the Greenwich Theatre as the run-down music-hall comedian Archie Rice in John Osborne's production of his own play, *The Entertainer*. Ironically, although the part seemed cruelly appropriate to Wall, his performance suffered from his inability to be anything other than a first-rate entertainer. He had no such problem with his own one man show, *Aspects of Max Wall* which opened on 3 February 1975 at the Garrick Theatre. It was such a success that he went on to an extended season at the Shaw Theatre and won the Variety Club of Great Britain's special award for 1975.

Nellie Wallace, music hall's greatest grotesque comedienne, born 18 March 1870 in Glasgow, where her parents were appearing at a local hall. She made her first stage appearance as a clog dancer at the Steam Clock Music Hall, Birmingham, in 1882, later working as a dancer billed as 'La Petite Nellie' and touring as one of the 'Three Sisters Wallace'. Turning solo she worked the provincial halls, appeared in pantomime and after her marriage to actor Bill Liddie, toured with a fit-up company in a wide range of parts but without any great success. She was a scream in the death scene of *East Lynne*, and on one occasion had the audience in hysterics when as Joan of Arc she made her entrance on a carthorse which literally sneezed her into the orchestra pit. After that it was back to the halls, and at Christmas 1894 she appeared at the Comedy Theatre, Manchester, as second girl and understudy to principal girl Ada Reeve (qv) in the pantomime *Jack and Jill*. The cast also included Connie Ediss, who went on to fame in musical comedy at the Gaiety, and George Robey playing a small part in his first pantomime. At the time of the Manchester pantomime Ada Reeve was pregnant, and as the show proved very popular and ran longer than expected it began to look as though Jack and Jill's walk up the hill had produced more than a pail of water (Jack was played by Ada's husband, Bert Gilbert). Finally on 9 March 1895 Ada Reeve was forced to leave the cast and Nellie Wallace took over as principal girl for the last weeks of the run.

After years of touring the provincial halls she made her first London variety appearance in 1903, and soon afterwards was a great success at the Oxford. By December 1910 when she appeared on the bill that opened the London Palladium, she was an established star, living up to her billing of 'The Essence of Eccentricity'. Dressed in a multi-coloured jumper, 'they bring out the figure so well', tartan skirt (allowing generous glimpses of red flannel), elastic-sided boots, skimpy feather boa, or a moth-eaten fur tippit, which she affectionately referred to as 'my little bit of vermin', and a hat with quivering feather, she was certainly one of the funniest women on the halls. With thin pencilled eyebrows and beak-like twitching nose, no one burlesqued the frustrated spinster with more devilish bluntness:

My mother said always look under the bed,
Before you blow the candle out, to see if
   there's a man about.
I always do, but you can make a bet,
It's never been my luck to find a man there yet!

Her extensive repertoire of songs, sung in a voice as comical as her appearance and punctuated by chuckling asides, and inimitable little yodels, included 'I Lost George in Trafalgar Square', 'I've Been Jilted by the Baker, Mr White', 'Blasted Oak', 'Half Past Nine', 'I Was the Early Bird after the Worm', 'Tally Ho' and 'Mother's Pie Crust'. She made several successful tours of America and with the decline of variety after the First World War turned to revue, starring in 1923 with Billy Merson in Albert de Courville's *Whirl of the World* at the Palladium (627 performances). In March 1925 she returned to the Palladium to star with George Robey, Marie Blanch and Lorna and Toots Pounds in *Sky High* (309 performances). Between 1931 and 1934 she took part in the early George Black 'Crazy' shows.

One of the few successful woman pantomime dames, her Widow Twankey ironing a basket of 'unmentionables' was a masterpiece of low comedy. Early in 1922 she replaced George Robey as Dame Trot in *Jack and the Beanstalk* at the London Hippodrome. Another noted London pantomime appearance was as the Wicked Witch Carabosse in *The Sleeping Beauty* at the Vaudeville Theatre in 1935. During the war she toured with ENSA and in February 1948 was one of the original members of Don Ross's *Thanks for the Memory* touring show. The company took part in the Royal Variety Performance at the London Palladium on 1 November 1948 and Nellie was her usual success singing 'A Boy's Best Friend is his Mother', but she later collapsed in the wings. She recovered to go on for the finale, but the next day was taken to hospital where she died on 24 November 1948.

Albert and Les Ward, improvising musical novelty act of radio and summer shows. Brothers, born in Cardiff, Albert on 22 April 1917 and Les on 4 September 1921. They first appeared at the New Theatre, Cardiff, in 1947 and in London at the Empress Hall, Earls Court, in May 1949. Their crazy comedy routines and zany singing to their own 'musical' accompaniment produced on everything from bicycle pumps to washboards introduced the craze for skiffle and made them firm favourites on radio and in variety during the 1950s.

Warren, Latona and Sparks, comedy acrobatic trio. Leslie Warren, Joseph Latona, and Maisie Sparks. All three were born in Sydney, Australia: Warren and Latona in 1920 and Sparks in 1922. Latona and Sparks met at dancing school and made their first appearance together in *Jack and the Beanstalk* at Christmas 1932. Teaming as a dancing acrobatic double, they toured the Tivoli variety circuit of Australia until Latona joined the army in 1940. During the

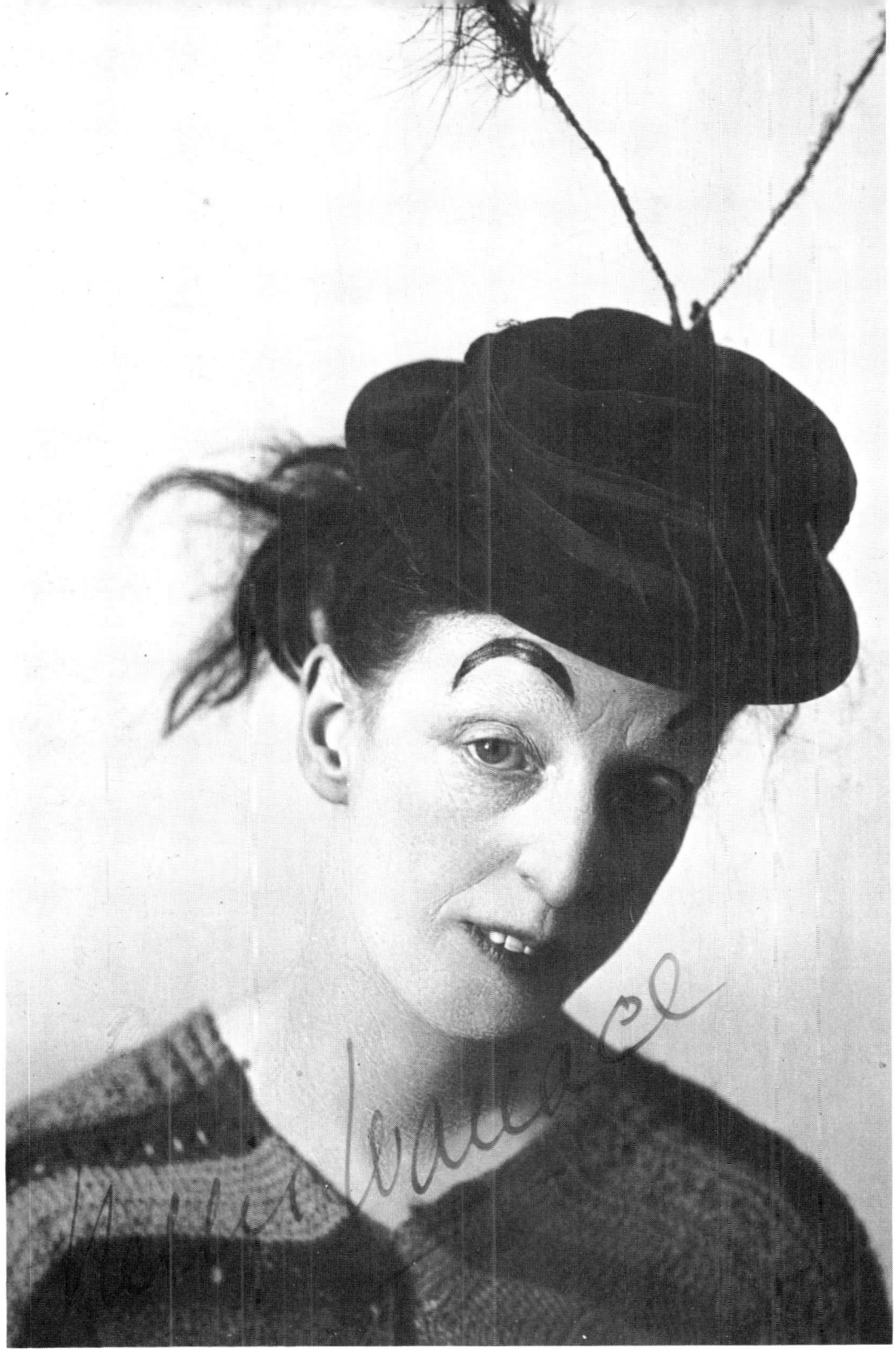

Nellie Wallace

war Maisie Sparks toured in variety with dancer June Juester, as the acrobatic dancing duo of 'June and Jeanette'. Leslie Warren came from a circus family known as 'The Martinettis' and worked as an acrobat from the age of three. After touring Australia, New Zealand and South Africa, the family act appeared for six months with the Blackpool Tower Circus, followed by an engagement at the London Palladium in July 1940. In 1944 Warren married Maisie Sparks and formed an acrobatic dancing act. On his discharge from the army Latona joined his old partner and her new husband and 'Warren, Latona and Sparks' toured for two years throughout Australia and New Zealand. They arrived in England in July 1948 for a month's provincial tour and, following a four-week music hall engagement in Paris, made their first London appearance in October 1948 in George and Alfred Black's *Sky High* at the Palladium. They appeared in the Royal Variety Performance at the Palladium on 1 November 1948 and again toured in variety.

Ben Warriss *see* **Jewel and Warriss**

Elsie and Doris Waters, comediennes famous as 'Gert and Daisy', one of the few successful female comedy double acts. Sisters born in London, they began their careers with Will Pepper's 'White Coons' concert party at the Pavilion, Southwold; Elsie as a vocalist and Doris doing a song-and-patter act at the piano. Summers on the pier were followed by winters entertaining at Masonics and the like. Their debut as a double act was at the St George's Hall, London, in 1923, but they continued the concert party social functions routine until 1927 when they toured their own company of seven, known as 'The Enthusiasts'. On 17 March 1934 they broadcast on the first of Henry Hall's radio 'Guest Night' programmes and on 8 May that year appeared in their first Royal Variety Performance. Between 1935 and 1937 they toured their own variety company and in 1938 made a second Royal Variety appearance.

During the war no radio variety show was complete without the cockney gossip of 'Gert and Daisy' and the latest news of their husbands, the mythical Bert and Fred. They made frequent tours for ENSA and at home entertained at ammunition factories with the radio show 'Workers' Playtime'. They made a number of propaganda films for the Ministry of Food and were both awarded the OBE in 1948. They continue to appear on old time variety bills and to play summer season—in 1970 at the Royal Hippodrome, Eastbourne.

Ada Webb, swimming novelty performer who appeared at music halls of the 1880s billed as 'The Queen of the Crystal Tank'. She first appeared at the age of 17 diving off the end of Llandudno pier and performing aquatic feats in a glass tank.

Elsie and Doris Waters, 'Gert and Daisy'

After an engagement of four months in Berlin, she was booked to appear as a winter attraction at Brighton, when even with temperatures at freezing point and with snow falling, large crowds gathered to see her dive daily off the West Pier. To Victorian England she was a daring novelty and she made her first appearance in London at the Washington Music Hall in 1887

Harry Weldon, comedian born in Liverpool on 1 February 1881. While working as a florist's assistant it was part of his job to deliver bouquets to the theatres and music halls of the Liverpool area, an occupation which kindled an ambition to try the stage himself. He made his professional debut at the Tivoli Theatre, Barrow, in March 1900 and his first London appearance at the Marylebone Music Hall in November the same year. After a few years as a solo comedian, it was as a member of Fred Karno's (qv) company that he made his name. As Stiffy, the goalkeeper in Karno's famous sketch 'The Football Match', he shot to fame and later developed it into his own music-hall act. When the sketch was booked for the London Coliseum in 1906 Karno engaged the 17-year-old Charlie Chaplin to play the part of the villain intent on bribing Stiffy to throw the match. Although there was jealousy and a good deal of animosity between the two, Chaplin wrote 60 years later in *My Autobiography* (1964): 'Although "The Football Match" was a burlesque slapstick affair, there was not a laugh in it until Weldon appeared. Everything led to his entrance, and of course Weldon, excellent comedian that he was, kept the audiences in continuous laughter from the moment he came on.' The sketch ran for 14 weeks in London, followed by a long provincial tour. Weldon later used the role of Stiffy in his own solo music-hall turn but his rather slow Lancashire style of comedy and curious 'gurgling' delivery went over better in the North than in the South. Stiffy was followed by a series of similar music-hall sketches, notably his famous boxing skit 'The White Hope', which introduced the popular catch phrase 'Tell them what I did to Colin Bell'. (Colin Bell was an Australian heavyweight who came to England to fight Bombardier Billy Wells at Olympia in June 1914. He was knocked out in the second round.) Weldon added, under his breath, 'but don't tell them what he did to me'. Other sketches included 'The Matador', 'Joe, the Crossing Sweeper' and 'The Policeman'. He made two command appearances at Buckingham Palace and appeared in the Royal Variety Show at the London Hippodrome in 1922. He was taken ill with dropsy in 1923 and although it seemed at first that his career was over, he made a good recovery, appearing at Christmas as Idle Jack in *Dick Whittington* at the Palladium. In 1924 he toured Australia and in 1925 married comedienne Hilda Clyder, with whom he toured South Africa in 1929. The tour was spoiled by his ill health and he died on his return to England, on 10 March 1930.

Señor Wences, Spanish ventriloquist, born Wenceslas Moreno in 1899. In his early teens he toured with a travelling circus, performing during the next decade as a bareback rider, acrobat, clown and juggler. Successful for many years in America with a ventriloquial juggling routine, he made his first appearance in London in cabaret at the Berkeley Hotel on 29 March 1937. Later that year he appeared in variety at the Victoria Palace and on 15 November took part in the Royal Variety Performance at the London Palladium. After the war, spent in the USA, he returned to England in 1948 for a season at the London Casino, followed by a variety tour of the UK.

Bessie Wentworth, singer of coon songs. Born Elizabeth Andrews in 1874, she first appeared in burlesque in 1891 and made her variety debut at the Tivoli Music Hall in 1894. She sang rather plaintive songs, wearing the costume of a plantation negro, but without blacking up. Her best was 'Looking for a Coon Like Me' by Harrington and Le Brun. She died at the age of 27 on 6 January 1901.

Gracie West, *see* **Revnell and West**

The Western Brothers, in fact cousins. Kenneth and George Western, famous in variety and on the air for their 'Old School Tie' and 'Hello Cads' topical songs-at-the-piano act. George Western originally played the piano with 'The Roosters Concert Party', teaming with Kenneth in 1925. In evening dress and wearing monocles, singing in drawled unison at a grand piano with a sophisticated air of blasé casualness, they were soon established as one of the most polished double acts of variety, cabaret and radio. Kenneth Western died in 1963, and George in 1969.

Jimmy Wheeler, boozy-voiced cockney comedian, born Ernest Remnant in Battersea, London, on 16 September 1910. Early in his career he was a professional ballroom dancer, and at the age of 17 appeared in the play *Crime* at the Queen's Theatre, London, and in 1928 in *The Trial of Mary Dugan* at the same theatre. In 1929 he worked a double act

The Western Brothers

with his father as 'Wheeler and Wilson', touring the UK in variety and revue, and in 1931 touring South Africa. He worked solo from 1949 and made the first of 30 appearances at the Palladium on 26 September that year. With his bookmaker's suit, pork-pie hat and shaggy moustache, ending his gruff cockney patter with the catch phrase 'Ay, Ay, that's yer lot', he became a popular comedian on radio and television, making five Royal Variety appearances. He died in October 1973.

Albert Whelan, 'the Australian Entertainer', credited with being the first artiste to use a signature tune, born Albert Waxman in Melbourne in 1875. He gave up a job as an accountant, and then as a mechanic, and in 1898 he and a friend went to make their fortunes in the Coolgardie goldfields of Western Australia, but instead of striking it rich were forced to sing and play the violin for their suppers, as the red-nosed comedians 'Whelan and Wilson'. On his return to Melbourne he toured with the first Australian production of *The Belle of New York* and appeared on small-time variety bills. His first London appearance was made as an 'eccentric dancer' at the Empire, Leicester Square, on 28 October 1901 and in November he repeated his success as Ichabod Bronson in a revival of *The Belle of New York* at the Adelphi Theatre,

Albert Whelan, 'The Australian Entertainer'

London. On the halls he presented a polished turn as a debonair man about town, strolling onto the stage nonchalantly whistling 'Der Lustige Bruder' (The Jolly Brothers' Waltz) as he casually removed and deposited his gloves, top hat, white silk scarf, coat and cane. He was rather like a man all dressed up with no place to go, who, as Maurice Wilson Disher put it in *Winkles and Champagne* (1938), 'is merely killing time between the cocktail party he has just been to, and the supper party he is just off to'. With perfect diction he would sing a ballad, musical monologue, and a comic song, of which 'The Poacher and the Bear', 'The Butterfly and the Bee' and 'The Old Top Hat' were among his favourites. He would play the piano and trot out a few stories, slipping in here and there some terrible puns, like the costermonger who sent the King some plums as the national anthem commands 'send him Victorias'. Just as his entrance took three minutes, so did his exit. Glancing at his watch and putting on his coat, scarf, hat and gloves, he strolled off to the warbled trills of his famous signature tune. When he was booked for his first appearance at the London Coliseum soon after it opened in 1902 he was given an eight-minute spot. Oswald Stoll was then trying to cram in four performances a day, and the harassed stage manager would have none of Whelan's protests that he needed six minutes just to get on and off. For a month he whistled his leisurely way onto the stage, took off top hat, coat, scarf and gloves and then put them on again and casually waltzed off. Even Stoll, who was a great disciplinarian, enjoyed the joke, and with full 18 minutes restored, Whelan made many appearances at the Coliseum and provincial Stoll variety theatres.

While appearing at the London Pavilion he was seen by an American vaudeville agent and booked to appear in New York in 1908. A great success, he returned to the USA the following year. Still billed as 'The Australian Entertainer' he appeared with Anna Pavlova in 1912 in a series of special matinees at the Palace Theatre. His first Royal Variety appearance was at the Victoria Palace in 1927 and in 1931 he teamed with Billy Bennett, replacing James Carew, in the black-faced cross-talking act 'Alexander and Mose'. As the new Alexander, the tall, lean 'always-a-gentleman' Whelan made an amusing contrast to the squat and portly 'almost-a-gentleman' Bennett. They appeared in variety and on the air, playing their separate acts on the first half of a variety bill and appearing together in the second as 'Alexander and Mose'. Like nigger minstrel corner men, their cross-talking went something like this:

ALEXANDER:	How's your brother all getting along.
MOSE:	He's been arrested for drinking eau-de-cologne.
ALEXANDER:	For drinking eau-de-cologne! What was the charge?
MOSE:	Fragrancy.

Whelan made several attempts to change his act, advertising 'No hat, no coat, no gloves, no whistle', but 'The Jolly Brothers' remained with him throughout his career. He died in 1962.

Tom White, character comedian and sketch performer, born in 1858. He originally worked the halls as a solo comedian and later formed a juvenile troupe of cockney street urchins billed as 'Tom White's Arabs'. The boys sang and danced and appeared in slapstick comedies and sketches, as pageboys, railway porters, pick-pockets etc., White as a straight man playing frustrated hotel-managers, stationmasters and policemen. After Tom White's early death at the age of 42 on 17 August 1900, the act was presented by Jack 'Pimple' Hipple, who had been with the troupe since August 1889.

Charles Whittle, born in Yorkshire in 1874, began his career as a blacksmith, appearing in his spare time as a comic vocalist at a local 'spits' with such success that he was soon 'top of the glass' (at the old tavern sing-songs the night's bill was often chalked on the mirror behind the bar). He gave up the forge for the footlights in 1897, making his first London appearance at the South London Palace in 1899. His songs included 'Billy Muggins', 'Nothing Like This in America', 'The Girl in the Clogs and Shawl', and the all-time music hall classics 'Let's All Go Down The Strand', 'We All Go the Same Way Home' and 'Put Me Among the Girls'. Except for a period of retirement, he went on appearing until 1938, and died in 1947.

Billy Williams, comic singer famed as 'The Man in the Velvet Suit'. Born William Holt Williams in Melbourne in 1878, he began his career at a racing stable and then worked as a golf instructor. In 1895 he joined a small variety company touring the outback and or his return to Melbourne appeared for Harry Rickards. With a letter of introduction from Rickards he arrived in England in 1900 and made his first London appearance at the Marylebone Music Hall, where he acted for a time as assistant manager. Disdaining the use of grotesque make-up and the costume of the usual comic singers of the day, he appeared instead in a well-cut velvet suit which became a feature of his billing. He was soon established as a singer of many good songs, including 'Why Can't we have the Sea in London?' 'Save a Little one for Me', 'Let's all go Mad', 'John, John, Go and Put your Trousers On' and 'When Father Papered the Parlour'. He made his home in England, buying a bungalow a Shoreham which he named 'The Kangaroo'. He was one of the first recording stars, his records selling in thousands. One record company alone issued 50 of his songs, and 'When Father Papered the Parlour' came out on over 30 different labels. After appearing at a hall in Islington he was taken seriously ill, and died at the age of 37 on 15 March 1915.

Billy Williams, 'The Man in the Velvet Suit'

Bransby Williams as Little Nell's Grandfather in 'The Old Curiosity Shop'

Bransby Williams, 'The Hamlet of the Halls'. Born in London on 14 August 1870, he started professional life as a tea sampler for a merchant in Mincing Lane, London. Later, while employed as a designer of wallpaper, he appeared as an amateur actor and musical entertainer. He made his first semi-professional appearance as a black-faced comedian at the Pavilion, Whitechapel, and for the next five years played working men's clubs as a comic singer, cartoonist, stump orator and nigger minstrel, also appearing with various stock and touring companies as a straight actor. He made his music-hall debut at the London, Shoreditch, on 26 August 1896, and the following week deputised for Dan Leno at the Tivoli, Canterbury and Paragon, Mile End. Billed as the 'Actor Mimic', he did impersonations of the leading actors of the day and music-hall comedians of the eccentric and grotesque variety. Even at that date his act was considered by some managements to be rather 'old hat'. Charles Morton gave him an audition but refused him an engagement at the Palace. He was, however, a success at most of the other London halls, particularly the Tivoli and Pavilion. Relying less on imitative acting, he developed his own interpretations of Shakespeare's more histrionic speeches and was a great success with a range of Dickensian character studies. With his own sketch company in 1890 he appeared at the Oxford as Sydney Carton in 'The Noble Deed', a lavishly produced scene dramatised from an incident in *A Tale of Two Cities*. A master of quick change, his one-man sketches included 'The Penny Showman', 'The Vicar's Christmas Eve', 'The Seven Ages of Man', 'Cameos and Characters', 'The Veteran's Birthday' and 'The Stage Door Keeper', the last giving great scope for his impressions of artistes of both the variety and legitimate stages. He also performed a solo version of *The Bells*, did the transformation scene from *Dr Jekyll and Mr Hyde* and acted out many of the more dramatic parts of Dickens, such as the death of Little Nell. His music-hall act usually opened with a lurid monologue, 'The Street Watchman' (also known as 'The Ole in the Road'), 'The Pigtail of Li Fan Fu', 'How We Saved The Barge', and his most famous 'The Green Eye of the Little Yellow God'.

He was commanded to appear for Edward VII at Sandringham on 3 December 1903, sharing the bill with soprano Carrie Tubb and a young pianist called Fred Norton, who later composed the musical success *Chu Chin Chow*. He took part in the Royal Variety Performance at the Alhambra in 1926 and in the 'Lambeth Walk' finale at the Coliseum in 1938. As an actor-manager he toured Canada in 1923 and 1927, Australia, New Zealand and South Africa in 1924 and 1925. His Dickens recital was the forerunner of the one-man show of Emlyn Williams and for years no Christmas Eve was complete without his television appearance as Scrooge in *A Christmas Carol*. In 1946, 50 years after his first appearance, he went on tour with his last stage production of *The Shop at Sly Corner*. He died in 1961 at the age of 91.

Fred Williams, born in Islington, in a theatrical family that included his brother, Arthur Williams, the original Lurcher in *Dorothy*, and his nephew Fred Emney, Senior (qv). His first appearance was at the age of 19 in the pantomime *King Frolic* at the East London Theatre, with a cast that included Herbert Campbell, Harriet Vernon and Marie Loftus. He and his friend Arthur Roberts (qv) were given a trial turn at Deacon's Music Hall, Islington, in 1876. Roberts was booked for a week and Williams engaged to act as chairman, a post he held for the next three years. He later toured the halls with a series of burlesque sketches, including 'The Jubilee Teapot', 'The Drudge', 'Little Marguerite' and 'Will Tell'. He was also a fine pantomime artiste, at his best in dame roles. He died on 6 June 1916.

Wilson, Keppel and Betty, internationally celebrated comedy dance act. Jack Wilson was born in Liverpool on 29 January 1894 and went to the USA as a boy. His first stage appearance was in vaudeville as a soft-shoe dancer at Bristol, Connecticut, in 1909. Joe Keppel was born in County Cork, Ireland, on 10 May 1895, making his first appearance with

Wilson, Keppel and Betty, 'Cleopatra's Nightmare', 1945

Robb Wilton

Van Arheim's Minstrels at Albany, New York, in 1910. Teaming as a comedy dance act, Wilson and Keppel played everything from 'medicine shows' to acting as 'curtain raisers' to Jewish drama. With Betty Knox they toured in vaudeville and burlesque, presenting their classic sand dance 'Cleopatra's Nightmare'. They made their first appearance in England at the London Palladium on 2 August 1932, appearing in the Royal Variety Show the following year. On settling in England, their comedy mime routines became famous in variety and pantomime and remained so for many years. (There is a nine-minute, 8-mm film of 'Cleopatra's Nightmare' in the National Film Archives). When Betty retired from the act in 1941 to take up journalism, her place was taken by her 17-year-old daughter Patsy. In 1943 they appeared with Flanagan and Allen, Florence Desmond and Eddie Gray in Jack Hylton's revue *Hi-De-Hie* at the Palace Theatre, London, making their second Royal Variety appearance in 1945 and their third in 1947. Jack Wilson died at Brinsworth House on 24 August 1970.

Robb Wilton, character comedian, born Robert Wilton Smith in Liverpool on 28 August 1881. Turning from an engineering career to the stage, his first appearance was with a stock company at the Theatre Royal, Garston, on 21 January 1899. During the next few years he played everything from the villain in melodrama to dame in pantomime. While waiting in the wings to go on in the role of a prison warder, he picked up a cap several sizes too small, and the audience's laughter as he made his entrance led to his first appearance as a solo comedian at the Lyric, Liverpool, in 1903, and a three-year contract to appear in variety for Walter de Frece. Following his London debut at the Holborn Empire on 24 May 1909, assisted by his wife Florence Palmer, he toured the UK, USA, Canada and Australia with his variety sketches, 'The Police Station', 'His Journey's End', 'The Magistrate', 'The Fire Station', 'Prison Guv'nor', etc. With his puzzled expression, deliberate manner of speech in a soft Lancashire dialect, meditatively fingering his face as he spoke, he became one of the best

Norman Wisdom, 1955

known and most popular of the radio and variety comedians. He reached the height of his popularity during the Second World War, with his frequent broadcasts recounting the doings of Mr Muddlecombe, JP, both on the bench and as Chairman of the Nether Backwash Rural District Council. Introducing his act with his immortal 'The day war broke out... my missus turned to me and said "Well, what are you going to do about it?"', he had a long list of lugubrious monologues; that of the blethering fireman—'Keep the fire going until we get there, lady'—of the air-raid warden and the Home Guard man—'In for the duration unless the war ends before'. He made a Royal Variety appearance at the Alhambra in 1926, and in 1943 performed his Home Guard Sketch at a command performance at Windsor Castle on the occasion of the present Queen's 16th birthday. He died on 1 May 1957.

Norman Wisdom, successful slapstick comedian who in the character of Norman, a simple youth in tight-fitting suit and flat cap, oafed his way to fame in the 1950s. Born in London on 4 February 1919, he first appeared with an army concert party during the war, and made his variety debut at Collins Music Hall on 17 December 1945. After provincial engagements in variety, pantomime and revue, he made his first West End appearance on 5 April 1948 in a variety season at the London Casino. The next morning the *Daily Mail* proclaimed 'A new star is born', and from his low spot on the Casino bill he went on to top the bill at the Golders Green Hippodrome. He soon discovered that being a hit as an unknown supporting act was one thing, to live up to expectations at the top of the bill was another. That summer he gained invaluable experience in *Out of the Blue* at the Spa Theatre, Scarborough, acting in sketches, appearing in production numbers, and working his own 12 minute speciality act. In the show he introduced the gormless character Norman for the first time, coming up as a volunteer from the audience to cause havoc with the magic act of David Nixon. The routine was such a success that when the summer season at Scarborough came to an end, Wisdom and Nixon appeared together in variety at the London casino. Norman went on to top bills at variety theatres in London and the provinces and appeared in the revue *Sauce Piquante* at the Cambridge Theatre, London

During the summer of 1949 he appeared in *Buttons and Bows*, Henry Hall's show starring Donald Peers at the Palace Theatre, Blackpool. This led to variety engagements and four consecutive pantomime seasons for Derek Salberg. Following a visit to the USA he was booked by Bernard Delfont to star in the Folies Bergère show *Paris to Piccadilly* at the Prince of Wales Theatre, London, and on November 1952 appeared in his first Royal Variety Performance at the London Palladium. In 1953 he starred in *Trouble in Store*, the first of a phenomenally successful series of comedy films. The film earned him a British Film Academy Award and made him a record star with the plaintive song 'Don't Laugh at me 'Cos I'm a Fool'. In musical comedy he was a great success in *Where's Charley?*, Frank Loesser's musical version of *Charley's Aunt* at the Palace Theatre, London, in February 1958, and in 1963 starred in Anthony Newley's musical *The Roar of the Greasepaint, the Smell of the Crowd*, which 'died a death' in Manchester without reaching the West End. He appeared in New York in 1966 with *Walking Happy*, a musical version of *Hobson's Choice*, and also starred with Noël Coward in Richard Rodgers's award-winning television musical version of Shaw's *Androcles and the Lion*. In 1969 he was nominated for an Oscar as best supporting actor for his role in United Artists film *The Night They Raided Minsky's*. After three years spent in the USA and on variety tours of Australia and South Africa he returned to England in 1971 to appear in summer season at the ABC Theatre, Great Yarmouth, and the following summer at Bournemouth. He has appeared in many British television programmes, including his own series, 'Wit and Wisdom'.

Vic Wise, comedian, born David Victor Bloom in Southampton in 1900. He went to South Africa as a boy and made his first stage appearance as a magician in Johannesburg on 7 August 1913. Later he toured the Fuller circuit of Australia as a variety and revue comedian, and then appeared in vaudeville in the USA. He came to England with a partner and first appeared with him as 'Campbell and Wise' at Collins Music Hall in August 1932. As a solo comic he became well known in variety and on radio with a Jewish-style comedy routine.

Wee Georgie Wood, music-hall's little boy who never grew up. Born George Bramlett, at Jarrow on 17 December 1895, he made amateur stage appearances from the age of six, and appeared with a semi-professional minstrel troupe known in Sunderland as 'The Local Lads'. In 1903 he joined Will Elliott's concert party, followed by Cosgrove and Burns' 'Merry Mascots', a pierrot company appearing that summer at Barnard's Castle. In 1904 he worked a single turn as a mimic at the Empire Music Hall, South Shields, and the following year appeared with Levy and Caldwell's Juveniles. A fellow member of the troupe was Stan Laurel, then working under his real name, Stanley Jefferson. He gave a benefit performance for Cosgrove and Burns at the Palace Theatre, Bradford, in 1908, working the sketch 'The Nursery at Bed Time'. Dressed in a white silk dress and long blonde wig trimmed with blue ribbons, he looked nearer five years of age than 13. After being put to bed by his nurse, played by Ethel Burns, he slipped out of bed and, seemingly oblivious of the audience, treated his Teddy Bear to impromptu impressions of music-hall artistes. The sketch was so successful that the special matinee became a week at the top of the bill and led to a contract with variety agent Ernest Edelston. He toured the nursery sketch in variety, making his first London appearance at the Shepherd's Bush Empire on 9 April 1908. He toured South Africa in 1909, and in January 1915 starred in 'High class vaudeville' at B.F. Keith's Colonial Theatre, New York.

For nearly 40 years he appeared in pantomime and variety, for much of the time with his famous sketches 'Mrs Robinson and her Son'. Dolly Harmer played his mother from 1917 until her death in 1956 and together they toured the USA, South Africa, Canada, Australia, and New Zealand. During the Second World War they worked for ENSA entertaining the troops in North Africa and the Middle and Far East. Another of Wee Georgie's stalwarts was Tom Blacklock, a member of his company from 1917 to 1928. Wee Georgie, Dolly Harmer and Tom Blacklock appeared in 'The Blackhand Gang' in the Royal Variety Performance at the Victoria Palace on 24 February 1927. A hard-working if somewhat contentious member of the Grand Order of Water Rats, he served as King Rat in 1936. He has for many years contributed his own personal jottings 'Stage Man's Diary' to *The Stage*.

Wood and Shepard, American burnt-cork comedians and musical double act. Wood first appeared as a solo vaudeville comic in 1876, later joining a succession of minstrel troupes and variety road shows. He teamed with Shepard, who had previously worked as a band master and cornet soloist with Lester Alfred's Minstrels, and together they worked for seven seasons with Rich and Harriss's Variety Company. They made their first appearance in England at the London Pavilion in May 1898, but were such a failure that they beat a hasty retreat to the USA a week later. Returning to London later the same year they were a greater success at the Alhambra and became a popular supporting act in variety throughout the UK and at the Folies Bergère, Paris.

Arthur Worsley, ventriloquist born on 16 October 1920. He began his stage career at the age of eleven at the Casino, Rusholme, Manchester, in 1931. He has been a star act from the age of 14 when he made his first London appearance at the South London Palace in June 1935.

Harry Worth, comedian famous as the dithering character of the BBC television series 'Here's Harry'. Born in Hoyland, near Barnsley, in 1918, he worked down the pit from the age of 14 and joined the RAF in 1941, appearing with a Gang Show in India. On leaving the forces he appeared as a ventriloquist with a concert party on the beach at Southport. He made his first London appearance at the Windmill in 1947 and, developing his own confused comedy style, went on to appear in variety at the London Hippodrome and to tour South Africa with Johnnie Ray. He was soon established as a very funny character comedian of variety and

Wee Georgie Wood

radio and the star of over 100 episodes of 'Here's Harry'. In 1971 he played the leading part in a BBC comedy drama series based on Evelyn Waugh's novel *Scoop*, that of the gardening correspondent who is sent to report on a war by mistake. He did a series for ITV in 1974 and toured in the lead of *Harvey*. He appeared, without great success, in 1975 in the West End play *Norman, Where Are You?* at the Phoenix Theatre.

Z

Zaeo, acrobat, gymnast and aerialist, born in Norwood, London, on 31 January 1866. At the age of 12 she was apprenticed to a circus owner named Wieland whom she later married. Her first performance was as an equestrienne at the Exhibition Palace, Dublin, in 1879, and as a trapeze artiste at the Alexandra Palace, London, in October the same year. In 1880 she appeared at the Westminster Royal Aquarium, followed by a world tour. She returned to the Aquarium in 1890, and posters advertising her performance showed her in a tight-fitting leotard and caused cries of 'indecent' from the Central Vigilance Society for the Repression of Immorality. The posters were withdrawn but she remained a great attraction at the Aquarium for over a year. She later appeared at the Palace Theatre and other London halls as a fire dancer, eventually retiring to run a number of side shows at the Royal Aquarium.

The Zancigs, Julius and Agnes Zancig, Danish-American mind-reading act, billed as 'The Two Minds with but a Single

Above: Harry Worth, 1969

Below: The Zancigs. 'Two Minds with but a Single Thought'

Thought'. After success at Hammerstein's Roof Garden, New York, they toured with Houdini's road show, described on the bills as offering a 'triumphant demonstration of the actuality of telepathy'. When the tour came to an end in the summer of 1906, the Zancigs came to England and made their London debut at the Alhambra, Leicester Square, followed by a tour of the UK. The act took the now familiar form of Julius going into the auditorium and asking his blindfolded wife sitting on the stage to identify objects belonging to members of the audience. The code that Julius and Agnes used was so ingeniously devised that they were soon credited with the powers of genuine mental telepathy. They never claimed to possess psychic powers and as members of the Society of American Magicians stated that 'if they lost their sight and hearing they could never do any of their tricks'. They did however make advertising capital out of a testimonial supplied by Sir Arthur Conan Doyle, who wrote: 'I have tested Professor and Mrs Zancig today and I am quite sure that their remarkable performance as I saw it is due to psychic-caused [thought transference] and not to trickery.' On Boxing Day 1906 the Zancigs were commanded by Edward VII to entertain at a party at Sandringham.

On their return to the USA the Zancigs headlined for many years in vaudeville and produced their own touring shows. After the death of Agnes Zancig, Julius appeared with several other partners but never again repeated the same polished performance that he and his wife had achieved. He eventually sold the secrets of his act to Houdini for his vast collection of magic and retired to California where he became a fashionable society astrologer with a side-line in crystal balls, complete with instructions, at $5 and $10 each. He died on 29 July 1929.

Zazel. 'The Human Cannon Ball'

Zaeo, at the Westminster Royal Aquarium, 1890

Zazel, a female human cannon-ball who appeared at the Westminster Royal Aquarium and other pleasure gardens and exhibition halls of London and the provinces during the 1880s. Like Zaeo, her unladylike antics upset Victorian sensibilities and caused a storm of protest from the moralists—reactions which ensured her success wherever she appeared.

Ann Ziegler and Webster Booth, husband-and-wife singing duo who, with their 'Only a Rose' signature tune, were the leading variety and radio duettists of the 1940s and early 1950s. Ann Ziegler was born in Liverpool on 22 June 1910 and gave her first recital in London at the Wigmore Hall in April 1934. After singing in the chorus of *By Appointment* at the New Theatre, London, she appeared in pantomime in Liverpool in 1935 and in Edinburgh in 1936. She made her New York debut in September 1937. Webster Booth, born in Birmingham on 21 January 1902, first appeared in *The Yeoman of the Guard* at the Theatre Royal, Brighton, on 9 September 1924, and toured with the D'Oyly Carte Company until 1927. After success as a concert singer he appeared at Covent Garden in 1938. For three summer seasons, 1940 to 1942, Ann Ziegler and Webster Booth appeared at the Opera House, Blackpool, and in December 1941 opened at the London Palladium in George Black's revue *Gangway*. During the war they became a household name on radio and in variety, appearing in the Royal Variety Performance on 5 November 1943. They were very popular in Australia and New Zealand during a tour in 1948, and eventually made Australia their home.